THE LAMP
OF GOD

THE LAMP OF GOD

A JEWISH BOOK OF LIGHT

FREEMA GOTTLIEB

Jason Aronson Inc.
Northvale, New Jersey
London

The author gratefully acknowledges permission to reprint from the following sources:

Origins of the Kabbalah by Gershom Scholem. Trans. by Allan Arkush. © 1987 Princeton University Press. Used by permission of Princeton University Press, Princeton, New Jersey.

Zohar: The Book of Enlightenment. Trans. by Daniel C. Matt. From The Classics of Western Spirituality Series. © 1983 by Daniel C. Matt. Used by permission of Paulist Press, Ramsey, New Jersey.

The Early Kabbalah, Joseph Dan, ed. Trans. by Ronald Kiener. From The Classics of Western Spirituality Series. © 1986 by Joseph Dan and Ronald C. Kiener. Used by permission of Paulist Press, Ramsey, New Jersey.

The Legends of the Jews, vol. 4, by Louis Ginzberg. © 1968. Copyrighted and used by permission of The Jewish Publication Society, Philadelphia, Pennsylvania.

Pesikta de-Rab Kahana. Trans. by W. G. Braude and I. J. Kapstein. © 1975. Copyrighted and used by permission of The Jewish Publication Society, Philadelphia, Pennsylvania.

Kabbalah: New Perspectives by Moshe Idel. © 1988 Yale University Press. Used by permission of Yale University Press, New Haven, Connecticut.

Library of Congress Cataloging-in-Publication Data

Gottlieb, Freema.
   The lamp of God : a Jewish book of light / by Freema Gottlieb.
   p.   cm.
   Bibliography: p.
   Includes index.
   ISBN 0-87668-898-9
   1. Light–Religious aspects–Judaism.   I. Title.
BM657.C3G67   1989
296.4–dc19   89–31234
                                                                      CIP

Manufactured in the United States of America. Jason Aronson Inc. offers books and cassettes. For information and catalog write to Jason Aronson Inc., 230 Livingston Street, Northvale, New Jersey 07647.

For my father, Rabbi Wolf Gottlieb (Yedidyah)—Poland, Scotland, and Israel, and for my mother, Betty (Bracha) Rosen, who passed on to me the Light.

Like many other Jews, my first experience of "Jewish Light" was as a child seeing my mother light the Sabbath candles.

There were four members of our small nuclear family of survivors from the European Holocaust. My mother lit one candle for each of us, and an additional candle. One day she told us why she lit the extra candle.

One Friday during the first year of her marriage in Vienna, just after the Anschluss, my father did not come home. Forgetting the time, my mother wandered about the city seeking news of him. It turned out that he was being detained by the Gestapo.

Because he was "sponsored" by a British citizen, and because just that day Neville Chamberlain made the pact of "Peace in Our Time" with Hitler, he was released. The Nazi who brought him the news in his cell also told him, "With this gun I would have shot you today. Instead, you are free for now."

The next Sabbath, my mother told us, and for all Sabbaths to come, she lit an additional candle for the Sabbath she had missed.

It was the power of that additional candle that gave me an insight into the way in which light speaks to us. It explained why, for instance, Jews kindle a "soul" light for the dead and why, after a death, Jews say the Kaddish prayer, extolling God's Greatness at the very moment when His world seems infinitely to have shrunk at the blasphemous loss of a soul—the Kaddish, says the Zohar, is a prayer that represents the rekindling of the Menorah light—and why, after the destruction of the Temple, when Jews had lost their sovereignty and their land and were doomed to millennia of persecution and pogrom, the seven-branched Temple candelabra was gifted with an additional branch.

It was this eloquent quality of light to speak for what we cannot see that inspired me to write this book.

CONTENTS

– II –
LIGHTS OF CREATION:
LEGENDS OF SUN AND MOON

– III –

LIGHT OF MAN   139

– IV –

LIGHT OF THE COMMANDMENT   185

– V –
LIGHTS OF MAGIC   275

– VI –
LIGHT OUT OF DARKNESS   315

– VII –
OUT OF THE DEPTHS   355

Preface

Universally, light is considered as precious and necessary as life itself. Every living organism – from the rhinoceros to the amoeba, from the sunflower to the infant in arms to the most sophisticated intellectual giant – responds to light on an instinctive and biocellular level. Even more than bread and water, light is one of those staples of physical existence that is both a celebration of life and an invitation to growth and self-transformation.

In all cultural eras, the vocabulary of light has been used to express the deepest movements of our inner life. At one time or another, light has come to represent the forces of Good, wisdom and enlightenment, spiritual abundance, and life itself. As an image of Supreme Value, light has been taken as a description of God Himself.

The light-loving Greeks viewed darkness and death with equal horror. Death was a passing away from the light. In many languages, beauty is associated with radiance: in German, Yiddish, and English, fairness and beauty are synonymous. The presence of someone we love is described in Hebrew as "bringing light to the eyes." A blind person, to both the ancient Hebrews and the Greeks, was considered almost like one dead, and the Talmud says that someone deprived of the sense of sight cannot fully enjoy what he eats. In fact, the gift of sight was valued to such an extent that the pleasure of looking at a beautiful woman was more intense than actually sleeping with her (*Yoma, Seder Moed* 8:74b–75a). When the Rabbis want to describe the pleasure that awaits the soul in the next world, they do not find it necessary to resort to descriptions of a houri-filled Paradise. Rather, the soul "basks in the radiance of God's Presence"—and there is no pleasure higher than that.

Light is vital to both physical and intellectual life. Through the process of photosynthesis, light promotes growth in stem, leaf, and root, producing flowers and the germination of seeds. This interaction of light and air, together with green pigment in plant life, produces the stores of energy known as starch or carbohydrate. Through this chain reaction of cause and effect, the sunlight absorbed in green plants is converted into the vitality of the human body and the energy in the human brain cells that produces ideas. In the most concrete physical way, light becomes life, vitality, and knowledge, and the capacity for ascendance from lower to higher forms of life.

This metaphorical quality of light as a link between lower and higher realms has been preserved in modern atomic science, which describes the behavior of light as both wave and particle—sometimes it has material manifestations, sometimes more spiritual manifestations.

Since Temple days and before, light has been enshrined at the very heart of Jewish religious life. Every holy day is ushered in by the kindling of candles by the mistress of the house; on *Hanukkah*, the Jewish winter Festival of Lights, eight candles are kindled; and on special anniversaries, a *neshamah* or soul light is lit in memory of the departed. Centered around light, in fact, are some of the most sensuous and attractive Jewish rituals. And it is here that the technicalities of law and the inner illumination of Judaism are at one.

With God's first utterance and command, "Let there be

Light!" (Genesis 1:2), the curtain was lifted on the pageant of existence.

The focus of the drama of Creation – and this book – is not so much on light in the abstract, but on "traveling light," or the attempt to bring light down to earth and to set it within a human frame of reference. One of the characteristics of light and fire is that they both spread. This, then, is the story, not of light but of Lamps, or varying powers of reception and response. And it is the story, too, of the Elevation of the Feminine, for the Lamp as pure Vessel is viewed as female – *Shekhinah* – in kabbalistic sources. In relation to God, the whole created world, Israel, the Temple, and mankind are categorized as female, containers for His light.

The *Midrash* says that God was "constrained to dwell with mortals in a Lamp" (*Bamidbar Rabbah* 15:9). This is certainly not to be taken literally as an allusion to magic genies, but as a way of imagining a possible meeting ground between God and the world. "The spirit of man is God's Lamp" (Proverbs 27:20).

The kernel of the problem is: How can spirit and matter dwell side by side? How can the Infinite be said to be contained within finitude? How can it be said that God breathed a soul into man? Or that He dwells in a temple, a land, a lamp, a human being, or even in a book? What is the relationship between a given object and the amount of yearning projected upon it?

This book was initially motivated by what amounted to a fixation with one dominant image – that of the *Menorah* and the seemingly incommensurable amount of emotion invested in this one artifact throughout the ages. Obviously, the meaning of the kindling of the seven-branched Temple *Menorah* was a duplication of God's initial kindling of the celestial lights, and the kindling of the eight-branched *Menorah* retained its cosmic dimension while also being a memorial to that original *Menorah* of the Seven (the seven lower natural *Sefirot*, branches or emanations, corresponding to the seven days of Creation), the ruined Sanctuary, and past glories of an exiled people.

Through the link between the *Menorah* and the *Sefirot*, the neo-Platonic Emanations of Divine light and bounty to mankind, the Jewish Candelabra was transformed into a cosmic archetype. And then, simply from being the history of a particular symbol, this became the story of light.

This book partially consists of a series of quotations, mined from sources that range from Psalms and the Prophets to the authors of the Talmud and the *Midrash*, Kabbalists, Hasidic Rabbis, and twentieth-century commentators. However, the treatment is not intended to be in historical sequence. It is of little use to know that although the Bible speaks of the *Menorah* and the *Midrash* speaks of God creating the world with the agency of Ten Powers, the first known link between the Ten *Sefirot* and the *Menorah* is to be found in the thirteenth-century manuscript of Rabbi Asher ben David.

Historically, the links developed stage by stage, but for today's reader the poetic associations exist simultaneously. For me, when God said "Let there be Light," those words encapsulated all that was to come – a fanning out, as it were, into all ten branches of the *Sefirot*. The light journey charted here from receptacle to receptacle works through fragmentation and individuation to a reintegration in newer and more pleasing wholes; this spiritual and poetic voyage draws on more than two thousand years of sources of Jewish "history of light." It does not pretend to delineate the history of concepts, only to present the living light itself as seen from a twentieth-century perspective, essentially the story of the transformation of the psyche, of a people, and of mankind.

The structure of the book follows the movement of "Primordial Light" down into the depths of history by means of successive waves of containment and expulsion of essential energy. Thus, after God's retreat within Himself (*Tzimtzum*), "light" is poured out through a series of emanations – the Ten *Sefirot* – into the colossal "Lamp" of Creation; into the Luminaries of Sun and Moon; into the Lamp-receptacles of the Temple and the People of Israel; then, after the destruction by fire of the outer wall of the Temple, the *Shekhinah* Light again voyages forth with Her children (the exiled Jews) into all the nations of the Diaspora. Amid the darkness of persecution and pogrom, She attempts to reverse the movement of descent and to initiate the path of return

by observance of special acts (or *mitzvot*, such as the commandment to kindle) that turn the entire physical world into a lamp.

Parallel with the fate and fortunes of the *Shekhinah* Light of
Israel and of a collective humanity is the smaller "lamp" of the
individual psyche. Here the dynamic also changes from one of
increasing individuation to an attempt to reintegrate the fragments. For essentially, "God's lamp is the human spirit" (Proverbs 27:20).

The narrative is interspersed with certain dominant images
of compression and explosiveness, unity and multiplicity, such
as rays of light, splinters of a rock, the facets and irradiations of a
jewel, the sparks and threads of a burning coal in the darkness of
which all nuances of color are contained; the "Lamp of Darkness" of the *Zohar*; the image of the seven-branched candelabra, a
Tree that serves to duplicate the kindling of the celestial lights;
and the *Sefirot*, a kabbalistic diagram of the cosmos, seen to
present one vast piping system of light, of blessing, and of
life-force.

"Light" was the first "thing of beauty" ever created by an
artist, the first Word, and the first image. This book therefore
meditates upon the meaning of such outward expressions as
clothes, jewels, statues, and colors, and the interplay of darkness
with light. As well as being a "Book of Lights," it is also a book
of symbols and aesthetics.

Made up of fragments and notes in addition to a linear
narrative, the text itself coheres around single images or "Words
of Torah," each a scintillation, a spark, a ray, that cumulatively
recomposes the Jewel.

Acknowledgments

My prime acknowledgment is to my sources, who are the real authors of this book. My ideas derive from a common stock – from the originators of the *Midrash*, of *Kabbalah*, from the *Maharal*, the *Sifat Emet*, and Rav Kuk to name but a few. Given their contributions, I was only employed as a kind of note-taker.

I should like to acknowledge the contribution of my teachers, whose words and personalities above all provided me with inspiration for my task. My first and most important teacher was my father. His last letter to me, which I received only after my return from the unveiling of his gravestone in Israel, was about *Midrashim* on the royal progress of the Sun seen as a human personality subject to moods both of melancholy and joy; at his bedside at night lay the "Lights" of that great twentieth-century Zionist and universalist poet, Rav Kuk. It was this memory that prompted me to ask my young friend and teacher, Micha Odenheimer, to give "learnings" from the writings of Rav Kuk to a circle of friends in Manhattan so that his light should shine there, too. These regular gatherings were invaluable in helping to bring my own work to completion.

A family and childhood friend and teacher, Rabbi Shmuel
Sperber of London and Jerusalem, illuminated for me the vi-
sionary thread that links the humanitarian rabbinic tradition
with prophetic fire. And it was my dear friend and teacher, Dr.
Yochanan Muffs, who pinpointed the role of the human being
within that rabbinic tradition in providing therapy and illumination for God Himself.

Dr. Michael Gruber not only encouraged me to keep going,
but also made many illuminating parallels between "light imagery" and the essential movements of disintegration and psychic
renewal. It was his advocacy of the practice of mental concentration (*kavannah*) that gradually made the archetypal image of the
Menorah yield up layer upon layer of Her mystery.

In a sense, this book also is a result of the cumulative
response of such friends as Naomi Mark, Mikhail Gurewitz, and
Naama Citroney who, when I told them the venture I was
engaged in, spontaneously lit up and came out with their own
insights.

The warmth and intimacy of the Carlebach Synagogue on
New York's Upper West Side provided a spiritual haven from
which continually renewing "Words of Torah" welled up.
Rabbis Elichaim and Shlomo Carlebach and, above all, Rabbi
Elichaim's wife Hadassah, afforded me their own original insights, as did Rabbis Saul Berman of the Lincoln Square Synagogue and Murray Schaum of Riverdale. My thanks also to
Dovid Silber of the Drisha Institute and to Dr. Solomon Mowshowitz, who made themselves available for queries bibliograph-
ical, philosophical, and halakhic in scope.

I am indebted to Dr. Moshe Idel of the Hebrew University
of Jerusalem. His facility with hitherto little-known esoteric
sources of *Kabbalah* has provided many of the mystical references
in this book. My thanks, also, to Professor Eliot Wolfson of New
York University, who gave me invaluable help to orient myself
in the oceans of *Kabbalah*.

Above all I owe a debt of gratitude to The Writers Room—
both the staff and the members of the board—for providing the
kind of environment in which inspiration can flow. Thanks also
to my fellow inmates—the writers—who form an ideal kind of

community during the long periods of enforced seclusion that writing entails.

Many thanks also to the Inland Book Company for providing free rent in the Room to a writer published by a small press and to The Writers Room for selecting me and Jason Aronson Inc. as a recipient. For their support, moral and financial, during a period of hardship, I must also mention Pen America and the Authors' League.

Warm thanks to Arthur Kurzweil, Editorial Vice President of Jason Aronson Inc., for his share in crystallizing the central concept of this book, and above all to my editor, Elena Le Pera, for her clarity, understanding, and wonderful ability to elicit from me what I really meant.

ONE

LIGHT

OF

THE

FEMININE

"To Dwell in Thy Midst. . ." (Exodus 25:8)

The Hand of God by Auguste Rodin. The Hand of God is the maternal shaping force out of which the human soul emerges. (*Copyright ARS NY/ SPADEM, 1988*)

"In the beginning, God produced a Lamp of Darkness" (*Zohar* 1:15a). Thus the *Zohar* greets God's introduction of the "Light of the Feminine" into His Creation.

Light is simply a metaphor for Existence and for Life. Therefore 'Light' has been taken as the perfect description of the *Ein-Sof*, the Infinite Essence of God Himself. As Primal Cause, He is the flame from whom all lesser lights and emanations catch fire.

"Before all things were created. . ." says Rabbi Chaim Vital, a disciple of the sixteenth-century Kabbalist and poet Rabbi Isaac Luria, "the Supernal Light . . . filled all existence and there was no empty space (empty, that is, because it was not filled with light). . . ."[1]

Before anything, except God, had any kind of personal identity or independent existence, before it could be said there was a thing such as perception, all that existed and was perceived was God's Heavenly Light.

"Before the worlds were created, all that existed were He and His Name."

3

THE GIVER AND THE RECEIVER

What is God's "Name," not His Unknowable Essence, but this perception of Him, the dark outline of His Endless Light? Light is the Glory radiating from His essence and the physical equivalent of His Name, characterized as feminine.

There are two aspects to light, traditionally distinguished as masculine and feminine, or Giver and Receiver. It was God's desire to give that made Him create a receptacle to receive His Light. If God is Infinite Light, what He "needed" in creating the world was something to contain it.

"He is One and His Name is One." What is God's "Name" but this "wish" to create the world, the "will to receive," the Vessel. The Gematria (numerical value) of *rotsen* (will), *shemoi* (name), and *tsinor* (vessel) are the same.[2] Therefore, God's will is His Name, the way He makes Himself known in the world – and that is the light that radiates through the first Primal "Lamp" or "Vessel of the Feminine."

This is why the prayer a Jewish woman says every day, "Blessed are You O Lord our God . . . who has made me according to His Wish," is a special compliment. Woman was made according to God's desire for a Vessel or "Lamp" to fill with His light.

As R. Yehuda Ashlag, a twentieth-century commentator on R. Isaac Luria, expressed it:

> As soon as the idea surfaced in the Mind of the Divine to create Man, there sprang forth a Lamp . . . a container . . . the "Will to Receive." And this Divine projection, though light to us, is dark compared to Him, a Vessel for His Endless light.[3]

Before God created the world, says the *Sefer ha-Bahir* (*The Book of Illumination*), He had a Lamp He loved better than any other object in His vast treasure house. This Lamp was His favorite. In moments of leisure He liked to take it out and look at it and touch it gently.

If before He created the world God was neither bored nor lonely, it was because of this Lamp. The only problem He faced was where to put it. There was no place it could be exhibited to advantage. It became of paramount importance that He create a space for it. So "the Divine essence contracted inward to form a primal space or vacuum to allow matter to come into being." And from then on, the Lamp, at first a mere plaything of the Divine, was transformed into a separate entity that would enable it to enter into a mutually satisfying relationship with Him.

Rabbi Azriel of Gerona said in the name of Rabbi Shimon bar Yohai: "A man has joy in the answer of his mouth" (Proverbs 15:23a). "A man has joy" – this is the Holy One. . . .

"In the answer of his mouth" – it is written, And God said, "Let there be light" (Genesis 1:3).[4] God was filled with absolute joy and wonder at the sheer responsiveness of His Creation. He expressed Himself, and something other than Himself answered. This was the first relationship to exist and the first exchange between Male and Female.

Not with work nor with effort did God create the universe, but with a mere word. And God said, "Let there be Light" (*Bereishit Rabbah* 12:10, 4:7). Thus the expenditure of energy on a Word kindled Light. Word and Light correspond.

But some say God created the world with even less effort than that, with not as much as a letter, with only the merest breath, with a *heh*. (This slight exhalation is the feminine ending in Hebrew.)

According to Lurianic *Kabbalah*, everything comes into being through the Letters of the Divine Name, and the crucial letter that allows the creation to flow into the world of substance is the *heh* of the Feminine realm of *Malkhut*. "With the Word of God were the Heavens made; with the breath of His mouth, all their host. . . . For He spoke and it was, He commanded and it became so" (Psalm 33:6,9).

"All letters demand an effort to pronounce them, whereas the *heh* demands no effort (*heh* is a mere aspirate); similarly, not with labor or wearying toil did the Holy One . . . create His world, but 'by the word of the Lord' (Psalm 33:6) and 'The heavens were made' " (*Bereishit Rabbah* 12:10).

Similar to what the *Midrash* says about God's Creation of

the world is what the Prophet Zechariah says about the mechanism of the *Menorah*:

> Not with labor or wearying toil . . . but with the Word of the Lord is paralleled by Not by power, nor by might but by My Spirit. [Zechariah 4:6]

MENORAH AS DIVINE ARCHETYPE

God's Word is like the inhaling and exhaling of breath, a flow that is symbolized by the cosmic *Menorah*.

God's Name can be seen as a Holy Family. In the transcendent world, Father and Mother – the *Sefirah* or celestial irradiation of *Keter* (Crown) and *Binah* (Understanding) – unite the *yod* and the *heh* of God's Name to produce the son (*vav*) and the daughter (*heh*) in the immanent world. The four letters of God's Name stand for the four essential components of life – Force, Pattern, Energy, and Substance.

> The second letter, *heh*, which represents the large complete vessel, is in the same form as the fourth letter, *heh*, being the Feminine *Sefirah* of *Malkhut*, because at the time of the Messiah She will be exalted to the plane of the second letter – that is to say, the Daughter will be united with Her Mother and thus already She has the same shape.[5]

God created the world with a *heh*, the *heh* of question, the *heh* of equal dialogue, a *heh* that does not accept tyranny, a *heh* that will question even God Himself and bring a delighted smile to the face of the Creator, a *heh* that the Nations do not understand: "Come let us argue together. . . . !" says God, desiring above all this dialogue that plunges Him right into the center of His creation.

A PLACE OF BUNDLING

The *Menorah* of the *Sefirot* was the first truly beautiful work of art to emerge out the Hand of God. This first *Menorah* was created of no other substance than light in a dark frame.

And these (the branches) are the *Sefirot* (the Emanations of the Divine Light), all of them interconnected in one another without any division like a cluster which includes everything, branches and leaves and grapes, bells and clappers and everything on a single bough. Everything grows and burgeons from one root, planted on one spot. Every quality is called after the place of its origin from which it derives nourishment and from which they grow and spread out at first, from one becoming two, then three, and so all of them, *ad infinitum.* It is of them Solomon says in his wisdom: "A branch of camphor is my beloved to me." And because of their closeness to their Creator He elevates them and calls them by name. And the sign for the seven Extremities growing out from the Place is a tree with interlocking branches without the intrusion of anything else.

The *Menorah* is entirely made of one substance – both sides, shaft, goblets, calyxes, and petals – all growing out from one source, without being confused for each other. And similarly with the six branches on top of each of which is a candle with the seventh candle on the middle shaft. All of them face opposite it, symbolizing the fact that the middle is the most important, maintaining everything in existence. In the *Menorah*, as in these seven *Sefirot*, it is the same, like a cluster symbolic of (the light) that is drawn through them from the *Ein-Sof*, the Light which is inserted in each lamp which is kindled and lit up because of the central light and therefore are the seven *Sefirot* in the Torah called "days and luminaries," hinting at the middle shaft which holds everything together, the oil of the central lamp from which the process begins and at which it is complete. The qualities of these lights are equal.

Because the *Shekhinah* is found without a division in this Tree of the Seven *Sefirot*, it is called a "place of bundling." About this Solomon says in his wisdom: "My beloved is to me a bundle of myrrh." And in another context, this heap is called a "bundle of life," for so it is written: "May the soul of my lord be gathered into the bundle of life." And it is called "the extremities of the holy place" because everything lives and grows from the Source of Life and the Source of Life emanates through them, preserving and sustaining them. It is not called that because of any intrinsic characteristic but because it sustains the places and the extremities which draw and emanate from the Endless.[6]

When God uttered the words "Let there be light!" He did not create anything new. What He did was what artists and fathers and mothers do – He took something inside Himself and projected it into the external world, pouring His light into the container of created space. With God's utterance "Let there be light!" the *Menorah* that was already there was set up on its pedestal for all to see.

Therefore, this first Feminine, in addition to being portrayed in Jewish sources as a consort, or even as a Mother (*Binah*, the *Sefirah* of Understanding), is more generally depicted as "the king's daughter" and the Jewel in His Crown.

Menorah, Hebrew for Lamp, consists of the root *nur*, "flame," symbolic of God Himself, and the prefix *mem*, thereby creating a vessel for the flame.

God had this *Menorah* in mind even before He created the sunlight. In the natural order of the world, first there is plant life, then there is a garden; first there is creation, then there is the Temple; first there is nature, then there is civilization. But according to both Aristotelian and Jewish thinking, the last thing to be realized is often the first in conception and the very point of it all. In a sense, therefore, the objective preexists what leads up to it.

First we set our sights on the goal, then we take the steps to attain it. "God looked into the Torah and created the world" (*Bereishit Rabbah* 1:1). According to this view the Torah is not simply Law that came into existence at a certain period of historical development. It is a Divine blueprint pointing to the secret formulas and principles underlying nature. And similarly with primordial light. First God dreamt of a *Menorah*, and then He created the light of the sun and the moon.

The Jewish *Menorah* existed with God before the natural backdrop to set it off had come into existence. There she lived like a young girl in her father's house before she is old enough to marry. Then, with a "Let there be Light!" God sent His *Shekhinah* (the Divine Presence, viewed as female) out under the marriage canopy of the cosmos.[7]

AND GOD CREATED LIGHT

When God decided to undertake Creation, complications quickly set in. What He did by disclosing His light was to create the conditions that made possible the existence of anything outside of Him. Only in this way could His light be seen. What in fact He created, according to the *Zohar*, was a frame of darkness to offset the light, or a "Lamp of Darkness."

The light mentioned in Genesis as God's first Creation was already no longer God, but a gift and expression of Him. As soon as God needed to find a "Place" for His light—a container or Lamp—the light descended and became feminized.

"The mere thought that He wanted (to create universes)," says R. Yehuda Ashlag, "triggered off from Him a Light. . . . That Light comprised everything, the entire universe and its abundance and creatures, celestial world, angels and souls, terrestrial worlds and all the inhabitants thereof."[8]

Though it may appear that with Creation God expanded His area of activity with the creation of numerous worlds and creatures, in fact "when (He) . . . decided to create all universes," says Luria's disciple R. Chaim Vital, "He constricted the light."[9] God, in a sense, set some limits on His infinity so as to make room for other things. By bringing out the light of creation, He made Himself dark and distant in relation to what He had created.

According to Luria's concept of *Tzimtzum* (contraction)—from all His beautiful Creation, the emanation of God's Light—God only created one new thing. "He who fashions light and creates darkness" (Isaiah 45:7). God created only Darkness, the Darkness that is a vessel for and absorbs all light, the dark ink of the Hebrew letters that contain the "light" of the meaning of a text. The only really new thing God created was a (feminine) Vessel for His Light.

> Only after the light had been fashioned, darkness arose, the light ruling in the sky, the darkness on the earth. [*Ozar Midrashim* 64b]

Light is known to exist by virtue of darkness. . . . One is the chair upon which the other sits; one is like the man who holds an object in his upraised hand, and the other is like the object thus held.[10]

"I saw that light gained an additional luster from darkness" (Ecclesiastes 2:13). A higher quality of light comes from darkness, through the transformation of darkness to light.[11] According to this typology, darkness is a vessel whose virtue resides in the fact that it absorbs the (superior, masculine) light.

BLACK FIRE ON WHITE FIRE

Of what is Torah composed? "Black fire on white fire." In this world we read the letters, which are black, and ignore the background, which is white. In reality we are living in a negative of the true print, and the letters in the "Heavenly Torah" are formed of white light, while the spaces are black, as in a negative. What we see as letters – the darkness – are only vessels, while the shining white spaces contain the real meaning.

The concept of *Tzimtzum* only exists for us; only to our eyes is the Lamp dark; to God even darkness is light. In general, the Hebrew letters, black or white, are themselves delineated as vessels for the light of the meaning they convey. They are the particular garb or form Torah takes when addressed to human beings. Rav Kuk compares them to "fiery horses" (also vessels) bearing us further than we could travel on foot, solely through the power of reason. "The power of the imagination (the fire) increases through its attachment to a letter of Torah (the horse), so that it ascends far higher than one could do on one's own, with a rapid flight and on a safe course."[12]

The joy that Torah gives to a person comes from the intensity of light compressed into the letters of the Torah, which are full of life-force and Divine delight. The (letters) are full of the light of life and an ennobling joy floods the soul, but even more than the fact of the joy that flows from the letters themselves, which are already imprinted on the soul, this joy flows from the tremendous spiritual life-force that is continually flowing from the upper springs far loftier than the letters imprinted recognizably on the soul. And their light and joy is far greater, filling (the soul) with happiness and wondrous delight unparalleled by all else.

Sometimes it is impossible for a person to learn because he is faced with such intense ecstasy, the general illumination that the sum total of all that is higher than the letters shines forth to him. So that it is impossible for him (at the time) to contract himself into the letters that he is learning. But if he receives this light with holiness and modesty, he will afterwards merit to be able to learn with great joy and a pure and renewed relish.[13]

What Rav Kuk is saying here is that sometimes the letters of the Torah cannot contain the powerful light compressed into them and that learning itself is too slow a process for the flash of illumination that is granted.

The same differentiation that applies to the dark and the light of letters and spaces has been made about the pronunciation of vowel and consonant. In a Hebrew text the vowels are omitted, except for educational purposes. We only read the consonants, which compose a majority of the letters, so that one might think the vowels are less important. Not so. The consonants, again, are viewed as vessels and guidelines for the breath or vocalization (which is the essential).

The Scroll of the Torah is (written) without vowels, in order to enable man to interpret it however he wishes . . . as the consonants without the vowels bear several interpretations, and (may be) divided into several sparks. This is the reason why we do not write the vowels of the scroll of Torah, for the significance of each word is in accordance with its vocalization, but when it is vocalized it has but one single significance; but without vowels man may interpret it . . . [extrapolating from it] several [different] things, many, marvelous and sublime.[14]

A similar differentiation as that between masculine and feminine is made in the distinction between the Lower and

Higher Torah, the Oral and Written Torah. The Higher, Mystical, or Written Torah given by God is masculine, while the Lower Oral Law is feminine and resides in the region of *Malkhut* (Kingdom).

The World to Come, which we have already stated is the world of Severity – either as punishment or as reward – is the crown of Kingdom, the Oral Torah. It is the hue of a black fire on white fire, which is the Written Torah. Now the forms of the letters are not vowelized nor are they shaped except through the power of the black, which is like ink. So too, the Written Torah is unformed in a physical image, except through the power of the Oral Torah. That is to say, one cannot be explained fully without the other. So too, the attribute of Mercy is not comprehended nor seen except by means of the hues of the attribute of Severity. Now the hues of the mark of black (which are the hues of the attribute of Severity) rise and expand and spread over the hues of white (which are the colors of the attribute of Mercy) that rise and cover the blackness. This is similar to the image of the light of a glowing ember, for the force in the colors of the flame rises and strengthens until the light of the ember is invisible due to the intensity of the flame which envelops it. When the colors of the flame increase and spread out one from another, then the physical eyes rule over the essence of the ember (by) physical, sensible sight.

So too (we find) that . . . with the advent of Will (symbolized by darkness), the shades of blackness are weakened and dissipated and dispersed from the unreflecting mirror above the white hues, which illuminate and sparkle and shine like the splendor of white sapphire. Then a few of the prophets . . . were able to perceive this splendor . . . each according to their merit: a spiritual perception and vision appropriate to each prophet. The shades of blackness that spread forth and sparkle from it are similar to the image of the flame that sparkles from the light of the ember, like the intensity of the hues of the small luminary in the midst of the intensely strong light of the sun, and (the small luminary) shines because of (the sun's) strength. It darkens the face of one who peers into it, and blinds anyone who persists and continues his gaze. And if he escapes the blindness by distancing himself from the rays of the sun, he (still) cannot see the light of the ether until he calms down and rests nearly for an hour or two. And due to the abundant intensity of its light and splendor, it is called the reflecting mirror. It illuminated the greatest of the prophets, peace be on him. For no other prophetic eye viewed it or united with it, save Moshe our teacher, peace be upon him.[15]

In addition to this distinction between two types of Torah – higher and lower – the typology of masculine and feminine also corresponds to the distinction between God and Man, light and Lamp. According to this pattern, mankind as a collective entity is personified as feminine, *Shekhinah*, while its regeneration can depend on the spiritual heroism of the *Tzaddikim*, the Jewish equivalent of knights of chivalry, who are stereotypically male.

JOURNEY OF THE FEMININE

God wanted to bestow all light, all joy, and all good upon the world (His feminine Consort). But (according to some interpretations) She was moved with the feminist urge toward a more egalitarian and ultimately, more intimate relationship, and did not want to be continually a taker. She therefore shut Herself off temporarily from the light and became entangled in a series of contractions (*Tzimtzumim*) to produce a whole chain of worlds. In the moment that the "Will" to create surfaced in the Divine, this Vessel or *Shekhinah*, and not the *Ein-Sof*, initiated the movement of *Tzimtzum*.

"The Will to Receive" that God created, whose essential nature was to draw down bounty from above, sought to restrict that light, so that instead of being a mere taker, She could weave a chain of universes that would reverse the movement of emanation by "giving glory" to their Creator. "In this 'Will to Receive,'" writes Ashlag, "resides the most exalted virtue of total bestowal."[16]

Thus it is the Feminine and not the Masculine who is here the initiator of creation. And though She descends the Sefirotic spiral in order to rise even higher, there is an element of darkness in Her action.

"In Herself only slightly darker than the Heavenly Light . . . this Darkness is Mother to all *klippot*, husks, shells, and veils between the soul and the Divine, mother of all appetite for self-gratification that leads to mortality."[17]

The *Shekhinah*'s audacious act of self-banishment presages all future exiles of *Knesset Yisrael*, and if Her separation from the Holy One parallels the original splitting apart of the male and female in the original hermaphrodite Adam, it is even closer to Lilith's conscious abandonment of Adam because Her exile was self-chosen. And although the adage "The Glory of the King's Daughter lies within" (Psalm 45:13) has been used throughout the ages to teach Jewish women modesty, according to *Kabbalah* the journey of the feminine has been an active voyage outward, away from God's Endless Light, to the realm of substance, physicality, and activism.

In the myth of the Fair and the Dark Beloved, one might have believed that the *Shekhinah* was all light. However, this is not so, and she is frequently depicted veiled in black garments.[18]

In the beginning, God created a "Lamp of darkness"—a "scintillating ember." In that ember was contained the quintessence of the whole world. The totality of creation achieved consummation in that glowing coal, and that glowing coal is everything we touch, our relationship to others, to our environment, to God, our relationship to ourselves.

With ten words, ten *Sefirot*, ten Vessels for the light, God created the world. With Ten Commandments God gave the Torah to Israel and to mankind on Mount Sinai. Both are implied in the glowing coal.

The question arises: what is the nature of the coal—blackness or shine? Either one can spit at the fire and put it out, or one can breathe evenly and blow the whole world into a glow.

Everything is that ember. It depends how we talk to it, how we breathe, whether our world is redeemed or destroyed. That coal is the world of nature, it is Torah, and it is the deepest point in our soul.

Just as the various qualities of the *Sefirot* penetrate one another in a powerful dramatic movement, so do the colors blend into one another. And just as all the *Sefirot* are contained in *Ein-Sof* (like the flame in the Burning Coal), so is there a type of blackness and darkness that contains all color.

THE *IYYUN* CIRCLE

The *Iyyun* Circle (thirteenth century) developed its own brand of mysticism in which the terms for differentiation from the One are slightly different from those in Sefirotic *Kabbalah*. According to Scholem, a responsum falsely attributed to R. Hai Gaon by an anonymous person from Provence delineated three lights (*sahsahot*) above the First *Sefirah*, hidden in the "root of roots"[19] – the Inner Primordial Light, or *Penimi Kadmon*; the Transparent Light, *Or Mesuhsah*; and the Clear Light, *Or Sah*. These were concealed either in *Keter* or in the *Ein-Sof*.

Thus the Ten *Sefirot*, together with these three additional lights, made up the equivalent of the talmudic description of God's Thirteen Attributes.

The *Iyyun* Circle was also involved with color symbolism.

And now behold and direct your heart to the first attribute, long and true and straight like a scepter. Regarding these matters, each of the attributes is called a flame. Now these flames are scepters, and the scepters are eyes, and each of the eyes themselves divide into five matters. Now these matters divide into sources, the sources into a structure, and the structure congeals. This congealment becomes a glowing ember, and it is to the ember that the five matters cling. For this reason the flame is linked to the ember.

From one source flows light, which in turn is divided into the two hues – whiteness and redness. From the second source flows the darkness composed of three colors – green, blue, and white – to the changing sources, and as they go forth their colors change. For when they are subject to the power of the primeval darkness they are not other than two colors like other darkness. But as they are drawn out, their colors change into many hues included in the five colors that we have already mentioned. These five colors are akin to a flame extending from ether,

refracting as they change. For we have already said that the two
flows are really one matter coming from the primeval darkness,
eluding form. When this form is altered, it paints itself through its
courses and the hues of its colors into ten, and each separate hue
contains the number ten, arriving at a total of one hundred. The
hundred returns again and again into utterance, calculation, and
the grouping of entities; calculation in calculation, utterance in
utterance, until they return to the sum of one, and one is the
essence.[20]

THE BURNING COAL

The image of the Burning Coal is frequently used in the writings
of Rabbi Isaac the Blind of Provence. The Burning Coal stands
both for *Keter*, or God Himself, and for the whole system of
Emanations from *Keter*, including that "knowable" part of the
Ein-Sof (*Keter*) that emanates, and this description still fits into the
category of Vessel and the Feminine. Here the Burning Coal is
the *Ein-Sof*, the flame refers to the *Sefirot*, and the *Sefirot* are
pictured as part of the substance of the Divine Light.

The parallel between the image of the threads of flame and
scintillations quivering in a Burning Coal, and branches and
roots drawn out of the Sefirotic tree, is also made by Rabbi
Isaac.[21]

The paths (of Wisdom, Torah, or the Sophia) are like the threads
of the flames which are the paths for the coals, and through the
flames man can see the coal (which is at their base) in the manner
of a skein, for by following the thread, he arrives at the place of
the skein. Similarly, man finds through the leaves, boughs and
branches, and the numerous trunks, the conduits which lead to
the essential and to the subtle reality of the root, invisible on
account of its subtlety and its inwardness.[22]

The burning coal appears in other kabbalistic literature with
similar symbolic delineations:

In spite of the fact that we make mention of attributes and names of the *Sefirot*, this is done in order to refer to them, not to divide between them. But He is One, united with them all, as the Intellect (to its) meaning, like the burning coal, which is linked to the flame.[23]

Whether it be burning coal or "Lamp of Darkness,"[24] both fit in with the concept of the *Sefirot* as an image of unity in multiplicity. And as Rabbi Asher ben David, a pupil of Rabbi Isaac, noted, so does the *Menorah*. Rabbi Asher for the first time highlighted the link that exists between the *Menorah* and the *Sefirot*, suggesting that the one was a microcosm and replica of the other (see pp. 7–8).

Just as all the branches of the *Menorah* were beaten out of a single block of gold, so (from the point of view of fire and spirituality) did all its flames originate from the same ember.

The *Menorah* is a place where all identities merge and, like the Royal Crown of Ibn Gabirol, is the reservoir of souls.

And God divided the light from the darkness. Up to this point the male principle was represented by light and the female by darkness; subsequently, they were joined together and made one. The difference by means of which light is distinguished from darkness is by degree; both are equal in kind, as there is no light without darkness and no darkness without light. [*Zohar* I:32a]

In Hebrew, words often have opposite connotations – for example, *davak*, to embrace and to contend. Mystically, separation here actually creates the conditions for union. Paradoxically, it was only when the rib of Adam was separated from him that God built it up into Woman and the two could embrace.

When God created the world, His light was concentrated into a single point to form a primal space or vacuum to allow matter to come into being. First, He retracted, then sent His light back again into the world.

So (according to Lurianic *Kabbalah*), first God "withdrew," leaving the abyss and darkness that were the fertile teeming grounds of Creation; then He projected Himself back into them, drawing out from Himself, as it were, a mere "thread" of His Infinite Light, which He spun and spun until "He draws forth Light as a garment" (Psalm 104:2).

This sliver of the "Supernal Light" fanned out into all ten emanations of light (the Ten *Sefirot*[25] of God's cosmic *Menorah*) and the whole creation.[26]

In the vacuum left by the *Tzimtzum*, lines of Divine Light pour in. Crystal vessels are formed but they cannot contain the richness, and therefore burst, leaving *klippot*—shards or hard husks covering seeds or germs of light—remnants of the withdrawal of the Infinite Light of the *Ein-Sof*.

This fragmentation of the Divine Light, which results in the externalization of Evil, is also called the "Breaking of the Vessels" or the "Death of Kings." The aim of Creation is to release those imprisoned sparks, that captive Princess. In Lurianic *Kabbalah*, the face (*Partzuf*) of the *Sefirot* of Divine Wisdom and Understanding (*Hokhmah* and *Binah*) become *Abba* and *Imma* (Father and Mother), whereas that of the Highest *Sefirah* of all is the *Arikh Anpin*, the Long-Suffering One. While the secret "face" of the *Shekhinah*, or the lowest *Sefirah* of *Malkhut*, is Rachel, who rules over the sphere of the Moon that has been diminished, the face of the other six *Sefirot* of Nature constitute the *Zeir Anpin*, the Impatient One, the personality who, in the cosmological process, is the "Holy One Blessed be He" in his relationship with *Shekhinah*.

The *Menorah* of the *Sefirot* is only feminine in the sense that it is a receptacle for God's Light. Otherwise, it is itself made up of a complex series of interactions between masculine and feminine components. Union between a masculine "point" of Endless Light, the *yud* of God's Holy Name, and the *heh* of the Celestial Mother or Divine Intellect, the *Sefirah* of *Binah* produces the ninth *Sefirah* of *Yesod* (the phallic *vav* of the Divine Name), which in our imagination can obviously be associated with the central shaft that also has the connotation of Feeder or Mother. Through *Yesod* the qualities of all the *Sefirot*, or the "Divine Image," flow with all the requisite procreative juices into the lowest *Sefirah* of Substance, or *Shekhinah*.

HE IS ONE AND HIS NAME IS ONE

"In the beginning God (that is, Endless Light) produced a Lamp (Vessel) of darkness" (*Zohar* I:15a). Before, "He is One and His Name is One." The expression "He" refers to the essence of the light. Therefore it is called "He," implying hiddenness and concealment, for the essence of the light is hidden and concealed. "His Name refers to the revelation and expression of light.[27]

"His Name" encompasses two levels—"The Names" and "The Name." "The Names" refers to the Ten *Sefirot* (of the Heavenly *Menorah*), for God staked out within Himself what was to become the Creation, whereas "The Name" refers to the level where the *Sefirot* are infinite and cannot be counted.

The Name or the Glory is another Name for the *Sefirot*, and also for the *Shekhinah* in a broader sense. (In a more precise sense, the *Shekhinah* denotes only the lowest of the *Sefirot*, *Malkhut* or Queen.)

There was complete unity between God and His *Shekhinah*. God's life and light pulsated harmoniously between lower and higher worlds, and harmoniously it was mirrored in the life of the Original Man, *Adam Kadmon*. This unity was brought about precisely because while God was united with the Higher Feminine, the *Shekhinah*—or the daughter—ruled over the lower regions. But then Sin, possibly the Sin of Adam, damaged the channels connecting lower and higher worlds. This exile of the *Shekhinah* on the vertical or transcendental axis corresponds on the horizontal or geographical axis to the exile of *Knesset Yisrael* from the Land of Israel.

Shakespeare's *Winter's Tale* is a variation on this theme. In the play the King himself is responsible for the rift that all but destroys the life of his family and of the Kingdom. Jealous of his Queen, he condemns her newborn child (a daughter) to death. His Queen dies brokenhearted, and the Kingdom simply withers. Redemption is finally brought about "from below," from the healthy peasant class who have adopted the cast-out baby. Only after the discovery in nature (similar to the *Sefirah* of *Malkhut*) of a younger version of the Queen is the Mother herself brought back to life and the health of the Kingdom restored.

The primordial Breaking of the Vessels is paralleled on a lower plane by the Sin of the First Adam, which brought about the creation of the material world. Since then, every sin brings about a confusion of particles of the good with the *klippot*, darkness with light, the holy with the impure. Each time man falls, he drags the *Shekhinah* down with him into further ruin. On the other hand, this degradation has its positive side. There is no part of the physical world so low or so abject that is not filled with fragments of *Shekhinah* Light. Scholem quotes Luria.

> Sparks of the *Shekhinah* are scattered in all worlds and there is no sphere of existence including organic and inorganic nature that is not full of holy sparks which are mixed up with the *klippot* and need to be separated from them and lifted up.[28]

During the upsurge of Hasidism in Eastern Europe in the seventeenth century, the Great *Maggid* seized on this brimming over of Creation with Divine Light as a totally positive event.

> The first thing one has to know is that God fills all worlds and that no place is empty of Him and that He is in all worlds, etc.

> That this is so can be observed from experience. For in all things there inheres the vital energy of the Creator, Blessed be He.[29]

But how is this impregnation of the Divine expressed? In the *Zohar* these "worlds" of Divine Light are likened to young women, just as they are in the Christian parable of the Ten Virgins. The *Zohar* says in Song of Songs 6:8, "and maidens without number." Don't read *Alamot*, "maidens"; read *Olamot*, "worlds—for there are an infinite number of worlds" (*Zohar* II:71b).

"And God was compelled to live with man in a Lamp" (*Bamidbar Rabbah* 15:9). What does this mean? In order to create a meeting point of the spiritual and the physical, God had to become involved in a descending spiral of emanations of His

Divine Light, the dark underside of which is indicated by His reverse action of hiding His Infinite Light in a series of contractions. That is, in order to reveal as much of Himself in the physical world as the physical world could take, He had to hide and only then disclose Himself.

The picture of all of subsequent history, therefore, is that of the pouring of liquid light into a set of womblike containers, each inherently Feminine in the sense of being totally receptive – the Ten *Sefirot*, Creation, the cosmic Lamps of Sun and Moon, the Holy Land, Zion, Jerusalem, the Temple, Israel, good people, mankind, each in relation to God's Endless Light takes up a feminine stance.

Ever since (according to Lurianic *Kabbalah*), the locus of light has been a series of loops – in, out, egression and regression, *hitpashtut* and *histalkut* – like the inhalation and exhalation of breath. If God expressed too much of His Light, there would be no room for the world; if too little, the world could not exist. Tension between the two types of movement is what keeps the world in motion. The more extroverted approach is related to what unexpectedly in Jewish typology is cast as the "masculine" mode of Grace and generosity, while the sterner quality of inwardness and restraint is linked to the feminine attribute of Judgment.

The movement was from light to Lamp – a continual process of compression of the light within a container. That container – whether it was the whole arena of Creation, the earth, the Tabernacle, the Land of Israel, Jerusalem, the Temple, the Holy Ark – was filled with an almost unbearable electric charge, destined to explode outward and irradiate the outermost corners of darkness.

It is said that the construction of the earth began at the center – the foundation stone of the Temple. This stone (the *Shekhinah*, or the soul of mankind) is located at the center of the Holy Ark in the center of the *Hekal*, the palace, which is at the center of the Temple, in Zion, in Jerusalem, in Israel. At that focal point the first ray of light came forth, illuminating first the Holy Land and then the whole earth. A beam of light rayed out from Creation and solidifed into the *Bet Hamikdash*. The link

between light and a stone might be some dead meteorite that fell
from outer space thousands of years ago:

> Rabbi Berekiah says in the name of Rabbi Yitzhak. "From the
> place (*Makom*) of the Temple, light was created," as the verse
> states. *And behold the Glory of the God of Israel came from the way of the
> east* (Ezekiel 43:2). "Glory" refers to the Temple. As is stated, *A
> glorious throne exalted from the beginning is the place of our Temple*
> (Jeremiah 17:12). [*Midrash Tehillim* 50:279; *Midrash Konen* 24–25;
> *Bereishit Rabbah* 3:4–5; *Vayikra Rabbah* 31:7]

SHEKHINAH

The name of God's Presence dwelling within the physical is
Shekhinah, traditionally viewed as feminine, only because She is
the inferior, passive aspect of the Deity – inferior in that She
descends, and passive in that, although She is dynamic in Her
all-absorbing relationship to Her Husband, She "owns nothing of
Her own" and is a mere vehicle for His Light.[30]

The root of the Aramaic word *Shekhinah* is "the act of
dwelling," of Immanence and "Being Present," or "The Divine
Presence." But in the Bible and in the Talmud, there is no
mention of the *Shekhinah* as a feminine personality. The closest
the Bible comes to it is the idea of Divinity "dwelling" on earth
in a sanctuary (*mishkan*) or Temple. The word *shaken* links the
Omnipresent with a particular locale and with a particular event
and by so doing gives the Transcendent God personality. What it
does not do is make His Presence feminine. If there is a sexual
connotation about God's Presence, it is as male within the
female – the Land of Israel, Zion, the Temple site, "the place
where the Lord your God will choose to rest His Name there"
(Deuteronomy 14:3).

The urge to "redeem" nature by choosing certain representative objects and investing them with spiritual import is fairly
universal. A selection is made of some particular thing, either
direct from nature or polished by human artistry, as a sample for
all the rest, and it is dedicated in God's service. Stones were

anointed with oil as memory markers for graves and as altars where sacrifices were made.

GIVING AN OPENING FOR THE DIVINE

One step further in this development is the wish to project human needs and vulnerabilities and, by supplying what is deficient, to bring the Divine within human comprehension. It is man's need for shelter that impels him to build a House for God, and it is the wish to live in God's sight and under His special Providence that prompts him to fashion a *Menorah*.

Jacob slept at *Bet El* (the House of God), with a stone (the *Shekhinah*, the soul of mankind) at his head. When he awakened from his dream of a ladder of light reaching from earth to heaven with angels ascending and descending, he exclaimed: "How awesome is this place! This is none other than the abode of God" (Genesis 28:17).

When Jacob arrived at the small town of Padan in Syria to find himself a wife and build the living "House of God," he found all the shepherds of the place gathered round the village well to help roll away the massive stone blocking the mouth of the well so that they could water their flocks. The stone was the *Shekhinah*, and the waters were the "descending light" that reveals itself through femininity. The mere sight of Rachel advancing toward him with her flocks streaming out behind her gave Jacob courage to roll the stone away singlehanded. Then, not only were the waters of the well released, but feelings were also, and Jacob did not shrink from expressing his pent up emotion. After this feat of virility in a foreign country, he broke down. He embraced his cousin and kissed her and wept because he saw that although they would marry, their time together would be brief; at the end she would not lie together with him in the same grave. In Rachel, Jacob saw the exile that would be the destiny of their children, and he understood that she would stand in for the *Shekhinah*, her prayers following her children into foreign lands.

Before there was a Temple or house of prayer, there was only an altar consisting of a stone or a tree stump. Oil was poured on stone or wood to dedicate it as an altar. The oil helped it to shine, either by polishing it or by being set alight.

ISRAEL AS A LIGHT UNTO THE NATIONS

Sacrifices were made at local shrines from the bounty and first fruits of the earth. First fruits of the womb were also dedicated to God until the Levites and the offspring of Aaron were chosen to serve as the priesthood, instead of the eldest in the family. It is in this sense, too, that Israel is chosen as a "priest" and "light" to the nations. Israel's chosenness lies in the fact that it is the quintessence or "first fruit" of mankind; after the dedication of this sample produce, the whole harvest of human civilization is there for enjoyment (Ramban on Genesis 1:1).

The original gift that man made to God was not a Temple, not a *Menorah*, but a symbol of his own life and continuity – his firstborn son. In a trial of faith, Abraham was tested for his readiness to sacrifice his most beloved possession, Isaac.

THE TRIAL OF ABRAHAM

Together, executioner and victim went to the scene of the sacrifice, to some as yet unknown place in the hills. Father and son went with one mind and one heart. Abraham built a rough altar and strapped Isaac and the wood on top of it. With the knife touching his throat and the flames of the sacrificial fire leaping up, Isaac saw the full radiance of the *Shekhinah* like a fire, and he was forever blinded.

At the time the setting was rough, but the fire of that sacrifice was destined to be transmuted into the illumination of the Golden *Menorah* that would never be put out. The readiness to give life itself was channeled into living art, the wish to embellish and dedicate some object, substituting for that ultimate sacrifice.

Because Abraham held back nothing, because of his dedication and readiness to give, he was transformed into the very prototype of blessing. Not only would he and the son who might have been killed become the recipients of blessing; they became channels through which blessing came to the world.

What is the connection between such primitive rites of sacrifice and blessing? Only a readiness to give beyond limit opens the channels for blessing as symbolized by the *Sefirot* and the Temple *Menorah*. And the site where Abraham was prepared to sacrifice his son became the place where the Temple sacrifice formalized an intimacy and give-and-take between Heaven and earth; a place where the prayers of Jews and non-Jews would be answered, even if people prayed from afar and only faced in that direction;[31] a place of encounter between God and people; a place of spiritual illumination; a place where God's Presence would be "seen," as symbolized by the *Menorah*. And all this because of the fire of dedication that induced two of the Fathers of Israel to offer up to God absolutely everything, including themselves.

Some polytheistic religions found an alternative to the actual sacrifice of human beings by their life-long celibacy and dedication to the god or goddess. Thus, in Euripides, Agamemnon's rash vow to sacrifice the first thing he sets eyes on entails his dedicating his daughter Iphigenia to Artemis and not the actual spilling of her blood.

Some rabbis say that Jephta, who made a similar vow, did not actually sacrifice his daughter to God—how could God or any of the legal authorities have tolerated human sacrifice!—but that she was henceforward barred from participation in normal human life and had to live apart, devoting her time to prayer. When Hannah offered her baby Samuel to serve in the Temple, this was a substitute sacrifice. Similarly, when the Jews dedicated gold and jewels either to the Sanctuary or even to the Golden Calf, it was the same instinct to give unstintingly, to melt themselves down in the crucible of fire and offer the molten metal up to Divinity that prompted their actions. Indeed, it was in part a recognition of their reasons for making the Golden Calf that made God provide an alternative command; "Make Me a Tabernacle. Make Me a *Menorah*," and provide an outlet for that instinct. The dedication of gifts and the sacrifice of animals were substitutes for the basic wish to give themselves to God by giving life to the Giver of Life. Sacrifice and Temple dedication are simply strategies to satisfy the same need without such dire measures.

Paradoxically, it was only when the Temple was destroyed that the ultimate sacrifice of martyrdom was called for. Christianity, like paganism, has human sacrifice at the center of its ritual, whereas Judaism's celebration of the Temple ritual provides an outlet for this basic human urge to give.

IN ACCORDANCE WITH THEIR MEANS

What really can man give to God? He can give God the produce of the earth, gold, jewels, animals, all that he prizes, but what does all this matter to God? Perhaps the only thing man can really give is himself, his soul, his consciousness, his life. Then all those other things can be given as the molds into which man pours his life.

Moshe heard the following three things from The Holy One, Blessed be He, and was taken aback.

When He told him: *Then shall they give every man a ransom for his soul* (Exodus 30:12), Moshe pondered: "Who is in a position to give a ransom for his soul?"

The Holy One, Blessed be He, told him: *I do not ask for ransom in accordance with My means but in accordance with their means. This they shall give* (Exodus 30:13).

R. Meir expounded: "The Holy One, Blessed be He, took what resembled a coin of fire from beneath the Throne of Glory and showed Moshe: 'This they shall give.'"

Similarly, when The Holy One, Blessed be He, told Moshe: *Command the children of Israel and say unto them, My food which is presented unto Me for an offering made by fire* (Numbers 28:2).

Moshe thought: Who is in a position to supply Him with sufficient offerings? If we offer to Him all the beasts of the field and lay on the altar all the trees of Lebanon it will not suffice for Him; as it says: *Lebanon is not sufficient fuel, nor the beasts thereof sufficient for burnt offerings* (Isaiah 40:16).

The Holy One, Blessed be He said to him: *I do not ask for*

offerings in accordance with My means but in accordance with theirs.
[*Bamidbar Rabbah* 12:3]

THE PLACE THAT THE LORD YOUR GOD WILL CHOOSE

It is the instinctive feeling that some places have a special quality to encapsulate the infinite that instills in man a compulsion for temple-building. In the wilderness, when the Israelites lived a nomadic existence in tents, the *Shekhinah* "lived" in a Tent of Meeting. When Israel's early kings, David and Solomon, built up the Land of Israel, they felt guilty about living in a palace while the Ark of God dwelt in a primitive tent. At Sinai, Israel celebrated its marriage to God, and there the relationship was consummated. With actual knowledge, a certain innocence and spontaneity in the love relationship inevitably had to go. Privacy was needed for full intimacy, and a greater reserve and modesty were necessary in public, simply because of the fullness of the union. God's appearances took place less frequently under a tree or on a mountain, but were more often formalized in the context of the Sanctuary:

A mortal king had a daughter whom he loved exceedingly. So long as his daughter was small he used to speak with her in public, or if he saw her in the courtyard he spoke with her. When she grew up and attained puberty, the king said: "It befits not my daughter's dignity that I should converse with her in public. Make a pavilion for her so that when I wish to speak with my daughter I shall do so inside the pavilion."

In the same way, when the The Holy One, Blessed be He, saw Israel in Egypt, they were in the child stage (of nationhood), as it says: *When Israel was a child, then I loved him, and out of Egypt I called My son* (Hosea 11: 1).

When He saw them by the sea, He spoke with them, as it says: *And the Lord said unto Moses: Wherefore criest thou unto Me?* (Exodus 14:15).

When He saw them at Sinai, He spoke with them, as it says: *The Lord spoke with you face to face* (Deuteronomy 5:4).

As soon as they received the Torah, they became His nation and said: *All that the Lord hath spoken will we do and obey* (Exodus 24:7). The Holy One, Blessed be He, observed: "It is not in keeping with the dignity of My children that I should hold converse with them in the open. *Make a Tabernacle for Me*, and when I have to communicate with them I shall do so from the Tabernacle." [*Bamidbar Rabbah* 12: 4]

Notwithstanding this view of the Temple as a manifestation of Israel's desire to give, the idea of Infinity accommodating itself to some limited space or receptacle still remains incomprehensible. Solomon lived with this problem as the Temple was rising up under his orders. During the dedication ceremony, he asked:

> Is it true that God can
>   dwell on earth
> when the Heavens
> and the highest Heavens
> of the Heavens
> Cannot contain You
> How much less this House
>   that I have built. . .
>   *Solomon's prayer*, Dedication of the Temple (I Kings 8:27)

Yehuda Halevi, the great Spanish-Jewish poet, paraphrases the problem:

> The whirling world cannot contain Thee;
> How then the chambers of a Temple?[32]

TO CONTAIN INFINITY

But God has the capacity both to extend His Light to fill all worlds and to contract it so as to be "present" at some particular location. Transcending all, His true greatness is expressed in His "humility," in His readiness to reveal Himself in the smallest detail of Creation. Paradoxically, Luria read his doctrine of *Tzimtzum* and the apparent retreat of God's Light into some "point" out of the *Midrashim* that describe God's ability to contract His *Shekhinah* into a particular locality—for example, the planks of the Tabernacle and the space between the Cherubim.

When God commanded Moshe, "Build Me a Sanctuary that I might dwell among you," Moshe found great difficulty in complying. Why? He found it inconceivable that something so vast could be contained in any place.

R. Yohanan bar Nappaha explained. Moshe heard God say, "Let them make Me a Sanctuary." Immediately he became very worried about how God could be confined within the four walls of a Tabernacle. But the Holy One reassured him: "I shall descend and contract My *Shekhinah* between [the planks of the tabernacle] down below (*Pesikta de Rav Kahana* 20a, 62a, ed. Mandelbaum, pp. 8, 33, 337).

Another explanation of The Almighty, we cannot find Him, excellent in power. When God said to Moshe: *Make a tabernacle for Me*, he exclaimed in amazement: "The Glory of The Holy One, Blessed be He, fills heaven and earth, and yet He commands *Make a tabernacle for Me!*"

Moreover, he saw prophetically that Solomon would one day build a Temple, much larger than the tabernacle, and yet would say to God: *But will God in very truth dwell on the earth? Behold, Heaven, and the Heavens cannot contain Thee; how much less this house that I have built* (I Kings 8:27).

If Solomon said this of the Temple, which was so much greater than the tabernacle, then how much more could this be said of the tabernacle? For this reason did Moshe say: *O Thou that dwellest in the covert, O Most High* (Psalm 91:1), which R. Judah ben R. Simeon explained, "He who dwells in the covert is Most High above all His creatures"; and what does it mean *In the shadow of the Almighty. . .* In the "shadow" of "the God" (*Bezal El*) "in the shadow," which Bezalel constructed; and for this reason does it say, *And abidest in the shadow of the Almighty.* God said: "Not as you think do I think; twenty boards on the north, twenty on the south, and eight in the west (suffice Me); moreover, I will descend and even confine My *Shekhinah* within one square cubit." [*Shemot Rabbah* 34:1–2]

The Holy One, Blessed be He, said to (Moshe), *Let them make Me a sanctuary, that I may dwell amongst them* (Exodus 25:8). Moshe thought: "Who is in a position to make a sanctuary in which He can dwell?" *Behold Heaven and the Heaven of the Heavens cannot contain Thee!* (I Kings 8:27).

Furthermore it says, *Do not I fill heaven and earth?* (Jeremiah 23:24). And it also says, *The heaven is My throne, and the earth is My footstool* (Isaiah 66:1).

The Holy One, Blessed be He, told him: "I do not ask for a sanctuary in accordance with My capacity, but in accordance with theirs. For should I desire it, the whole world could not hold My Glory, nor even a single one of My attendants. I only ask of you twenty cubits to the south, twenty to the north, and eight to the west."

Accordingly, Moshe said: *The Most High who dwells in the covert* – namely, The Holy One, Blessed be He, who dwells under cover in the world and sees everything but is not Himself seen, is eager to abide in our shadow. [*Bamidbar Rabbah* 12:38]

The problem is similar to the one posed by the Roman emperor who was a contemporary of Rabban Gamaliel (ca. 100 C.E.). To the latter the skeptic derisively alludes to not one but many *Shekhinata* in the mistaken belief that to multiply the One God is to defuse His Power:

You say that God is in every congregation of ten. But there are many such congregations. How many can God be in? Can there be many *Shekhinata*? [*Sanhedrin* 39a]

The answer is obvious; although God is One, the way He manifests Himself to people is manifold. Rabban Gamliel replies:

Like the Sun – He shines over all. The Sun is only one of God's multitude of servants. If it can shine over the entire world, God's Glory certainly can. [*Sanhedrin* 39a]

A heathen once asked R. Joshua ben Karhah: "Why did God choose a (lowly) thornbush from which to speak to Moshe?"

Karhah replied: "Were it a carob tree or a sycamore tree, you would have asked the same question; but to dismiss you without any reply is not right, so I will tell you why. To teach you that no place is devoid of God's Presence, not even a thornbush."

R. Eliezer said: "Just as the thornbush is the lowliest of all trees in the world, so Israel was lowly and humble in Egypt; therefore did God reveal Himself to them and redeem them." [*Shemot Rabbah* 11:5]

When God told Moshe to tell Israel that the Name He must go by was "I am that I am," He was trying to communicate to them the nature of the God they would have to deal with. God is a developmental personality who contracts His *Shekhinah* and expands it at will.

I am that I am (Exodus 2:14). God said: "When I so wish it, one of the angels who is a third of the world stretches out his hand from heaven and touches the earth, as it says: *And the form of a hand was put forth, and I was taken by a lock of my head* (Ezekiel 8:3). And when I desire it, I make those of them sit beneath a tree, as it is said: *And recline yourselves under the tree* (Genesis 18:4). And when I desire, My glory fills the whole world, as it is said: *Do not I fill heaven and earth? saith the Lord* (Jeremiah 23:24). And when I wished it, I spoke with Job from the whirlwind, as it is said: *Then the Lord answered Job out of the whirlwind* (Job 40:6). And when I wish, I speak from a thornbush." [*Shemot Rabbah* 111:6]

Sometimes God can appear to man like an angel with hair-raising physical dimensions; sometimes He can appear in one spot on earth "under a tree," allowing those to whom He appears to sit at ease; sometimes His *Shekhinah* fills the cosmos; sometimes it speaks from awe-inspiring natural events, such as a storm; and sometimes God speaks from the lowliest of hills or trees, such as Sinai or the minute thornbush. In fact, says *Baba Batra* 25a, "The *Shekhinah* is in every place!"

AS IF YOU HAVE TAKEN ME

A special building or place can induce the descent of the *Shekhinah*, as it says: "And you shall make Me a Sanctuary and I will dwell in it" (Exodus 25:8). However, the Rabbis distinguish between the People's dedication, crowned by the reward of the Divine Presence dwelling among them, and a mere adulation of fine buildings:

It was only when the Ark of the Covenant, containing the Two Tablets of stone on which were engraved the Ten Commandments, entered Solomon's temple that the Cloud of Glory filled the place (I Kings 8:5-14).

The place which Thou has made for Thy dwelling place, Lord, for Thy sanctuary, Lord, which Thy hands prepared (Exodus 15:17). This implies the necessity of building a sanctuary below, corresponding to the sanctuary above wherein the Holy One is daily served and worshipped. [*Zohar* III:59b]

The *Midrash* says that on hearing the news that God was going to send His *Shekhinah* to dwell in the Sanctuary down below, the angels were worried that they, who depended for their staple diet on *Shekhinah* radiance, would somehow suffer in the move. What would be left for them? God reassured them that though the Tabernacle would be filled with Divine Presence, the Heavens would not suffer any reduction in splendor.

Similarly, because the *Shekhinah* is infinite, it can rest in the Sanctuary without the rest of the world being depleted of the fullness of Divine Presence.

He made the pillars of (the palanquin) of silver. . . the inside thereof being inlaid with love (Song of Songs 3:10). Rabbah Azayiah said . . . "This refers to the *Shekhinah*."

One verse says *So that the priest could not stand to minister by reason of the cloud, for the glory of the Lord filled the house of the Lord* (I Kings 8:11), and another verse says, *And the court was full of the brightness of the Lord's glory* (Ezekiel 10:4). [The *Yalkut* and *Tanhuma* adduce, instead of this verse, *Behold heaven and the heavens of the heavens cannot contain Thee* (I Kings 8:27).]

How can these two verses be reconciled? R. Joshua of Siknin said in the name of R. Levi: To what can the tent of meeting be compared? To a cave adjoining the sea, which the sea overflows when it becomes rough. Though the cave is filled, the sea loses nothing. So the tent of meeting was filled with the glory of the Divine Presence, and yet the world lost nothing of the *Shekhinah*. [*Shir HaShirim Rabbah* 3:10]

The problem, which the Roman emperor did not wholly realize, is not that the multiple appearances of Divinity make God multiple; there is more than enough *Shekhinah* to satisfy everyone; the question is simply one of receptivity.

And they shall make an Ark of acacia wood (Exodus 25:10). Thus it is written, *The Almighty, we cannot find Him, excellent in power* (Job 37:23). Job said to his companions: Do you imagine that even all you have said exhausts all His praise? All the things you have said, *why These are but the outskirts of His ways* (Job 26:14). Elihu said: *The Almighty, we cannot find Him, excellent in power.* He that hears this verse may exclaim, "Perhaps, Heaven forbid, this is blasphemy!" But this is what Elihu meant: We will never find God's strength (fully) displayed toward any of His creatures, for He does not visit His creatures with burdensome laws, but comes to each one according to his strength. For know thou, that if God had come upon Israel with the full might of His strength when He gave them the Torah, they would not have been able to withstand it, as it says, *If we hear the voice of the Lord our God any more, then we shall die* (Deuteronomy 5:22). God, however, came upon them according to their individual strength, for it says, *The voice of the Lord is with power* (Psalm 29:4). It does not say "with His Power" but "with power"—that is, according to the capacity of each individual. [*Shemot Rabbah* 34:1–2]

It was easy for God to contract His *Shekhinah* within one plank of acacia wood; the challenge was for human beings to receive the *Shekhinah* with their limitations.

I have commanded you (says God) concerning many acts of taking in order to make you worthy of Divine reward . . . I said to you: *That they take Me an offering* (Exodus 25:2), with a view that I should dwell among you; as it says, *And let them make Me a sanctuary that I may dwell among them* (Exodus 25:8).

The Holy One, Blessed be He, as it were said: "Take Me and I will dwell among you." He does not say: "that they take an offering," but *that they take Me an offering,* as if to say "It is Me Whom you take." I said to you *That they take unto you pure olive oil . . . for the light* (Exodus 27:20). But do I require your light? Lo, it is written, *The light dwelleth with Him* (Daniel 2:22). It is only in order to make you worthy and to atone for your souls, which are compared to a lamp; as it says, *The spirit of man is the lamp of the Lord, searching all the inward parts* (Proverbs 20:27). On this occasion, also, when I told you, *Ye shall take on the first day.* [*Vayikra Rabbah* 30:13]

And what is that "pure oil" that Israel must "take" as one takes a wife, for self-completion? It is the *Shekhinah* that is taken – God Himself. Another explanation is that each person takes his life in his hand; he must tap into the depths of his own being. It is only that kind of "taking" of pure oil that is rewarded with the light of the *Shekhinah.*

God has given . . . the Torah to Israel and He said to them: *It is as if you have taken Me.* [*Shemot Rabbah* 33:7]

THE HUMANITY OF GOD

Ideally, say the rationalists, one should be able to worship God without any props. For a God transcendent and omnipresent does not need to dwell in any particular place; in fact, He does not have any "needs" at all. However, the *Hasidim,* the Kabbalists before them, and the writers of the *Midrash* have a different and far less cold-blooded approach. If man really wishes to "attach" himself to God, he must do so in the same way that he cares for the most precious thing in his life. Just as he loves a woman, food, music, or life itself, so must he love God; he must color his love with his whole humanity and not "transcend" it.

And this is precisely the point where God and humanity meet. As soon as the Transcendental enters into a relationship with the finite, He is in that dimension and no longer infinite – and the central concept of Judaism is that God relates to man. For man, God is not transcendent; certainly the character sketch we get of Him from the Bible is not cold and unemotional. He is all that man cares for, and that is why God lets His *Shekhinah* rest on the Sanctuary.

Ramban (Nachmanides), and many of the greatest of the Kabbalists and later the *Hasidim*, believe that there is indeed a sense where God "needs" to gain an entry into the physical world through His Presence in our lives—He does indeed "need" our light. And this need on God's part for human love is the whole meaning of *Shekhinah* and all the sexual and erotic accoutrements surrounding Her.

The Bible says explicitly—not once, but many times—that God wants to dwell in the Land, God wants to dwell in the Sanctuary

> The dwelling of the *Shekhinah* below (in the midst of the Jewish People) is a supreme and not a vulgar desire on the part of the Most High. [Ramban on Exodus 25:8]

In fact, say the commentators, the whole of Israel's early history—the liberation from enslavement, the exodus from Egypt, the journey through the wilderness—was for one purpose only—that the *Shekhinah* should live with the Jewish People (Exodus 29:46).

This is like a suitor who takes a woman out on dates, gives her presents, writes to her, phones her. Why? Because at the end of it all he hopes to marry her and to live and share his life with her. (The root of *Shekhinah* means "intimacy," from the Hebrew word *Shokhen*, neighbor.) This closest of all possible relationships is symbolized by the love dynamic between a man and a woman. When the Jewish People came on pilgrimage from the most farflung corners of Israel and beyond to celebrate the Festivals in the Temple, the curtain was drawn away from the Holy of Holies to reveal the Cherubim, one male, one female, their bodies interlocked in passionate embrace. Then the pilgrims were told: "Look! You are beloved before God as the love between man and woman" (*Yoma* 54a).

The real sphere of activity of the *Shekhinah* is below. [*Bereishit Rabbah* 19:7]

God's desire for the physical heart of man is viewed by the Kabbalists as almost biological. Rabbi Isaac of Acre (fourteenth century) explains how the very highest spiritual passion, far from transcending the body, inheres and is dependent upon much that is superficially repulsive, by comparing the sacrifices in the Temple to sexual intercourse. As he describes it, one scholar asked another how it was possible that animal sacrifice, with all its disgusting concomitants, such as the burning of fat, sprinkling of blood, and acrid smell of the burning of skin and hair, should help to sustain the world. His colleague replied that a child coming upon a man and woman in the act of intercourse might through ignorance ask the same question, yet out of precisely such primitive appetite, spirituality gains sustenance.[33]

As the "Previous" Lubavitcher Rebbe, R. Yosef Yitzhak put it:

> The ultimate purpose for the creation of the spiritual and physical world lies in God's desire to have a dwelling place in the lower world and that man's domination and transformation of his physical nature will reveal the Presence of God even on this material plane; and though the soul descends from the spiritual heights and becomes clothed in a physical body with animal desires which cover up and obscure the soul's light, nevertheless the soul (through its service in Torah and *Mitzvot*) will be able to refine and purify the body, its animal desires, and its surrounding environment as well. And through this the individual can bring about the revelation (of the *Shekhinah*) in his own personal Temple.[34]

COSMIC CORRESPONDENCES

The Most High desired to dwell below. As a result, everything below is a reflection or mirror image of its idealized (Platonic) essence above, and even in the waters there are correspondences and mirror reflections of the earthly reality.

> R. Berekiah began . . . *For all that is in the heaven (is) in the earth* (I Chronicles 29:11). You will find that everything God has created in the heaven, He has also created on earth. (R. Berekiah is referring to Platonic replicas of Ideal Essences.)
>
> Of heaven are we told: *Above Him stood the Seraphim* (Isaiah 6:2); of earth: *Acacia wood, standing up* (Exodus 26:15). (The planks of acacia wood of the Holy of Holies were supposed to represent the fiery host of angels guarding the Celestial Throne. But also they were transplanted *Sefirot* channeling Divine light.)
>
> Of the throne above we read, *(Then Solomon sat on) the throne of the Lord* (I Chronicles 29:23). And of that below: *Thou throne of glory, on high from the beginning, thou place of our sanctuary* (Jeremiah 17:12). (By this time, not only are correspondences made between above and below, but also exchanges. King Solomon sits on the Supernal Throne, while the Temple below is referred to as *Thou Throne of our Glory, on high from the beginning.*)
>
> Referring to "above," we read, *And the light dwelleth with him* (Daniel 11:22), and to "below," *That they bring thee pure olive oil, beaten for the light* (Exodus 27:20).
>
> What is more, those that are below are dearer to Him than those above; as a proof, you can see that He left those things that were on high and descended to dwell with those that were below, as it says, *And let them make Me a sanctuary, that I might dwell among them* (Exodus 25:8). God instructed Moshe, *After their pattern*: as thou seeest above, so make below.
>
> It does not say in this context, "He set up acacia trees," but *(he made the tabernacle) of acacia trees standing up* (Exodus 26:15) in the same way as they were stationed in the heavenly host. For instance, just as above there are *Seraphim* (fiery angels) standing, so below there are acacia trees standing; just as above there are stars, so below there are stars.
>
> R. Hiyya ben Abba said: This shows that the hooks of gold in the tabernacle showed like stars in the firmament.
>
> "And" so to speak, (said God), "if thou makest (the likeness

of) this heavenly one below, I shall leave My heavenly Council above and descend and confine My divine presence within the midst of you below." [*Shemot Rabbah* 33:4; *Shir HaShirim Rabbah* 3:11]

Perhaps the Temple, which according to the Talmud resembled a forest of golden fruit trees (*Yoma* 82, 83), was called "Lebanon" after the splendid Lebanese cedars it was made of; or perhaps it was so called after the *Levanah*, the Moon, symbol of feminine beauty and *Shekhinah*.

So the Temple contained at its heart a wild burning forest, all of gold. What was this forest but the golden branches of the *Menorah* springing from one ingot of gold? What was this forest but the cosmological Tree of the *Sefirot*? And what, in fact, are the *Sefirot* but the transplantation (or emanation) of light from within God Himself. The authors of *Bereishit Rabbah* called emanation "uprooting," the transplantation of divine shrubs with supraterrestrial roots into the Creation.[35] A parallel is drawn between the verses "And the Lord God planted a garden eastward in Eden" (Genesis 2:8) and "The trees of the Lord have their fill; the cedars of Lebanon which He has planted" (Psalm 104:17). R. Hanina says of this pair of verses, "They (the *Sefirot*) were like the horns of the locusts, and the Holy One . . . uprooted them and transplanted them into the Garden of Eden" (*Bereishit Rabbah* 15:1).

The *Sefirot* are compared to horned locusts because it was believed the horny membrane covering them was made of the same substance as the body, just as the Tree of Life is said to bear fruit with the same taste as its root. This is to hint at the idea that the *Sefirot* were an intrinsic part of the Divine Light, but projected onto a physical plane.

"CUTTINGS" FROM EDEN

Rabbi Ezra of Gerona says that the "gathering of the roses" mentioned in the Song of Songs refers to emanation that brings an inflow of Divine light and blessing into the world of nature. According to Rabbi Ezra, the process that gave rise to the *Sefirot* was not simply an act of creation out of nothing, but rather an act of "uprooting" of various potencies from their primeval preexistence in the bosom of the Creator and their transplantation within the terrestrial paradise.

Eden was filled with trees and plants and flowers, produced from cuttings transplanted straight from the *Ein-Sof*. These Adam and Eve were given the gratifying task of tending. Each plant was guarded by an angel or a star. Had Adam and Eve not eaten the forbidden fruit during the last hours before *Shabbat*, they and the shrubs and the *Sefirot* would have been transplanted back into the Celestial Eden for *Shabbat*.

A link is then made between Lebanon and the Garden of Eden, so that the movement of light is from God to nature to civilization – epitomized by a man-made building (the Temple) constructed of the cedars of Lebanon, inside which forests of pure gold were re-created. "Cuttings" from Eden were transplanted directly into "Lebanon," or the golden man-made forest of the Holy Temple:

> When King Solomon built the Sanctuary, he planted therein all kinds of (trees of) golden delights, which were bringing forth fruit in their seasons, and as the winds blew at them, they would fall off, as it is written: *May his fruits rustle like Lebanon* (Psalm 72:16). However, when the enemies of the Jewish People forcibly entered, (these cedars) withered, as it is written: *And the flower of Lebanon languishes* (Nahum 1:4); and the Holy One, blessed be He, will in the future restore them, as it is said: *It shall blossom abundantly and rejoice, even with joy and singing; the glory of Lebanon shall be given unto it* (Isaiah 35:2). [*Yoma* 39b]

The *Midrash* says that trees provide an environment especially benign and healthful to man, just as the Temple does for the Jewish People.

> All the trees were created for man's companionship. All the conversation of mankind concerns the earth: Has the earth produced, or has the earth not produced? And all mankind's prayers

concern the earth: "Lord, may the earth yield (fruit)"; or, "Lord, may the earth prosper!"

All the prayers of Israel, however, are for the Temple: "Lord, may the Temple be rebuilt!" And, "When will the Temple be rebuilt?" [*Bereishit Rabbah* 13:2–5]

The Temple existed to atone for the sins of Israel and to provide a wave of regeneration and cosmic renewal, just as the forests renew man's natural environment. And, in a sense, the Temple, like the *Menorah*, is a cosmic Tree extending from above down, and from below up, drawing into the material world the abundant energies of the Infinite, at the same time transmitting sap of prayers and sacrifice to renew the fabric of the cosmos. For, as trees demonstrate, Creation is a living organism – everything in it affecting everything else. The *Menorah* – and the Sanctuary in which it lived, like certain olive trees in Greece and Italy that hold up the structure of a house – did not serve solely as a lamp bearer, but also as a Tree.

The original *Menorah* is seen as an inverted cosmic tree extending from above down, drawing into the material world the abundant energies of the Infinite. Man also is like an inverted Tree, with his roots in Heaven, drawing down light and blessing from his skyborne branches and *Sefirot*.

WHEN THE LAND YIELDS HER FRUITS

Before the Dispersion, when the Temple was standing, the Jews were an agricultural people. Produce and the fruits of the land meant survival. Nevertheless, the choicest were brought to the Temple with great pageantry. Selection of the *Bikkurim* (first fruits) – for example, for the Festival of *Shavuot* – was from the first and the finest. The kind of beauty that arises spontaneously from this outflow of nature to civilization – from the outlying agricultural settlements of the Land of Israel to Jerusalem – is demonstrated by this cavalcade of offerings from the length and breadth of the Land in tribute to the Holy City, she who is the "joy of all the earth."

How were the *Bikkurim* set aside? A man goes down into his field. He sees a fig that ripened, a cluster of grapes that ripened, or a pomegranate that ripened. He ties a reed-rope around the fruit and says: "Let these be first fruits."

How were the first fruits taken up (to Jerusalem)? All (the inhabitants of) the cities that constituted the sector assembled in the city of the sector and spent the night in the open place thereof without entering any of the houses. Early in the morning the officer said: "Let us arise and go up to Zion, unto the house of the Lord our God."

Those who lived nearby brought fresh figs and grapes, but those from a distance brought dried figs and raisins. An ox with horns bedecked with gold and with an olive crown on its head led the way. The flute was played before them until they were near Jerusalem. They sent messengers in advance and ornamentally arrayed their first fruits. The governors and chiefs and treasurers (of the Temple) went out to meet them. According to the rank of the entrants they used to go forth. All the skilled artisans of Jerusalem would stand up before them and greet them: "Brothers, men of such and such a place, we are delighted to welcome you."

They used to play the flute in front of them till they reached the Temple Mount; and when they reached the Temple Mount, even King Agrippa would take a basket and place it on his shoulder and walk as far as the Temple Court. As they approached the court, the Levites sang the song: "I will extol Thee, O Lord, for Thou hast raised me up and hast not suffered mine enemies to rejoice over me."

The rich brought their first fruits in baskets overlaid with silver or gold, whilst the poor used wicker baskets of peeled willow branches, and they used to give the baskets and the first fruits to the priest. [*Bikkurim* 3:1–5]

A certain Rabbi Hanina, who was poor, was very wistful when he saw his more fortunate brothers bring sacrifices and peace offerings to the Temple.

He said to himself: "All of them are bringing up peace offerings to Jerusalem, but I am not bringing up anything. What should I do?"

Immediately he went out to the quarry of his city and found there one stone. He went and he hewed it and he polished it and he dyed it gold.

He said, "I am taking on the responsibility to get this to Jerusalem."

He tried to hire porters and begged them: "Please bring this stone up to Jerusalem for me."

They replied: "Give us 100 pieces of gold in payment and we shall bring your stone up for you to Jerusalem."

He said to them, "But where should I have 100 pieces of gold or even 50 to give you?"

Immediately God prepared for him 50 angels who looked like ordinary people. They said to him: "Master, give us five selahs and we shall bring up your stone for you to Jerusalem. However (we shall do this) only on condition that you take your share of the burden alongside us." The next moment they found themselves in Jerusalem.

He wanted to pay them but they had disappeared.

. . . People informed him: "It appears the Ministering Angels helped you bring up the stone to Jerusalem." Immediately the Sages joined together and gave him his share of the pay he had earned together with the Angels. [*Shir HaShirim Rabbah* 1:1,2–4]

Not only Israelites, but also their allies showed their friendship by sending gifts for the Temple. Solomon had close ties with other nations and included in the Temple service prayers and sacrifice for their benefit. They in turn brought up gifts to the Temple. Solomon's close friend Hiram, King of Tyre, supplied the Temple with gold and with cedarwood, the acacia in which the *Shekhinah* itself rested, so that the whole edifice was referred to as "Lebanon," literally, a shining white or yellow moonlike substance with purifying properties. Mysteriously, because of Hiram's romantic gift, it is as if there were a golden orchard of a Lebanon planted right in the building's heart, a secret Eden.

During the last years of the Second Temple, two royal converts, King Munbaz of Adiabene and his mother, Queen Helena, also gave lavish gifts.

King Munbaz made all the handles of the vessels that were used on the Day of Atonement of gold. Helena, his mother, made a *Menorah* over the Temple gate. She also made a golden table on which was inscribed the chapter concerning the woman who had gone astray (Numbers 5:12–31). When the sun rose, sparkling rays proceeded from it (the golden table) and all knew that it was time to read the *Shema.* [*Yoma* 37a–b]

Miracles were known to have occurred in connection with these gifts. When a certain Nicanor returned from Alexandria with two gates for the Temple, he was caught in a storm at sea.

Thereupon they took one of his doors and cast it into the sea and yet the sea would not stop its rage. When, thereupon, they prepared to cast the other into the sea, he rose and clung to it, saying: "Cast me in with it!" They did so, and the sea dramatically stopped its raging. He was deeply grieved about the other (door). As he arrived at the harbor of Acco, it broke through and came up from under the sides of the boat. Others say: A monster of the sea swallowed it and spat it out on the dry land. . . . Therefore, all the gates in the Sanctuary were changed for golden ones, with the exception of the Nicanor gates, because of the miracles wrought with them. But some say: Because the bronze of which they were made had a golden hue. R. Eliezer ben Jacob said: "It was Corinthian bronze, which shone like gold." [*Yoma* 8a, 37b–38a]

(In the Second Temple) all the building was overlaid with gold except the backs of the doors. R. Isaac said: This statement of the *Mishnah* refers to the Second Temple; but in the First Temple even the backs of the doors were covered with gold.

We learn (*Yoma* 44b) that seven kinds of gold were employed in the Temple: good gold, pure gold, chased gold, beaten gold, gold of *mufaz,* refined gold, gold of *parvayim.*

"Good gold" means literally "good," as it says, *And the gold of that land is good* (Genesis 11:12), commenting on which R. Isaac said: "It is good to have in the house, it is good to take with on a journey."

"Pure gold": so called because it could be put in the furnace and come out without losing anything. (It was entirely free from dross.)

R. Judah said in the name of R. Ammi: Solomon passed a thousand talents of gold through the furnace a thousand times until he reduced them to one talent. R. Jose said in the name of R. Judah: It happened that the candlestick of the Temple was heavier than the candlestick of the wilderness by the weight of one Gordian denarius, and it passed through the furnace eighty times until it lost the excess. At first it lost dross, but subsequently it lost only very minute quantities.

"Chased gold": so called because it made all goldsmiths shut up their shops. "Beaten gold" is gold that is drawn out like wax. Hadrian had an egg's weight of it; Diocletian had a Gordian denarius of it; the present Government has none of it and never had any.

"Gold of *mufaz*": (Some say) it resembles sulphur flaring up in the fire. . . . Rabbi Abun said it was called after the country of its origin, Ufaz.

Different explanations were given for "Refined gold": The School of Rabbi Jannai said that it was cut into pieces the size of olives and given to ostriches to eat, and it issued from them refined.

The school of R. Judah ben Rabbi Simeon said: They used to bury it in dung for seven years and it came out refined.

"Gold of *parvayim*": Resh Lakish said: It was red, resembling the blood of a bullock (*par*). Some say it produced fruit (*perot*). For when Solomon built the Temple, he fashioned out of this gold all manner of trees, and when the trees in the field produced their fruit, those in the Temple also produced fruit, and the fruit used to drop off and it was gathered and put aside for the repair of the Temple. When. . . an image (was) set up in the Temple, all those trees withered, so it says, *And the flower of Lebanon languisheth!* (Nahum 1:4). But in the time to come, the Holy One, blessed be He, will restore them, as it says, *It shall blossom abundantly* (Isaiah 35:2). [*Shir HaShirim Rabbah* 3:10]

In the two verses plant processes of withering and blossoming are applied to the Temple. Josephus, wanting to impress the Romans with the glories of Jewish civilization, assumed that the *Menorah* had to be made of gold (*Antiquities of the Jews* 12:238), but he was wrong. Although the original *Menorah* of Moshe was fashioned out of one golden ingot, even the candelabrum of the Temple did not have to be made of gold. When the Maccabees rededicated the Temple in 165 B.C.E., they were unable to use the golden *Menorah*, which had been defiled by the Syrians.

At first, according to the Talmud, this band of warriors made a *Menorah* of iron overlaid with tin (or wood). They took seven iron swords, covered them with zinc, and used them as a *Menorah* (*Megillat Taanit; Pesikta Rabbati* 2:1).

However, when the Maccabees became high priests and kings, when they grew richer, they made it of silver; when they grew richer still, they made it of gold" (*Avodah Zarah* 43b, *Rosh Hashanah* 24b).

THE LAMP WITHIN THE TEMPLE

Most of the materials dedicated to the Temple, such as R. Hanina's stone, if not made of precious metal, were polished and burnished to shine with the special luster that is a hallmark of beauty. Little wonder that the Temple and the whole of the Holy City, presented a breathtaking spectacle. The Rabbis said:

> He who has not seen Jerusalem in her splendor has never seen a desirable city in his life. He who has not seen the Temple in its full construction has never seen a glorious building in his life. Which Temple? . . . The allusion is to the building of Herod. Of what did he build it? . . . Of yellow and white marble. Some there are who say, with yellow, blue and white marble. The building rose in tiers. . . . He intended at first to overlay it with gold, but the Rabbis told him, Leave it alone for it is more beautiful as it is, as it looks like the waves of the sea. [*Sukkah* 51b]

Frequently, the irridescence of precious metal creates the effect of flames. The Temple, built stone by stone out of Israel's and mankind's sense of dedication, blazed with glory and was full of *Shekhinah* Light.

It is the basic association with light and fire that links the Temple with the Lamp inside it, that essential part of the inner furniture that sometimes takes on the symbolism of the whole. Just as the *Menorah*, a sign of God's Presence, blossomed from a single lump of fiery gold ("A pure candlestick came down from Heaven . . ."), so it is said that when the Third Temple is built, no human hand will have any part in its construction. It will arise out of a Divine Fire, and human hand will have no power against it.

The flow of Divine Light generated by the Holy Temple and by the *Menorah* within the Temple is also associated with the idea of the *Sukkah*. (God's Tent of Meeting in the desert, forerunner of the Temple, is referred to in English as a tabernacle.) *Sukkot* is the Temple festival par excellence. The desert Sanctuary and both Temples were dedicated during the *Sukkot* season.

The *Midrash* lists seven festivals of dedication – among them the dedication of Jerusalem after it had been enclosed by walls and the purification and dedication of the Temple by the Hasmoneans on *Hanukkah*. (The very word *Hanukkah* means dedication in Hebrew.) All these dedications are accompanied by light and by fire. The Dedication of the World to Come will also be "celebrated with the light of lamps" when the "light of the moon shall become like the light of the sun and the light of the sun shall become seven-fold" (*Pesikta Rabbati* 26).

Since Temple days the Festival of *Sukkot* had associations with the kindling of the seven-branched *Menorot*:

> There were three golden candlesticks with four golden bowls on the top of each of them and four ladders to each, and four youths drawn from the priestly stock in whose hands were held jars of oil containing one hundred and twenty log (*measures*), which they poured into the bowls. [*Sukkot* 51a]

Wicks made out of the wornout drawers and girdles of the priests were made to float in the oil and the lamps were kindled. The illumination was so intense that "there was not a courtyard in Jerusalem that was not illumined by the light of the place of the waterdrawing. A woman could sift wheat by the illumination of the Place of the Water-Drawing" (*Sukkot* 53a).

The combustion of oil produces energy in the form of light and fire. In biblical times it was the anointing, and not the crowning, of the King that was all-important and that surrounded his forehead with an aura of light as God's chosen. In the same way, when we kindle the oil of the *Hanukkah* lamp – that "Sanctuary in little" – an act of crowning as well as of dedication takes place as the flames spring up.

THE CROWNING OF A QUEEN

What is oil but the supernal influx descending upon the highest *Sefirah* – that of *Keter*, or Crown. From the earliest times, the kindling of the *Menorah* has been associated with crowning. The *Menorah* was lit with pure olive oil, symbolic of the flow of Divine energy to an earthly (female) receptacle. The *Midrash* suggests that the olive tree brought light to the world in the days of Noah because the dove that Noah sent out after the flood had abated to find out if there was any dry land in sight returned with the leaf of the olive tree in its mouth (*Vayikra Rabbah* 31:10).

Oil is also a sign of purity and fertility. The oil of *Hanukkah* remained untainted because it was found in a sealed cruse. Similarly, in the Christian parable of the five wise virgins and the five foolish virgins, the girls who saved their oil are themselves little jugs of oil, or *Menorot*, sealed and pure. They have something to give their husbands, while the five foolish girls do not. The parable ends: "Then shall the kingdom of Heaven be likened unto ten virgins who took their lamps and went out to meet the bridegroom" (Matthew 25:1).

Clearly, the Ten Virgin *Menorah*-Bearers are in themselves ten *Menorot* (Bearers of the Light), as in the ten *Menorot* of Solomon and the ten *Sefirot* through which light is drawn into the material world. On *Hanukkah*, the little cruse of oil bore the seal of the High Priest – the guarantee of its purity; and the lights of *Hanukkah* are "holy" ("dedicated") and cannot be used for mundane purposes.

The *Menorah*, when its light springs up, is a bride bedecked with jewels under the wedding canopy. And if, according to Jewish tradition, every bride is a queen at the time of her wedding, then the *Menorah* lights compose a wedding garland and the diadem of a Queen.

It is likely that the images of *Menorot* and virgins were combined in the early literature and were considered the embodiment of both God's spirit and the creative force at work in Nature. The *Midrash* describes Israel's act of kindling almost in terms of an incarnation: "The Holy One, Blessed be He, was forced to dwell [the same root as *Shekhinah*] with Israel in a Lamp" (*Bamidbar Rabbah* 15:9).

Both the *Menorah* and the Sanctuary of which the *Menorah* is a replica in miniature are compared to crowns, and the dedication of both is through oil.

> *With the crown with which his mother crowned him* (Song of Songs 3:11). This means that just as a crown is set with precious stones and pearls, so the Tent of Meeting stood out because of the blue and purple and scarlet and fine linen (with which it was decorated). [*Shir HaShirim Rabbah* 3:11]

The Festival of *Sukkot* is like a coronation of God in His Palace. The ritual of waving the palm branch and citron is a means of paying homage to the "King of Kings." The same ceremony is reenacted in metallic motifs with scepter and orb in the coronation of a human sovereign. The scepter (*lulav*) is a phallic symbol of masculine force (*Yesod*), while the orb (*etrog*) is simply the world, or *Malkhut*.

The first *Hanukkah* was celebrated, with the waving of palm branches, as a belated Festival of *Sukkot* (II *Maccabees* 10:6–7), whereas long before the historic events that gave rise to the *Hanukkah* of the Hasmoneans, *Sukkot* was the original festival celebrated by the illumination of golden *Menorot*. It certainly seems that the seven-branched *lulav* is a vegetable version of the Golden Temple *Menorah*. What is more, the *lulav*, when taken together with the date, is the one tree that is both masculine and feminine, like the *Menorah* – both a phallus and a receptacle. The sight of waving palm branches, or *Sukkot*, across the Land of Israel is like the wonderful sight of the kindling of many beacons, or *Menorot*. The panorama presented across the hills of Zion is like a living crown.

The image is that not only of a crown hovering over the head, but of a roof or protected enclosure.

Sukkot commemorates the early stages of Israel's relationship with God in the wilderness. This was an arduous nomadic journey before the construction of the Temple, when the Jewish people camped out in *Sukkot* (makeshift and uncomfortable booths) and followed a Pillar of Fire by night and a Pillar of Cloud by day (symbolic of God's Presence) wherever it might lead. As a reward for their faith, immediately after the Revelation at Sinai, God instructed Moshe to tell the People to make Him also a tabernacle (*Mishkan*) so that He might "dwell in their midst" (Exodus 25:8). So, God's Tabernacle is a crown for faith.

The *Sukkah*, like the Temple and like all Creation, represents a feminine space, symbolic of God's Presence (*Shekhinah*), and His special care. There is a Jewish saying, forged in the unsettled conditions of exile: "A man's wife is his true home." (He may have to flee his physical abode, but she provides shelter and love for him in exile.) Similarly with the Tabernacle. Although the physical structure of the Temple was destroyed, the *Shekhinah* (internal spirit of the *Mishkan*) is with the Jewish People in good and bad times – a faith demonstrated by Israel's willingness to abandon comfort year by year to celebrate the Festival of *Sukkot* in a flimsy hut.

CLOUDS OF GLORY

Rabbi Akiva made the surprising statement that the Children of Israel did not dwell in actual booths, but that God provided for each and every one of them clouds of glory (His Divine Providence). Rabbi Akiva continues:

> *Sukkot* . . . means only clouds of glory, as it is said: *And the Lord will create over the whole habitation of Mount Zion and over her assemblies, a cloud and smoke by day, and the shining of a flaming fire by night; for over*

all the glory shall be a canopy. And there shall be a pavilion for a shadow in the daytime (Isaiah 4:5–6). [*Mekilta de Rabbi Yishmael* 1:175]

The *Mishkan* thus represents the People's dedication, crowned by the Divine Presence dwelling among them. If the *Sukkah* is symbolic of the tents of the Israelites and their faith in God, it also symbolizes the reward of that faith and the building of a central *Mishkan*. Just as the Israelites projected their own physical needs and provided God with a Tent, so God, by allowing His Cloud of Glory to rest on the *Mishkan* also, as it were, snipped out individual Clouds of Glory for each tent in the encampment. The real security for each Israelite was not the flimsy, collapsible canvas overhead, but a personal sense of God's Presence.

The Pillars of Cloud and Fire (or "Glory") represent two aspects of *Shekhinah*. When the Sanctuary was set up, both hovered in the form of Clouds of Glory over the Tent. Of them, the *Mekilta* asks:

> But how is it possible to say this (that they followed Pillars of Fire or of Cloud)? Is it not written: *The whole earth is filled with His glory?* (Isaiah 6:3). Why then did these Pillars appear at one particular place?
>
> R. Antoninos explained this with the following example: A king once sat in judgment and remained in court until after dark. His children also remained in court so they could accompany him home. When they left his palace, he took a lantern and carried it, lighting the way for his children. His officers and nobles saw this and offered to carry the lantern for the king. The king told them: "I do not carry the lamp because I lack someone else to carry it. I carry it to show my love for my children."
>
> R. Antoninos explained that the same is true of God. He reveals His glory before His children as an expression of (His) love for them. [*Mekilta* 25a on Exodus 14:21–2]

"Clouds of Glory" were a brilliant radiation of *Shekhinah*, a nurturing maternal Presence hovering over the tent, or crowning of the people's head. God's protective Providence – Clouds of Glory – has become synonymous with a *Sukkah*, spread out over

Israel like a pavilion or a tent, like the wings of a bird. The concave space suggested by all these images is inherently feminine. If the Cloud is associated with the maternal quality of the 'Presence,' it is also linked with the Mothers of Israel.

> You find that as long as Sarah lived, a cloud hung over her tent; when she died, that cloud disappeared; but when Rebekah came, it (the cloud) returned.
>
> As long as Sarah lived, her doors were wide open; at her death, that liberality ceased; but when Rebekah came, that open-handedness returned.
>
> As long as Sarah lived, there was a blessing in her dough, and the lamp used to burn from the evening of the Sabbath until the evening of the following Sabbath; when she died, these ceased, but when Rebekah came, they returned. [*Bereishit Rabbah* 60:15]

Not only is the *Sukkah* compared to the Clouds of Glory; the ideal *Sukkah* is made of the same glorious fabric as those clouds. Also, the *Menorah*, symbol of *Shekhinah* within the *Mishkan*, is compared to them.

The *Sukkah* is covered by foliage – in Hebrew, *Sikhakh* – a delicate green tracery or froth, light as the breath of a baby, figuring Clouds of Glory in plant form. The density of the *Sikhakh* is crucial from a halakhic point of view, as there must be a certain amount of light and a certain amount of shadow. The *Sukkah* has, in fact, been compared totally to the *Tzel*, or "shadow" of the Most High – the shadow of her wings providing protection for Israel. Indeed, the word *sikhakh* comes from *sokhaikh*, the cocooning of the wings of the angels.

THE "FABRIC" OF THE *SUKKAH*

Man has two souls – his individual egotistical soul and the soul that belongs to the whole of mankind. That is why sleeping in a *Sukkah* is so important: It is all-encompassing; we have no control over our destiny. Body and soul are given over to the sensuous and spiritual experience. In the same way, says Rabbi Azulai, to sleep in Israel gives man a new soul – a collective soul.

To be capable of true self-sacrifice (surrender of the soul), one must be open to what is beyond oneself – the small soul must be capable of growing into the larger soul. And this also is the link between the individual light and the *Menorah*, a crown of lights in which each light remains distinct. The *Menorah*, the *Sukkah*, the Temple, Israel, even *Shabbat* are all-encompassing. They demand absolutely everything of a person – nothing is held back – and in return, they give man a new soul; a totally new quality of experience.[36]

An extravagant hypothesis about the fabric of the *Sukkah* has been suggested. At the time of the Redemption, the Tabernacle uniting the whole of Israel will be cut from the skin of Leviathan.

> *Rabbi* in the name of R. Johanan said: The Holy One . . . will in time to come make a tabernacle for the righteous from the skin of Leviathan; for it is said: *Canst thou fill tabernacles with his skin* (Job 40:31, Isaiah 40:3). [*Nezikin* 11; *Baba Batra* 5:75a]

What does this mean? There are two parallel legends – one concerning the Hidden Light that was too dazzling for the world and was therefore hidden for the righteous until the time of the Redemption and the other concerning Leviathan, male and female, who were so powerful they would have swallowed the world. What did God do to prevent this? He killed the female and chained the male. The flesh of the female was pickled for the righteous to feast on during the time of the Redemption.

The female Leviathan and "First Light" are obviously synonymous, and the fabric of the *Sukkah* at the time of the Redemption is extended from nothing other than *Shekhinah* Light.

A related myth is that of the Moon (female), whose size was diminished until the Redemption. She, too, is a symbol of *Shekhinah* and pure femininity.

SOLOMON AND THE FEMINIZATION OF LIGHT

Spatialization, or the impregnation of the womb of Creation, immediately implied feminization. As soon as God required a "Place" for His Light, the light "descended" and became feminized. The container (womb) and what fills the container are considered feminine. So if the *Shekhinah* is seen as feminine, so are Temple, *Menorah*, and Holy Land. So, also, the human soul is seen as feminine – whatever the person's sex. The *Neshamah*, like Jerusalem and like the *Shekhinah*, is sometimes known in stories as the "king's daughter" because that part of *Kabbalah* that involves light imagery is nothing but a spatialization or unfolding of spirituality.

In *Midrash Mishle*, the *Shekhinah* appears for the first time as a separate entity from God.[37] Little wonder that Her very first words in Jewish literature were spoken in defense of King Solomon's right to enter into the Future Life. There are countless reasons why She should have considered Solomon Her champion and favorite in the world below. He was the one who built a Place for Her in Jerusalem. He pursued many women in order to find Her. His love of many women and his amassing of great wealth were all to find Wisdom and to demonstrate in his own Kingdom and in his life the splendor of the Kingdom of God. Under Her influence He wrote Ecclesiastes and the Song of Songs.

Solomon, great king as he was, was held *persona non grata* by the rabbis. Not only did the Men of the Great Assembly want to exclude Ecclesiastes and the Song of Songs from the biblical canon on the grounds that Ecclesiastes was too cynical and world-weary and the Song of Songs too sensuous and erotic, but they also considered officially excluding Solomon from the life of the world-to-come.

Solomon's Beloved, the Shepherdess of the Song of Songs, had Her dark counterpart waiting to undermine all that he dreamt of.

On the same night that Solomon completed the work of the Holy Temple, he married Batia, the daughter of Pharaoh. There was great jubilation because of the Temple and jubilation because of Pharaoh's daughter, but the jubilation for Pharaoh's daughter exceeded that of the Temple; as the proverbs says: "Everybody flatters the king." At that instant the Holy One, blessed be He, conceived the plan of destroying Jerusalem.

Our Rabbis say: "Pharaoh's daughter brought him a thou-

sand kinds of musical instruments and ordered that they be
played to him that same night. What else did she do? She spread
a canopy above his bed and set therein all manner of precious
stones and pearls that glittered like stars and constellations, and
every time Solomon wished to rise he would see these stars and
constellations, and so he went on sleeping until four hours after
sunrise."

Now Israel were grieved, for it was the day of the dedication
of the Temple, and they could not perform the service because
Solomon was asleep and they were afraid to wake him, out of
their awe of royalty. They went and informed Bathsheba his
mother, and she came and woke him up and reproved him.
Hence it is written: *The burden wherewith his mother corrected him*
(Proverbs 31:1). R. Johanan said: "This teaches that his mother
bent him over a column (scolded him severely) and said to him:
'*What, my son* (Proverbs 31:2). Everyone knows that your father
was a God-fearing man. Now they will speak thus: Bathsheba is
his mother; she brought him to it!'" [*Bamidbar Rabbah* 10:4]

Samson Raphael Hirsch tells us that the promise "And I
shall dwell in your midst" is dependent not merely on compli-
ance with certain technical strictures concerning the construction
of the Sanctuary but upon a whole ethical stand. The promised
reward extends far beyond the mere presence of God in the
Temple. It means His closeness in every aspect of the national
and private life. The Sanctuary was destroyed once, and the
Temple twice, not because of any defect in architecture, but
because Israel's public and private life at the time simply did not
justify God's Presence there.[38]

Though there was nothing wrong with giving splendid
expression to true religious feeling, the trouble came when attachment to sumptuous forms and ceremonies (whether expressed in Temple sacrifices or the outward observance of the
commandments) was at the expense of genuine self-dedication:

Thus says the Lord . . . Mend your ways and your deeds
and I shall dwell among you in this place. But don't trust in
the lying words of those who say: The Temple of the Lord,

The Temple of the Lord, The Temple of the Lord. Rather should you really mend your ways and your doings by having just relationships between man and man. [Jeremiah 7:3–5]

The atrophy of inward dedication among the People to match the outward appearance took from the Temple its spiritual reason for existence and necessitated its destruction. To save Israel's inner potential for holiness, the outer husk of the building had to go.

RETREAT OF THE *SHEKHINAH*

From the ark she moved onto the cherub
From the Cherub onto the other Cherub
From the second Cherub onto the threshold of the Temple
From the threshold into the court of the Priests
From the court onto the altar in the court
From the altar onto the roof of the Temple
From the roof onto the wall
From the wall into the city of Jerusalem
From the city onto the Mount of Olives
From the Mount of Olives into the desert.

(*Rosh Hashanah* 31a)

The *Shekhinah* fell back from Her proud Dwelling-place; at each of the nine stations, equivalent to nine out of the ten *Sefirot*, she became more remote. She spent three and a half years on the Mount of Olives, crying out three times a day: "Return, you backsliding children, Return!" (Jeremiah 3:22).

In the desert She waited six months for Israel to repent. When they failed to do so, She cried in desperation: "Let them perish!" (*Rosh Hashanah* 31a).

Then She made up Her mind: "I shall go and return to My

Place (in Heaven) till they acknowledge their guilt." [*Pesikta de Rav Kahana* 13:11, ed. Mandelbaum, p. 235]

Solomon's self-indulgence and love of pleasure and luxury may have prompted the rabbis to propose debarring him and his writings from Eternal Life, but history has judged otherwise. Solomon may have sinned in the grand style, but it was done in a passionate pursuit of wisdom. So he came to be known as *Yedidyah*, the "Lover" or "Beloved of God," and he used his experience and great passions to gain love and knowledge of God.

THE BEST OF SONGS

In defense of the "Song," Rabbi Akiva made his famous declaration: "All the Writings are holy. But the Song of Songs is the 'Holy of Holies.'"

Rabbi Akiva said: Far be it from anyone in Israel to dispute that The Song of Songs (is part of the canon). For the whole world only existed, so to speak, for the day on which The Song of Songs was given to it. [*Shir HaShirim Rabbah* 1:1]

No longer are we speaking of the Song of Solomon but of the "Song of Songs" of Israel. So complimentary is it to *Knesset Yisrael* that She has adopted it.

We say with the *Midrash*: the "Song of Songs" – the best of songs, the most excellent of songs, the finest of songs. Let us recite songs and praises to Him who has made us a theme of song in the world, as it says, *And they shall shout aloud the songs of the Temple* (Amos 8:3) – that is, the praises of the Temple. [*Shir HaShirim Rabbah* 1:1]

Obviously the People of Israel is being compared with the Temple – God's resting place below. The building itself is an objectification of the People. In fact, the People as a whole and every one of its individuals together are God's true dwelling-place.

R. Johanan said in the name of R. Aha, who had it from R. Simeon ben Abba: "Let us recite songs and praises to Him who will one day cause the holy spirit to rest upon us, let us sing before Him many songs." In all other songs either God praises Israel or they praise Him. . . . Here, however, they praise Him and He praises them. He says to Her: *Behold thou art beautiful, my beloved* (Song of Songs 1:16). And She says to Him: *Behold thou art beautiful, my beloved, verily pleasant* (Song of Songs 1:17). Another commented: "A double Song." And he was capped: "Double and reduplicated."

She says to Him, He says to her: "You are beautiful and holy. Holy and beautiful are You!" [*Shir HaShirim Rabbah* 1:1]

DAUGHTER OF SPLENDOR

A traditional response, when faced with great beauty and excellence, is to wonder: Whose daughter is she and where is she from? Of what culture is she a part? Where did she absorb those good manners and who instilled in her such fine qualities? Where is the place of her glory?

These are the questions Eliezer asked of Rivkah after receiving kindness from her at the Well, the questions Odysseus asked of Nausicaa. The simple pastoral clothes these wonderful women wore only enhanced their regal natures. All the externals surrounding Perdita of Shakespeare's *A Winter's Tale* summed up in her beauty; the way she carried herself, the way she moved, the way she danced—betrayed that she was no shepherdess but the "Daughter of the King":

> When you sing,
> I'll have you buy and sell so, so give alms,
> Pray so; and, for the ord'ring your affairs,
> To sing them too: when you do dance,
>   I wish you
> A wave o'the sea, that you
>   might ever do
> Nothing but that; move still, still so,

And own no other function: each
  your doings,
So singular in each particular,
Crowns what you are doing
  in the present deeds,
That all your acts are queens.

A Winter's Tale (IV:3)

For the same reasons, the *Shekhinah* in exile is often pictured in the marketplace crying Her wares, and the Beloved of the Song of Songs is a Shepherdess. These disguises, by very contrast, spell out the royalty and divinity of the King whose daughter she is. Similarly, in the *Kedushah*, it is the highest praise to say: "Where is the Place of His Glory!" And when the *Bahir* was written down—by the early Middle Ages at the latest—this "Glory" was now feminized, and the same encomium was addressed to Her. In fact, both the King and His Daughter come in essence from the same place. Although "place" suggests the idea of "vessel"—a feminine receptacle—God or Endless Light is also referred to as the "Place" because He pervades and transcends everything. Rav Ashlag, the twentieth-century commentator on Lurianic *Kabbalah*, has described "light" as the "Place" of the Creation, whereas the *Midrash* says that although God is "the Place of His world, His world is not His Place" (*Bereishit Rabbah* 67:9).

But the *Bahir* sees place as essentially feminine:

What is meant by *the whole earth is full of His Glory* (Isaiah 6:3)? That is, the "earth," which was created on the first day and corresponds in the higher spheres to the Land of Israel, full of the Glory of God.

And what is it? . . . (of which it is said) *Blessed be the Glory of God from His* (read here by the *Bahir* as *Her*) *Place* (Ezekiel 3:12). But what is the Glory of God?

A parable: It is like a king who had in his chamber the queen, who enraptured all of his legions; and they had sons. These sons came every day to see the king and to pay him homage. They said to him: "Where is our Mother?" He replied: "You cannot see her now."

Then they said: *"May She be blessed wherever She is."* From this it follows that no one really knows Her Place.

A parable: A king's daughter came from afar and nobody knew from where she came, until the people saw that she was capable, beautiful, and excellent in all that she did. Then they said: "Truly this one for sure is taken from the form of the light, for through her deeds the world becomes luminous."

Then they asked her: "Where are you from?"

She said: "From My Place."

Then they said: "If that is so, the people in your place are absolutely marvelous!"

May She be praised and blessed in Her Place. [*Bahir,* no. 90]

The meaning of this last parable is that the King's Daughter is essentially *Place Personified.* If she comes from the "Form of the Light," this only means that she is the spatialization of Light, the Light of God's Immanence and *Shekhinah.*

FROM THE "FORM OF THE LIGHT"

The *Bahir* talks of God's "Bride" or "Daughter" as a personification of all His Kingly Splendor. The Bride is the "Heart" of God, the Hebrew Gematria of which is *lev,* or 32, representing the thirty-two paths of Wisdom leading to the Center.[39]

It is like a king who was in the innermost chamber and the number of the chambers was thirty-two, and a path led to each chamber. Did it suit the king that every one could take his paths and enter into his chambers at will? No!

Did it suit him not to display openly his pearl and treasures, jewels and precious stones? No!

What did He do? He took the "daughter" and combined in her and in her garments (that is, manifestations) all the paths, and whoever wishes to enter the interior must look this way.

And in His great love for her He sometimes called her "my sister," for they had come from the same place; sometimes He

called her "my daughter," for she is His daughter, and sometimes
He called her "my mother." [*Bahir*, no. 43]

This "daughter" is pure object and jewel reflecting the
Divine radiance to man – possibly she is the Torah. In herself she
has utterly no personality, but is merely and consummately a
"Beautiful Vessel."

The *Bahir* asks whether Abraham had a daughter. This
question implies that this daughter was the *Shekhinah*. The narrative continues in the form of a parable:

> It is like a king who had a perfect servant. . . . Then the king said:
> "What should I give to this servant or what should I do for
> him?. . . Lo, I have made a beautiful vessel, and inside are
> beautiful gems to which none can be compared, and they are the
> jewels of kings. I shall give them to him, and he may partake of
> them instead of me." That is what is written: "God blessed
> Abraham with 'all things.'" [*Bahir*, no. 52]

The *Shekhinah* here is pure objectivization of Divine royalty
and splendor. She is the priceless jewel called *Soheret*, bartered
back and forth in the marketplace. While early Jewish kings
rarely wore crowns but were simply anointed with oil, they
hung their jewels on their queens. The queen's function in the
world of substance is to be a Jewel-Bearer. Her physical attributes
and embellishments are not her own. Essentially a tiny beje-
welled masklike figure, *Malkhut* serves to reflect the splendid
image of the king.

In addition to serving as figure for the Image of God, the
precious stone, jewel, or the Pearl is both *Sophia* (Torah or Divine
Wisdom) and the collective soul of man – the soul of the individual fragmented into the separate rays and sparklets of this
Jewel.

All the luster of gold and precious stones employed in
decoration of the Temple are only the external expression of the
People's desire to dedicate their best to God's service, whereas
the images of light and fire are hints at a corresponding desire on
the part of the *Shekhinah* to dwell with the People.

Gold (*zahav* in Hebrew) is broken down in the *Bahir* into

three separate letters standing for Three Divine Attributes in the divine—*z* for the masculine element, *h* for the feminine of the human soul, and *b* for the union of the two, with the male actually inside the female. This is illustrated with a story:

> *The royal princess, her dress embroidered with golden mountings!* (Psalm 45:14). This is like a king who had a daughter, good and beautiful, gracious and perfect, and he married her to the son of a king and gave her garments, a crown, and jewels, and gave her to him with a great fortune.
> Can the king now live without (outside) his daughter? No!
> Can he always be with her all day? No!
> What did he do? He made a window between himself and her, and whenever the father and the daughter needed each other, they would come together through the window. [*Bahir*, no. 36]

Here the *Bahir* is talking about the relationship between spiritual and physical. The "daughter" is God's gift of Divinity to the physical world, whereas the window is the way He still keeps contact with her.

Torah is like a jewel with an infinite number of facets, flashing and refracting the light of Truth according to the complexion of the human soul. Ben Bag Bag said: "Turn it and turn it (the Torah); for everything is in it" (*Avot* 5:21).

According to the *Bahir*, this jewel is the "stone that the builders (the Patriarchs) rejected, which has become the chief cornerstone" (Psalm 118:22). The *Bahir* interprets Habakkuk 3:2 in the following way:

> A king had a valuable jewel . . . and when he rejoiced, he hugged it and kissed it, set it upon his head, and loved it. Habakkuk said to him: Even though the kings are with you, that jewel is the ornament of your world. [*Bahir*, nos. 49, 51]

THE *SHEKHINAH* AND *KNESSET YISRAEL*

Between the time of writing the *Bahir* and the *Zohar*, not only had the *Shekhinah* been feminized, but it had also coalesced with an idealized archetype of *Knesset Yisrael*:

Rabbi Jose began to speak on the words: *The Song of Songs, which is Solomon's* (Songs of Songs 1:1). Said he: "This song King Solomon poured forth when the Temple was erected and all the worlds, above and below, had reached their perfect consummation. And although . . . the exact time it was sung is a matter of dispute by the members of the Fellowship, we may be certain it was not sung until that time of absolute completion when the Moon – the *Shekhinah* – came to her fullness and was revealed in the full perfection of her radiance, and when the Temple had been erected in the likeness of the Temple that is above.

"The Holy One, blessed be He, then experienced such joy as He had hardly known since the creation of the world. When Moshe set up the Tabernacle in the wilderness, another such was raised in the heavenly spheres. . . . But when the first Temple was completed, another Tabernacle was erected at the same time, which was a center for all the world, shedding radiance upon all things and giving light to all spheres. Then the world was firmly established, and all the supernal casements were opened to pour forth light, and all the worlds experienced such joy as had never been known to them before, and celestial and terrestrial beings alike broke forth in song, and the song that they sang is the 'Song of Songs,' or, as we render, 'Song of the Singers,' of those musicians who play before the Holy One, blessed be He.

"King David composed 'A Song of Ascents'; King Solomon composed the 'Song of Songs.' Now what is the difference between the two? Do we not interpret both titles to mean each and both the same thing? Yes, indeed, this is so, for both (songs) are certainly one, but in the days of David all the singers of the spheres were not yet set in their rightful places to sing the praises of the King, because the Temple was not yet in existence. For, as on earth, the Levites are divided into choirs, so it is above, and the upper correspond to the lower. But not before the Temple was erected did they take up their right places, and the lamp (of *Malkhut*), which before gave no light, began then to shed radiance abroad, and then this song was sung to the glory of the Supernal King (*Tiferet*), the King to whom peace belongs. This Song is superior to all songs of praise that have ever been sung. The day when this Song was revealed on earth was perfect in all things. Therefore this Song is the 'Holy of Holies.' "[40] [*Zohar* II:143a, b]

"David endeavored to prepare the maidens (the celestial spheres) and to adorn them for the Matrona's presence so that She and her maidens might be manifested in beauty and grace.

"When Solomon came he found the Matrona and the virgins thus adorned, so he in his turn aspired to lead the Bride to the Bridegroom. He brought the Bridegroom to the place where beneath the marriage canopy the Bride awaited Him, and drew them together with words of love, that they might be united as One in perfection, in perfect love. Therefore Solomon produced a more sublime song than all other men.

"Moshe, by building the Tabernacle, brought about the union of the Matrona with the world here below; Solomon brought about the perfect union of the Matrona with the Bridegroom above: he first led Him to the canopy, and then brought them both down to this world. . . .

"(The Holy One married the *Shekhinah* to Moshe in the lower world) and she became, as it were, the Bride of Moshe. . . . As soon as She was united with (him), She descended to this world and united Herself with it, and She became firmly established in this world as never before.

"But no man since Adam . . . has ever brought about love and union above except Solomon, who, as we have said, first prepared that union and then invited the Bridegroom and the Bride to the House he prepared for them.

"Blessed are David and Solomon his son who have furthered the Supernal Union. Since the day when the Holy One said to the Moon, Go and make yourself small, She was never again joined in perfect union with the Sun until Solomon arose." [*Zohar* II:144b–145a]

According to this passage from the *Zohar*–and as David's Psalms seem to indicate–Solomon and David were concerned with bringing the reign of the Heavenly Kingdom down to earth and uniting Divinity and the world. When the *Zohar* says David wished to "adorn the Queen and the maidens," it is referring to the *Shekhinah* and the *Sefirot*. The *olamot* (worlds and capsules of concealment of Divine Light and of mutually coexisting worlds that are hidden within the visible world) become *alamot* (virgins), and "Queen" is a reference to the most physical *Sefirah* of *Malkhut*, over which the *Shekhinah* reigns. "Queens and maidens" also refers to Israel and the nations. What David wanted in his beautiful psalms was to "adorn the queen," in preparation for a coronation-wedding, and what Solomon wanted in his many love affairs was to reunite God and His feminine counterpart, the *Shekhinah* above and *Knesset Yisrael* below.

> *Great is the Lord and highly to be praised in the city of our God, in the mountain of his holiness* (Psalm 48:2). When is the Lord called "great"? When *Knesset Yisrael* is to be found with Him: *in the city of our God is He great. In the city of our God* means "with the city of our God". . . and we learn that a king without a queen is not a (real) king and is neither great nor praised. Thus, so long as the male is without a female, all his excellency is removed from him and he is not in the category of Adam, and moreover he is not worthy of being blessed. [*Zohar* IV:5a,b]

Here the quality of "greatness" is contingent. A king needs subjects and a city to be called a great king. This shadow-reputation is signified by his feminine counterpart, his queen. In Hebrew, the expression "great in" is overtly sexual, as in "great with child." The male is inside the female when his potency is proved. So God's desire to "dwell in thy midst" also makes use of sexual imagery. He sends out His Indwelling Presence, His *Shekhinah*, the feminine shadowy part of Divinity, to dwell in the *Mishkan* (the Place of Dwelling).

Rabbi Abba began:

> *Have them take Me a gift from everyone* (Exodus 25:2). A parable: There was a king among his people, but the queen was not with the king. As long as the queen was not with the king, the people did not feel secure; they could not dwell safely. As soon as the queen came, all the people rejoiced and dwelt safely.

> So, at first, even though the Blessed Holy One performed mira-

cles and signs through Moses, the people did not feel secure. As soon as the Blessed Holy One said, "Have them take My gift. I place My Dwelling in your midst," everyone felt secure and rejoiced in the rite of the Blessed Holy One.

As it is written: *On the day that Moses consummated setting up the Dwelling* (Numbers 7:1), the Bride of Moses came down to earth.[41]

The *Mishkan* is here a female image, the "Queen" without whom the people can have no confidence in their king.

In the story, four people are involved. The kings represent both Moses and God. The Queen is the *Mishkan*. Just as Moses is God's representative vis-à-vis the People, so the Queen is the People's representative to the King. For the People, the Queen is an intercessionary figure without whom they feel they have no connection with the king. So it was with the *Mishkan*, which was an idealized essence of *Knesset Yisrael* within the royal palace.

Knesset Yisrael refers not only to a human group but also to the *Shekhinah*, the feminine-receptive element within the Godhead, designated elsewhere as Queen, Kingdom, Jerusalem, Temple, Sabbath, Glory, and Moon.

In fact, the Queen here is many things; she is God's Indwelling Presence, but she is more human-feminine than Divine. She is the beautiful daughter of the People who is their one warm human link with the remote King in the royal palace. The origin of the *Shekhinah* as one of the People (*Knesset Yisrael*) is made clear on page 66, where the relationship of the King with His People parallels that of the King with His Queen. This is why, allegorically, Esther clad in her "royal robe" is the personification of Queenliness, or of the *Shekhinah* pleading with the King for the life of her people. Indeed, another name for the *Shekhinah* is *Knesset Yisrael*, an idealized, glamorous embodiment of the sovereign spirit of Israel. On another level of interpretation, Moshe (heroic male) is the human representative faced with the task of bringing down the Divine, or that part of the Divine that can so be brought down—categorized as feminine—another name for which is the Lower Torah. There, Moshe (humanity) wins

Torah (God's "daughter"), and through him she becomes the bride of Israel and of mankind.

There is a play on the Hebrew when celebrating the "completion" of the construction of the *Mishkan*. The Hebrew for "finishing," "yearning," or "perfecting" (*kallah*) almost means bride, because there is a Jewish notion that man is not complete until he is married, and union with woman marks the completion of the original structure of the human being, which was hermaphroditic. Therefore, the completion of the *Mishkan* marks the wedding of Israel with God, or Moshe with the *Shekhinah*.

Therefore, when the People received the Torah, husbands and wives had to separate for three days. Moshe had to leave his wife Zipporah in order to wed the Torah (alias for the *Shekhinah*), thus bringing Her into the ranks of Israel.

Everything on earth has its heavenly counterpart. Similarly, there is a Temple below and a Temple above, a Jerusalem on earth and a Celestial Jerusalem, Jews below and an idealized entity called *Knesset Yisrael* above, an earthly individual and a heavenly "partner," an "I–Thou," a fallible human being and a person "in the world of light." Just as in nature everybody has a shadow, so in the spiritual world everyone has a "light" or "sun."

THE CELESTIAL BRIDE

This "light" counterpart is His essential self, His suprasensory personal guide, a figure of light. According to Rabbi Moses Cordovero (1522–1570), the great mystic of Safed, each Jew has two souls—his own soul and his twin soul in the spiritual sphere—his soul typified as feminine and a celestial bride and crown of light for his head.

> Man stands between the two females, the physical female . . . and the *Shekhinah* who stands above him to bless him.[42]

Not only is there the workaday female—the "wife"—whom there is the obligation to cherish so as to give joy to the *Shekhinah*, but in the Divine pleroma there are two other females. The *Sefirah* of *Malkhut*, *Shekhinah*, or *Knesset Yisrael* that governs the material world is Rachel, or the "daughter," corresponding to Leah, or the "mother" of the *Sefirah* of *Binah* (Understanding) in the transcendent sphere. The *Kabbalah* of the Ari (Rabbi Isaac Luria) is more concerned with creating "unifications" between Mother and Daughter than with creating harmony between *Keter* and *Malkhut*, the masculine and feminine aspects within the Godhead.

The *Zohar* describes beautifully what happens when Moshe draws closer to the *Shekhinah* and the spiritual stripping that takes place in seven stages in order to arm Moshe, representative of masculine-kind, with the innermost secrets of the Torah.

The Old Man continued:

Human beings are so confused in their minds.
They do not see the way of truth in Torah.
Torah calls out to them every day, in love,
but they do not want to turn their heads.
Even though I have said that Torah removes a
       word from her sheath,
is seen for a moment, then quickly hides away—
       that is certainly true—
but when she reveals herself from her sheath
       and hides herself right away,
she does so only for those who know
       her intimately.

A parable.
To what can this be compared?
To a lovely princess
beautiful in every way and hidden deep
       within her palace.

She has one lover, unknown to anyone; he is
       hidden too:
Out of his love for her, this lover passes
       by her gate constantly,
       lifting his eyes to every side.
She knows that her lover is hovering by her gate constantly.

What does she do?
She opens a little window in her hidden palace
    and reveals her face to her lover,
then swiftly withdraws, concealing herself.
No one near the lover sees or reflects,
    only the lover,
    and his heart and his soul and everything within him
    flow out to her.
And he knows that out of love for him
    she revealed herself for that one moment
    to awaken love in him.
So it is with a word of Torah.[43]

Part of the fascination of Divine revelation is in the captivating alternation of concealment with disclosure and illumination.

In the *Midrash* it says that the emanations of Creation
proceeded by God "drawing forth light like a garment," and it
seems that is also how knowledge unfolds:

R. Simeon ben Jehozadak sent a message to R. Samuel bar
Nahman, saying: "I understand that you are a master of storytel-
ling; so tell me whence light went forth to the world?" (In other
words: Where is the Place of His Glory.)

R. Samuel bar Nahman replied: "The Holy One covered
Himself with a white robe, and the world–all of it–was made
bright by the radiance of His majesty."

But since R. Samuel bar Nahman gave his reply in a whisper, R. Simeon ben Jehozadak pressed him further: "Why whisper? Is not what you have just whispered said right out in the
verse," *Who coverest Thyself with Thy light as with a garment* (Psalm
104:2)?

Thereupon R. Samuel bar Nahman answered: "It was told
me in a whisper, so I answered you in a whisper. Indeed, had not
R. Isaac expounded in public the theme that light came into
the world from the robe with which the Holy One covered
Himself, it would have been prohibited to say so in public (even

in a whisper)."[*Pesikta de Rav Kahana, Piske* 21, trans. Braude, pp. 341–342]

A *Midrash* compares the Tabernacle to a robe and Israel to the "cantankerous" wife of a king (God) (*Bamidbar Rabbah* 12:7). The King asked His wife to make him a splendid robe. Being goodhearted, she complied. All the while she was busy with this labor of love, her faculties and skills were engaged, and she stopped complaining. But when the King saw her task was almost completed, he tensed himself for the next round of grumbles.

Another *Midrash* compares God's command to Moshe – "Build Me a Tabernacle!" – to the ordering of a new outfit from the royal tailor.

> R. Berekiah in the name of R. Bezalel said that God was like a king who showed himself to his servant in a beautiful robe and adorned with diamonds and said to him, "Make me one like this."
>
> He said: "My lord the king, how can I make one like this?"
>
> So the Holy One, blessed be He, said to Moshe: "Make Me a tabernacle."
>
> He said before Him: "Sovereign of the Universe, how can I make one like this?"
>
> He replied: "See and make."
>
> He said to Him: "How can I make one like this?"
>
> He replied: "After their pattern: as thou seeest above, so make below." [*Shir HaShirim Rabbah* 3:11]

Shekhinah is the archetype of this garment or of the descent of veil upon veil of God's Light.

But what is this "Presence" whose entry into the Temple even in the Bible is celebrated by clouds of glory. Neither in the Bible nor in the Talmud, where this Presence begins to be called *Shekhinah*, is there any question of its being feminine or in any way independent from God.

However, the love song between Solomon and his Shepherdess is read by the writers of the *Midrash* as a parable of the love between God and Israel (personifed as a woman). Because of this bond, He sent His *Shekhinah* to dwell in the Sanctuary they had built for Him. The *Shekhinah* itself is not feminine, but simply part of the Divine.

In the Talmud also, the Voice of the *Shekhinah* is the Voice of God addressing man; never is there any idea that the Voice of the *Shekhinah* might enter into dialogue with God! The Indwelling aspect of God, the God Who appears in places and to individuals, is named *Shekhinah* on earth and *Kavod*, the "Throne of Glory" or simply "the Glory," in the celestial mystical realms. In *Merkavah* literature, such as the "Measure of the Body," Gershom Scholem has pointed out that the *Shekhinah* is even quantified.[44] But there is never an indication that we are talking about anything specifically feminine, only God as He appears to man.

> Its radiance, however, is so great that the angels must cover their faces with their wings so as not to see it. The ministering angels are removed from the *Shekhinah* by myriads of parasangs, and the body of the *Shekhinah* itself measures millions of miles.[45] [*Shemot Rabbah* 32:4]

Here God's *Shekhinah* is so concretized and reified that its vast proportions are even measurable. It is God Present in the world almost as a physical object. It is God as pure mask, but certainly with no personality of its own. Even the tremendous physical dimensions attributed to the *Shekhinah* are only an attempt to express a spiritual concept—prophetic insight and the radiant vision of God.

In late *Aggadata,* such phrases as "Where *Knesset Yisrael* was exiled, there the *Shekhinah* accompanied them," link the fate and fortunes of the *Shekhinah* with a feminine personification of Israel. In retrospect, the two were simply telescoped into one large Feminine collectivity. In fact, this connection is already made by Jeremiah, who visualizes not the *Shekhinah* but *Knesset Yisrael* as constituting the most intimate undergarments of the Divine: "For as the girdle cleaveth to the loins of a man, so have I caused the whole House of Israel to cleave unto Me" (Jeremiah 13:11).[46] It is appropriate that only in the exile referred to by

Jeremiah and in the separation of Jews from their land and their sovereignty–a typically feminine state of disempowerment–God's *Shekhinah* should become inextricably linked with the Jewish People.

On the one hand there was the mysterious Unknown God. On the other there was the Face He presents to the world–the *Shekhinah* (*Kavod*), the human Form on the Throne of Glory in the Vision of Ezekiel. To guard against any mushrooming of pantheistic heresies and to protect the principle of the Unity of God, philosophers such as Rambam and Saadia isolated the Glory or the *Shekhinah* from God and viewed it as God's "first Creation" ("First Light") rather than as part of Him. The *Kavod* came to be regarded in much the same light as the active intelligence of the neo-Platonists, an angelic mediator between God and man. In fact, according to the Platonists, each of the ten Spheres had an angel or Intelligence that directed it in much the same way as the *Shekhinah* ruled and guided the realm of *Malkhut*.

The name of the angel that negotiated between God and Man was *Metatron*, a sublimation of Enoch who is said to have changed his body into pure flame and his spirit into that of *Metatron*. The numerical value of *Metatron* is the same as that of God's Name, *Shaddai*. The aspect of God as Almighty was thus handed over to *Metatron* as vice-regent. But the derivation of the name is *Mater*, or *Matrona*, Mother or Mistress, as if originally God's intermediary with the world was His feminine aspect, the *Sefirah* of *Binah*. It is in this context of intermediaries and subsidiary powers–masculine and feminine–that the narrative of Passover liberation insists that the Jewish People were redeemed from Egypt "not through an angel, not through a Seraph, but by God himself."

Over the Generations, what the *Kavod* or the *Shekhinah* came to represent was the collectivity of the souls of mankind or of *Knesset Israel*, while God himself remained inscrutable. Rambam (Rabbi Moshe ben Maimon, Maimonides), by severing the umbilical cord between God and the "Presence" while protecting God from polytheism of various brands, was also implying that all the Divine manifestations and examples of Divine Providence in the Bible were in some sense a human projection (actions of the *Kavod* or the *Shekhinah* or lofty imaginings on the part of *Knesset Yisrael*) and that God Himself was above that.

The surprising thing about this development is that while Rambam and other Jewish philosophers acted to protect the purity of Jewish monotheism, most Jews of the time came out against this cold-blooded rationalism as an influence of Greek and Arab philosophy. The *Kabbalah*, on the other hand, which was developing concurrently within the very heart of the People and which visualized the *Kavod* and the *Shekhinah* as a feminine part of God, passed unchallenged and was accepted as the secret core and heart of Judaism.

THE GARMENT OF SEVEN COLORS

In contrast to the crystalline light of *Ein-Sof* designated as masculine, the *Shekhinah* (feminine) appears decked out in all the colors of the Seven *Sefirot*.

> [L]ovely in mirrors and visions, colors and hues; all these appear in the mirror that does not shine.[47]

Dyed in all the seven colors of the *Sefirot* and the wondrous illusions of the "Glass that does not shine," the *Shekhinah* – She whom the poet T.S. Eliot in "Ash Wednesday" envisages as "the Lady of the spiral staircase," successively strips off all the garments that had been necessary for the descent in order to allow for the ascending light of the transparent vision granted Moshe that "sees God face to face" (variation on the *Zohar* III:99a).

Ezekiel compares the image of God's Presence to "the appearance of the Rainbow in the clouds on a rainy day" (Ezekiel 1:28). The *Shekhinah* has also been depicted as wearing dark garments, the black that contains all color. Therefore, the multicolored flames of the Burning Coal are identical with the iridescence of all seven colors of the rainbow – one of Her many names – symbolizing the covenant, or bridge of light, between God and man.

"Behold, I have placed My bow in the cloud and it shall be a sign of the covenant between Me and the earth," was God's promise to Noah after the Flood. "When I cover the earth with clouds, the rainbow will appear in the clouds, and I will remember My covenant between Me and you and every living creature among all flesh, and the waters will never again become a flood destroying all flesh. When the rainbow is in the clouds, I will see her and remember the everlasting covenant" (Genesis 9:13–16).

The Old Man opened and said, *Moses went inside the cloud and ascended the mountain* (Exodus 24:18).

What is this cloud?

The one of which it is written: *I have placed My bow in the cloud* (Genesis 9:13).

We have learned that the Rainbow took off Her garments and gave them to Moses. Wearing that garment Moses went up the mountain; from inside it he saw what he saw, delighting in the All, up to that place.

The Comrades approached and threw themselves down in front of the Old Man. They cried, and said, If we have come into the world only to hear these words from your mouth, it is enough for us.[48]

God stretched out the heavens as a garment. These are the veils of *Shekhinah* Light. When Adam and Eve were driven out of Eden, God cut garments of light for them. Joseph's "coat of many colors" was the garment of *Shekhinah* vision. Jews wear the *Tallit* as a reminder of the care and protection of Heaven. Man swaddles himself in the *Tallit*, colored blue and white like the sky, to remove himself from all distraction and to concentrate on prayer in the miniature Tent of God's personal Providence. The *Tallit* creates for him the conditions of a Temple or the blue and crystal of the Heavens.

Symbolic meaning flows from one object to another. The Temple, the Temple *Menorah*, the *Sukkah*, and the *Tallit* are all symbolic of holy space and the care of the Presence that fills that space. The *Kippah* (head-covering) a man wears on his head is a sign of *Yirat Shamayim*, awe or the fear of Heaven that is the response to Providence and Presence and to the terrifying beauty of the Heavens.

In the wilderness, a Pillar of Cloud by day and a Pillar of Fire by night symbolized God's Presence to the Israelites, and Clouds of Glory rested over the Tent of Meeting. According to one of the early alchemists, cited by Carl Jung,[49] the anima or feminine part of the self is also represented by a "subtle imperceptible smoke." Paradoxically, the Presence of the *Shekhinah* is manifested by a cloud on the one hand and by Glory or Radiance on the other.

After forty years of wandering in the desert, God tells the Israelites: "Your garment has not withered on you . . . these forty years" (Deuteronomy 8:4). About this Rashi comments that the Clouds of Glory, like a good Heavenly Housewife, pressed and laundered their garments and kept them in good repair. And when their infants grew up, their clothes grew with them. This phenomenon, Rashi concludes, is exactly like the lizard whose skin expands with him. Rashi's explanation is based on *Devarim Rabbah* 7:11–12.

> The clothes they wore did not get old, but those they packed away in their trunks did get old.
>
> R. Eliezer, the son of R. Shimon bar Yohai asked R. Simeon ben Jose, his father-in-law: "Did then the Israelites take with them leather garments into the wilderness?"
>
> The latter replied: "The clothes which they had on them were those wherewith the ministering angels had clothed them at Sinai; therefore they did not grow old."
>
> He further asked him: "Did the (Israelites) not grow so that the clothes became too small for them?"
>
> He replied: "Do not wonder at this. When the snail grows, its shell grows with it."
>
> He then asked him: "Did not the clothes need washing?"
>
> He replied: "The (pillar of) cloud rubbed against them and whitened them."
>
> He asked him: "Seeing that the cloud consisted of fire, were they not scorched."

He replied: "Do not wonder at this. Asbestos is cleansed only by fire."

So, too, as their clothes were of heavenly make, the cloud rubbed against them without damaging them.

He asked him: "Did not the vermin breed in them?"

He replied: "If in their death no worm could touch them, how much less in their lifetime!"

He asked: "Did they not emit an evil odor because of the perspiration?"

He replied: "They used to play with the sweet-scented grass around the well, the fragrance of which permeated the world."

Whence this? For it is said, *And the smell of thy garments is like the smell of Lebanon* (Song of Songs 4:11). And whence was all this excellency derived?

From, *Thou art a fountain of gardens, a well of living waters* (Song of Songs 4:15). [*Devarim Rabbah* 7:11–12]

Since the Fall of Adam, Man's soul has been naked. God gave him a body in this world so that he could use it to do *Mitzvot*, which would sculpt him into God's image and clothe him in garments of light when he returns to God.

GOD'S BODY OF LIGHT

Therefore did Rabbi (Judah the Prince) refer to his clothes as "Those who honor me" or "My Dignity." The clothes referred to are the equivalent for man of God's Glory; they are feminine, as is the *neshamah*, for ultimately each snippet of a soul will be pieced together to form the external beauty and image of God – His celestial garment or outward covering, equivalent to His Vessel or His Lamp. In other words, God's Body or the instrument He employs in the material world is the human soul.

If a man is (sufficiently) worthy, a covering is made for him; if he is not worthy (even of this), a necklace is made for him, for it is said: *And necklaces about thy neck* (Proverbs 1:9).

If he is (sufficiently) worthy, a necklace is made for him;

if he is not worthy (even of this), an amulet is made for him; as it is said: *And thou wilt bind him for thy maidens* (Job 40:29).

The rest (of Leviathan) will be spread by the Holy One, blessed be He, upon the walls of Jerusalem, and its splendor will shine from one end of the world to the other; as it is said: *And nations shall walk at thy light, and kings at the brightness of thy rising* (Isaiah 40:3). [*Nezikin* 11; *Baba Batra* 5:75a]

Leviathan's fins radiate brilliant light, obscuring the light of the Sun. His eyes are "moons," fringed with "eyelids of the dawn." They shed such splendor that the whole sea is illuminated.

There is a belief that a special holiness is attached to fingernails and toenails. Parings are therefore burned and not swept up with dirt or garbage. This is because the First Couple was totally covered with a thin membrane of horn (*keren*) made of the same material as fingernails. This transparent substance served as a window all over man's body. It made walls of flesh disappear. The inner and outer worlds reflected each other, and man had in front of him the soul he presented to the Creator at each moment of life. The *keren* was the real "coat of light"; it emitted rays or horns of light over the entire body surface like those cast by the face of Moshe our Teacher.

When Adam and Eve were driven out of Paradise, God gave them "coats of *or*," coats of skin – that is, leather coats. Some say God gave them coats of light (the brilliant hide of Leviathan). The Heavens, in fact, also were a tent or garment of light formed of the upper parts of the sea creature.

But after Adam and Eve sinned, the Holy One took the great light of Leviathan with which He had created the world and concealed it in a treasure-house to bring it out in the future for the benefit of the righteous.[50]

Originally, man's body was made of light, and only after the Fall did it congeal into a grosser substance. Therefore, it is the task of everyone to use his physical organs to serve God in such a way that He will restore that original body.

Rav Huna says, "One who is careful about the *mitzvah* of *tzitzit* – that is, the commandment to wear fringes on the corners of one's clothes–will acquire luxurious garments." This refers to the world after death, when the dead will again come to life. "Luxurious garments" is especially related to the resurrection, for the dead will arise in their garments, as the Talmud states.

Cleopatra the queen once asked Rabbi Meir: I know that the dead will return to life, as is written. *And they will sprout from the city, as the grass from the earth* (Psalm 72:16). However, when they arise, will they be naked or will they be dressed?

Answered he: Let us compare this to wheat: a grain of wheat, although planted naked, emerges wearing several layers of garments; *Tzaddikim* (saints), who are buried in garments, will certainly arise fully clothed. [*Sanhedrin* 90b]

Rav Huna is talking about spiritual garments, whereas Cleopatra is preoccupied with externals and takes him quite literally. Egyptian to the core, she believes in the Resurrection, but the realistic physical details of how it is to happen also interest her. As we see from the gear surrounding the mummies in the Pyramids, the Egyptians were all for surrounding the dead with his favorite objects and possessions so as to make the transition to the afterlife easier. They did not anticipate any great transformation between this world and the next. As an arbiter of fashion, Cleopatra cannot help but express an interest in clothes. In fact, the garment or body of light to which Rav Huna is referring is an inner light that is projected outward.

In the Talmud, garments refer not to anything outward and worldly, but, on the contrary, to the most inward part of a human being–his soul–and the doctrine of transmigration is described in terms of some kind of celestial laundering.

A king once gave his servants royal garments.

The wise kept them clean, but the fools dirtied them in their work. When the king demanded the garments back, he was pleased with the wise but angry with the fools. Of the wise he said: "Let my robes be placed in my Treasury and they can go home in peace." Of the fools he said: "Let my robes be given to the fuller, and let them be confined in prison." [*Shabbat* 152b]

Garments and Light are both synonymous for the soul, as is demonstrated by the similar story of the Wise Virgins in the Christian Gospels. In the *Bahir*, these garments change owners, alluding to the transmigration of souls.

A king had servants and he dressed them in garments of silk and embroidery. When the servants went astray, the king pushed them away from him, removed their garments, and threw them out. He took the garments and washed them well, until there were no longer any stains on them, and arranged them in order. He then engaged other servants and dressed them in these garments without knowing whether they would be good servants. Thus they partook of garments that had already been in the world and that others had worn before them. [*Bahir*, no. 86]

Beauty and art are expected to reflect this inner radiance. As the twentieth-century philosopher Rav Kuk said at the inauguration of the Bezalel Art School in Israel, in Judaism "all kinds of embellishments are allowed," embellishments of art objects and embellishments of personal appearance.[51] In medieval times the peddler was a welcome figure to the women of the household because he sold unguents, cosmetics, and ribbons to enhance their beauty. The Talmud says, "A man should teach his daughter Greek, for it will be like jewels to her."

When the Sanctuary was being built, the ornaments offered by the Israelite women were given special honor. Despite the protests of Moshe, the mirrors that had been used to attract men were used in the Temple to fashion a salver that would strengthen the harmony between male and female energies. The Israelite women's surrender and dedication of their personal ornaments shows that ultimately what they wanted to beautify was greater than their own sensual satisfaction.

Something of the same self-sacrifice is demonstrated in the story of Rachel, wife of Rabbi Akiva, who sacrificed her youth so that her husband could study. To pay for his schooling, she cut off her luxuriant hair—"the crown of a woman's head"—and sold it in the marketplace. When Rabbi Akiva returned as a great scholar to the acclaim of all Jerusalem after many years away from his wife, Rachel, now haggard and work-worn, flung herself at his feet, only to be pushed aside by the dignitaries. But Rabbi Akiva intervened and said that instead of honoring him they should honor her, for his scholarship was due to her sacrifice.

He placed a special diadem on her shorn head, a "Jerusalem of Gold." One can only imagine what this looked like – a crown and a panorama with the skyline of the City etched on her forehead.

ATARAH: A ROYAL CROWN

There is no absolute conflict between the flesh and the spirit. The whole *Sefirah* of Substance is seen as God's Kingdom, or *Malkhut*, in which His Presence or *Shekhinah* holds sway.

The *Midrash* says that Sarah (or Princess) was the physical kingdom or "Crown" of her husband and that her realm contained ten subdivisions that added glory to the whole.

> And God said unto Abraham: As for Sarai thy wife, thou shalt not call her name Sarai, but Sarah (Princess) shall her name be (Genesis 17:15).
>
> R. Joshua ben Karhah said: "The *yud* which the Lord took from Sarai soared aloft before God and protested: 'Sovereign of the universe! Because I am the smallest of the letters, Thou hast withdrawn me from the name of that righteous woman!'"
> [*Bereishit Rabbah* 47:1]

Sarah's original name was Sarai. The numerical value of *yud* is ten and *heh* is five. God removed the *yud* from her name and split it up into two *heh*s, or fives – one for her name, which became Sarah, and one for her husband Abram, who became Abraham, "Father of multitudes," an indication of his greatness. So Abraham was crowned through Sarah, but Sarah was not crowned through Abraham.

It is written: *A virtuous woman is a crown to her husband* (Proverbs 12:4).

R. Aha said: "Her husband was crowned through her, but she was not crowned through her husband."

The Rabbis said: "She was her husband's mistress. Usually it is the husband who gives the orders, but we read here, *In all that Sarah says to you, obey her*" (Genesis 21:12). [*Bereishit Rabbah* 47:1]

While the Babylonian Talmud described the central shaft of the *Menorah* as the representative of the *Shekhinah* (*Megillah* 21b) and the most important and "honored" part of the Lamp (*Menahot* 98b), the Alexandrine Jewish philosopher Philo (first century C.E.) sometimes named the central shaft "Sophia" (Wisdom) and sometimes "Sarah." Although all the *Menorah*'s branches derive oil from this shaft, "Sarah" only shines toward God. Therefore, though she has children, she is the Eternal Virgin. And although She is active in the world and takes on the labor of a man, in Her relationship to God She is purely feminine—a receptacle of His light.

The *Menorah* gives light from one part only—"the part looking toward God. . . . It sends its beams upward toward the One, as though feeling that its light is too bright for human eyes to look upon it."[52] In Philo's partially Greek imagination, the beauty of particular beings and creatures is seen as a reflection of a higher Beauty.

By the seventeenth century, these neo-Platonic ideas of the ascent of Beauty from material to spiritual realms via a series of reflections and correspondences was an accepted part of Hasidic thought. The *Maggid* of Mezeritch describes how Beauty or radiance signals the *Shekhinah*'s entry into the physical lower regions. Sarah stands in for the majesty of the *Shekhinah*. If Sarah, of all the Mothers, is shown as being especially preoccupied with personal adornment, it is because of her name, which is the clue to what she represents. Her form reflects Divine rule. Therefore, as the prototype of royalty, she is duty bound to adorn herself and care for her appearance. According to the *Maggid*, she acted not out of petty personal vanity, but in order to "honor the image of the King" entrusted to her.

The intention of Sarah in all her adornments and embellishments was only for the sake of heaven, as someone who embellishes the image of the King. Namely, there is a connection between the supernal vitality, which is the spark of the *Shekhinah*, and man. Therefore, if someone adorns himself, he (should) do it in order to hint at the adornment of the *Shekhinah*, and his beauty is from the splendor of the *Shekhinah* (that is, the *Sefirah* of Royalty, or *Malkhut*, which also is the *Sefirah* of Physicality).[53]

It is said that Abraham was so involved with Sarah spiritually and emotionally that he never actually looked at her. But when the pair crossed the river from Israel into Egypt, a realm of darkness and sensuality, he happened to glance down and saw her reflection in the water. He was amazed at how beautiful she was: "Behold! How beautiful you are!" He was so deeply involved with her that to see her face in water–in *Kabbalah*, "water" is a feminine image for descending light–was to see an image of an image of that initial radiance.

Beauty–one's own or that of another–should be regarded as a symbol of the beauty of the *Shekhinah*, recommends the *Maggid* in a passage totally reminiscent of Plato's ascent of Love.

If one sees a beautiful and adorned human being, (he should think) that this (object of beauty) . . . is in the image of God, and he should reflect that what he is looking at is the beauty and adornment of the image of the King.

And this was the intention of Sarah when she adorned herself. Namely, as it is said: "Go out and see, daughters of Zion." That is to say: Go out of your corporeality and see the spirituality of a thing, since the corporeality of any particular thing is only a symbol and hint at the Supernal Beauty. Here a spark of beauty, out of the Beauty of the World of Beauty, is dwelling below. And it is necessary to be resolved that this beauty should be quenched as a candle (in the light of) noon, in comparison to the Supernal Splendor and Beauty.[54]

This image of a wavering candle signifying a combination of passionate spirit and speedily depleting resources symbolizes both an individual's life and personality and fleeting physical loveliness.

The *Shekhinah* is in a sense only a jeweled mask of the Divine here on earth – the glory of His Kingdom made visible. But through the *Shekhinah*, the physical pulsates and tries to come alive.

JEWELS OF THE BRIDE

Another name for the *Shekhinah* or for *Knesset Yisrael* is *Atarah*, Ornament or Crown. She is God's Jewel, His "Daughter," whose accomplishments do Him credit.

The Ari (Rabbi Isaac Luria, sixteenth century) is primarily concerned with "unifications" of the two feminine principles of Above and Below, Leah and Rachel, Mother and Daughter, rather than with a direct reconciliation of male and female. Even earlier, in the *Zohar*, the kindling with oil of the *Menorah* by *Knesset Yisrael* is described as the coronation of the "Supernal Mother." This emerges in the context of an episode in the *Zohar* in which four rabbis in search of the ultimate hear the Voice of the *Shekhinah* echo from a Cave: "Lamps shall give light from the lampstand." The *Zohar* continues:

> Here the Community of Israel (a female image) receives the light while the Supernal Mother is crowned, and all the lamps are illumined from her. [*Zohar* V:150a]

By the single act of kindling the *Menorah*, Israel is identified and united with the creative aspect of God through the symbol of the *Menorah*.

It is interesting to note that the central shaft of the *Menorah*, in addition to being feminine – *Shekhinah* or Sarah – has also taken on some of the emblematic qualities of the Sun, feeder of lesser lights. The Sun of Transcendence of the world beyond the Cave in the Platonic myth, in the *Zohar* penetrates the cave. It is from this lower depth that She Herself becomes a source and a feeder for the realms of transcendence.

The position of the *Menorah* or Crown described here is not horizontal but vertical, each lamp clearly standing for one of the *Sefirot*. The Community of Israel (Rachel, or the "Daughter") receives the light below, while the Supernal Mother is crowned above. "Just as the *Shekhinah* is below, she is on high; just as *Knesset Yisrael* conducts herself on earth, so is the Feminine essence within God."[55]

In the text from the *Zohar*, by resorting to metaphors of oil and fire, a link is established between the image of a *Menorah* and the image of a Crown. In the *Sifre* the kindling of the *Menorah* is also described as a kind of crown. A mosaic has been found in *Beit Shearim* in which a person "wears" a *Menorah* on his head like a hat or a crown.[56] And the Arab mystic Rabi'a was seen by a disciple with a lamp or Jewish *sakhina* (*Shekhinah*) on a chain shining over her head like a crown or like the rays of light in the form of an aureole shining around the face and head of Moshe.

> While she was still praying, he saw a lamp above her head, suspended without a chain, and the whole house was illuminated by the rays from that light. This enveloping radiance – *sakhinah* (*Shekhinah*), cloud of glory, indicating God's Presence – corresponds to the halo on the head of God's saints.[57]

Woman has often been characterized as the Vessel, the physical means for ascent, a "ladder of light" – she either can help her husband rise or she can bring him down. (The same is true of a husband, but these "feminine" images, lovely as they are, have not been created by women.)

Just as the Islamic woman saint Rabi'a had a lamp – the *Shekhinah* – above her head like an aureole or Crown, so does the Jewish mystic. Ascent is from the body to the soul to the *Shekhinah* Light; each is a support for the next rung in the ascent; each is a female image. But this description of Woman – through whom man can rise, and not as an end in herself – has also been turned on its head. For if she is the ladder, she is also the *Atarah* (or Diadem), and a Crown for God Himself.

Rabbi David ben Yehuda he-Hasid (early fourteenth century), who preceded the Ari, was preoccupied with unifications of the masculine and feminine aspects of the Deity. Ideally, these

are indissoluble – *hu ve-hu*. *Hu* is He or God; *ve-hu*, literally "And
He," is taken for the feminine aspect of *Malkhut* or Kingdom.
These two are described as the "Upper Eye" and the "Lower
Eye."[58] According to Rabbi David, *Keter* is the aristocratic house-
holder and *Malkhut* is the housewife who actually does the work.

A crown is an outward vessel or ornament denoting kingship. A crown's usual position on the head makes it an ideal
image for the Highest of the *Sefirot*. There are occasions, however, when this same externalization of royalty or *Shekhinah*
descends into the Lower regions. The more logical equivalent of
a Crown when it descends from the "Head" of Divinity would
be a throne or a footstool, all three being symbols of royalty.
Isaiah has called Israel and the Temple God's "footstool" and also
His Throne, and the same terminology has been used by the
Hasidim for the relationship of body to soul and soul to *Shekhinah*:

> The body becomes a throne for the soul . . . and the soul a throne
> for the light of the *Shekhinah*, which is above his head, and the
> light as it were flows all around him, and he sits in the midst of
> the light and rejoices in trembling.[59]

Throne, Crown, and Footstool all signify simply God's
visible rule from shifting perspectives. God Himself is signified
by *Or* (Light), whereas the prefix *Mem* is the attachment that
"contains" light in a lamp. This visible form of royal splendor is
shaped like the Hebrew letter *Mem*, which has an opening, in the
same way as *Menorot* (Lamps) was written in the description of
the Creation in the *Zohar* (Genesis 1:14–16):

> A king had a throne. Sometimes, he took it in his arms, some-
> times he put it on his head. They asked him why? (He said it was)
> because it was beautiful, and it made him sad to sit on it. They
> asked him: "And where does he put it on his head?" He said: "In
> the open letter *mem*." [*Bahir*, no. 25]

Frequently the feminine is described as *Vessel*, seat, or opportunity for the masculine, and the sexual position is the male
above the female. But if so, then in the story the King loves His

Glory – the Vessel – too much to treat Her with the indignity of sitting upon Her. Rather He would prefer holding Her in His arms, sometimes even raising Her higher than Himself, and causing Her to sit on His head like a crown or like the *Tefillin* of the Head.

Beauty of bodily form in *Ben Sira* (25, 26) is compared to "the shining lamp on the holy lampstand" – the long phallic base supports the aureole of the receptacle. In this case, the masculine image is the supportive one.

In *Kabbalah*, "Crown" has an additional significance – that of a source of Divine influx (of light, oil, Life, and procreative juices). God, therefore, is called *Keter* because He is the "Head" and Source of Divine Light to all channels of all the *Sefirot*. The lowest feminine *Sefirah*, on the other hand, is called *Malkhut*, or Kingdom, because She is supposed to receive and to reflect this light. She does not. Ever since the *Tzimtzum*, the "Queen" has shut herself off from all the *Sefirot* of light by means of the Curtain and has carved out for herself a "lamp of darkness." Her intention is to reverse the whole process of Creation, to return the light of all ten *Sefirot* to its source in the Endless. This "Returning Light" – the telescoping of the light in which all ten *Sefirot* are clothed – has its source in the "Queen" herself, illuminating from below to above.

Therefore, as every source is called a "Crown," the Queen's desire to put herself on a level with the Giver and Creator of the World is answered, as she herself becomes a Crown to her lord. In a complete reversal of roles, *Malkhut* or *Knesset Yisrael*, by observing the *Torah*, assists God in keeping the world in existence. She helps Him "emanate power to His attributes," that is, light or oil to the *Sefirot*[60] in the manner of a Crown (*Atarah*).

> In spite of the fact that it (the Queen) is beneath (the other *Sefirot*), sometimes it ascends to *Ein-Sof* and becomes an *Atarah* (Ornament) for the head (of all the *Sefirot*), and for this reason is it called *Atarah*.[61]

> The counting of the ten *Sefirot* began with *Atarah* – to let you know that it is also *Keter;* and if you will reverse the *Sefirot*, then

Malkhut will be the first . . . as they have neither beginning nor end – the beginning of thought being the end of the action.[62]

Therefore the relationship of God to physical Creation, is like the spiral of the ten *Sefirot*, resembling the coil of a snake, with the tail ending up in the head – "in my end is my beginning" – each having its source in the other.

You must realize that *Atarot* (Numbers 32:3) alludes to two crowns: the upper crown and the lower crown. For just as He is called *Keter Elyon*, so *Malkhut* is called *Ateret*, which means crown. . . . When *Ateret Yisrael* joins Herself with *Keter Elyon* and rises to *Ein-Sof*, they are called *Atarot*.[63]

Rabbi Ashlag asks what happens if, contrary to the law of the Torah, a bride does not wait to receive a ring from her Beloved but gives him one instead? Does that constitute a legal marriage?

In Jewish tradition the woman is passive. She "takes," whereas the man, as the superior, initiates and "gives." In cosmological terms, God is the Giver of Light, creatures are "takers," and *Knesset Yisrael*, as the quintessential Creature, is the essence of Femininity, the ideal vessel for the Divine Light. But what happens if the Bride gives her Beloved a ring or other object of value? Has she defied modesty? Or can the man say about her gift: "By this you will become betrothed to me," as if he had been the giver.

The Talmud implies that although technically the Bride has acted against the Law, if the man is secure enough, his masculinity will not be jeopardized by her generosity: "If he is meritorious," says the Talmud, "the ceremonial procedure may be reversed" (*Kiddushin* 7). In this case, what difference does it make whether she receives a physical object, such as a ring, or the personal gratification of knowing that her gift has been accepted by the man she respects enough to marry.

A certain strength of character is necessary in order to be able to receive. Then giving and receiving become the same, and the marriage is accomplished through the special privilege and pleasure the woman has received in being able to give to the man. If giving creates closeness in human relationships, then it certainly does so in the relationship between God and Israel.

What does it mean that the Feminine Principle is crowned? It means that She comes into her own – She becomes her husband's crown at the moment of union.

The same idea is conveyed in the *Lekha Dodi*, R. Solomon Alkabetz's "Song of Welcome to the Sabbath Bride," in which She is described as Her Husband's crown. By lighting the *Menorah*, the passive receptacle of God's goodness, she in turn "feeds" Him, and the light that is radiated back to the Source becomes His crowning joy.

Not only does She act as an ornament for Her Husband, but, just as He is essential to Her and the source of Her Life, so She is the source of His entry into the physical world. She is His Shepherdess, allowing Him to graze in the pasture grounds of *Malkhut*. For had Israel not accepted the Torah, God would have reversed the whole of Creation. Therefore Creation and the role God allows Himself to play in it depend on whether Israel keeps the Torah. Playing on the description of Israel as a "shepherdess" the Midrash explains, "She who sustains Me; She who gives me to graze." In effect, "Israel sustains its Father in Heaven" (*Shir HaShirim Rabbah* 1:9).

This idea has been expressed succinctly in the explanation of the verse, "You are My witnesses, says the Lord . . . and I am God" (Isaiah 43:10), which the Rabbis say means that if Israel were not to live up to its mission to act as witnesses for God, it would be as if God did not exist.

THE ORAL LAW

How does *Knesset Yisrael* take the initiative where God is concerned? One way is through the continuing development of the Torah. Although God gave the world and Israel, above all, His Written Revelation, it is through the genius of Israel and its very human voice that the Oral Law develops.

Rav Kuk has pointed out that although the Written Torah – God's "voice" – is infinitely superior to the human voice of the

Oral Law, there is a deeper sense in which the opposite is true. For the Written Law depends for its full realization on the human voice of *Knesset Yisrael*.

In the Oral Torah (rabbinic Judaism), says Rav Kuk in his *Orot Ha-Torah*, we are forced to come down from the transcendent realms of God's Torah and wake up to practical living.

Superficially, the Oral Law is naturally lower than the Written Law. One is God's transcendent Torah; the other belongs to Israel as representative of humanity. The Oral Law, suggests Rav Kuk, is the 'voice' of an ideal *Knesset Yisrael*:

> We feel (he says) that the spirit of the People's connection, like a burning coal, with the Law of Truth has created the special nature of the Oral Torah. The Oral Torah essentially is filtered through the character of the Jewish People and is an expression of her authentic nature.[64]

Though the Written Law is Israel's highest link with God, it was given to Jews to bring out their own spiritual nature. And how is this Jewish genius best manifested but in the development of the Oral Law. In this sense, therefore, the Oral Law is higher than the Written Law. Rav Kuk lends this idea credence with a talmudic quote: "Dearer (to God) are the words of the Scribes than the words of the Written Law."

Above all things, Rav Kuk implies, God desires the realization of human potential. Only for this purpose did He give Israel the 'Heavenly' Torah. And above all, He wishes to evoke the human dialogue and response contained in the Oral Law.

But how can the Oral Law cease being theory and come alive? If it is the authentic "voice" of the Jewish People, then the Land of Israel is the true physical dimension of the Jewish spirit. Only when the Land is rebuilt, with all Jews living there, "organized like a country, with a Temple and a kingdom, a priesthood and with prophecy, judges and civil authorities, will the Oral Law really come alive," maintains Rav Kuk.

In exile, the Oral Law like *Knesset Yisrael*, is almost cut off from the Heavenly Torah. The mystical meaning of the Torah (the Bible and the Prophets) is very far removed from daily life;

only enough of a connection remains to give rabbinic Judaism the vitality to survive. However, each day mainstream Judaism, like the *Shekhinah* herself, descends lower and becomes more alienated from the source of her inspiration.

> Until the day will dawn when the light of life will rise from the treasure of eternal redemption and Israel will do valiantly and be replanted in her land and be efficiently administered along the lines of God's kingdom of *Malkhut*.
>
> Then the Oral Torah will begin to sprout from the depths of her being and will rise up, up, up, and the light of the Heavenly Torah will shine on her with new rays. And the light of the soul of God, the Life of worlds will be revealed below through Israel's triumph; He will shine in the light of the seven days of the light of the Sun and the light of the Moon together. . . . And their light will draw direct from one another and the earth and the People will respond with the whole beauty of life.[65]

So in a sense *Knesset Yisrael* is not only God's Beloved, but also a Source for His self-realization. She is called His Mother because She nurtures Him into Creation. *Knesset Yisrael* nurtures this "child" as God nurtures the world.

> *Behold Shlomo the King, with the crown with which his mother crowned him on his wedding day, the day of the rejoicing of his heart* (Song of Songs 3:11). "The Crown with which his Mother crowned him on his wedding day," that is, the *Shekhinah* descended to the Temple once Solomon had completed it. [*Bamidbar Rabbah* 12:4–8]

The *Shekhinah* is the crowning glory of Solomon's efforts to build a place in Creation for the Divine Presence. The *Shekhinah* is both the "Mother" who blesses his efforts by descending and the *Atarah* or Crown.

The King was not the earthly Shlomo but the King who is the very essence of Peace (*shalom*). And who bound the crown? *Knesset Yisrael*, by saying, "*May God reign forever and ever!*"

To which God responds: It is as if you have bound a bond of Kingship on My head.[66]

Therefore, in this *Midrash,* while God is the King, Israel herself is the Mother and dispenser of Crowns.

> The Crown with which His mother crowned Him: This is like the parable of a king who had an only daughter of whom he was very fond, so that at first he called her "daughter"; still not satisfied with that, he called her "sister," and still not satisfied with that, he called her "mother."
>
> So The Holy One, Blessed be He, loved Israel exceedingly and called her "daughter," as it says, *Hearken, O daughter, and consider* (Psalm 45:11); still not satisfied with that, He called her "sister," as it says, *Open to me, my sister, my love* (Songs of Songs 5:2); and still not satisfied with that He called her "mother," as it says, *Attend unto Me, O My people, and give ear unto Me, O My nation – u-le'umi* (Isaiah 51:4), where it is written *ul'immi* (and to my mother).
>
> R. Shimon bar Yohai rose and kissed him (the speaker) on his head, saying, "Had I come only to hear this explanation from your lips, it would have been worth it." [*Shir HaShirim Rabbah* 3:11]

God lavishes on Israel names of the greatest intimacy but "lover" or "wife" are not included. Whereas the man–woman relationship is based on the attraction and tension of polarities, a daughter comes from the same flesh as a father, a sister is even closer because she shares his background and childhood memories and, until marriage breaks up the bond, she is the female form of the self. That is why both Abraham and Isaac called their wives "sisters" – because they shared so much. A mother, however, is the source of identity. That is also why in Jewish law the mourning period for a mother is a year, whereas for a wife it is only thirty days. (One can only have one mother.)

Therefore, in describing the closeness of the man–woman love relationship with Israel, God successively calls Israel by the name of the sister–daughter–mother – blood relationships in ascending order of affection.

To achieve this intimacy, *Shekhinah* wants no longer to be the passive beneficiary of God's Bounty, but wishes to do something for Him in return, even if it means for a time shutting Herself off completely from Heaven's Light. So, instead of being identified with something transcendent, such as God Himself, *Shekhinah* becomes earthly and attaches Herself to the fate, fortunes, and way of life of a particular people who, like Her, are in a state of exile.

By reversing the movement of Creation, it is the wish of this feminine collective entity—*Shekhinah, Knesset Yisrael*—to present as a gift the entire created world and all the stages of Emanation through which She has traveled back to God. She longs that all rays and "sparks of holiness," all jewels, all commandments, all prayers, and the souls of all humanity should combine in Her to form a single diadem, and that She should become Her Husband's Crown.

THE TEARS OF RACHEL

According to Jewish tradition, the Cave of Machpelah, is the burial place of Adam and Eve, co-founders of humanity. The Fathers of Israel are also buried there, together with their wives— Abraham and Sarah, Isaac and Rebecca, Jacob and Leah.

Rachel is buried elsewhere, and her tomb is not peaceful. Not that Rachel was excluded from sharing her husband's last rest because she was unworthy to enter the Tomb of the Fathers, but her fate is a unique and lonely one. What may initially have started as her punishment has grown in the hearts of the Jewish people—her children—into her special glory.

At first it was not Rachel who cried, but rather Jacob, who fell in love with her at the first moment he set eyes on her. Jacob, in exile far from Israel and his family, one day joined the shepherds who were standing around the village well in Haran. He asked them why they were not watering their sheep. They answered that a large stone blocking the water was too heavy for them to move and they were waiting for the other shepherds to return so that they could all move the stone together. When Jacob looked up and saw Rachel coming toward him with her sheep, he was imbued with such strength that he was able to move the stone single-handedly. No sooner had he removed the physical block, than he seemed to lift an emotional obstacle as well, thus allowing him to express his joy and grief. Spontaneously he kissed her and broke down in tears. The Rabbis explain that what Jacob saw at that very instant was not union, but separation – she would be buried apart from him on the road the Children of Israel would take into exile.

Jacob had to pay his future wife's father, Laban, in hard labor before he could marry her. The Torah says that the seven long years he worked for Rachel were like seven days because he loved her so much (Genesis 29:20). Even then Rachel eluded him. Rachel had an older sister, Leah, whom her father was determined to marry off before his younger, prettier daughter.

The morning after the wedding Jacob awakened to discover he had been tricked into marrying the wrong woman. His father-in-law, Laban, had cheated him and had put Leah under the veil. But, say the Rabbis, Jacob felt doubly betrayed because his own Rachel had given away the secret password between them so that her sister would not be put to shame. When Jacob protested to his father-in-law, Laban agreed that for another stint of hard labor, he could also marry the woman he really wanted. And this is how, against his will, Jacob married the two sisters.

The seemingly tragic story of Jacob's involuntary involvement with two sisters, Leah and Rachel, was a necessary prelude, say the Rabbis, to the building of the House of Israel. The struggles and jealousies of these women were necessary to incorporate the special heroic qualities of each. And through this ordeal God's three modes of relating to *Knesset Yisrael* – as sister, as daughter, and as mother – are worked out.

The two sisters represent two seemingly disparate types of women, yet in reality the two constitute different aspects of essential femininity. Since the time of the early desecendants of Adam described in the Bible, men frequently found it convenient to marry two wives – the older, plainer and more respected of the two to bear the children, supervise, and sometimes actually do the housework, and the other more attractive younger woman, the "daughter" in relation to the first wife, to hold the husband's affections while staying youthful by never having children. This arrangement might have been convenient for the nonmonogamous male, but it satisfied neither woman's natural longing for erotic love and for motherhood.

Although Jacob did not actively seek out this selfish arrangement—as far as he was concerned the younger of the two, Rachel, was not only his senior wife, but his only one—the division of roles between Rachel and Leah almost fits into this cruel paradigm.

The two together are All-Woman, Leah the fecund Mother, while Rachel, say the Rabbis, shared with the Land of Israel the beauty of the hind, symbol of eternal virginity. Each time they had intercourse, her vagina is alleged to have come together as if she were still a virgin. Her bone structure was too narrow to have children, and each occasion Jacob made love to her was like the first time.

The two sisters are taken by the Kabbalists to compose the basic Virgin–Mother components of the *Shekhinah,* Leah being equated with the transcendent *Sefirah* of *Binah,* or Understanding, God's Mothering aspect, while Rachel is the wayward, adventurous "daughter," the lower *Shekhinah* who manifests herself in the bottommost *Sefirah* of *Malkhut,* the world of darkness, physicality, and dispersion, where *Knesset Yisrael,* her other manifestation, is exiled.

But these stereotypes do not really fit the women. In fact, the real Rachel and Leah admired and were jealous of each other precisely because each wanted to develop the shadow-complementary part of herself.

After Rachel's supreme act of self-sacrifice in surrendering her marriage-rights to her sister, she became entangled in a series of substitutions that inexorably separated her from her lover. Ever after tears have always been associated with her name. When Rachel was moved by her sister's tears, her heart expanded to embrace the grief of the *Shekhinah.*

When Jacob lost Rachel, a void was left in his heart that no rival wife could fill. The *Shekhinah* herself softly took up residence in the heart of the mourning Jacob, affording him consolation among the mourners of Zion.

And Rachel – if her sister took her place as first wife in the marriage, if the *Shekhinah* took her place in Jacob's heart – where then was she?

Jeremiah, Prophet of the exile, imagines her far from dead. It is as if Rachel were exiled on the boundary to a foreign land and not buried in the grave together with her husband and the other Fathers and Mothers of the Jewish People, so that when her children were exiled, She could shake off death to shed those tears that became her own special gift. Her selfless compassion toward her sister permitted Rachel to change places with the *Shekhinah* Herself to better intercede for Israel.

A cloudy, anguished figure, she strains forward to reach out to a People and to a future not yet clothed in the grateful imagination of her People nor given substance and vitality by their sorrowful poetry, which would soften the full force of the catastrophe.

> A Voice is heard on the Heights
> Wailing, bitter weeping –
> Rachel weeping for her children
> She refuses all comfort. . . .
> Thus says the Lord:
> Restrain your voice from weeping
> Your eyes from shedding tears:
> For there is a reward for your labor,
> declares the Lord:
> They shall return from the enemy's land.
> Your children shall return to their country.
> And there is hope for your latter end,
> declares the Lord.
>
> (Jeremiah 31:15–18)

But was the principal loss and grief Rachel's? Did she in fact have so many children? Surely it was Leah, not Rachel, who should have been the one to mourn far greater losses – that Rachel considers all hers. It is Rachel's barren womb that cries out for the misbegotten in a frightful amorphous compassion.

And her disinterested concern for her sister's descendants

will be more easily heard as prayer than that of the natural mother. She pleads: "Have mercy on Your children. Not mine. Not hers. But Yours!"

Convinced by the logic of her own life and the self-sacrifice that is at the very core of her experience, the answer will finally be heard:

> Rejoice, thou barren, thou that didst not bear.
> Break out into exultation and laugh aloud.
> For more are the children of the desolate
> than the children of the married wife,
>   saith the Lord.
> For the Lord has called
> as a woman forsaken and vexed in spirit
> and a wife of one's youth, can she be rejected,
>   saith the Lord your God.
> It is true that for a short moment I had forsaken you
> But with infinite mercy shall I gather you in. . .
> O thou afflicted, tossed with tempest
>   and not comforted.
> All your children shall be taught of the Lord
> And great shall be the peace of your children.
>
> (Isaiah 54:1, 6–8, 11, 13)

For each child is essentially a star that gives light, unique and precious, a still flame, the joyous and tranquil shining of which is reflected in the Jewish mother's eyes. When the Sabbath candles are lit, those eyes assume a serenity and a radiance of immeasurable gentlenesss, as the mother confronts the unknown future awaiting her children with blessing. She regards steadily the light she has kindled – with faith, a veil is lifted, at the raging conflagration depicted there, the hands move blindly forward in sign of protection or protest, as if shielding from sight would avert calamity. Not a blessing but a shriek is heard. Still, the weeping of Rachel is given substance by that sound.

For when a human being weeps and sheds tears (and shares another's grief as his own . . .) he also causes tears to be shed on high. In fact, the Lord God of Hosts travels in an eternal drought, longing from His very soul to shed so much as a single human tear, and only human tears can bring God Himself relief. *Oh, that My Head were waters and my eyes a fountain of tears that thereby I might also weep for My dead* (Jeremiah 8:23).[67]

A mother holds a sick child in her arms. It is evening, and there is no light to distinguish the features of the baby's face. She listens to its intermittent breathing, which grows softer and fainter, until it stops altogether. A deathlike coldness seizes the mother's heart. Is the child dead? She cannot tell. She begins to cry softly, questioningly. The baby, hearing the voice of its mother, is sure to join in. If not, the mother will know her child is dead. Then her voice will mourn indeed, with the terrible abandon of unstinted grief. So she begins her soft and tentative keening as she rocks back and forth. There is no response. Higher and higher the mother's voice rises, deeper and deeper in agony.

Israel might still respond out of the Exile to the Mother crying out to it from outside the borders. For her appeal is directed equally to her children and to her God, and through her God Himself she is pleading with them. "Return, my children, Return. Are you still alive? When will you finally listen and bring untold comfort with your return?" Only with their return will Rachel's arduous labor pangs be over, and her own unique destiny completed.

SHEKHINAH-ATARAH

When Israel prays, *Shekhinah-Atarah* ascends to the head of God and sits there like a Crown. The collective prayers of Israel become the very essence of Prayer, Prayer incarnate, a shadowy female entity identical to the *Shekhinah*.

Prayer is God's Partner, and She sits on His left side like a bride, and He is Her bridegroom. And she is called "the daughter of the King," and sometimes she is called *Bat Kol* (the daughter of a

Voice) after the name of her mission . . . for the name of the
Shekhinah that is with Him – that is the tenth Kingship, which is
the secret of all secrets. [Rabbi Eliezer of Worms, *Sefer ha-Hochmah*
55b]

[The sound of] the prayer[s] of Israel . . . [continuously]
ascends to the firmament above their heads, and goes to sit on
the Head of the Holy One [where it] becomes a crown [*Atarah*]
. . . for [Prayer] sits there like a crown . . . and the *Atarah* of the
Holy One is 600,000 parasangs in size, corresponding to the
600,000 Israelites, and the Name of the *Atarah* (Crown) is . . .
(Israel) . . . and when the Crown (*Keter*) ascends, they run and
prostrate themselves and speedily go to put their crowns on. . . .
And so the prayers (and) the Crowns (*Atarot*) that ascend to the
throne are like a throne, and the throne is made of a sapphire
stone (Ezekiel 1:26).[68]

R. Judah bar Simon said: "A parable. This is comparable to
one who made an *Atarah*. Somebody else passed, saw it, and said
(to him): 'With whatever you can adorn it, precious stones and
jewels, do so and put (them) in it, since it is intended to be on the
head of the King.'"
So God said to Moshe: "With whatever you can praise Israel
to Me, and embellish them, do so, for by them I gain glory." As
it is said, *Israel, by whom I will be glorified* (Isaiah 49:3). [*Tanhuma, Ki
Tisa* 8]

Atarah, therefore, also means the silver neckline embroidered around the *Tallit* (prayer shawl). At key moments in prayer,
the *Tallit* is used as a headcovering – the *Ateret* then encircles the
head – an imitation of "Him who stretches out light as a garment."
Prayers make up part of the *Atarah* or bridal diadem, which,
as we have seen with the *Tallit,* is both a necklace when worn
around the shoulders and a tiara when covering the head. And
when the rosary[69] of all the prayers is told, the complete diadem
of tears rises to sit on the head of God.[70] Thus Prayer, like the
kindling of the *Menorah,* is another act of crowning of the king.
Just as in a coronation all the bejeweled ritual objects and the

anointing are intrinsic parts of kingship, so the highest aspects of Divinity are successively robed and sacramentally ornamented by each level of the ascent of the *Atarah*. It is as if that jewel or emanation of light takes on reality only after it has been transmuted in the depths of the human consciousness and the human heart. Only then can it make up the "Jewels of the Bride."

NOTES

1. Rabbi Chaim Vital, *Etz Chaim, Shaar Egolim VeYashar* 2.
2. Rabbi Yehuda Ashlag, *Ten Luminous Emanations of Rabbi Isaac Luria,* trans. Levi I. Krakovsky, vol. I (Jerusalem: Research Center of *Kabbalah,* 1969), pp. 4, 44, 72.
3. Ashlag, *Emanations,* vol. I, p. 41.
4. Rabbi Azriel of Gerona, *"Wisdom and the Elements,"* quoted in Joseph Dan, *The Early Kabbalah,* trans. Ronald C. Kiener (New York: Paulist Press, 1986), p. 100.
5. Ashlag, *Emanations,* vol. I, p. 86.
6. Joseph Dan, "Interpretation of the Tetragrammaton," in *Kabbalat Rabbi Asher ben David* (Jerusalem: Hebrew University Publication, 1980), pp. 1–2. First discussion linking *Sefirot* with the *Menorah.* See also p. 17.
7. This explanation of the Creation as a Feminine piece of art radiating with God's Light is based on the *Bahir,* and on Gershom Scholem's explication of it in his *Origins of the Kabbalah,* ed. R.J. Zwi Werblowsky, trans. from the German by Allan Arkush (Philadelphia: Jewish Publication Society, 1987), pp. 162–180.
8. Ashlag, *Emanations,* vol. I, p. 20.
9. Rabbi Chaim Vital, *Etz Chaim, Shaar Egolim VeYashar* 2.
10. Louis I. Newman, *The Hasidic Anthology* (New York: Scribner's, 1934), p. 264. Aaron of Apt, *Keter Shem Tov,* p. 14a, Slavuta, 1784, quoted in Ethics 5:14; Singer, p. 202.
11. *Bosi l'Gani,* the last series of discourses written by the "Previous" Lubavitcher Rebbe, published on the day of his passing (New York: Empire Press, 1980), p. 13.
12. Rav Abraham Kuk, *Lights of Torah,* trans. from the Hebrew by the author (Jerusalem: Mossad, 1965), p. 4.
13. Rav Kuk, *Lights,* pp. 1–3.
14. Bahya ben Asher, *Commentary on the Pentateuch on* Numbers 11:12,

in *Kitvey ha-Ramban,* a collection of the writings of Nachmanides and others, ed. H. D. Chavel, quoted in Moshe Idel, *Kabbalah: New Perspectives* (New Haven: Yale University Press, 1988), p. 214.

15. Rabbi Isaac the Blind of Provence, *The Mystical Torah–Kabbalistic Creation,* an interpretation of *Midrash Konen,* translated from a manuscript found in the Jewish Theological Seminary of America (New York: Enelow Collection, no. 699) in Joseph Dan, *The Early Kabbalah,* trans. Ronald C. Kiener (New York: Paulist Press, 1986), p. 76. Rabbi Isaac was the son of Rabbi Abraham ben David of Posquieres (the RaBaD, c. 1120–1198). Rabbi Isaac's name – the Aramaic *Sagge-Nehor* or "full of light" – the Hebrew for a euphemism – means the opposite of what it does in English! Since Rabbi Isaac wrote so much about light and color, it is difficult to know if in fact he really became blinded by the radiance of the *Shekhinah,* as did Isaac, his namesake in the Bible.

16. Ashlag, *Emanations,* vol. I, p. 58.

17. Ibid., pp. 19–20.

18. For the vision of the *Shekhinah* "dressed in dark clothes" see Moshe Idel, *New Perspectives in Kabbalah* (New Haven: Yale University Press, 1988), p. 315, n. 58.

19. Gershom Scholem, *Origins of the Kabbalah* (Philadelphia: Jewish Publication Society, 1987), pp. 349–350.

20. *Sefer Ma'ayan Hokhmah,* Ms. 8330, Hebrew University, in Joseph Dan, *The Early Kabbalah,* pp. 49–53.

21. It was also Rabbi Isaac, as far as we know, who in his commentary on the *Sefer Yetzirah* first gave the ten *Sefirot* the symbolic weight attached to them by most of subsequent *Kabbalah.*

22. Ms. 198 Christ Church College, fol. 25b, quoted in Scholem, *Origins,* p. 281.

23. Rabbi Shem Tov ibn Gaon, "Keter Shem Tov," in *Maor Va-Shemesh,* fol. 25a, quoted in Idel, *Kabbalah,* p. 138.

24. The *Zohar* was written toward the end of the thirteenth century. Its contents could have been very ancient indeed.

25. The first mention of the *Sefirot* or emanations to be found in Jewish sources was in the *Sefer Yetzirah* (3rd–6th centuries C.E.).

26. According to the Aristotelian–Ptolemaic cosmology adhered to by the Jewish and non-Jewish world until the end of the Middle Ages, the earth was surrounded by nine other rotating concentric spheres (or *Sefirot*), including the moon, the sun, the

various planets, the stars, and the diurnal sphere, each of which was guided by an "Intelligence," "soul" or internal moving force. To this world view the theory of emanations, which has its source in Greek neo-Platonism, added a transcendent dimension, showing the origin of the material world from a spiritual First Principle. God, the ultimate source of motion, is also the primal source of the light that expands outward and travels through the various emanations or spheres until it reaches our world.

27. This interpretation of "Name" and "Names" is based on Ashlag, *Emanations,* vol. I, pp. 44, 72.

28. *Sefer HaGilgulim,* chap. 18, and *Sefer HaLikkutim,* fol. 8c, quoted in Gershom Scholem, *Major Trends in Jewish Mysticism* (Jerusalem: Schocken, 1941), p. 280.

29. The *Maggid* of Mezeritch, R. Dov Baer, *Or HaGanuz,* fol. 8c, trans. Moshe Idel, Jewish Theological Seminary Summer Session, New York, 1987.

30. Philo, *De Congressu,* quoted in Erwin R. Goodenough, *Jewish Symbols in the Greco-Roman Period,* vol. 4 (New York: Pantheon, 1954), p. 84.

31. See Chapter 5 this volume, p. 309.

32. "God in All," from *Selected Poems of Jehuda Halevi,* trans. Nina Salaman, ed. Heinrich Brody (Philadelphia: Jewish Publication Society, 1924), p. 168.

33. See Rabbi Isaac of Acre's *Me'irat Einayim,* quoted in Moshe Idel, *The Mystical Experience in Abraham Abulafia,* trans. J. Chipman (Albany: State University of New York Press, 1988), p. 203.

34. *Bosi l'Gani,* p. 10.

35. R. Ezra of Gerona, "Commentary on Song of Songs," ed. H. Chavel, in *Kitvey ha-Ramban* 11:504, quoted in Moshe Idel's *Kabbalah: New Perspectives* (New Haven: Yale University Press, 1988), p. 181.

36. As retold by Manitou, R. Leon Ashkenazi, in a lecture I attended in Jerusalem during *Sukkot* 1986.

37. See Scholem, *Origins,* p. 165, and his comparison of *Midrash Mishle* 47a, ed. Buber with a similar passage in the Talmud (*Sanhedrin* 104b), in which Solomon's defense is taken up by "the Daughter of a Voice."

38. Based on Samson Raphael Hirsch, *The Pentateuch: Commentary on Exodus,* vol. 2, trans. Isaac Levy (London: Soncino Press, 1956).

39. The Hebrew for 32 is 30 = L and 2 = B, standing for *leb* or the Heart, the innermost sanctum reached by the 32. The *Maharal* says there are thirty-two *Tzitzit*, or fringes, on the *Tallit*, the shawl worn by a man in prayer as an imitation of how God emanates light to the world. Together these thirty-two channels transmit radiance from the *Shekhinah* at the heart of creation.

40. "Rabbi Akiva says: 'All the Writings are holy, but the "Song of Songs" is the Holy of Holies' " (*Shir HaShirim Rabbah* I:1,11).

41. Daniel C. Matt, *The Zohar: The Book of Enlightenment* (Ramsey, NJ: Paulist Press, 1983), p. 130.

42. Moses Cordovero, *The Palm Tree of Deborah*, trans. Louis Jacobs (London: Vallentine Mitchell, 1960), p. 117.

43. Matt, "The Old Man and the Beautiful Maiden," in the *Zohar*, pp. 123–124.

44. Scholem, *Major Trends*, pp. 110–115.

45. See *Shiur Komah*, and Chap. 2 of this book on the measurements of the Body of God, *Adam Kadmon*, and the *Shekhinah*.

46. Scholem, *Major Trends*, pp. 110–115.

47. See Rabbi David ben Yehudah he-Hasid, *The Book of Mirrors* (*Sefer Mar'ot ha-Zove'ot*), ed. Daniel C. Matt (Chico, CA: Brown Judaic Studies, Scholars Press, 1982), 19:21.

48. Matt, the *Zohar*, pp. 123–124.

49. Carl Jung, *Psychology and Alchemy,* in *Collected Works*, 2nd ed. (Princeton, NJ: Princeton University Press, 1968), vol. 12, p. 278.

50. See Ginzberg, *Legends,* vol. 5, pp. 42–46.

51. Rav A.Y. Kuk, *Selected Letters*, trans. into English and annotated by Tzvi Feldman (Israel: Ma'a lot Publications, 1986), *Igrot* 158, pp. 190–198.

52. Philo, *De Congressu*, in Goodenough, *Graeco-Jewish Symbols,* vol. 4, p. 86.

53. The *Maggid* of Mezeritch, *Or ha-Ganuz*, fol. 8c, trans. Moshe Idel for a course on Hasidism at the Jewish Theological Seminary, Summer 1987.

54. Ibid.

55. *Seder Rabbah de-Bereishit Schäfer Synopse*, par. 745, quoted in Idel, *New Perspectives*, p. 196.

56. Abba Eban, *My People: the Story of the Jews* (New York: Behrman House, 1968), p. 114.

57. Margaret Smith, *Rabi'a the Mystic and her Fellow-saints in Islam*

(Cambridge, England: Cambridge University Press, 1928), p. 7.

58. *The Book of Mirrors*, p. 27.

59. Rabbi Dov Baer of Mezeritch, The Great *Maggid,* from the "Creation section," *The Hidden Light,* quoted in Scholem, *Major Trends,* pp. 335–336.

60. See Idel, *New Perspectives,* p. 163.

61. *Commentary on a Kabbalistic Song,* in Koriat's *Ma'or va-Shemesh,* fol. 3a, quoted in Idel, *New Perspectives,* p. 197.

62. Idel, *New Perspectives,* p. 197.

63. R. David ben Yehuda he-Hasid, *Sefer Mar'ot ha-Zove'ot,* 228:18–20, 29–30. See Matt, *The Book of Mirrors,* pp. 26–27.

64. Abraham Isaac Kuk, *The Written Torah and the Oral Torah,* in *Orot Ha-Torah Harav,* trans. Freema Gottlieb, 2 vols. (Jerusalem: Mossad Harav Kuk, 1965), pp. 1–3.

65. Kuk, *Orot Ha-Torah,* pp. 1–3.

66. See Idel, *New Perspectives,* p. 192.

67. Rabbi Chaim Vital, *Etz Ha-Da'at Tov,* part II (Jerusalem, 1982), fol. 5b, quoted in "Theurgical Weeping" by Moshe Idel, *New Perspectives,* pp. 197–199.

68. See Idel, *New Perspectives,* pp. 193–195.

69. Focus on the concept of the *Atarah* has led me to see a striking resemblance between it and the Roman Catholic rosary. The use of a set of worry beads was also adopted by Islam in the ninth century. All these customs probably go back to a common source, the earliest record of which dates back to the late second-century Indian (Brahman) meditative practice of repeating all ninety-nine Names of God together with His Supreme Name while focusing on the beads of a necklace. This technique may not have originated in India, however, but might well have traveled from the Near East, especially since there is archaeological evidence in Nineveh of two women wearing this form of ornament.

The rosary has been part of the Eastern Orthodox and Roman Catholic meditative practice since the fourth century and has been associated with prayer by the tenth. I believe the origin of this very ancient meditative technique is associated with the neo-Platonic notion of Divine emanations and that individual beads or 'jewels' originally represented the *Sefirot,* a meaning of which is 'sapphire' or jewel. Interestingly, one of the first forms taken by the rosary in the sixth century Order of Cluny was that of knots, as in the Jewish *Tefillin* or *Tzitzit*, the fringes attached to a four-cornered garment, especially the *Tallit*. I believe the mystical meaning of these strings or straps with their knots is to symbolize the flow of Divine Grace (the strings, straps, or transmitters, a masculine image), with the vessel of containment (the knot or bead, feminine), that can focus and help us to receive the light. The knot serves the purpose of a tourniquet that stops the flow of blood through the arteries from completely depleting the body.

The notion of a female intercessor, or Prayer personified (Rachel, *Knesset Yisrael*, or the *Shekhinah*) presenting these 'jewels' back to God was adopted by Catholicism in the eleventh century during the Crusades. Only at this time did the rosary become associated with Mary, just when a parallel development was taking place in Jewish mystical feminine imagery. Interestingly, it was at precisely this period that the mystical Hebrew love-Poet, Yehuda Halevi sang the praises of Zion as a distant Beloved, and Crusader troubadors used the same accolades for the Holy Land as they did for Mary. Both woman and country are the epitome of physical beauty and an incarnation of the Divine. It was during their journeys to the Holy Land that the Crusaders must have adopted the Arab and Jewish mystical stance vis-à-vis the feminine into their own religious practice. Even the beads of the rosary, arranged in five sets of ten (the Ten *Sefirot* and the feminine Hebrew letter *Heh* are called 'Glories,' the Glory being a possible reference to the Jewish mystical figure of the *Kavod* [the *Shekhinah*] on God's sapphire throne).

It is possible that the whole Catholic portrait of the Virgin Mary as intercessor is borrowed from Jeremiah's depiction of Rachel mourning for the Children of Israel. Rachel had a son Joseph who was also stripped and humiliated; even the name is borrowed for Mary's husband. However, although Rachel is seen by the rabbis as endowed with special virtue to be able to plead the cause of the Jewish People, she always retains her humanity. Indeed, Jeremiah's picture of her rising from the grave to weep for her children is questioned by the rabbis as too supernatural.

Rachel weeping for her children. Rachel was dead. Who wept? It was the exiles who allowed themselves the luxury of weeping as they passed by her grave: *Rachel weeping for her children.* Who is 'Rachel,' not the dead Mother, but the 'daughter,' ever identified

with the questing soul and essence of *Knesset Yisrael*. This being
the case, there is certainly no idea that the Jewish People should
pray to her, rather than to God. Rather, Rachel, totally identified
with an ideal *Knesset Yisrael* (essential humanity), presents its very
life essence–tears–to God as a gift (see *Bereishit Rabbah* 71:2).

70. The Hebrew for prayers is *Tefillot,* which is related to *Tefillin.* In
those ancient texts of the *Atarah* of Rabbi Eliezer of Worms, when
the *Shekhinah* sits on God's head, it is in the form of the *"Tefillin* of
the Head."

TWO

LIGHTS

OF

CREATION:

LEGENDS

OF

SUN AND MOON

Ceremony for the Appearance of the New Moon. Celebrants raise themselves up three times on their toes and declare, "As I dance toward you and cannot touch you, so may my enemies never be able to touch me." (*Courtesy of AR/The Jewish Museum, The Jewish Theological Seminary, New York*)

God revealed light to the world on the first day of Creation, while the natural luminaries, the Sun and the Moon, were created only on the fourth day. One school of thought believed that the Sun and the Moon were actually created on the first day and only suspended on the heavenly tent on the fourth day (*Hagiga* 12a), while others said that the light God disclosed on the first day was different in essence from the lights that came after. Only after the first day did He pour His light into the natural containers, the Sun and the Moon.

The Sun is called *hammah* because it is hot, *Shamash* because it is God's great Servant. *Shamash* was once the name of a pagan sun deity. Indeed, the animated descriptions in Jewish sources of the passionate goings-on of the Sun and the Moon owe much of their verve and sparkle to their earlier divine status. Even after Abraham proclaimed belief in the One Invisible God, worship of the natural deities, the Sun, the Moon, and the stars, lingered on.

Many centuries later we find that Manasseh, King of Israel, erected statues in honor of heavenly hosts on Temple altars (II Kings 21:3–5). Job describes the secret compulsion at the sight of the Sun or the Moon "walking in brightness" to kiss one's hand in their direction out of sheer adoration (Job 31:26–28).

The Sun was pictured as a heroic war god riding on a horse or a chariot (Ezekiel 7:6,17), and it was the custom to turn rooftops into altars on which horses were dedicated for sun worship (II Kings 23:12). In Jewish biblical sources the equestrian skills of the Sun were still being celebrated – The Sun chariot was supposedly stationed at the western entrance to the Temple (Ezekiel 8:16).

The door to the Temple was originally in the Eastern wall. But this was inconvenient because the worshipper, on entering, had to do a swift about-turn in order to keep facing east. When the Ark found a permanent home on the wall opposite the entrance, this resulted in the disrespectful act of turning one's back on the Ark. By the time of the Prophets, suspicions were raised about the sun-worshipping implications of subordinating everything to this eastern orientation, so the eastern portal was bricked up. In the conflict between the traditions of having a door in the eastern wall and not turning one's back on the Torah Ark, the Torah won and was transferred to the Eastern wall, while the door was moved to the west, directly opposite. This meant that while the Eastern orientation was retained, the prime focus was again on the Torah and not on the rising sun. The *Mishnah* describes this shifting of emphasis:

> Our fathers, when they were in this place, turned their backs to the Torah and their faces toward the east and they bowed eastward to the Sun. But we have our eyes to the Lord. [*Sukkot* 54]

Although the door was shifted from east to west to make way for the Torah Ark, the compromise that was reached detracted in no way from the eastern primacy of the Sun. Although the worshipper bowing toward the east is showing respect to God and the Torah, the fact that an eastern orientation has been retained bears witness to the potency of the Sun image. Because the rising sun restores life to the natural world, the Torah that spreads spiritual light is placed in the East.

Among the various connotations for the image of the "Sun" is that of God Himself. In the synagogues of Na'aran and Bet

Alpha (sixth century C.E.) there is a representation of a solar deity driving a chariot with four steeds under the rays of the moon and the stars. The deity is surrounded by two circles of the zodiac divided into segments of the various signs. The winged female figures at the corners of the central panel represent the four seasons. Here, pagan symbols are assimilated and invested with Jewish liturgical significance. The whole motif could be an allusion to the "Chariot Mysteries" that were part of the upsurge in the secret study of Jewish mysticism at that time.

In Jewish sources, the heavenly bodies are depicted as persons endowed with intelligence, gusto, intense passions, and a very highly developed sense of ego. For example, while the Moon and the Sun are rivals, the Sun is very flustered and "ashamed" when people regard him as an object of worship (Isaiah 24:23, 27). He also has a sense of vocation and purpose in life – to shine is his whole reason for being, and as he shines he sings (Malachi 1:2; Joshua 10:12; *Midrash Tehillim* on Psalm 19:11). Even with all this, the Sun is no power seeker and is prepared to sacrifice His own career to prevent idolatry.

The words "Sun" and "light" are often used synonymously – both representing the life source. Everyone possesses an inner power or light, or daimon; sometimes this is called a "Sun," as in this tale from the *Midrash*:

> *The Sun also rises* (Ecclesiastes 1:5). The birth of Rabbi (Judah the Prince) took place on the day Akiva died. The Almighty never permits the Sun of one righteous man to set without causing that of another righteous man to arise and shine forth. [*Bereishit Rabbah* 63:1]

Here the "Sun of the righteous" is equivalent to the man's whole life.

The *Midrash* is saying, in effect, "The King is dead; long live the King," referring to the saints who keep Israel and the world's "bridge of light" with God in good repair. There is a chain of progression and transmission of the secrets of life among righteous people, just as there is of biological life in successive generations. And the burning torch that is being passed on is symbolized by the image of the "Sun."

The Sun is the jewel of the Heavens (*Apocrypha, Ben Sira* 26:16). *The Sun runs his course as a bridegroom. He exits from a bridal chamber. He sits upon a throne with a garland on his head* (Psalm 19:6). Three letters of God's Name are written on the Sun's heart. [*Pirke de Rabbi Eliezer* 6]

THE TWO GREAT LIGHTS:
MASHPIAH AND *MIKABEL*

In Genesis 1:16 the Sun is referred to as *ma'or,* a light or a torch, suspended (as on a bracket) in the firmament. Created on the fourth day, the Sun is the larger of the two Great Lights (Psalm 136:2). "And He formed the Sun and it gave forth light" (*Bereishit Rabbah* 6:2).

It was God's original intention that the Sun alone should give light on earth (*Bereishit Rabbah* 6). The Babylonian Talmud mentions a plant, *arane* – "adoration" – growing in the marshes – so named because it adores the Sun and turns in pursuit of it (*Shabbat* 35b). Had the Sun been the only visible light on earth, this temptation toward sun worship would have been irresistible.

There is only one overriding Unity and that belongs to God Himself. Other than this, the world is rich in variety. So, to avoid the idolatry that would inevitably have resulted had the Sun been the only natural luminary in the world, God also created the Moon.

However, according to another opinion, originally the two "Great Courtiers" or the Two Great Lights, the Sun and the Moon, were created equal (*Pirke de Rabbi Eliezer* 6).

> On the fourth day, He created together the two luminaries of which one was not greater [in size] than the other. They were equal as regards their height, qualities, and illuminating powers, as it is said: And God made the two great lights (Genesis 1:16).
>
> Rivalry ensued between them. One said to the other, "I am bigger than you."
>
> The other answered, "No, I am bigger than you!" [*Yalkut Shimoni* 1:5]

According to the *Zohar,* the "two Great Lights" referred to in Genesis 1:16 are the "higher world and the lower world; when the Masculine (the Sun) and the Feminine (the Moon) are manifested together, they are both called by the masculine gender. (That is to say, they are both equal.) Because the upper world is called 'great,' the lower world, which is united with it, is also called 'great'; but as soon as the above and the below part, and are separate, the one is called 'great' and the other 'small'. . .as when the Moon separated Herself from the Sun. She is called (a) small(er, lesser light)" (*Zohar* IV:147b–148a).

It was the Moon (the Feminine), the potentially lesser of the two, who had the most to lose from a divorce and who was the jealous and contentious partner. Not only did She quarrel with the Sun face to face; She brought her case to God Himself, declaring it not fair for "two monarchs to share the same Crown."

Her complaint went as follows: "O Lord, why did You create the world with the letter *Bet* (the second letter in the Hebrew alphabet, meaning 'two')?" She was really asking why God had created two lights instead of one light—Herself.

"You created the heaven and the earth, the heaven being greater than the earth. You created fire and water, water being stronger than fire, and now You have created the Sun and the Moon. Isn't it becoming clear that one of them should be greater than the other?[1] [*Midrash Konen* 25–26; *Bereishit Rabbah* 60b; *Shebu'ot* 9a]

But God replied that He was perfectly aware that She was trying to manipulate an advantage at the Sun's expense. Because she tried to detract from another, God diminished her, and as a punishment for encroaching on another's territory, He decreed that She should retain only a sixtieth of Her light.

Then the Moon asked plaintively: "Why should I be penalized so severely for having put forward a reasonable argument?" (*Hullin* 60b).

God relented: "In the future I will restore Your light, so that it will again be like the light of the Sun."

Still the Moon was not satisfied: "O, Lord," said she, "and the Light of the Sun, how great will it be in that day?"

Then God became even angrier: "What, you still harbor a grudge against the Sun? By My Life, in the world to come His light shall be seven-fold the light He now sheds" (*Midrash Konen* 25–26; *Bereishit Rabbah* 6:3; *Hullin* 60b; *Shebu'ot* 9a).

He makes Peace in His high places (Job 25:2). Said R. Levi: "None of the planets that travel in the sky see what is ahead of it, only what is behind. Like a man coming down a ladder facing behind him. So that each planet thinks: 'I am the first.' That is, 'He makes peace in His high places.'"

Said R. Shimon bar Yohai: "Because the sky is made of water and the stars of fire, yet they live together without hurting each other. That is why it is written: 'He makes peace in His high places.'" [*Yalkut Shimoni* 1:5; *Devarim Rabbah* 5:12]

God keeps the peace even between Sun and Moon, and an essential law of modesty and mutual respect binds them as man and wife (*Rosh Hashanah* 23b, 24a).

Abaye said: "R. Johanan has said: What is meant by the verse, *Dominion and fear are with Him, He maketh peace in His high places* (Job 25:2)? Never did the Sun behold the concavity of the New Moon nor the concavity of the rainbow. It never sees the concavity of the Moon, so that she should not feel humiliated. It never sees the concavity of the rainbow, so that the worshippers of the Sun should not say, 'He is shooting arrows (at those who do not worship him)'" (the rainbow in this case having the appearance of a bow bent by the Sun against the earth). [*Rosh Hashanah* 23b–24a]

But what did God do so that there would be peace between them?

He made the one larger and the other smaller, as it is said, *The greater light to rule the day and the lesser light to rule the night and the stars also did He make* (Genesis 1:16). [*Yalkut Shimoni* 1:5]

But how did this lack of equality make for peace? Not only did God reduce the size of the Moon. He also set Her to rule in a lesser environment, that of darkness and night, in this way polarizing their separate spheres of influence so they need not bicker.

And God divided between day and between night (Genesis 1:18). This was an actual division, like the story of the king who had two viceroys, one ruling in the city and the other in the country. And they both competed with each other.

One said: "I want to rule by day."

And the other said: "I want to rule by day."

And the king called the first one and said: "Day will be your limit."

And he summoned the other. "Night will be your limit."

That is the meaning of Who forms the light and creates the darkness. He makes peace in His high places (Isaiah 45:7). When the Sun and Moon were created, He made peace between them. [Yalkut Shimoni 1:5]

Yet, according to some opinions, the Sun and Moon thrived by being open to each other and borrowing from each other's light (Bamidbar Rabbah 26:4).

God consoled the Moon by telling her that, unlike the Sun, who only ruled by day, She would rule by day as well as by night. The Moon is frequently visible while the Sun is still above the horizon (Bereishit Rabbah 3:7). When She objected that in daylight the light of a candle is pointless, God compensated Her by dowering Her with a train of stars as if to say: You may now be smaller than the Sun and rule in a darker element, but add the brightness of all the stars and the galaxies who attend upon you at night, and you are not so badly off in comparison (Hullin 60b; Bereishit Rabbah 6:3).

According to another version of this myth, when God punished the Moon, She plummeted and tiny threads came loose from Her body, falling away like meteors and stars.[2]

And the stars (Genesis 1:16). Rabbi Aha said: "Imagine a king who had two governors, one ruling in the city and the other in a province. Said the king: 'Since the former has humbled himself to rule in the city only, I decree that whenever he goes out, the city council and the people shall go out with him, and whenever he enters, the city council and the people shall enter with him.'"

Thus did the Holy One, blessed be He, say: "Since the Moon humbled Herself to rule by night, I decree that when She comes forth, the stars shall come forth with Her, and when She [disappears], the stars shall go in with Her." [*Bereishit Rabbah* 6:4]

In Joseph's dream, the Sun and Moon and eleven stars bowed down to him—his Father, his Mother, and his whole family (Genesis 37:9).

But the Sun and Moon were created on either the first or the fourth day, before Man and Woman, who were created on the sixth. Therefore, Sun and Moon, standing for essential masculinity and femininity, existed even before man, as an idea within God Himself. The Moon is a symbol of the feminine: "The seed of the date has a split like a woman. Paralleling it is the power of the Moon" (*Bahir,* no. 198). "Women spin their wool or flax by the light of the Moon" (*Sotah* 6, 1; *Gittin* 89a).

The Moon was intended to be the loveliest of all God's creations—and the very symbol of Beauty.

Though originally God was unique in His world, even He has chosen to live with others, as symbolized by His beloved Moon—the *Shekhinah.*

In the initial stages of Creation, the world (feminine, symbolized by the Moon) was totally immersed in the light of the Sun (God).

And the Lord spoke unto Moses, saying: Speak unto Aaron . . . when thou lightest the lamps (Numbers 8:1).

Rabbi Judah discoursed here on the verse: *Which is as a bridegroom coming out of his chamber* (Psalm 19:6).

"Happy is the lot of Israel . . . to whom He gave . . . the Tree of Life [sometimes symbolized by a *Menorah*]. Now the Tree of Life extends from above downward, and it is the Sun which illumines all. Its radiance commences at the top and extends through the whole trunk in a straight line. . . . When the trunk shines, first the right arm of the tree is illumined and from its intensity the left side catches the light. . . . [*The Sun*] *goes forth . . . as a bridegroom* to meet his *bride, the beloved of his soul, whom He receives with outstretched arms. . . . He rejoices as a strong man to run his course* (Psalm 19:6) so as to shed his light on the Moon.

"Now the words *when thou lightest the lamps* contain an allusion to the celestial lamps, all of which are lit up together from the radiance of the Sun." [Numbers 8:1–12,16; *Zohar* V:148b–149a]

Here the whole structure of the *Menorah,* compared to a Tree, especially the central shaft, is phallic and masculine after the image of the Sun or source from which the whole train of emanations descend. Thus the *Menorah* and the central shaft (the Feeder) can sometimes represent masculine or feminine.[3]

As the *Midrash* pinpoints the relationship between Sun and Moon, the Bible describes the creation of man, and then – because "it was not good for him to be alone" – the creation of woman. Just as the world experiences *Tzimtzum,* or the apparent withdrawal of the Divine Light in order to achieve its own autonomy, so man was put to sleep so that Adam or humankind should split up into man and woman. Only in this way could man experience need and dependency upon the other and not set himself up as a god.

And just as the Moon was shortly followed by an attendant train of stars, so, where Woman was, her children were not far behind. From being a Unity, the world thus proceeded at an escalating pace to propagate a rich variety of species.

This movement was one of compression, and then of expansion of creative forces, of combustion and reintegration. It was one of splitting and individuation, from the One to the Many, from the "Light of Lights" (God) to the natural luminaries, the Sun and the Moon, to the stars that are the torn-off rags of His "garment of light," and to the many, many lamps of humankind.

The Midrash asks why Israel is compared to the stars, and not to the Sun and the Moon. This is curious, because Israel in its entirety as *Knesset Yisrael,* God's beloved, *is* compared to the

Moon. The answer may be that although ideal Israel–Israel as a unity–comprises the light of the Moon, the Jewish People, composed of myriads on myriads of individuals, is compared to Her children the stars.

> *Behold you are . . . as the stars of heaven for multitude* (Deuteronomy 1:10). Why did He bless them to be as the stars? Just as there are ranks above ranks amongst the stars [some being placed higher in the heaven than others], so too in Israel there are numerous gradations; as the stars are unsearchable and innumerable, so too are Israel past finding out and without number; as the stars (shine) from one end of the world to the other, so too are Israel (to be found from one end of the world to the other).
>
> Moshe asked God: "Why didst Thou not liken Thy children to the Sun and the Moon, which are greater than the stars?" God answered him: "By your life, the Sun and Moon are destined to be put to shame in the time to come." As it is written, *Then the Moon shall be confounded, and the Sun shall be ashamed* (Isaiah 24:23). "But the stars will never be subjected to shame." [And neither, for that matter, will Israel. Rather, God will come to the vindication of His People.] For so it is written, *And ye shall know that I am in the midst of Israel . . . and My People shall never be ashamed* (Joel 2:27). [*Devarim Rabbah* 1:14]

Why should the stars not be put to shame while the Sun and the Moon will be? Because Sun and Moon have become very self-important, whereas the stars know they are only fragments. This arrogance is true also of the relationship between Sun and Moon themselves. The Sun is a this-worldly power, while the Moon has been humiliated by being reduced in size.

More precious to God is the "broken vessel" or the "broken heart" than the one who thinks of himself as complete. For only where there is a feeling of defectiveness is there a drawing down of *Shekhinah* Light. And that is why Israel is compared to the Moon, because She sometimes is only a fragment of Her potential. And that is why Israel is also compared to the stars. Fragments of brightness and not a complete vessel, they reach out to one another, and so they never will be put to shame.

The image of the central shaft of the *Menorah* has been

compared to God and to images of Sun and Moon, seen as "feeders" of the planets. However, imagistically, if we stand back and look at the *Menorah* or at a whole panorama of blazing *Menorot,* there is nothing it reminds us of more than of all the stars in the nighttime sky. The entire heaven is the Tree and the planets are the lights on this gigantic *Menorah.*

The "children of Israel" are the also the "children of the Moon," the fragments She has been forcibly made to shed when She was diminished. The Moon in her present depleted state plus these compensatory fragments make up the glory that was once Hers. It is to recover Her own "Primordial Light" that She is drawn down to the world of the physical, identifying with *Knesset Yisrael* in the sphere of *Malkhut.* Just as Rachel preferred to cut herself off from burial together with Jacob in the "Cave of the Fathers" and to follow the Children of Israel into exile, the *Shekhinah* separates Herself from God in the sphere of transcendence to accompany Her "children," the "starry" fragments of the human soul.

The Two Great Lights: Who were they? The "Great Light" (the Sun) corresponds to God, while the "Lesser Light" (the Moon) corresponds to Nature (or *Elohim,* the Feminine). When the Two are together, they are Great; but when Feminine Nature is divorced from God, She is defective, as in the writing of *Meorot* (Lights) in the Torah.

When the Moon is separate from the Sun, then shells upon shells, emanations upon emanations, are created.

> They are all coverings one to another, brain within brain and spirit within spirit, so that one is a shell to another . . . extension after extension, each forming a vestment to the other, being in the relation membrane and brain to one another. Although at first a vestment, each stage becomes a brain to the next stage. The same process takes place below, so that . . . man combines brain and shell, spirit and body. [*Zohar* I:19b–20a]

This whole process, in which an image is both a light and a mask, is all for the ultimate good of the whole, "to give light upon the earth."

The relationship of Sun and Moon, in the capacity of Giver
and Receiver, represents not only masculine and feminine, but
the whole chain of transmission of leadership and learning. As
Socrates was aware, this is a relationship that also exists between
men. The Teacher draws down the light of ideas for his students.
In handing down knowledge, the Sun is the Teacher and the
Moon the Disciple, the Sun the Giver, and the Moon the recipient, the Sun radiates and the Moon reflects. Therefore the
Talmud says: "The face of Moshe was as the face of the Sun and
that of Joshua like the Moon"–which has no light of its own but
is a "reflection," or a mirror[4]–(*Nezikin* 11; *Baba Batra* 75a). Similarly, Rabbi Shimon bar Yohai, the mentor figure in the *Zohar,* is
known in that book as the "Holy Lamp," because he was an heir
to the Jewish mystical tradition or *Kabbalah.*

HODESH: SYMBOL OF FORGIVENESS AND RENEWAL

The Hebrew word for Moon is *Yerah*–the Wanderer, also *Lebanah*–a milky white radiance. *Lebanah* is also the name of the
Temple that atones for sins and makes them as white as snow.
The Moon, also called *hodesh*, or new month, is the symbol of
forgiveness and renewal.

The Canaanites worshipped the Moon as the "Queen of
Heaven" (Jeremiah 3:18; 44:17). In the time of Gideon, moon-
shaped ornaments adorned the necks of the Midianite camels
(Judges 7:21,26). The Bible refers to "the precious things put
forth by the Moon" (Deuteronomy 33:14), and the Moon was
believed to have the power to influence the growth of certain
plants and the tides of the ocean.

Originally, since the Sun stood for the dominating superior
authority, God or the masculine principal, it was taken to represent Jacob's guardian light. How do we know this? When the
Angel of Esau wounded Jacob on the thigh, the Sun came out and
healed him. As Jewish history unfolded, however, it became
evident that worldly power does not always go hand in hand
with virtue. A set of substitutions was therefore introduced,
whereby the Sun, standing for secularism and visible worldly

power, became the Lamp of Esau, Edom, or Rome, and Western culture, while Israel took the Moon as her light.

Since then, Israel identifies with the Moon, and her holy days and festivals are governed by the lunar calendar. The Talmud says that "an eclipse of the Moon is bad for the Jews" (*Sukkah* 29).

> Our rabbis learn: When there is an eclipse of the Sun, it is a bad sign for the nations of the world. When there is an eclipse of the Moon, it does not portend well for Israel, because those who used them as a symbol feel impoverished. It is comparable to a teacher who comes to school with a strap in his hand. Who gets worried: The pupils who are accustomed to make mistakes day by day are worried. [*Sukkah* 29]

To compensate the Moon for having diminished Her size, God promised that the Jews would measure the months by the Moon. The Moon raised the further objection that the Sun also had some say in the calendar. God again comforted her – certain Saints would share her attenuated crown. Just as she was (affectionately) called the "Little Moon," so they would be called by the diminutive.[5] But the Moon remained unconsolable.

> [When] the Moon complained to God and said: "O Lord, why did You create the world with the letter *Bet* ?" . . . God replied: "That it might be known unto My creatures that there are two worlds."
>
> The Moon then asked: "O Lord, which of the two worlds is the larger, this world or the world to come?"
>
> "The world to come is the larger."[6]

The two sisters Jacob married, Rachel and Leah, also became identified with Sun and Moon because of their distinct qualities. Leah, the intended mate of Esau, is symbolized by the Sun, or worldly power. Wedded to Jacob's spirituality, however, from her descends the royal line of David and the Messiah, who are God's power in this world.

Rachel and Joseph, on the other hand, have the Moon as

their symbol. They are the light of Israel shining in darkness and exile; much of what they have to deal with is a complicated, mysterious dream life. But the Torah tells us not to despair, but rather to look at the Moon. She always returns to the ascendant, although sometimes one might almost believe she has been completely extinguished.

When Adam and Eve realized they had sinned, they wept bitterly; the heavens, the Sun, the stars, and all created beings joined in their lament till the very throne of God. Even the angels and heavenly beings went into mourning at the Sin of Man. Only the Moon found something to laugh at. That is why God became furious and obscured her light. Instead of shining continually like the Sun, She waxes and wanes, and must be born and reborn.

On reflection, God regretted that He had punished the Moon. Why had She laughed? While the Sun and the Heavens saw only what was occupying the center of the stage at the moment–the sin that had blighted Paradise–the Moon was farsighted and able to "laugh at the time to come." She knew how to live with darkness. And her Lamp did not go out at night.[7] It is because of this infinitely mysterious capacity for self-renewal that Israel counts by the Moon.

The story of the Moon having been initially created equal to the Sun, of her demotion, and promised restoration speaks of the special destiny of one who suffers in exile and whose full vindication is yet to come.

If Israel measures her calendar by the Moon, most Jewish festivals except New Year (*Rosh Hashanah*) fall when the Moon is full, that is, in the middle of the month. The New Year, of course, is celebrated at the beginning of the month when the Moon is entirely hidden. This is why the Festival is described as the Day of Concealment (*Keseh*), the day when the Moon is veiled in a cloud. So when Satan brings his case for the persecution against Israel on *Rosh Hashanah*, which is also known as the Day of Judgment, the Sun is his only witness, as the Moon is then invisible. Ten days later, however, on the Day of Atonement (*Yom Kippur*), both testify together. But in the meantime Israel has had a chance to repent.[8]

The *Zohar* highlights this link between Israel, and the festivals of *Rosh Hashanah* and *Yom Kippur* even more emphatically. It stresses that the progress from the Day of Judgment (*Rosh Hashanah*) to the Day of Atonement (*Yom Kippur*) checks the self-righteous power of the Sun (this world) while permitting that of the Moon (spirituality) to grow from concealment (*Keseh*) to full disclosure (*Kippur*).

> Rabbi Eliezer said: This day is called the concealing (*keseh*) for the day of our feast, because the Moon is still concealed and does not shine. Through what then will it shine? Through repentance and the sound of the *Shofar* (ram's horn), as it is written: *Happy is the People that know the sound of the Shofar: they shall walk in the light of Thy countenance* (Psalm 89:16).

Pirke de Rabbi Eliezer says that the Moon dwells "between cloud and between thick cloud" (Job 38:9), as between two dishes, and that its going forth is "like a ram's horn."

> On this day (*Rosh Hashanah*), the Moon is covered, and she does not shine until the tenth day, when Israel will return with a perfect repentance so that the Supernal Mother will give Her light. Hence, this day is called the Day of Atonements (*kippurim*), because two lights are shedding illumination, since the higher lamp is illumining the lower. For on this day the Moon receives illumination from the Supernal Light and not from the light of the Sun. [*Zohar* V:100b–101a]

All the symbolic valencies between Sun and Moon have been revolutionized. No longer is the Moon depicted as the deficient and jealous female in relation to a beneficent Sun. Only the repentance of Israel brings out the full light of the Moon, Supernal Mother, whereas She (the Mother) receives Light from God Himself, and not from the Sun.

In the many variations of the myth of the reduction of the Moon, the Moon's sin and Her punishment are frequently turned to the positive. She was punished for trespassing into Her neighbor's terrain by having Her light diminished. On the other hand, Her humiliation is also seen as Her virtue, the stars being given to Her as Her reward for lack of ego. Her ability to shine both by day and by night, in this world and the next, is Her strength that makes Her fit to become Israel's symbol. In full realization that, if She had erred, it was because He created Her with ambivalencies and inconsistencies, God regretted demoting Her. On the first of every month, He had to have a he-goat brought as a sin-offering because He had been unfair. Not only this, but He made *Rosh Hodesh*, when the young Moon begins to appear, an occasion for forgiveness and renewal, rather in the nature of *Yom Kippur* (*Hullin* 60b; *Bereishit Rabbah* 6:3,7; *Pirke de Rabbi Eliezer* 4 and 51; *Targum Yerushalmi* on Genesis 1:16 and Numbers 28:15).

He who sees the New Moon is like one who receives the radiance of the *Shekhinah* (*Sanhedrin* 98b). The people needed to know the day of the official New Moon in order to calculate the dates of festivals such as *Pesach* and *Yom Kippur*. When witnesses in faraway Babylon saw traces of the New Moon, beacons were lit from hill to hill, until news was brought to the *Sanhedrin* in Jerusalem and the New Month was officially sanctified. Later, when the Samaritans intentionally misled the *Sanhedrin* by kindling false beacons, the practice of lighting beacons was discontinued, and messengers were sent to Jerusalem instead (*Moed, Rosh Hashanah* 22b).

The relay of beacons kindled to announce the New Moon parallels how the emanations and *Sefirot* were imagined on a vertical plane to convey Divine blessing to man. The concept has been compared to one candle lighting another candle, lighting another, and so on, until there is a panorama of light, without the original candle's suffering any diminution. It is also a probable source for the image of the *Hanukkah* lamp, made up of many separate lights, all of which serve to create a glow. This picture of the transmission of light is an ideal image for many physical and nonphysical processes.

The *Menorah* is compared to both Sun and Moon and the whole planetary system. The Talmud describes how the Sadducees wondered about the Pharisees' (the Rabbis') peculiar habit of "immersing the *Menorah* in liquid (oil) on a festival day." "Come and take a look at the Pharisees immersing the light of the Moon (the *Menorah*), they exclaim" (*Tosefot Hagiga* 3:35).

When the Moon is full, the ceremony of *kiddush ha-levanah*, or the sanctification of the Moon, takes place after *Havdalah* (the ritual dividing the *Shabbat* or Festival from the weekdays). The ceremony is held outdoors. Celebrants face the Moon and bless God for having brought about her renewal. Raising themselves up three times on their toes, they say: "As I dance toward you and cannot touch you, so shall my enemies be unable to touch me." Then everyone greets each other, "*Shalom aleichem. Aleichem shalom.*" (Peace be to you. To you, Peace.) The Messianic faith is then affirmed in the words, "David, King of Israel, is alive and well!"

But what has the royalty of David to do with the Moon? It was at the Feast of the New Moon that David escaped with his life when Saul would have put him to death. During the New Moon itself, of course, the Moon is invisible. Similarly, concerning King David when he was a wanderer and a fugitive before he came into his own, it could be said that his fortunes were symbolized not only by the Moon in her fullness but by the Moon in all her aspects and guises.

THE BLESSING OF THE SUN
(*BIRKHAT HA-HAMMAH*)

In two and a half days the Moon covers the distance traced by the Sun in thirty days (*Midrash Tehillim* on Psalm 19:13). The solar cycle takes twenty-eight years, the lunar nineteen. We begin the cycle of the sun with *Birkhat Ha-Hammah*, the Blessing of the Sun, a service of thanksgiving for creation of the Sun. The rite takes place on the first Wednesday of the month of *Nisan* after the Morning Prayer, when the sun is still about ninety degrees above the eastern horizon. Based on various Psalms, the rite ends with thanksgiving to God for sustaining us "until this day" and the hope that we will attain the days of the Messiah, when the light of the Sun will be sevenfold (Isaiah 30:26).

Rabbi says: "The ascent of the Moon is not like the rising of the Sun. The Sun shoots up vertically like a staff, while the Moon spreads its light abroad horizontally here and there." [*Yoma* 28b]

R. Gamliel said to the Sages: "This formula has been handed down to me from my grandfather's house:[9] Sometimes She (the Moon) traverses (the heavens) by a roundabout route and sometimes by a shortcut."

R. Johanan said: "What reason does the house of Rabbi suggest for this? Because it is written, *Who appointest the Moon for seasons, the Sun knoweth His going down* (Psalm 104:19). It is the Sun that knows His going down, but the Moon does not." (Her speed varies.) [*Rosh Hashanah* 109, 25a].

The Moon is made of light, the Sun of fire. The Sun has a human face, the Moon has the likeness of a woman.[10]

The tail of Scorpio rests in the River of "Stop-the-Light." The Great Bear has mercy on her children (Job 38:32).

Why does the Great Bear follow in the track of the Pleiades. Because she says to her: "Give me my children." What had happened? When the Holy One sought to bring the flood on the world, He took two stars from the Pleiades and brought the flood on the world. And when he wanted to stop the flood, He took two stars from the Great Bear and stopped the flood. [*Sefer Aggadah* II:40; Berakhot 58–59]

The Pleiades plump out the sweetness of the fruit and Orion dresses each one and knots it to the bough. [*Bereishit Rabbah* 10:6]

THE SUN TAKES A BATH

When looking down, His face and horns are of fire. When looking up, of hail. If the Sun did not change His modality from time to time, alternating between heat and cold, the earth would perish (*Pirke de Rabbi Eliezer* 6).

God set the Sun in the second firmament. "If He had placed it in the one nearest earth, everything would have been consumed" (*Midrash Tehillim* on Psalm 19:13; *Pesikta Rabbati* 24:186a).

How do we know that the Sun and the Moon were in the second firmament? As it is said: *And God set them in the firmament of the Heavens* (Genesis 1:17). This is a full (inclusive) verse that the Men of the Great Assembly explained as follows: You have made the Heavens, the Heavens of the Heavens and all their host. Where is the host set? In the second Heavens, which are above the Heavens. As it is written: *Let the Heavens tell His righteousness* (Psalm 19:12). In the future the heavens will testify how magnanimously God has dealt with His world by not setting them in the first Heavens. If He had (done so), the Creation would not have been able to endure the heat of the day. [*Yalkut Shimoni* 1:5]

When it comes time for the Sun to go out (on His royal progress), the Holy One weakens his force by plunging him into a shower of water so that he should not shoot out and consume the world. [*Bereishit Rabbah* 6:6]

The Phoenix is a flying creature . . . with the feet and tail of a lion and the head of a crocodile; his appearance is of a purple color like the rainbow. . . . He is the guardian of the terrestrial sphere. . . . He runs with the Sun on his circuit and he spreads out his wings and catches up the fiery rays of the Sun.[11]

If he did not intercept them, neither man nor any other living creature would remain alive. "On his right wing the following words are inscribed in huge letters, about 4,000 stadia high: 'Neither the earth produces me, nor the heavens, but only the Wings of Fire.' "

The Phoenix attends the Chariot of the Sun and goes with Him, bringing heat and dew according to God's instructions. In the morning when the Sun starts on His daily round, the Phoenix sings and every bird flaps his wings.[12]

When the Sun descends in the west in the evening, He dips down into the ocean and takes a bath in a stream of fire, the River *Nehar Dinur* ; His fire is extinguished, and He dispenses neither light nor warmth during the night. But as soon as He reaches the east in the morning, He bathes in a stream of flame, which imparts warmth and light to Him, and these He sheds over the earth.

In the same way, the Moon and the stars take a bath in a stream of hail before they enter upon their service for the night.[13] "The Sun bows before God and declares his obedience to His commands."[14] [He is a courtier offering homage to a king.] [*Pirke de Rabbi Eliezer* 6]

The Sun is subject to God's Will. "If He ordered, [the Sun] would cease to shine" (Job 9:7). Another name given to the rising Sun is "Daystar" (Psalm 19:5–6). The Sun sings and is joyous and performs His task voluntarily (Malachi 1:11; Joshua 10:12).

THE SUN AND THE MOON GO ON STRIKE

Everything was created for a purpose. Why were the Sun and the Moon created? They were created to shine. To shine was their work in the world and their natural gift. And yet there came a time when, for even higher reasons, they threatened to desist from the activity they loved the most.

The Sun, the great Lamp of our world, is affected by all He looks upon. Once upon a time, when the world was young, the Sun shone with a mild and moonlike radiance, reflecting an innocent world.

At that time the Sun enjoyed so much going to work that He sprang up of his own free will without having to be wakened. Out He strode in full regalia on His ceremonial round, rejoicing as he went and singing under His breath.

Then the world fell upon bad times and became corrupt, and the Sun shrank into Himself and refused to face up to His duties.

"No, Lord," He cried piteously, closing His eyes at all the corruption that tarnished His gaze. "Spare me such a sight. Let me remain at home on the other side of the Mountain."

Both He and His sister the Moon were all clean and silver-pure after their morning shower. The two joined forces and went on strike. They stamped their feet.

"Enough! We refuse to go out and muddy ourselves by shining on mankind and all his evil work. We are pure and sensitive souls. Everything we see affects us. After all our elaborate toilette how can You expect us to go out and dirty ourselves again by looking at the mess mankind has made of things."

"Who do you think you are!" God thundered. "You have absolutely no choice in the matter. When I give the word, out you go. Do you think you are people that you can stand here debating about ethical choices?"

"Besides, isn't shining your purpose in life? What else do you have to live for? Don't you think the role you have been assigned is important enough? In fact, your relationship to all living things is closely modeled on Mine. With your light and your warmth, you can draw up the plants and flowers from the earth and so create a veritable Paradise. What do you have to complain about?"

"Just wait," said the Sun. "You think that with a little cooperation on my part You have created a Paradise, but what You have on Your hands by creating man is something quite different. Now don't put the blame on me if—since You are invisible—those senseless beings fall down and worship me as soon as I appear. I wouldn't want to mislead anybody, and that is why I prefer to remain under cover."

Meanwhile, as the Sun kept God talking, an ice age crept over the earth. Immediately, the angels took action. They descended and drove the Sun out into the world with the lashes of whips like a beast at bay. He shot out, bloodied and ruddy, with the gaping wounds inflicted on Him by the angels, but most of all, by the sights He saw of human corruption.

In His reluctant passage He crossed many cities and many countries. Here He beheld battle and carnage, there murder committed on the sly in back alleys. All He saw made Him grow red in the face, until His earlier mellow light was lost entirely and He was ready to sink for shame.

> (As evil has a defiling and debilitating effect) toward evening, the Sun grows weaker and feebler toward sunset, until He plummets from the horizon like a drop of blood, for blood is the sign of corruption. [*Berakhot* 9:13d, 59b]

"The Sun has an angelic escort; one set conducts Him out in the morning, and another leads Him home at night" (*Pirke de*

Rabbi Eliezer 6). The angels remove the crown of the Sun in the evening and bring his rays to heaven to be polished afresh. But if in His daily round the Sun's rays happen to gleam for a moment on the face of a single good person, they linger there trembling. One can almost hear a sigh of relief and spiritual refreshment. And in one moment that harsh look melts in the milky radiance with which He initially set out.

> Said the Koretzer: "We read: *What profit has a man of all his labor wherein he laboreth under the sun* ? (Proverbs 1:3). What reward is due man for all his labors in God's service in addition to the recompense of being alive, and of beholding the Sun shine upon him bringing him the joy of life and light?"[15]

> Every day the Holy One sits in judgment on the globes of Sun and Moon, which are reluctant to go forth to shine upon the world. What reason do they give? "People burn incense to us, people worship us."
> R. Judah ben Shunem said: What does the Holy One do? He sits in judgment on them and they go forth and shine upon the world against their will. Hence it is written: *Every morning does He bring His judgment to light* (Zephaniah 3:5). [*Vayikra Rabbah* 31:9]

Sun and Moon are reluctant to carry out their natural function since people might worship them as idols. All creatures turn with instinctive gratitude to worship in the direction of light, but the luminaries want to protect themselves from Divine wrath. There is a *Midrash* that Abraham learned to worship an Unseen God only after bowing down to the visible luminaries of Sun and Moon.

OCEANIC CONSCIOUSNESS

When Abram was 3 years old, he began wondering: Who created the Heavens and the earth and me also? All day he prayed to the Sun. In the evening the Sun set in the west and the Moon rose in the east. When he saw the Moon and the stars he said: "This one created the Heavens and the earth and me, and these stars are his courtiers and servants." He stayed up all night praying to the Moon. In the morning the Moon set in the west and the Sun rose in the east. He concluded: "None of these have any power. They have a Master. Let me worship Him." And he bowed down. [*Sefer Aggadah* I:24; *Baba Batra* 10a; *Bereishit Rabbah* 38:13]

His attitude to Sun, Moon, and stars became such that "just as an illuminated castle must have a master, the same [must be] true of a world with such a sky" (*Bereishit Rabbah* 39:1).

So, despite the apprehensions of Sun and Moon, their light, in fact, instils a cosmic sense of wonder akin to religious faith. That sense of awe before the majesty of the heavens is a strain that runs through the Psalms.

The heavens declare the glory of God, and the skies proclaim His existence. [Psalm 19:2]

Lift up your eyes to the stars and see who has created these. He numbers them all like an army. He calls them all by name. [Isaiah 40:25-26]

O Lord our God, how dear is Your Name in all the earth, because Your Glory is set upon the Heavens. . . . O that I should see Your Name, the Moon and the stars that You have founded, the work of Your fingers. [Psalm 8:2,4]

He makes the Great lights, for His love is infinite. [Psalm 136:7]

Our rabbis learn: "Whoever sees the Sun on his circuit, the Moon in her plenitude, and the stars on their courses and the planets in their order should say: 'Blessed is the One who makes the Creation.' " [*Vayikra Rabbah* 23:8]

Said R. Shimon the son of Pazi: Said R. Joshua the Son of Levi in the name of the Son of Kapra: "Whoever knows how to meditate on the cycles and the planets and doesn't do so, about him

Scripture says: *And to the work of God you do not look, and His handiwork you do not see."*

Said R. Shmuel ben Nahmani: Said R. Jonathan: "From where do we know it is a religious duty to meditate on the cycles and the planets? As it is said: *And you shall observe them and do them for that is your wisdom and your understanding in the sight of the nations* (Deuteronomy 4:6). That is to say, meditation on the cycles and the planets." [*Shabbat* 75]

Shmuel used to say: "The pathways of the skies are as clear to me as the pathways of Nehardea (his own city), except for the comet that emits a long scepter of light and only appears in the sky in fragments. I don't know what it is. And we have a tradition that it does not pass Orion, for if it did pass Orion, the world would be destroyed. But we see that it did pass Orion. Its effulgence passed, which made it appear as if it did."

Rav Huna the son of R. Joshua says: "That is the lower part of the sky that is torn and turns and appears like the light of the sky." [*Berakhot* 58a–b]

According to the Rambam, the existence of the heavens is in itself a hymn to the Creator. Therefore, the study of astronomy, science, and philosophy is recommended as conducive to the love and fear of God (Maimonides, *Moreh Nevuchim* 1:44). From this we see that Sun and Moon had little to be afraid of. What they really loathed was shining upon evil, egotistical, and power-seeking individuals. Just as they reflected the Divine Majesty to men, so when they were forced to give light to the wicked, they became tarnished by the human evil they were forced to countenance. During the revolt of Korach, they refused to shine till justice was done to Moshe (*Nedarim* 39b; *Sanhedrin* 110a).

On the other hand, there are occasions when the Sun shines equally on all, oblivious of human tragedy.

Moshe lamented the People's destruction. "Be accursed, O Sun; Why was your light not extinguished in the hour when the enemy invaded the Sanctuary!" The Sun replied: "I could not grow dark. The Heavenly Powers would not permit it. Sixty fiery scourges they dealt me and they told me: God said let your light shine forth." [*Aichah Rabbah* 24:47–48; *Nedarim* 39b]

But, according to the following two versions, it is not the wrongdoings of man but the dazzling quality of the Supernal Light that makes the Sun and the Moon reluctant to go out. They themselves are wrapt in religious awe.

Day in and day out, the Sun and the Moon cover their eyes before the Supernal Light, and they are reluctant to go out.

What does the Holy One do? He lights their way. And they progress by His light, as it is said: *O Lord, they make progress by the Light of Your Face!* (Psalm 89:16).

When they are ready to set, they don't know where they are going, so dazzled are they by the Upper Light. So they stand still in the firmament and delay their departure.

But the Holy One showers before them arrows and torches and lightning bolts. And they stumble forward in the direction He aims. As it is said: *Sun and Moon stand in their place. By the light of Your arrows they move forward. By the gleam of the lightning of Your spear* (Habbakuk 3:11). [*Midrash Tehillim* on Psalm 19:11]

In the firmament they linger like celestial horses pawing the ether and reluctant to re-enter the stable. Like divers they hesitate before plunging into their opposite element. For the Sun must sink into a bed of darkness, and the Moon must dissolve in liquid sunlight.

Rabbi Eliezer says: "The world is like a vestibule whose northerly direction is not divided off. So that when the Sun touches the northwesterly corner, it curves and goes up above the firmament." Rabbi Joshua says: "The world is like a tent with the northerly direction divided off, so that when the Sun touches the northwesterly direction, it is concealed and goes behind the flap. As it is said: *It progresses forward to the south and makes a circuitous bypass to the north* (Ecclesiastes 1:6). It progresses forward to the south by day and makes a circuitous bypass to the north by night." [*Baba Batra* 25b]

Both the lights of Sun and Moon have a hidden side and are modest before the glory of the Light above. The Moon waxes and wanes throughout the month. She is hidden by the night. And the Sun grows and declines throughout the day. Here the modesty is on the part of the beholder, who cannot look at the Sun directly. This shows how light is directly connected with darkness, the visible with the invisible.

In the "future time," God will bring forth the Sun from this cover and the wicked will be consumed by its heat (*Nedarim* 8b; *Midrash Tehillim* on Psalm 19:13).

Light and Splendor are veiled just as a bride is covered with a veil because "the Glory of the King's Daughter lies within" (Psalm 45:13).

> Said Rav: "At the time when the Two Great Courtiers leave to take permission from their Sovereign to go on their rounds, their eyes grow dim from the radiance of the *Shekhinah*. Though they ask to go out and give light to the world, they themselves cannot see a thing.
>
> "What does the Holy One do for them? He shoots arrows in front of them to illumine their way. That is why it is said: *The Sun and the Moon stand in exaltation. By the light of Your arrows they journey, by the gleam of the lightning of Your javelins*" (Habakkuk 3:11). [*Vayikra Rabbah* 31:9]

Even the Sun, principal light of our world, goes "blind" before the blaze of the Supreme Source of light, and even He is dependent for light upon God.

How is the Sun similar to God Himself? It is impossible to behold God (or to look directly at the Sun) (*Hullin* 60a).

The Sun is an image for God Himself, for the "Light of Lights," because one cannot look at it directly. In this respect the Sun is superior to man. For the Sun's progress depends on the light of God's Face, while such clarity was something to which even Moshe our Teacher could not aspire. As it is said, Moshe our Teacher begged God: "Show me Your Glory!" (Exodus 33:18). This was the greatest thirst of his life. But God replied: "You cannot see My Face for no man can see Me and live"

(Exodus 33:20). In fact, Moshe is said to have faced the world from behind a mask, serving the function of our sunglasses.

The Sun

Like a bridegroom the Sun
Dons his robe that is spun of light,
Which emanated from You
Yet in no way diminishes Your light.

Taught to go westward round
With obeisance profound To his Lord
He by service so loyal
To a master so royal is a Lord.

While his homage each day
Serves to mark and display Your glory
It is Your hand that invests
The robe on which rests His glory.

Solomon Ibn Gabirol[16]

Israel said: *O send out Thy light and Thy truth; let them lead me* (Psalm 43:3). Great is the light of the Holy One. The Sun and Moon light up the world. But whence do they derive their radiance? They snatch a few of the sparks of the celestial light, as it is said, *The Sun and the Moon . . . at the light of Thine arrows they go, at the shining of Thy glittering spear* (Habakkuk 3:2).

Transcendent is the light on high, for only a hundredth part of it was given to all mankind. As it is said, *He knoweth what—mah,* Hebrew for one hundredth—*is in the darkness* (Daniel 11:22), darkness signifying the life of this world. "Therefore," says God, "have I made the Sun and the Moon that they shall give you light." As it is said, *And God set them in the firmament of the heaven to give light* (Genesis 1:17). [*Bamidbar Rabbah* 15:9]

R. Abina said: "The globe of the sun, says God, is one of my servants, and when it goes forth into the world no created being can feed its eyes on it. Do I then need your light." "But, as R.

Aha said: *The Lord was pleased for His righteousness' sake to make the Torah great and glorious* (Isaiah 42:21), which means: "I have no other intention than to make you worthy of divine favor." [*Vayikra Rabbah* 31:8–9]

What the Sun is to natural life on earth, so God is to Israel and the spiritual life. Isaiah says that in the time of redemption, "Israel's Sun will never more go down, for God will be Your everlasting light" (Isaiah 30:26).

THE ROYAL COURSE OF THE SUN

The royal course of the Sun is divinely ordained (Psalm 74:16).

Said Antoninus to Rabi: "Why does the Sun rise in the east and set in the west?" Rabi replied: "If it were the other way round you would also question me about that."

Antoninus responded: "This is how I will phrase my question: Why does the sun set in the west?"

Rabi replied: "In order to greet his Master (since we have it as a tradition that the *Shekhinah* lies in a westerly direction). As it is said: *And the heavenly hosts bow down before You* " (Nehemiah 9:6).

But Antoninus persisted: "Could the Sun not have gone halfway through the sky and given His salutations and made an exit?"

So Rabi concluded: "For the sake of the workers and the wayfarers (for whom otherwise it would have grown dark too soon)" (*Sanhedrin* 91).

The sages of Israel said: "The wheel is fixed and the planets revolve." But the sages of the nations say: "The wheel revolves but the planets are stationary." Said Rabi: "The rejoinder is that if the wheel rotated, the planets would revolve and turn with it in every direction, but we have never found the Great Bear in the south and Scorpion in the north."

The Sages of Israel maintained: "The Sun travels down from the firmament by day and up from the firmament by night. But the sages of the nations believe that by day the Sun travels below the firmament and by night He *also* travels below the firmament." Said Rabi: "Their words are more plausible than ours because the water springs are cool by day and boiling hot by night (since the Sun heats them up from below)."

R. Nathan said: "On sunny days, the Sun travels at the top of the sky. That is why the whole world steams but the deep springs are cold. And in the rainy season the Sun travels in the depths of the sky. And that is why the whole world cools off but the deep springs are boiling."

The Sun travels on four paths. During *Nisan, Iyyar,* and *Sivan,* it travels on the mountains to melt the snows. During *Tammuz, Av,* and *Elul,* it travels in populated areas so as to ripen the fruits. During *Tishri, Marheshvan,* and *Kislev,* it travels in the seas, to dry out the rivers. During *Tevet, Shevat,* and *Adar,* it travels in the wilderness so as not to dry up the seeds. [*Pesahim* 94b]

"The Sun stays in a bag, but in the month of *Tammuz* it comes out of the bag to ripen the fruits." [*Sefer Aggadah* I:9; *Midrash Tanhumah II; Tetzaveh* 98].

Rabbi Eliezer the Great says: "As soon as the fifteenth of *Av* comes around, the strength of the Sun is weakened" (*Baba Batra* 121).

Rabbi Yonatan says the Sun moves like the sail of a ship, like a ship with 365 ropes (the number of days in the solar year), or like a ship sailing from Alexandria with 354 ropes (the number of days in a lunar year). The Sun ascends 366 steps into the heavens, then descends 183 steps to the east and 183 steps to the west.

Three hundred and sixty-five windows created the Holy One for the world's use, 182 in the east, 182 in the west, and one in the middle of the sky through which the Sun came out for the first time at the Creation of the World. [Jerusalem Talmud, *Rosh Hashanah* 82]

There are 366 windows in the firmament through which the Sun successively emerges and retires. The Sun could complete his course from south to north in a single instant; 365 angels hold him back, however, with 365 grappling irons. Every day one loses his hold, and the Sun must thus spend a year on his course (*Midrash Tehillim* on Psalm 19:11).

> Said Rabbi Shimon bar Yohai: We don't know whether the Sun and the Moon blossom in the atmosphere or if they flow from heaven, or even if they are going in their accustomed path. It's a very difficult subject that is impossible for people to understand. [*Bereishit Rabbah* 6:8]

"Truly the light is sweet, and a pleasant thing it is for the eyes to behold the Sun" (Proverbs 11:7).

Three things are a foretaste of the world-to-come – *Shabbat* , sexual intercourse, and sunshine (*Berakhot* 57b). Yet – "Sunlight breaking through the clouds is hard to bear" (*Yoma* 20b) – the Sun also scorches and consumes evildoers (Psalm 121:6; Isaiah 40:9, 10; Isaiah 50:9,10).

The Sun annihilates evildoers and heals the righteous. "But unto you shall the Sun of righteousness arise with healing in his wings" (Malachi 4:20).

Abraham possessed a precious stone that healed the sick. When he died, God set the stone in the sphere of the Sun (*Baba Batra* 166).

The *Menorah* symbolizes the life force, God's flow of bounty to the world under the image of the Sun. But the fact that the *Menorah* is the symbol of both the Sun and the solar system shows that what the Sun stands for belongs to both the Divine Realm and to human reality. Indeed, the royal course of the Sun typifies the progress of the good man toward perfection.

> But the path of the just is as the shining light, that shines more and more until the perfect day. [Proverbs 4:18]

"The Sun passes paradise in the morning and hell in the evening." Dawn is a reflection of the roses of paradise; but sunset mirrors the fires of hell (*Baba Batra* 84a). The stream of fire in which the Sun bathes is identical with the River of Flame (*Hagiga* 13b; *Shemot Rabbah* 15:6; *Pirke de Rabbi Eliezer* 51). The River *Nehar*

Denur, in which angels conceived by God's Word were born, praised God and were reabsorbed into the fiery stream (*Pirke de Rabbi Eliezer* 51).

The Sun appears to be red during sunrise and sunset and golden in between, but really He is pure white. He appears to be red in the morning because He passes by and reflects the red roses of Eden, He appears to be red in the evening because He reflects the fires of *Gehinnom* (Hell), and He appears to be golden in between because of the dazzle of His rays.

The Sun is so transcendent that we cannot see Him. Only when the red roses of Eden, the blood of *Gehinnom*, or His own razzle-dazzle lend Him color can we mortals see His light.

"There is nothing new under the Sun. . ." (Proverbs 1:9)– under the Sun, but not over the Sun.

The Sun sings in honor of God while pursuing His course (Joshua 10:12) (*Midrash Tehillim* on Psalm 23).

The progress of the Sun in his circuit is an uninterrupted song of praise, and only His singing makes His motion possible. Therefore, when Joshua bid the Sun to stand still, he had to command Him to be silent. His song of praise hushed, the Sun stood still (*Midrash HaGaddol* 1:41–42; *Pirke de Rabbi Eliezer* 6; *Midrash Tehillim* 19:168–170; *Baraita de Ma'aseh Bereishit* 50; *Kohelet* 86; *Zohar Hadash* on Genesis 4:19; *Enoch* 2:114).[17]

The Sun and the Moon give thanks and glorify God; if they did not give praise they would cease to exist (Enoch 41:7).[18]

Joshua commanded the Sun to be still (Joshua 10:12). At first the Sun refused. He argued that He did not see why He had to listen to man. Since He had been created already on the Fourth Day of Creation, whereas man was not created until the sixth, surely He was the superior. Then Joshua reminded the Sun that, in the story of Joseph's Dream, Sun, Moon, and eleven stars had bowed down and acknowledged man's supremacy (*Midrash Tanhuma* on Ahare Mot 426).

Before the Sun agreed to keep quiet, He wanted Joshua to give Him some assurance that God's praises would not cease. The man agreed, therefore, to take up the song himself (*Bereishit Rabbah* 74:11) (*Midrash Tehillim* on Psalm 23).

NOTES

1. See also Louis Ginzberg, *Legends of the Jews*, trans. Henrietta Szold (Philadelphia: Jewish Publication Society, 1968), pp. 23–24.
2. Ginzberg, *Legends*, vol. 1, p. 26.
3. See Chapter 1 this volume, pp. 79–81, where the central shaft was equated with Sarah or the *Shekhinah*.
4. See Chapter 1, p. 72, on the "glass that does not shine."
5. Jacob, David, and Rachel were the youngest of their families.
6. Ginzberg, *Legends*, vol. 1, pp. 22–23; vol. 5, n. 100.
7. Here I link the Moon (*Malkhut*) with Sarah, who "laughed" when she gave birth to *Yitzhak* (laughter), and in praise of whom Abraham allegedly wrote the "Woman of Valor" (Proverbs 31:25), saying that she would "laugh in the time to come."
8. An anonymous Midrashic source with variant retellings by Medieval writers including *Machzor Vitry* and the *Zohar*.
9. Rabbi Gamliel's grandfather was Rabbi Yehuda Ha-Nasi (Rabbi), compiler of the *Mishnah*, of which the Talmud is an elaboration. As the seventh generation descendant of Hillel, he was *Nasi* (Prince, or Patriarch), an office that remained in Hillel's family for four hundred years. He died about 200 C.E. Hillel was a direct descendant of King David.
10. See *Greek Apocalypse of Baruch* 9.
11. See Ginzberg, *Legends*, vol. 1, pp. 27, 32–33; vol. 5, n. 152.
12. Ibid., vol. 1, pp. 32–33.
13. Ibid., vol. 5, n. 154.
14. Ibid., vol. 1, p. 25; vol. 5, n. 104. See also *Pirke de Rabbi Eliezer* 51, 56.
15. *Nofeth Tzufim*, Pinchas of Koretz (Warsaw, 1929), p. 53, in Louis Newman, *Hasidic Anthology* (New York: Scribner's, 1938), vol. 5, p. 396.
16. Variation on Solomon Ibn Gabirol, *Selected Religious Poems,* ed. Israel Davidson (Philadelphia: Jewish Publication Society, 1924), p. 19.
17. Ginzberg, *Legends*, vol. 1, pp. 24–25, 102; Greek Apocalypse of Baruch 6.
18. Ginzberg, *Legends*, vol. 1, pp. 24–25.

THREE

LIGHT
OF
MAN

Rabbi Dr. Zeev Gottlieb. The light of the face: "The splendor of Adam's countenance was the image of God" (Jerusalem Talmud, *Hagiga* 2:77a). (*Courtesy of the author*)

God's first words to Creation were: "Let there be Light!" (Genesis 1:3). We may think light was created on the first day, but it is written that God set the Sun and the Moon in the firmament on the fourth day. So when was light created – on the first day or the fourth?

When was man created? It seems that man was created last, in keeping with the saying that that which is most precious is kept till the end. Yet there is some indication that man was present, at least in imagination, from the very start.

These contradictions may be resolved by recourse to the myth of the "Hidden Light." The light God created on the first day, or even before, was far different in quality from the natural luminaries of the Sun and the Moon – they simply were one of a series of natural receptacles into which the light was subsequently poured:

According to R. Eliezer:

The light which The Holy One, Blessed be He, created on the first day, if a man had only been present, he would have been able to see by its means from one end of the world to the other.

141

But then God previewed the history of man. As soon as He saw the generation of the Flood and the Tower of Babel and viewed their corruption, He immediately hid the light from them.

And for whom did He hide it? For the righteous in the time-to-come. [*Hagiga* 12a]

THE HIDDEN LIGHT

Before the creation of the Sun, the Moon and the stars, which also have been called "times" because their circuit delimits the length of a day – it is very difficult to understand what days and hours mean. To add to the confusion, Man apparently was the last thing God created before the advent of the *Shabbat*. Without the presence of man and his artificial imposition of a time-frame on "reality," it is absurd to speak of distance and time. The *Midrash* realizes it is speaking hypothetically when it intentionally mixes up past and future tenses in describing what a human being might have or actually did experience before.

> The Light God created before Sun and Moon would have enabled man to see the world at a glance from one end to the other. [*Pirke de Rabbi Eliezer* 3]

But other teachers of the *Mishnah* maintain that the light created on the first day was the natural illumination of the Sun and the Moon, which were only hung in place in the firmament on the fourth day.

> But the Sages say: "It (the light created on the first day) is identical with the luminaries, for they were created on the first day, but they were not hung up (in the firmament) till the fourth day." [*Hagiga* 12a]

What this seems to imply is that the essence of light was created on the first day, while its particular manifestation (or vessel in which it was poured) was not fixed until the fourth. And "First Light," whether created on the first day or even before, was entirely different in quality to the light that came later:

R. (Meir) thus said: "Why is it written *And God said, let there be light, and there was light* (Genesis 1:3)? Why does it not say (as it does with all other creations), *and it was so?*

"But this teaches us that the light was very intense, so that no created thing could gaze upon it. God therefore stored it away for the righteous in the Ultimate Future." [*Bahir*, no. 190]

The first light that God created was not physical like that created on the fourth day. Of all God's creations, only light is singled out for approval: "And God saw the light that it was good" (Genesis 1:4). The other objects were generally part of His plan, but the light was the quintessence.

In Hebrew, "And it was so" – by which all the other creations are described – means "And it was established," placed, pigeonholed. "So" – and not otherwise. But the essence of light is its fluidity, its defiance of definition and constraint. It dazzles, it emanates, it travels, it is visible through veils and bodies of varying degrees of opacity and darkness. Light is a matter of nuance and degree and can be perceived in myriads of guises; by its very nature it is capable of transformation and of transforming the state of anything with which it comes in contact. Therefore the Bible does not say, as it does of God's other Creations: "And it was so."

A similar question to that raised about light can be raised about man. When was man created – on the sixth day or on the first?

And God Said: Let there be light. This refers to the actions of the righteous. *And God saw the light, that it was good* (Genesis 1:4). This means that God delights in people's good actions. [*Bereishit Rabbah* 11:5]

In "First Light" God saw the "image" of human goodness and the souls of the righteous.

R. Samuel ben Ammi said: "However many meritorious acts and good deeds a man laboriously performs and lays up to his credit, it is not enough repayment for the simple breath that issues forth from his mouth. *Neither is the soul filled* (Ecclesiastes 6:7).

"Three are insatiable: The earth, woman, and the soul. The earth, since it is said, *The earth is not satisfied with water* (Proverbs 30:16).

"Whence do we know this of woman? It is written, *She eats (enjoys adulterous intercourse), and wipes her mouth, and saith: I have done no wickedness* (Proverbs 30:16).

"How do we know this of the soul? It is written, *Neither is the soul filled* (Ecclesiastes 6:7).

"Six times is the word *soul* written here (in Leviticus 5), corresponding to the Six Days of Creation. The Holy One, Blessed be He, says to the soul: "All that I have created in the six days of creation I have created for your sake alone, and you go out and sin!" [*Vayikra Rabbah* 4:2]

Primordial Light was not external to man, an object he had to consume with his eyes. Rather, it was an attribute that he himself possessed, and the brilliance emitted was an intrinsic part of his physical presence. "The primordial light, which was created on the first day, is identical with the luster of Adam that he retained over the Sabbath" (*Bereishit Rabbah* 11:2; 12:6).

If we are told that Primordial Light extended man's vision "from one end of the world to the other," we are also told that *Adam Kadmon* extended "from one end of the world to the other." Logically, his vast horizons must have had something to do with his vast physical dimensions, and both had more than a little to do with Primordial Light. "The light by means of which the First Man was created allowed him to see from one end of the world to the other."[1]

R. Judah said: "The first man extended from one end of the world to the other, for it is said, *Since the day that God created man upon the earth, and from one end of heaven to the other.* As soon as he sinned, the Holy One blessed be He, placed His hand upon him and diminished him, for it is said: *And laid Thine hand upon me.*" [*Hagiga* 12a]

Original Man, the *Midrash* corroborates, filled "one end of the world to the other."

R. Tanhuma in the name of R. Banayah and R. Berekiah in the name of R. Liezer said: "He created him as a lifeless mass extending from one end of the world to the other; thus it is written, *Thine eyes did see mine unformed substance*" (Psalm 139:16).
    R. Joshua ben R. Nehemiah and R. Judah ben R. Simon in R. Liezer's name said: "He created him filling the whole world. How do we know (that he stretched) from east to west? Because it is said, *Thou hast formed me behind (ahor) and before (kedem)*. From north to south? Because it says, *Since the day that God created man upon the earth, and from the one end of heaven unto the other* (Deuteronomy 4:32). And how do we know that he filled the empty spaces of the world? From the verse, *And laid Thy hand upon me* (as you read, *Withdraw Thy hand from me*)" (Job 8:21). [*Bereishit Rabbah* 8:1]

Man only saw "from one end of the world to the other" because in himself he extended that far. His original breadth of vision has a physical cause. And when God diminished his physical dimensions, He not only took away from Adam's prophetic insight, but Adam also became less of a person. The essential loss was no external Paradise but an impoverishment in what it meant to be human.
    The *Shiur Komah* (measurement of God's body)–an enigmatic excursus into Chariot mysticism–describes the "body" of the Creator in a style similar to that used of the Beloved in the "Song of Songs."[2] Here, enormous figures are given for the length of each organ of the body of God and of His *Shekhinah* in order to hint at some deep level of enlightenment and vision on the part of the mystic.
    The stupendous measurements of the body of the *Shekhinah* are cosmic and reduce any attempt at visualization to absurdity. The Creator is 236,000 parasangs tall–according to another tradition, the height of His soles alone is 30 million parasangs. But "the measure of a parasang of God is three miles, and a mile has 10,000 yards, and a yard three spans of His span, and a span

fills the whole world, as it is written: Who hath meted out
heaven with a span."³

To talk about God's body at all is to speak in metaphors.
God's body is the external, most visible part of Him, by which
He is known. It is His Name, his *Shekhinah,* or even *Adam Kadmon,*
the human perception of the Divine, the "figure of a Man" sitting
on God's Throne in Ezekiel's vision (Ezekiel 1:26). So when we
read that, before Man's sin, he was of tremendous size and
extended from one side of the world to the other, we are reading
of the "Image of God" or the "Glory"–that is, the human
perception of God based on reflection.

Here, light and the angle of seeing have become a faculty of
soul. The ideal way of seeing carries within it its proper source of
light, no matter what it shines on. In fact, the light is not even a
matter of a personal subjective slant on the world outside so
much as a quality intrinsic to man himself: "The splendor of
Adam's countenance was the image of God" (Jerusalem Talmud,
Hagiga 2:77a). Primordial Light is Primordial Man–Man in all
his unfallen splendor as the image of God. The human unfallen
image of God is what is really meant by Primordial Light.

> Splendor of the face was only one of seven precious gifts that
> God presented to Adam before the Fall. Some of the others were–
> life eternal, tallness of stature, the fruit of the soil, the fruit of the
> tree; the luminaries in the sky in the time to come, the light of the
> moon will be like the light of the Sun and the light of the Sun will
> be sevenfold. [*Bereishit Rabbah* 12:6; *Bamidbar Rabbah* 13:12; *Shir
> HaShirim Rabbah* 30:3; *Midrash HaGadol* 126–130]

What happened to all this human splendor of soul after
Adam sinned? His skin was like a bright garment, shining like
his nails. Then this brightness vanished and he appeared naked
(*Bereishit Rabbah* 20:11).

Enoch, an early descendant of Adam, is said to have walked
with God in his lifetime, so that when he died his body was
entirely consumed by flame, while his soul was transformed into
the angel Metatron, God's representative to the wandering Israelites in the wilderness.

It is the duty of Metatron, whose own body was consumed entirely by the flames, to initiate into the Torah the souls of children who have died in infancy (such as the babies in the crematoria) (*Avodah Zarah* 3b) and to offer the souls of the righteous in the heavenly Temple as an atonement for the Jewish People (*Bamidbar Rabbah* 12:15).

Metatron was also known as the "angel of the Divine countenance," who, according to the *Zohar* and later *Kabbalah*, embodies "the highest splendor"–that is, the light of soul that Adam forfeited by his sin (*Zohar Hadash* 42d, 68a).

Metatron, too, represents the *Shekhinah*. He is described in the *Zohar* as her body, or her "son" (*Zohar* I:94b). Metatron rules in the Realm of Formation. He is the first of Creation, the human being created in God's likeness who revealed himself to Moshe and to Ezekiel. According to Cordovero, the first words in the Torah, "In the beginning God created," refer to Metatron, since he is the quintessence of man, the *Kadmon* incarnate in all the *Tzaddikim* of all times.[4]

"Adam is the only being who was created by the Hand of God. The rest of creation sprang from the word of God."[5] (The "word" of God is more abstract and removed from feeling than the Hand. The Hand of God is equivalent, not to One but Ten, *Sefirot*–Sayings, or Fingers, of God.)

"God created the heavenly beings with His right hand and the terrestrial with His left" (*Menahot* 36b; *Sifre* 35d). He created the whole world with one hand and man and the Temple with both (*Avot de Rabbi Nathan* 1:8; *Ketubot* 5a; *Pirke de Rabbi Eliezer* 7; *Mekilta Bahodesh* 6:69b; *Alphabet of Rabbi Akiva* 24–25). Why the Temple in particular? Because it is a "world-in-little" fashioned by man for God's glory.

> R. Samuel ben Ammi said: "From the beginning of the world's creation the Holy One, blessed be He, longed to enter into partnership with mortals." [*Bereishit Rabbah* 3:9]

When did He succeed? "On the day that the Tabernacle was completed" (Numbers 7:1). How is this? "Ten crowns adorned the first Day" (*Bereishit Rabbah* 3:9). What were those crowns but the Ten *Sefirot?* And those Crowns came into their own only when the *Shekhinah*–the last of those Crowns–dwelt on earth, which did not happen until "the day that the Tabernacle was completed."

Before any humans existed, the Torah has God, in His capacity as *Elohim*. God's attribute of strict Judgment and natural limitation put forward the suggestion: "Let us make man" (Genesis 1:26).

To whom was He talking? The classical commentators say He consulted the Angels who were against the idea. The angels said that man would destroy everything. But the *Zohar* makes an implicit comparison with Jacob who, before he left the house of Laban to return to Canaan, turned to ask consent from his wives. The suggestion is that God consulted the Feminine impetus in Creation before producing man. But the *Zohar* says something even more startling and radical. A wife makes no decision, says the *Zohar,* without asking permission of her husband. Who then consulted whom? The *Zohar* seems to suggest that it was the Feminine Mother impulse in God that asked permission of Her reluctant Husband and that She created man. The *Zohar* takes *Elohim* as the Feminine, the Vessel, subject to restriction. Thus it was God in His Feminine aspect who said: "Let us make man," asking permission of masculine Transcendence and Grace.

The *Zohar* then reverses again the roles to the conventional, comparing the case to that of a king who wants to build a palace. He does not build it with his own hands, but calls in an architect. This architect, or *Oman* in Hebrew, is the Feminine Wisdom in God that existed before Creation.[6] According to the principles of art and the natural limits of form, She created the world.

> When He desired anything built in the way of emanation (*Azilut* –in the realms of Transcendence), the Father said to the Mother by means of the Word (*Amirah*), "Let it be so and so!" and straightway it was so, as it is written: *And He said, Elohim, let there be light, and there was light* (Genesis 1:3), that is, One (God) said to *Elohim, Let there be light:* the master of the building gave the order, and the architect carried it out immediately.
>
> When He came to the "world of separation," which is the

sphere of individual beings, [the Feminine impulse took the initiative]. The architect said to the master of the building: *Let us make man* (Genesis 1:26) (the equivalent of *Let there be light* in the sphere of Transcendence). *In our image, according to our likeness* (Genesis 1:26). [*Zohar* I:22a–b]

"In our image": This is light in the sphere of transcendence. "According to our likeness": This is man in his immanence in nature. According to the *Zohar,* it was not the Angels, but the Masculine Transcendent God who saw that man would sin and was reluctant to create him, whereas the Mother took the initiative. Therefore man, created in the "image of *Elohim*" was formed after the image of the Mother, "since the Father was not willing to share in his creation."

What is more, when Adam sinned, his Mother also went into disgrace and was dismissed from the celestial palace. (The *Shekhinah* went into exile.) And division was effected between the Father and the Mother. Like Rachel, the *Shekhinah*'s yearning for Her children proved stronger than Her love for Her husband.

The companions of Rabbi Shimon seized on the (sexist) notion that man in his lowest aspect should be in the image of woman, whereas the ideal transcendent man, the "man of emanation," should have been totally male. But Rabbi Shimon disagrees and says that man in his very highest aspect is both male and female.

That is why it says: *And God said, "Let there be light"* (Genesis 1:3). *Let there be light.* From the side of the Father. *And there was light.* From the side of the Mother.

And this is the man "of two faces." This "man" has no "image and likeness." [*Zohar* I:22a–b]

(This represents the ideal relationship between the sexes also figured in the Cherubim embracing each other in the Temple below.)

Only the Supernal Mother had a name combining light and darkness–light, which was the supernal vestment and which

God created on the first day and then stored away for the righteous, and darkness.

Because the darkness was destined to sin against the light, the Father was not willing to share in man's creation and therefore the Mother said: "Let us make man in our image after our likeness."

"In our image" corresponds to light.

"After our likeness," to darkness, which is a vestment to light in the same way that a body is a vestment to the soul, as it is written, *Thou didst clothe me with skin and flesh* (Job 10:11).

He (Rabbi Shimon) then paused, and all the friends rejoiced and said: "Happy is our lot that we have been privileged to hear things which never were disclosed till now." [*Zohar* I:22a–b]

In an earlier Midrashic explanation of God's invitation: "Let us make man," we are told He "took counsel [not with the angels or with some Feminine Partner but] with the souls of the righteous."

As it is written: *These were the makers* (potters) *and those that dwelt among the plantations and hedges: there they dwelt with the king in his work* (I Chronicles 4:23). *These were the makers:* They are so termed on account of the verse, *Then the Lord formed* (made) *man* (Genesis 2:7). *There they dwelt with the king in his work:* with the Supreme King of kings, the Holy One, blessed be He, sat the souls of the righteous with whom He took counsel before creating the world. [*Bereishit Rabbah* 8:7]

Therefore, the Feminine plastic power in God, the Maker or "Potter," could be said to comprise "the souls of the Righteous" before man himself had come on the scene. It was man's potential for Good that decreed his creation. Each stage of his potential for self-realization – the "Ten Crowns" or Ten *Sefirot* – served as chisels in his formation.

Created in the image of God, Adam is a microcosm of the world. Both the cosmos and Man are comprised of Ten *Sefirot*. The human faculties mirror the *Sefirot* of the cosmos. Mystical union can be attained through the Ten *Sefirot,* or attributes intrinsic to human nature, through which man can capture the flowing emanation of the Divine.

R. Jacob Joseph of Polonnoye said in the name of R. Yisrael Baal Shem Tov:

> I received it as a mystical tradition from my teacher that there are Ten *Sefirot* in man, who is called a "world-in-little." For the Thought, which is called Father, after the *Tzimtzum,* which is called Mother (through all the *Sefirot*). . . . [7]

Not only are there shifting correspondences between inner and outer world but even extension of the *Sefirot* in man's psychic universe, according to the Rabbi, is made up of a series of *Tzimtzumim.* The identical process by which the world originally came into being—an ejaculation of "light" from the Father into the Vessel or Lamp of the Mother—produces a further series of contractions and extensions, which become Father and Mother in turn.

> With Ten Sayings God created the world, although a single Saying would have sufficed (to show how precious is the world that was created for the sake of man).
>
> He who saves one soul, it is as if he had saved an entire world, that was created by Ten Words . . . not one world, but many worlds; for man who is comprised of Ten *Sefirot* contains within him worlds within worlds. And someone who causes one person to perish is to be regarded as if he caused the destruction of the entire world, that was created by means of Ten Words. [*Avot de Rabbi Nathan* 31:90; *Avot* 5:1; *Rosh Hashanah* 32a]

Of what do these worlds consist? These are not just the many children or souls he might bring into the world, but the Divine Image that lies within him. For each of these many worlds represents the Ten Divine Words, *Sefirot* within *Sefirot,* the innumerable lights of the celestial *Menorah.*

> [T]here is a great supernal power in man, which cannot be described, and as man possesses (this), it is not right to destroy his

form and his soul from the world. And one who kills a person, what is the loss he brings about? He sheds the blood of that (person), and he also diminishes the form (of humanity in general)—that is, he diminishes the power of the *Sefirot* (or Divine creativity).[8]

THE PRIMORDIAL LIGHT OF
ADAM KADMON

Rabbi Akiva said: "How beloved is Man because he was created in the Image, as it is said *For in the Image God made man*" (*Avot* 3:16). What is this "Form" or "image of God" but the human archetype—*Adam Kadmon.*

As soon as man appeared, all was achieved, both in the upper and lower worlds, for all is contained in man. [*Zohar* V:48a]

As the entire Creation unfolded in the course of Creation Week, it basked in unmitigated dazzling *Shekhinah* Light. The Sun and the Moon may have been set in the sky on the fourth day as a contingency measure, but as the Sun only partook of a one-hundredth part of the original Primordial Light, their use was not called for—is a lamp necessary in sunlight!—until the end of the succeeding *Shabbat.*

The light God created before Sun and Moon *would* have enabled man to see the world at a glance from one end to the other.
And God saw the light that it was good and God divided between the light and between the darkness (Genesis 1:5).
R. Judah son of R. Simeon said: "He divided it off for Himself. It is like a king who sees a fine portion and says: 'Save that for me!' So God created the world and He created a great light and He said: 'No creature can use it, only Me!' That is why it says: *And light dwells with Him*" (Daniel 2:22).
Said R. Abin Ha-Levi: "The Holy One took it and wrapped Himself in it like a *Tallit.* [9] The Heavens were fashioned from the light of God's garment."

But the Rabbis say: "He divided it off for the righteous at the time to come. This can be compared to a king who had a fine portion and He said: "This is for my son." [*Pirke de Rabbi Eliezer* 3]

This notion of the Primordial Light eclipsing the light of the Sun echoes the following description of *Adam Kadmon,* the sole of whose heel also eclipsed the light of the Sun in splendor.

Said R. Levi in the name of R. Menasheh: The apple of the heel of the First Man outshone the disk of the Sun.
    The human habit of a man's making himself two of any-thing, one for himself and one for his son, is scarcely to be marveled at. So Adam was created for God's use and the disk of the Sun was created for Adam: (Before he sinned), if the breadth of Adam's heel shone more than the disk of the Sun, how much more glorious than the Sun was the radiance of his face! [*Midrash Tanhuma* on *Ahare Mot,* p. 426]

Here, while man is God's lamp or globe or toy, the Sun is man's. Just as a baby is infinitely more real than a toy, so the splendor of the human soul and *Adam Kadmon* eclipse the light of the Sun. The story of the "two of anything" resembles that of the King (God) who keeps the light that eclipses the Sun both for Himself and for his righteous son. Since Primordial Light eclipses the Sun and the splendor of *Adam Kadmon* eclipses the Sun, *Adam Kadmon* can be considered the equivalent of Primordial Light.
    What is Primordial Light but the reservoir of all souls existing in God Himself! Therefore it can be said that the essence of the human soul is drawn from the Primordial Light and is superior to the lights of the cosmos that were created for man's sake.
    Obviously, Primordial Light and Primordial Man come from the same essence, by comparison with which the Sun palls. And in the future the hidden light that will reemerge many times as intense as the illumination of Sun and Moon will be the lost inner light of Israel and of mankind.
    Intrinsically the soul of *Adam Kadmon,* drawn from the reservoir of Souls, is quintessential light and was the very "idea"

on which the whole of the subsequent drama of Creation was based. And if the soul of man can be equated with Primordial Light, there is no contradiction in the timing of man's advent on the scene. Though the creation of man was completed only six hours before *Shabbat,* in a sense he existed from the beginning of Creation because he was the reason and intent behind the very first creative utterance: "Let there be Light."

Six hours before the advent of *Shabbat,* Eve induced man to eat from the Tree of Knowledge of Good and Evil, and the luster of "First Light" was removed from the world.

THE NATURE OF MAN'S SIN

Adam and Eve's existence in Eden before the sin was both an intellectual and an agricultural enterprise. Some say that the plants themselves were celestial shrubs, cuttings from the *Sefirot.* The Six *Sefirot* of nature were revealed to Adam and Eve in the shape of the Tree of Life, and the last *Sefirah* was revealed in the form of the Tree of Knowledge. Strangely, the Feminine was associated with Knowledge and the Masculine with Life-Force, though the reverse might have been expected. Adam, with Eve's encouragement, was tempted to concentrate on the feminine characteristics of the *Shekhinah* (Knowledge), to the detriment of the (masculine) quality of the biological life. As a result, the intellect became alienated. Man concentrated on the Tree of Knowledge (the *Shekhinah*) to such an extent that he interrupted the stream of energy that joined Her to the Tree of Life (the six masculine *Sefirot* or The Holy One, Blessed be He). Adam's sin consisted of severing the channels between *Malkhut* and the higher *Sefirot* and breaking the harmony between knowledge and Life, thus bringing about a second "exile of the *Shekhinah.*"[10]

After Adam's sin on the eve of *Shabbat,* God gave Creation thirty-six hours of grace:

The thirty-six hours are made up of twelve hours on the eve of the Sabbath, twelve on the Sabbath night, and twelve on the Sabbath-day. [*Bereishit Rabbah* 11:2, 12:6; *Berakhot* 8:5]

THE FIRST *SHABBAT*

Over *Shabbat* the sentence was suspended, only coming into effect after the termination of the Holy Day. For *Shabbat* comes with a special blessing. What is its nature?

> *And God blessed the Sabbath day.* How did He bless it? With light. When the Sun set on the night of the Sabbath, the light continued to function (even during the night).
>
> R. Liezer said: "He blessed it in the matter of a lamp, and this happened in my case. I once lit a lamp for the Sabbath night, and when I came at the termination of the Sabbath, I found it still burning and not at all diminished." [*Bereishit Rabbah* 11:2]

The miracle R. Liezer is referring to concerns sources of light energy – not dissimilar to the miracle of *Hanukkah*. We may believe that He who does not work on the six days to prepare the physical conditions conducive to the enjoyment of *Shabbat* (light, warmth, food, etc.) will not have *Shabbat*. This is true, but so is the opposite. *Shabbat* in itself is a source of physical blessing for the whole of the week. For *Shabbat* is a generator of light.

If R. Liezer thought this element of the miraculous occurred with artificial, man-made candles on any *Shabbat* of the year, what must have happened during Adam's first *Shabbat* in Paradise when there were only the God-given luminaries of Sun and Moon? "The luminaries enjoyed a reprieve and were not smitten until after the end of *Shabbat*" (*Bereishit Rabbah* 11:4–5).

> *I have descended into the nut grove* (Song of Songs 5:1). For thirty-six hours the *Shekhinah* light blossomed forth in Creation. Then a husk or *Klippah* was created to guard the fruit. [Kalever Rebbe]

The *Shekhinah* Light that descended into the physical world developed a husk like the shell of a nut. Although the shell or *Klippah* cannot be eaten – and for that reason is "bad," constituting a barrier to immediate enjoyment of the kernel – it also serves as a protection for the nutrients that lie within.

With the departure of *Shabbat,* Adam was driven out of Eden, which was closed against him by "Cherubim with a fiery revolving sword" to cut him off from the Tree of Eternal Life. These fiery Presences who guarded the Greater Eden were only an enlarged form of the *Klippah* that guards each atom or "fruit" of the cellular structure, similar to the horny membrane of fingernails and toenails. It is questionable whether Adam was driven out of Eden or whether the simple withdrawal of Primordial Light made Eden sink inward within each physical cell and behind the "husk" of the material world as we know it.

Since Adam concentrated on the Tree of Knowledge to the detriment of life, the human brain is "contained in a shell that will not be broken" till the End of Days. Only then "will the husk be broken and the light shine out into the world from the brain without any covering on it" (*Zohar* III:69b).

> And God said: *Let there be light, and there was light* (Genesis 1:3).
>
> That was not an occasion for rejoicing, since the world did not merit the use of that light, as R. Judah ben Simon said: "The light which The Holy One, Blessed be He, created on the first day was such that man could see thereby from one end of the universe to the other. When The Holy One, Blessed be He, foresaw that the conduct of the generation of Enoch and the conduct of the generation of the Flood would be corrupt, He deliberately hid it from them. This is indicated by what is written, *From the wicked their light is witholden* (Job 37:13). And where did He hide it–in the Garden of Eden, as it is said, *Light is sown for the righteous, and gladness for the upright in heart* (Psalm 97:11). [*Vayikra Rabbah* 11:7]

Adam's or Man's activity, or that of the *Tzaddik*, can in effect control the godhead–bringing it closer or driving it away. It says in the *Midrash* that "the real home of the *Shekhinah* is in the lower world. But Sins drive away the feet of the *Shekhinah*" (*Bereishit Rabbah* 19:7).

In one sense, after the Sin of Adam it was not God who drove man out of Eden, but man who had already banished God and the *Shekhinah* from an Eden that was transformed into a wilderness as a consequence. With the disappearance of this special form of light energy, thorns, thistles, and malignant growths proliferated where before paradise reigned.

If God "hid" the light, that does not mean He withdrew it.

Where did He hide it? Various possibilities have been put forward, but the best hiding place is where one would never think of looking–in the temporary, painful chaos of everyday life. Eden may have been an externalization of Adam's spiritual state. According to R. Chaim Vital, Adam's sin caused him to sink from the realm of "making" (*Asiyah*)[11] into that of the *Klippot,* which was the gross material world of the physical. Paradise, therefore, can be seen as the reservoir of all souls, and the "clippings" of the *Sefirot* or "roses" were these scintillations of soul entrusted to the care of Adam and Eve. When they sinned, all these fragments of soul became separated and had to enter separate bodies.

After the Sin of Adam, possibly Eden itself fell, too, and was transformed into the world that we know, with Primordial Light gone underground, shrinking into the innermost recess, and *Klippot* acting as the fiery angels on guard at the entrance. The same barrier of fire with which God fenced off evil also provided the division between darkness and light.

On the verse "And God divided between the light and between the darkness" (Genesis 1:4), the great biblical commentator Rashi says, based on the *Midrash,* that under circumstances in which light and dark became inextricably mixed, God took measures to salvage pure Primordial Light for the righteous.

The separating of the light from the dark only came into effect at the termination of *Shabbat.* Only when, paradoxically, the spiritual light of the *Shekhinah* was dragged down into the demonic realm of evil and darkness so that there was no place so abysmally low and evil that it was entirely bereft of some sparks of *Shekhinah* Light did God, as a precautionary measure, make the first *Havdalah,* separating the "First Light" and concealing it. "God concealed this light from the wicked, saving it up for the righteous in the world-to-come" (*Pirke de Rabbi Eliezer* 3).

The stories of the concealment of the *Shekhinah* Light are similar to those about the reduction in the dimensions of man and the diminution of the light of the Moon. In Jewish mysticism, the Moon represents the sphere of *Shekhinah, Malkhut,* or the whole physical world in which we live. And this is how the Moon, usually taken as a feminine symbol, can be the representative of the whole of mankind and the Jewish People.

When Adam and Eve discovered they had sinned, they cried bitterly, and with them wept the heavens, the Sun and the stars, and all created beings and things till the very throne of God. Even the angels and celestial beings were grieved by the transgression of Adam. Only the Moon laughed. That is why God grew angry and obscured her light. Instead of shining steadily like the Sun, the whole day long, she grows old quickly, and must be born and reborn again and again.[12]

It seems from this story that the waxing and waning of the Moon is a punishment. But taken in another sense, this continual movement makes Her the symbol of the human capacity for growth and renewal.

Legend says that only with the termination of *Shabbat* and the concealment of "First Light" did God teach man the secret of fire – which constituted the first of a series of man-made "lamps" or light sources.

Samuel said: "Why do we recite a blessing over a lamp (fire) at the termination of the Sabbath? Because then it (man-made lamps) was created for the first time."

R. Huna in Rab's name and R. Abbahu in R. Johanan's name said: "At the termination of the Day of Atonement, too, we recite a blessing over it, because the fire rested the whole day." [*Bereishit Rabbah* 11:2]

Here "fire" is used in the sense of human creativity, desire, and even evil, which reach some kind of resolution during the Day of Atonement.

In commemoration of these two events – the withdrawal of "First Light" and the possibility of the kindling of lamps – every week at the end of *Shabbat* we, too, make a division between "light and darkness," "good and evil," while also thanking God for creating the "brands of the fire."

The *Havdalah* ceremony marks the distinction between the Jewish and Greek ideas of God. In the Greek legend, Prometheus "stole" fire from the gods. In the Jewish story, God did not begrudge man knowledge or eternal life or even divinity; it was man who cut himself off from those gifts while God, in a compassionate effort to give man a substitute means for survival, made him the gift of fire and the power to kindle *Menorot*. The fire He gave him, however, contained within it the germs of absolute evil and of total self-annihilation – as we see in the capacity brought within human reach by atomic fission.

At the first nightfall, Adam was amazed to see the sun slowly sinking below the horizon and the entire world growing dim. Everything seemed to become void and outlines blurred so that he became afraid that the Serpent had swallowed the Sun. He did not know what had happened. He was convinced the world was destroyed and that it was reverting to its state before creation. Both he and Eve wept and repented until dawn. Then, through their tears, they saw the rebirth of light. It must have seemed to them that the world had been saved from a cataclysm. They sacrificed to God a unicorn "whose horn was created before his hoofs" (*Avodah Zarah* 8a; *Avot de Rabbi Nathan* 1).

This is the short blessing a Jew says before going to sleep at night:

> Blessed are You O Lord My God, King of the Universe Who causes the bonds of sleep to fall on my eyes and slumber on my eyelids, and Who gives light to the pupil of the eye. May it be Your will, O Lord My God and God of my fathers, that You should let me lie down in peace and let me stand up in peace for a good life. . . . May You illumine my eyes from the sleep of death. Blessed art Thou, O Lord My God, who lights the whole world with His Glory. [Prayer before going to sleep, in the *Siddur*]

"The Cock heralds the light, admonishing man not to forget to praise his Creator."[13] The very first blessing a Jew says in the morning thanks God for "giving the Cock the understanding to distinguish between day and night."

After Adam and Eve were driven out of the Garden, they were both subject to all kinds of fears. In a single day the sun came and went, and the gradual disappearance of the light they had come to take for granted must have been terrible for them. In the cycle of the year, the days grew shorter and shorter, and with each day there was less light. Adam and Eve's first experience of winter convinced them that the world had been darkened on their account.

When it is time for man to leave the world, the Angel that introduced him to the world reappears, and the man weeps so that his voice reverberates to all ends of the world; yet only the cock can hear. Then the Angel reminds him: Against your will you came into this world, and against your will you will leave it and give reckoning to the Supreme King of Kings.[14] [*Midrash Tanhuma, Pekude* 3; *Niddah* 11a–b, 16d, 30b; *Sanhedrin* 96a; *Avot* 4; *Zohar* II:11a–b]

(Then after Adam died) was the Sun darkened and the Moon and the stars for seven days and Shem in his mourning embraced from above the body of his father, and Eve was looking on the ground with hands folded over her head, and all her children wept most bitterly (*Life of Adam and Eve* 26).

Eve rose up and went outside and fell on the ground and began to say: "I have sinned, God of All, I have sinned against Thee."

Even thus prayed Eve on her knees; and behold the angel of humanity came to her, and raised her up and said: "Rise up, Eve from they penitence, for behold, Adam thy husband hath gone out of his body. Rise up and behold his spirit borne aloft to His Maker" (*Life of Adam and Eve* 26).

And Eve rose up and wiped off her tears with her hand, and the angel saith to her, "Lift up thyself from the earth."

And she gazed steadfastly into heaven and beheld a chariot of light borne by four bright eagles [and] it was impossible for any man born of woman to tell the glory of them or behold their faces – and angels going before the chariot – and when they came to the place where Adam was, the chariot halted and the Seraphim.

And [she] beheld golden censers . . . and the smoke of incense veiled the firmaments. And the angels fell down and worshipped God, begging him to pardon Adam, "for he is Thy image and the work of Thy hands" (*Apocalypsis Moises* 33:1–15).

And I, Eve beheld two great and fearful wonders standing in the presence of God and I wept for fear, and I cried aloud to my son Shem and said, "Rise up, Shem, from the body of thy father Adam and come to me, and thou shalt see a spectacle which no man's eye hath beheld" (*Apocalypsis Moises* 34:1–2).

Then Shem arose and came to his mother and to her he saith: "What is thy trouble? Why weepest thou?"

And she saith to him: "Look up and see with thine eyes the seven heavens opened, and see how the soul of thy father lies on its face and all the holy angels are praying on his behalf and saying: 'Pardon him, Father of All, for he is Thine image!' Pray my child, Shem, what shall this mean? . . . But who are the two negroes who stand by during the prayers for thy father Adam?" (*Apocalypsis Moises* 35:1–4).

Then Shem tells his mother that they are the Sun and the Moon and they fall down and pray on behalf of my father Adam.

Eve saith to him: "And where is their light and why have they taken on such a black appearance?"

And Shem answered her: "The light has not left them, but they cannot shine before the light of the Universe, the Father of light; and on this account their light has been hidden from them"[15] (*Apocalypsis Moises* 36:1–3).

According to Lurianic *Kabbalah,* the first being that emanated from light was *Adam Kadmon.* He was the total pattern of the Divine Light flowing from the *Ein-Sof* into the *Tzimtzum* (from a higher to a lower type of nothingness, or empty space resulting from the contraction of Divine Light). From his eyes, nose, and mouth branched forth the *Sefirot,* the lights of which were preserved in "bowls" or Vessels of crystalline purity. The lights of the three upper *Sefirot* were harmoniously contained in their bowls, but those of the six lower *Sefirot* of nature (the *Zeir Anpin*) burst their Vessels as a cathartic process to divide the evil from the good and externalize it in the form of *Klippot*. The cataclysmic event of the "Breaking of the Vessels" can be regarded as a kind of catharsis, rather like the natural cycle of disintegration and rebirth.

> Just as the seed must burst in order to sprout and blossom, so too the first bowls had to be shattered in order that the light–the Cosmic Seed–might fulfill its functions.[16]

Before the Fall, *Adam Kadmon* was a cosmic being. His original appearance, including his vast dimensions, was purely spiritual. The original appearance of *Adam Kadmon* before he was exiled into his body was made up of 613 organs corresponding to the 613 commandments.

But, says Scholem, the original sin of the First Man paralleled on a lower level the "Breaking of the Vessels" on the level of theosophy. Only after the Fall was Adam diminished and solidified into substance, and a division set in between body and spirit. As man's spiritual state was reduced, so was the quality of light emitted by his physical organs. With man, the *Shekhinah* (or the Moon) also fell into the world of materiality. This *Shekhinah* in exile is called Rachel, whose spirit paces the boundaries, reaching out to her children in Dispersion even though this entails separation from her husband.

After the initial breaking of the Vessels, a new stream of light bursts forth from the forehead of *Adam Kadmon,* presenting the *Sefirot* in new configurations. These facets, or *Partzufin* (countenances), of God make up a personal God interested in the fate of man. It is the essence of *Tikkun* to restore these dispersed lights and *Partzufin* to their place in the structure of Original Man.

Fulfillment of the commandments in the physical world presents a way for man to carve out and regain his original spiritual stature and the reunion of the *Sefirah* of *Malkhut,* or Rachel, with the six masculine *Sefirot*.

As far back as the *Midrash* it says God showed "First Man" the fate of various key figures among his descendants who all came from specific limbs of his original structure. "Whatever comes into being, its name was given long ago" (Ecclesiastes 6:10).

What is the meaning of *And it is known beforehand what man is* (Ecclesiastes 6:10)?

While Adam was still a lifeless mass, God showed him all the righteous people that would descend from him; some there were that hung on Adam's hair and others on his head; some on his forehead, on his eyes, nose, mouth, ears; some on his ear-laps.

The proof is that when Job sought to dispute with God, saying: *Oh that I knew where I might find Him, that I might come even to His seat. I would order my cause before Him* (Job 23:3), God answered him: "You wish to dispute with Me. *Where were you when I laid the foundations of the earth?*" (Job 38:4).

Said R. Simeon ben Lakish: "God said to him: 'Job, tell Me where was your essential source suspended? On (Adam's) head or his forehead? Or on which limb? Only if you know on which limb your source was can you argue with me.' " [*Shemot Rabbah* 40:3]

From the text, God's reply to the human being who dares to enter into dialogue with Him – "Where were you when I created the world?" – seems the rejoinder of a bully who crushes any counterargument through sheer force.

According to R. Simeon ben Lakish's midrashic interpretation, however, God is, on the contrary, seriously advising Job on how to facilitate dialogue: get down to essentials. Find your source in *Adam Kadmon* and talk to Me from that vantage point of strength. Talk to Me as 'Image of God' to God Himself.

Adam's soul contained within it all the future souls of man as so many sparks of Primordial Light, a kind of Jungian collective unconscious, composed of glimmers of future time rather than time past.

The *Tzaddikim* are a return to Adam in the sense that they are in touch with Primordial Light. There are instances of rare individuals, or *Tzaddikim,* whose powers of spiritual self-actualization are like those of Adam before the sin and who allegedly possess the corresponding physiological characteristic of *Adam Kadmon* as transmitters of light energy.

THE SHINING FACE OF THE *TZADDIK*

The "shining" of the body or the face of the *Tzaddik* is part of the mystical experience. In his book on the thirteenth-century proponent of ecstatic *Kabbalah,* Abraham Abulafia, Moshe Idel describes how a disciple of the Master, named Shem Tov, woke up one night after having spent two months in deep meditation on the permutations of the Divine Names and realized a light was shining from his own face. At first he could not believe it; yet, wherever he went, the light followed him, even when he cowered under a blanket. "And so the soul of the righteous man shines, and in every place where the righteous go, their souls shine."[17]

There are various tales describing the Baal Shem Tov's special powers of clairvoyance that expressed themselves physically through a light on his face. Aware of the reaction people might have to this physical phenomenon, when he was a young man and had not yet become known as the leader of the *Hasidim,* the Besht, like Moshe, is said to have frequently resorted to a mask.[18]

A guest spent *Shabbat* in the home of the young Baal Shem Tov, and, everyone slept in one room.

> At midnight the guest awoke and saw a large fire burning on the stove. He cried out, thinking the house was on fire. Then he saw a great light, fell back, and fainted.
>
> When he revived, the Besht said to him: "You should not have looked at what is not permitted you."[19]

When the Baal Shem Tov opened the *Zohar,* he was able to see at a distance. How was this possible? The Baal Shem Tov was such a great human being (*Tzaddik*) that in the letters of the *Book of Splendor* he was able to detect the Primordial Light that had been Adam's normal mode of seeing before he ate the forbidden fruit. In this way, he was gifted with Adam's capacity to see from one end of the world to the other because he himself possessed primordial splendor.

The prime example of the radiance that comes from knowledge of the hidden light of the Torah is that of Moshe. According to various *Midrashim,* not only did Moshe's face emit rays as a grown man, but even when he was in the womb, his parents' house is said to have been filled with light.

> When his fetus was fully formed after forty days, the skin of his face shone (Exodus 34:29). When he was weaned, it shone. All this to indicate to you the purity of his matter . . . like the heavenly sapphire-like material.[20]

Not only was the Holy Ark that contained the Torah filled with light, so was the little Ark in which Moshe was hidden as an infant. When Pharaoh's daughter opened this Ark, she was dazzled by the light within that convinced her Moshe was no ordinary child. According to legend, Yocheved, Moshe's real mother, fitted him out in his cradle with a little marriage canopy—all these arks and canopies are enclosures for the rainbow-colored *Shekhinah* Light. It is usually the desire of every parent to see his/her child under the marriage canopy, but as Yocheved was abandoning him to his fate, she prepared him when he was still a baby for the Holy Day of his marriage. And Moshe was not lacking for a bride even at that age. Just as the Torah dwells in the Holy Ark and is surrounded by radiance, just as the *Shekhinah* fills the Tabernacle, so the Egyptian Princess found the *Shekhinah* closeted together with the baby Moshe under the small marriage canopy prepared for him by his mother.

According to legend, at that time the *Shekhinah* also took the daughter of Pharaoh under Her wings because she had saved the life of the one who was to give the Torah to Israel. From then on the name of the Princess was changed from Daughter of Pharaoh to *Batiah*—Daughter of God. With the name change, another change may also have taken place—Daughter of God for the

Shekhinah. But although the light under the bulrushes may be taken to be *Shekhinah* radiance, it also is the light of Moshe's own soul, or his *anima.*

The relationship of God to Israel in the Torah and in the *Aggadata* (stories) of the Talmud is compared to the love relationship between husband and wife. When the feminine elements in the Godhead were personified as the *Shekhinah,* or Divine Wisdom, in order that "what happens on high be repeated below," Moshe as representative of the mystic or mankind becomes the husband of the *Shekhinah.* This startling allegory only becomes explicit in the *Zohar,* although in Proverbs the philosopher is compared to a man who has married a virtuous wife.

To explain why it is necessary to have Moshe couple with the *Shekhinah,* the *Zohar* says that the People needed reassurance. They needed to feel secure in their relationship with God and to know that He was not too aloof from their lives. So when Moshe, their living link with God, disappeared on Mount Sinai for forty days, the people made the Golden Calf as an intermediary between themselves and the Unknown God. When Moshe reappeared, the only thing that would satisfy them was for him to bring God's Presence—as inscribed in the Torah or enshrined in the Sanctuary—down to earth. Sexual intercourse is a metaphor for this act of bringing down and realization in the physical.

It was not enough for the people to know that all the signs and wonders they had seen came from a divine source, or even that God was in a sense "married" to an idealized feminine personification of Israel. As the people of a patriarchal society, they had to reverse the relationship, and a man, one of them— Moshe, as prototype of the Mystic—had to "marry" and dominate the feminine aspect of God.

In some extraordinary way the *Zohar* depicts Moshe, in his very thirst for transcendence, as superior even to the Divine Presence, which becomes feminized on its journey down. This is shown by the imagery of garments and colors. While the purpose of differentiating the *Shekhinah* from God is to show the Divine come down to earth and dressed in the many veils and colors of our illusions, the prophetic insight of Moshe is crystalline, as one who ascends and returns to his source in the One. Thus, Her insight is full of dreams and imagery and beauty – the "opaque glass" or leaden-backed mirror that reflects all the fragmentary colors of illusion – whereas his vision is transparent – piercing through to God Himself. Therefore when it comes to the nature of the relationship, He is above and She is below.

Similarly in *Kabbalah,* although the self-chosen exile of the Feminine (the *Shekhinah*) and Her elevation provide the center to the whole drama of existence, another way of looking at the same process is that the onus is on man (the *Tzaddik*). It is up to him, both individually and collectively to effect a *Tikkun* by rescuing the Princess lost as a result of the sin of Adam.

The *Shekhinah,* or the Moon, is taken as the collective representative for individual masculine endeavors, the individual "points" or scintillations in Her bouquet. Thus, though the *Shekhinah* descends in order to turn Her passive (feminine) stance relative to God into the more dynamic action of raising up the whole of the Created world, how close or how far the *Shekhinah* Light comes down depends on man and on the generations of the *Tzaddikim.* Mankind, and the *Tzaddik* in particular from the period of the *Midrash* on, was endowed with the capacity of bringing the *Shekhinah* closer to our world or driving it further away.

In relation to the lower spheres, the *Shekhinah* takes on an active (male) stance made up of the heroic deeds of the individual *Tzaddik,* while in relation to God she remains feminine and entirely passive.

As soon as Adam sinned, the *Shekhinah* started packing Her bags to depart from Eden. God's Presence was on the move, both in form of a Voice, echoing and vibrating throughout the Garden, and in the form of Fire and "traveling" light.

And they heard the voice of the Lord God traveling in the garden toward the cool of the day (Genesis 3:7). R. Halapay said: "We know (from here) that a voice may travel; but we do not yet know that 'traveling' can apply to fire. Where do we learn that? From a verse in another place: *And the fire traveled down upon the earth*" (Exodus 9:23).

R. Abba ben Kahana said: "It (the Fire of the Divine Presence) repeatedly leaped and ascended. The real home of the *Shekhinah* was in the lower world."

[W]hen Adam sinned, She departed to the first firmament; when Cain sinned, She ascended to the second firmament; when the generation of Enoch sinned, She ascended to the third; when the generation of the Flood sinned, to the fourth; with the generation of the separation of tongues, to the fifth; with the Sodomites, to the sixth; with the Egyptians in the days of Abraham, to the seventh.

But to counterbalance these, there arose seven righteous men: Abraham, Isaac, Jacob, Levi, Kohath, Amram, and Moshe, and they brought Her down again to earth.

Abraham brought Her down from the seventh to the sixth firmament, Isaac from the sixth to the fifth, Jacob from the fifth to the fourth, Levi from the fourth to the third, Kohath from the third to the second, Amram from the second to the first, while Moshe brought Her right down below.

R. Isaac said: "It is written, *The righteous shall inherit the land and dwell in it* (cause the *Shekhinah* to dwell in it) *for ever* (Psalm 37:29): Then what are the wicked to do—are they to range in the air! What it means is that the wicked did not permit the *Shekhinah* to dwell on earth." [*Bereishit Rabbah* 19:7]

The highest note of the five-toned accordion of soul, has its celestial roots in the *Shekhinah,* and when that highest part loses contact with the lower soul, the *Shekhinah* Herself is given no grounding.

The Soul of Man (feminine) contains five different powers that enable Her to escape from the body every night, rise to heaven, and fetch new life for man.

When a baby is conceived, its Soul, which is holy and pure and a part of God's Glory, is forced to leave that higher world and enter the depths of the womb. Before entering the womb, She is borne aloft to Paradise by an Angel who shows her the righteous sitting there in their glory, with their crowns *in* their heads. . . . A light is set above her, the light of the *Menorah,* which enables her to see from one end of the world to another.[21]

"With their crowns *in* their heads." The Hebrew does not say "upon" but "in," as if their crowns were an intrinsic part of them and impossible to remove. That is the difference between the life of the saints in the next world and the life of ordinary people in this world.

THE LADDER OF LIGHTS

What are these crowns? They are man's five souls, extending upward like a ladder, one above the other, drawing down the light of the *Ein-Sof*. And, contrariwise, acting as a source of spiritual nourishment for the *Ein-Sof*—that is, for God Himself.[22]

In this world, spirituality is very much dispersed, extending out into all the realms of the *Sefirot*. So one may believe that the soul is concealed within the body, but the opposite is also true—that people walk about with a spiraling ladder of lights and crowns leading up to God Himself. From higher soul to lower soul, the light reaches us. Some people have even their lowest soul—somewhere far out in the stratosphere—attached to them by a kind of umbilical cord, like the string of a kite. And to all appearances they might have no soul at all.

As for the righteous, they will sit "with their crowns *in* their heads"—that is, with all five levels of soul rooted in their very being.

We can picture the Seven *Tzaddikim* like the well-known Russian dolls that nest inside each other. On the one hand, Seven *Tzaddikim* represent the various stages of emanation of nature. On the other, one man includes all seven stages (or seven organs) within himself. In a sense, all eras of history form stepping stones from the generation of one *Tzaddik* to another to create the idealized picture of the true human archetype, *Adam Kadmon,* or the "Image of God" known in Persian Sufism as the "Man of Light."

Just as in *Kabbalah* each of the seven stages or *Sefirot* is represented by a particular color, so in Persian Sufism there is a connection between fragmentary "colored photisms" and the composite picture of the "physiology of the man of light."

[T]he seven subtle organs (*latifa*) are the seven centers typifying the Abodes of the seven great prophets in the man of light. The growth of the man of light thus recapitulates inwardly the whole cycle of Prophecy. The idea of this growth, which is the liberation of the man of light, can be [seen] even in certain types of Iranian paintings (from Manichean painting to the Persian miniature). Finally, the physiology of the man of light, whose growth is accompanied by colored photisms each having a precise mystical significance, is an integral part of a general doctrine of colors and of the very experience of color.[23]

This man of light or quintessence of mankind is depicted in the seven-branched *Menorah*. The Kalever Rebbe describes how, through the virtue of elevating the *Menorah*, the soul burns from ascent to ascent with the strength of Abraham, Yitzhak, Yisrael, and all the *Tzaddikim*.

Sometimes these stages are separate individuals or *Tzaddikim*, sometimes they are levels included in the one person, such as *Adam ha-Rishon* (First Man).

> R. Hama ben Hanina said: "The Holy One . . . made ten canopies for Adam in the garden of Eden; for it is said: *You were in Eden the garden of God; every precious stone was your covering – the cornelian, the topaz, and the emerald, the beryl, the onyx and the jasper, the sapphire, the carbuncle, and the emerald, and gold*" (Ezekiel 28:13). R. Johanan said: "The least of all (these) was gold, since it is mentioned last." [*Berakhot* 58a; *Shabbat* 34a; *Sanhedrin* 100a; *Nezikin* 11; *Baba Batra* 75a]

Sometimes seven *Tzaddikim* are spoken of, sometimes ten, to correspond with the Seven *Sefirot* of nature and with the Ten *Sefirot*. Sometimes we are speaking of generations and not of individuals, but always what is indicated is levels of development and self-transformation.

There were ten generations from Adam to Noah to show you how long-suffering God is. He let generations come and go until

He brought on them the waters of the Flood. There are ten generations from Noah to Abram to tell you how long-suffering God is. He let the generations come and go until our Father Abram came and received a reward for all of them. [*Avot* 5:2]

There were ten generations from Noah till Abram, and of all of them the Holy One only spoke to our Father Abram who received the reward for all of them.

Said R. Berekiah in the name of R. Nehemiah: "This can be compared to a king who in his procession from place to place lost a pearl from His crown. The King stopped and his entourage stopped.

"They paced back and forth. The local people enquired: 'Why did His Majesty and his court stop here?' The courtiers replied: 'His Majesty lost a pearl from his royal crown.' He gathered the dust and piled it up into heaps and brought sieves. He sieved through the first pile and found nothing; in the second, nothing; but in the third he found the pearl. A public proclamation was made: The King has found his Pearl"

So the Holy One said to Abram: "Go for yourself. For you I waited. Why did I need to establish a connection with all the preceding generations. Only for your sake." That is why it says: – *Who has chosen Abram – And found his heart faithful before You* (Nehemiah 39:10). In Abram God found His Pearl, the renewal of the primordial light of mankind. [*Bereishit Rabbah* 39:10]

God ordered Abram to "go out," not just for himself and for his own destiny, but also so that God could show his nature to the world. Abram was like a sealed vial of perfume that God wanted the nations to savor and enjoy. His favorite was like a vial of sweet perfume sealed until the right time – saved until later. This precious vial was the cruse of pure oil that miraculously lasted for the eight days of *Hanukkah*.

It was not only that God ordered Abram to leave for the Land "that I will show you," but He wanted to display Abram's nature to the world like a glorious jewel. He therefore had a precious stone hung around Abram's neck. Whoever saw it was immediately healed.

So from Abram's singular jewel, or his righteousness – He was on "one side of the world and everybody else on the other" – came all the stars in the nighttime sky, the whole nation of Israel.

> When The Holy One, Blessed be He said to Abraham: *Get thee out of thy country . . . and I will make of thee a great nation* (Genesis 12:1), the latter replied: "Lord of the Universe! What benefit do I derive from all these blessings since I am about to depart from this world childless?"
>
> Said God to him: "Art thou sure that thou wilt no longer give birth to a child?"
>
> The reply was: "Lord of the Universe! My planet tells me I will be childless."
>
> "So thou art afraid of the planet!" God retorted, "As thou livest, it will be as impossible to number thy offspring as it is to number the stars of heaven."
>
> [God said to him: "Talking of astrology, Leave such petty calculations to the astrologers. You have the vision of a Prophet, with far wider horizons than they. *Get thee out.*]
>
> *And He brought him outside* (Genesis 15:1). R. Joshua said in R. Levi's name: "Did He then lead him forth outside the world?" This means that He showed him the streets of heaven, as you read, *While as yet He had not made the earth, nor the outer spaces* (Proverbs 8:26).
>
> R. Judah ben R. Simon said in the name of R. Johanan: "God raised Abraham up above the vault of the heavens. That is why He said to him: 'Look now toward heaven, look down,' as if to signify to look down from above."

From that radically altered perspective God turned to Abraham and asked: "And now, can you in fact count the stars?" Abraham was speechless at the infinite vistas streaming down below him.

> Then God said to him: *So shall be thy seed!* (Genesis 15:5); that is: Just as thou seest all these stars and canst not count them, so [numerous] will thy children be, for none will be able to number them. [*Shemot Rabbah* 37:6; *Bereishit Rabbah* 44:12]

The *Tzaddik* is the prototype of the Hero or the Great Individual. Not only is he a just man who keeps the commandments, but he is like a favorite child of God for whose sake He might alter the whole mechanism of nature.

Abram, says Rashi, when he left for the "Land that I will show you," left the known for the unknown. He literally went beyond the destiny written out for him in the stars. The light emanating from Abram after this, like the light emanating from all God's *Tzaddikim,* transcends the natural brilliance of the planets.

There is a seemingly universal belief, as we have already noted in connection with the Baal Shem Tov and with the "antlers" of light and the mask of Moshe, that light crowns the head and radiates from the face of God's saints. This is epitomized in the function of the High Priest as transmitter of light-energy. We are told that the sign that the High Priest was filled with the Holy Spirit was that his face "glowed like torches" (*Vayikra Rabbah* 21:11).

The Levites served a unique function among the People as guardians of the *Menorah* even when the Temple had been destroyed.[24] Their whole purpose, as we see in the Blessing of the Priests still said on Festivals–"May the Lord cause His countenance to shine upon you" (Psalm 67:2)–was as conductors of the Divine light to Israel. While the *Kohanim* (the Priests) bless the assembled gathering, the latter are not permitted to look in their direction. The reason given is that the congregation might become blinded by the radiance of the *Shekhinah.* But what in fact would they see? They would see ordinary humans (*Kohanim*) blessing them, when the idea is for the *Kohanim* to make themselves invisible, their own personalities transparent before the Divine light. In Islamic mysticism saints are called "God's eyes." They have entirely negated their ego, so that God "sees" and radiates through them. This "transparent" function is illustrated by the glow on the face of the High Priest when he emerged from the Holy of Holies on *Yom Kippur,* a mirroring of *Shekhinah* Light.

The question has frequently been raised how *Yom Kippur* (a fast) resembles *Purim* (a festival in which feasting plays a prominent role). The similarity lies, I suggest, in the likeness between the function played by Queen Esther in the *Purim* story and the role of the High Priest on *Yom Kippur.* The plight of the High Priest on the one occasion in the year when he, as representative of Israel, was required to enter the Holy of Holies and seclude himself with the Divine, was similar to that of Esther when she went to the King. If she had not "found grace" in his eyes, and if the tyrant had not extended his scepter, her head would have rolled from her shoulders. Similarly, the High Priest in Temple times, and every Jew nowadays, is invited to penetrate to an intimacy with God on *Yom Kippur* not available on other days of the year. This might be a privilege but, as we know from the story of Nadav and Avihu, the sons of Aaron who entered the Holy of Holies uninvited, it was not without its attendant pitfalls. If due care is not taken, there is a danger the result could be–not "favor" and light and reconciliation, but the outbreak of a destructive fire.

The nature of the High Priest when he penetrated the Holy of Holies, was both masculine and feminine. In entering that Holy resting place of the *Shekhinah,* he played a male role, but in relation to God, like Esther, who also put on "royal garments" for her ordeal of life and death, he was the "feminine vessel" for Divine favor to *Knesset Yisrael,* who were awaiting in high suspense for his reemergence. The moment when he reappeared, unscathed, as it were, from the fire, was greeted in Temple times as the high point of *Yom Kippur.* The light radiating from his face at that moment was a sign of God's entire acceptance of the prayers of *Knesset Yisrael,* and therefore, because of the renewed closeness of that primal relationship, erotic images both masculine and feminine have been used to describe it.

The radiance of the *Shekhinah* enveloping him has been said to resemble "the image of the rainbow in the cloud"–that is "a rose set in the middle of the garden of sweet love," "the clear light set in (God's) diadem," and "the love etched on the face of a bridegroom."[25]

The role of the *Kohanim* in relaying light to Israel was one shared by prophets and *Tzaddikim.* The *Midrash* says of Elijah and of the *Tzaddikim* in general that in them God shows mankind what He will bring about in the Hereafter. What God only will permit Himself in the Hereafter, He already allows His *Tzaddikim* in this world:

> Thus God will resurrect the dead, and Elijah resurrected the dead. . . . God (will) bless the little (quantity) and Elijah blessed the little (in quantity). . . . God has blessed childless women with children and so has Elijah (now in this world). [*Bereishit Rabbah* 77a]

According to interpretations clearly articulated in Hasidism and *Kabbalah*–but already present in the *Aggadata* of the Talmud–the *Tzaddik* is capable of attaining such intimate knowledge and attachment to God (*Deveikut*) that, like the High Priest, he too is able to bring godly "light" energies down to earth that sometimes manifest themselves as blessings in the most physical sense.

In the Talmud, too, among the various appellations and descriptions of the *Tzaddik,* he is called *Yesod,* the Foundation of the world. "The world is based on one pillar and this is called *Tzaddik* because it is written: 'The *Tzaddik* is an everlasting foundation'" (Proverbs 10:25; *Sanhedrin* 12b).

In *Kabbalah, Yesod* is the phallic symbol, also called "the life of the worlds," and the "symbol of the covenant"–the ninth (masculine) *Sefirah*–leading all the higher preceding energies into the last womblike *Sefirah* of *Malkhut.* Thus it is "man" or the *Tzaddik* who impregnates and elevates the whole physical-female realm over which the *Shekhinah* has sway.

LIFTING THE SPARKS OF ONE'S SOUL

The *Tzaddik* is capable not only of raising himself up, but the whole physical world. He is compared to a ladder with angels ascending and descending and to channels sending the divine flow to man (*Likkutei Yikkarim* 37a). He is a mediating link between heaven and earth and connects upper and lower worlds.[26]

But the individual *Tzaddik* is capable of bringing redemption to Israel and mankind because only he contains an image of the fragmentary souls of all men. Rabbi Nachman of Bratzlav says that the *Tzaddik* is called "covenant of peace" because he contains within him the "general viewpoint of the Jewish People."[27]

In a process closely akin to projection in psychological terms, "every individual sees in the *Tzaddik* his own share, or his image" says the Great *Maggid* (*Likkutei Amarim* 32a). Thus the process goes both ways. Not only does the *Tzaddik* contain within him a little bit of all men, but vice versa – all men see reflected in him the image of their own potential. In this way, not only is the *Tzaddik* a stepping stone in universal and national salvation, but he brings his followers closer to the realization of personal redemption in context of their own lives.

Drawing on various alchemy texts, Jung says that people are surrounded by multiple luminosities, like so many sparks or points of light, and that these portray the psyche as a multiple consciousness – that is, a multitude of luminous particles that in their sum constitute the Self. This impressionist panorama represents the total content of archetypes of the collective unconscious.

These fragmented "sparks" of an original integral consciousness correspond to the Breaking of the Vessels and the challenge imposed on man of effecting a *Tikkun,* or reintegration of the individual rays. Already an aspect of Lurianic *Kabbalah,* this concept was taken over by Hasidism and internalized. No longer are the sparks part of a purely cosmological process; they represent the fragmentation and reintegration of the individual psyche. And this is so even when what is described may seem to belong to the external world of objects. In fact, they are fragments of the original soul of the *Tzaddik* waiting to be reintegrated again within him:

In Hasidism, the *Tzaddik* only reflects on a heroic cosmic scale what is going on in the soul of every individual. Everyone is composed of various fragments or sparks of lower vitality that he tries to elevate and reintegrate with his highest self through a process known as *Deveikut,* or attachment to the Divine. According to the Baal Shem Tov, an individual's *Nefesh,* or animal soul is mirrored in his possessions. So the Baal Shem was quoted to have told his grandson, Ephraim of Sedylkov, that "all that belongs to man, be it his servants and animals, be it his household effects – they are all of his sparks which belong to the root of his soul and he has to lift them up to their upper root."[28] What is operative here is a kind of animism.

The Preacher Mendel of Baer, a friend of the Baal Shem, found similarly that even the food and drink a person consumes belonged to him originally. They are the divine sparks that fell away from Adam after he sinned and became intermingled with the sticks and stones of the vegetable world.

> There is a great mystery: Why did God create the food and drink for which man longs?
> The reason is that these are full of sparks of Adam, the first man, which after his fall wrapped themselves up and hid away in all the four spheres of nature, in stones, plants, animals and men, as they strive to return to cleave unto the sphere of holiness, and whatever a man eats and drinks is actually part of his own sparks which he is under an obligation to restore . . . that is, they are there in exile, in strange forms and clothing and be it known to you that all things that serve the needs of man are esoterically his own sons which have gone into exile and captivity. [Commentary on Psalm 107, *Perush al Hodu*][29]

Rabbi Jacob Joseph of Polonnoye says in the name of R. Isaac Luria that in a sense all the objects we meet, all relationships, all experiences, down to our business transactions, and even the person we are married to are all "spiritual fallout" from our soul. Character is fate, *karma,* part of a person's spiritual state: "If a man deserves it by his good deeds, then he meets the sparks, which by his very nature belong to him."[30]

Success and failure depend on "the state of his sparks." And not only do all experiences, both pleasant and unpleasant, arise from an individual's very nature, but they are given to elevate him – "because everything serves man to concentrate his mind and to lift up the sparks of his own soul."[31] Personal salvation, says the Rabbi of Polonnoye, is the only means at man's disposal to bring about redemption on the cosmic plane and rescue the fragmented sparks of *Shekhinah* Light; therefore every single mundane action on the part of the individual could help to bring the Messiah.

Economic materialists might be interested to know the *Maggid* of Mezeritch's conviction that property changed hands only when a given owner had exhausted the particular sparks that were part of his soul. Moreover, this form of transfer is carried out by ordinary people, and not only by the *Tzaddikim*. [32]

The Rabbi of Polonnoye also believed it was frequently necessary to travel to places where one might pick up and reintegrate the lost sparks of one's soul. "Every single individual in Israel has to go to such places as contain sparks from the root of his own soul in order that he might free them."[33]

It is possible that encounters between friends and lovers could have arisen because both are part of the same entity. According to the Talmud, man was originally created as an androgyne (*Berakhot* 61a). To this the *Zohar* adds that if we are worthy, we may meet the partner to whom we were originally joined before being sent out into this world (*Zohar* 1:91b).

The main source of this animistic doctrine was Chaim Vital—surely his name is emblematic of his teaching!—who, in his famous work on transmigration of souls maintains:

> There are sparks that are near to a man, and others that remain at a distance and all depends on his actions. You ought to know that a *Tzaddik* is able by his deeds, to reassemble the sparks of (his various souls), his *Nefesh,* his *Ruach,* or his *Neshamah,* and to lift them up from the depth of the "husks."[34]

In addition to the sparks being fragments of the individual soul, they are also transpersonal. Belonging to the collective unconscious, they float from one ego to another with the insouciant impersonality of objects or motes of dust; yet it is they who are the broken-up rays of God's "Jewel."

The *Midrash* comments on the verse: "In Your Presence is the fullness of joy" (Leviticus 30:2) with a play on the word *sheva*—seven—and *sova*—fullness.

There are seven groups of *Tzaddikim* who will in the future welcome the *Shekhinah*. [They are Her Knights – that is, there are seven stages in receiving Her Presence.]

What does it signify that we speak every day of the "world to come" and we do not know what we are saying? The *Targum* translates "world to come" as "world which comes" – in the present tense. What does that mean? That teaches that before the creation of the world, a plan was formed to create a great light for illumination. Then a great light was created that no creature would be able to bear. God foresaw that no one would be able to bear it; then he took a seventh part of it and gave it to them in its place. As for the rest, he hid it for the world to come. He said: If they show themselves worthy of this seventh and guard it, I will give them the rest in the other world, which means "the world which comes," which has already been coming since the six days of Creation. [*Bahir,* no. 106]

"Light is sown for the righteous." So says the *Noam Elimelech.* The meaning of "the time to come" refers not only to the time of the Messiah, but also to the whole of subsequent history that will unfold after that and to the righteous who will spring up in every generation and in every period. If they deserve it, the hidden light will be revealed again to them periodically throughout history. The whole of human history will be jeweled with epiphanies.

The light was sown in the earth (*adamah*) – that is, for mankind (*adam*). As seed is buried in earth, so a germ of light remains only potential in the human soul. It is left to the *Tzaddik* (man) to bring it to reality.[35]

The "hidden" Primordial Light that God concealed during Creation is disclosed to individuals and to generations at specific moments of moral revelation in the History of the Patriarchs and of the Nation – for example, the birth of Moshe, the Burning Bush, the Exodus from Egypt, the Parting of the Red Sea, the Revelation at Sinai. And what happened to the fathers is a symbol for future Jewish history.

"First Light" is present in all of existence, and those with sufficient vision see it even now. The righteous are gifted with the prophetic insight to see what others cannot because their souls already reflect that light. In a sense they are even creating it. For what is that light but the "Divine Image" – the collective soul of man in its readiness to reflect the Divine.

Every human being is like the cruse of oil of *Hanukkah*, mostly sealed, a little revealed. What we have to do is to bring out more and more of that light.

Everybody has a special light burning for him in the higher world, totally different from the light of every other person. When two friends meet in this world, their lights up above unite for a moment, and out of the union of the two lights, an angel is born. However, the angel is only given sufficient strength to live one year. If the two friends meet again within the year, they give the angel a further lease of life. But if they do not see each other for that length of time, the angel wastes away and dies for lack of light. The Talmud bids us, when we see a friend we have not seen for a whole year, to bless God for "raising the dead." This is a strange commandment indeed, since neither of us has died. Whom then has God raised from the dead? Surely none other than the languishing angel whose lease of life is renewed each time we meet.[36]

The *Tzaddik* contains within him the light of the Messiah. Therefore, like the Messiah, he can bring the redemption.

R. Simeon ben Lakish maintained: He (man) was the latest in the work of the last day and the earliest in the work of the first day. For it is said: *And the spirit of God hovered* (Genesis 1:2) refers to the soul of Adam, as you read, *And the spirit of the Lord shall rest upon him* (Isaiah 11:2). [*Bereishit Rabbah* 8:1]

The startling suggestion is made here that the spirit of God *is* the Soul of man. How is that link made? Not only is man God's image but it also says God "breathed into man the spirit of life." This suggests that man was inspired with a breath of "the spirit of God" that hovered over the Deep. Therefore man goes right back to the very beginning of Creation. Thus, although physically man may have been God's "latest creation," his soul was present as part of the Divine Spirit that hovered over the abyss!

> Man was both the first and last work of the Creation. His soul was created on the first day—*The spirit of God moving upon the face of the waters.* This was the Soul of man, the soul of the Messiah. [This is a striking case of "The last is the most precious." But also "last in realization, first in thought."] [*Hagiga* 12a; *Bereishit Rabbah* 8:1; *Midrash Tanhuma,* 13:111, 32; *Tehillim* 139, 529; *Sanhedrin* 38a]

"And the light dwelleth with him" (Daniel 2:22) alludes both to the Primordial Light and to the King (Messiah) (*Bereishit Rabbah* 1:6).

There is a *Midrash* that says "in the beginning" the Messiah was all dream and no fruition. When the First Man saw by means of "First Light" that God had not allowed David the lifespan of even one single day, he realized he must do something. So he took seventy of his years and gave them to David.

What this means is that the soul of Adam, David, and the Messiah are connected and come from the same source as stages in the unraveling of human development.

> David (father of the Messiah) asked God: "When will *that* light come?" He replied: "When the end is reached and Jerusalem is rebuilt I shall bring it. As it is said: *Arise, shine for thy light is come*" (Isaiah 60:1). [*Pirke de Rabbi Eliezer* 3]

If the query of David, when his grandson (the Messiah) was due, was answered by God in terms of the national redemption, then in the sequel seventeen centuries later when the Baal Shem Tov (presumably closer to Redemption) asked the Messiah himself when he was arriving, the answer is based on personal and individual salvation. God speaks of the objective light of Jerusalem—the Messiah—in terms of the dissemination among ordinary individuals of illumination and knowledge of God—enlightenment. The Messiah replies:

By this shalt thou know it (the time of my coming): when your
teaching will become renowned and revealed throughout the
world, and when thy springs will be dispersed abroad, imparting
to others what I taught you and you apprehended so that they too
will be able to perform contemplative unifications and ascents of
the soul *like you*. Then shall all the *klippot* ("shells") perish and it
will be a time of acceptability and salvation.[37]

Thus in the twentieth century, redemption has been
viewed as an illumination from within; the "springs," as we
have seen, referring to the "feminine light," is a quality that the
soul of man sheds on his environment. Rav Kuk describes it in
this way. "From the illumination of our souls, flashes of light
will shine on the world. These meanings will all together fill the
world with abundance."[38]

NOTES

1. A variation on *Bereishit Rabbah* 12:6, quoted in Alexander Altmann, "Gnostic Themes in Rabbinic Cosmology" in *Essays in
   Honor of J.H. Hertz,* ed. Isidore Epstein (London: Goldston, 1943),
   p. 30.
2. Scholem, *Major Trends,* p. 63.
3. *Merkava Shalmah* 38a, quoted in *Major Trends,* pp. 63–64. See n. 81,
   p. 365.
4. Based on Aharon Weiner, *The Prophet Elijah in the Development of
   Judaism* (Boston: Routledge and Kegan Paul, 1900), pp. 97–99;
   also *Zohar* I:899.
5. Ginzberg, *Legends,* vol. 1, p. 49; *Rashi on Genesis* 1:27; *Alphabet of R.
   Akiva* 59:13.
6. "Then was I by him as one brought up with Him; and I was daily
   His delight, playing constantly in front of Him" (Proverbs 8:30).
   Oman, meaning "nursling" or child brought up in the home, has
   the double meaning of "artist."
       Solomon is here talking about the Divine Wisdom, categorized
   as feminine. It is this verse that inspired the *Zohar* to see the natural
   aspect of God (*Elohim*) both as feminine and as a (playful?) architect. It seems that there was a tradition of women potters and

metalworkers in Sephardic lands. See especially Chapter 5 in this volume on the female potter who hands out judgments on *Yom Kippur.*

7. *Toldot Yaakov Yoseph,* fol. 86a, quoted in Idel, *New Perspectives,* p. 150.

8. *Sefer ha-Ne'elam,* Ms. 817, fol. 17 Paris, quoted in Idel, *New Perspectives,* p. 180.

9. See *Tallit* as the "dress" man weaves for himself in this world to clothe himself in the future life, Chapter 1, pp. 76–77.

10. The first exile of the *Shekhinah* was after the Breaking of the Vessels.

11. *Asiyah* is the lowest of the four worlds between the *Ein-Sof* (the Infinite) and our earthly cosmos, according to Cordovero and the Kabbalists of Safed.

12. Ginzberg, *Legends,* vol. 1, p. 80, based on *Slavonic Apocalypse of Baruch 7.*

13. Ginzberg, *Legends,* vol. 5, p. 62, based on *Greek Apocalypse of Baruch 7.*

14. Based also on Ginzberg, *Legends,* vol. 1, p. 58.

15. These variations on the sequel to the story of Adam and Eve were probably collected by a Jew of the Diaspora sometime between 60 and 300 C.E. The *Apocalypsis Moises* and the *Life of Adam and Eve,* quoted in R. H. Charles, ed., *The Apocrypha and Pseudepigrapha of the Old Testament,* vol. 2 (Oxford, England: Clarendon Press), p. 149.

16. Based on Menahem Azariah Fano, *Yogat Olam* (1648), *Emek Ha-Melekh* 24b, in Gershom Scholem, *Major Trends,* p. 268.

17. R. Moses Taku, *Ketav Tammim,* quoted in Moshe Idel, *The Mystical Experience in Abraham Abulafia,* trans. Jonathan Chipman (Albany, NY: State University of New York Press, 1988), p. 148, n. 38.

18. *Baal Shem Tov,* literally the Master of a Good Name. The Hebrew acronym, the Besht, became his signature.

19. *Shivhei ha-Besht,* trans. and ed. Dan Ben-Amos and Jerome R. Mintz (Bloomington, IN: Indiana University Press, 1970), p. 30.

20. *Sa'are Zedeq,* Ms. 8, 148, fol. 33b–34a, quoted in Idel, *Mystical Experience in Abraham Abulafia,* p. 148, n. 38.

21. Ginzberg, *Legends,* vol. 1, pp. 57–59; *Niddah* 16b, 30b, 39a; *Sanhedrin* 96a, *Berakhot* 17; *Zohar* II:11a–b.

22. Man's five souls are: *Nefesh* (his animal soul), *Ruach, Neshamah, Hayyah,* and *Yehidah,* at one with the Supernal Light.

23. Henry Corbin, *The Men of Light in Iranian Sufism* (Boulder, CO: Shambhala, 1978), p. 12.

24. The Hasmoneans were descended from Aaron and the Priesthood. Aaron was promised that, while the light of the seven-branched Temple *Menorah* might be extinguished, the light initiated by his descendants, the Maccabean heroes would remain with the Jewish People forever (*Bamidbar Rabbah* 15:6).

25. Meshullam the Great ben Kalonymus, tenth century C.E., based on *Wisdom of Ben Sirah*.

26. *Likkutim Yekarim* ascribed to R. Meshullam of Zhabaraz (Lemberg, 1863), fol. 37a.

27. Rabbi Nachman of Bratzlav, *Likkute Moharan,* pp. 100, 104, quoted in Aharon Weiner, *The Prophet Elijah in the Development of Judaism* (Boston: Routledge and Kegan Paul, 1978), p. 130.

28. *Degel Mahane Efrayim,* Koretz, 1819, fol. 38a, quoted in Gershom Scholem, *The Messianic Idea in Judaism* (New York: Schocken Books, 1978), p. 189.

29. Quoted in Scholem, *Messianic Idea,* pp. 189–190.

30. Ibid.

31. Rabbi of Polonnoye, *Toledot,* ff. 84b, 90b, quoted in *Messianic Idea,* p. 189.

32. Based on the *Maggid* of Mezeritch, *Likkutim Yekarim,* 1972, quoted in *Messianic Idea,* p. 192.

33. *Ketonet Passim,* Lvov, 1866, ff. 35 a–b, quoted in *Messianic Idea,* p. 191.

34. Chaim Vital, "On Transmigration of Souls," quoted in *Messianic Idea,* pp. 190–191.

35. Based on an oral Torah learning of Rabbi Murray Schaum of Riverdale, NY.

36. Jiri Langer, *Nine Gates* (Edinburgh: James Clarke & Co. Ltd., 1961), p. 218.

37. The Baal Shem Tov, in a letter to his brother-in-law Rabbi Gershon of Kutov, Koretz, 1791, trans. and ed. Norman Lamm, *Tradition* 14 (4), 1974.

38. Abraham Isaac Kuk, *The Lights of Penitence,* trans. Ben Zion Bokser (New York: Paulist Press, 1978), p. 351.

FOUR

LIGHT

OF

THE

COMMANDMENT

Friday Night. "Delight of *Shabbat*": The observance of any of God's commandments kindles a light. (*Courtesy of AR/The Jewish Museum, Jewish Theological
Seminary, New York*)

The first command God gave to the world at the Creation was "Let there be light." This was not addressed to any particular people or even only to man; it was directed at the cosmos. Since then, all other commands have only been amplifications and particularizations of that first proclamation that light be let into the world.

THE COMMANDMENT TO KINDLE: AN IMITATION OF CELESTIAL LIGHT

The "commandment to kindle" is perhaps the most beautiful of all the commandments in the Torah and a sensuous demonstration of the impact they all exert, but in a less visible way. Says the *Sifat Emet* (Rabbi Yehuda Aryeh Leib Alter, the second Gerer Rebbe (1807–1905): "The *Mitzvot*, they are called *Nerot!*" (The Commandments, they are called Lamps!).

In the Torah there is only one "commandment to kindle" – addressed, not to the individual, but to the descendants of Aaron who were to fulfill the lighting of the seven-branched *Menorah* in the Sanctuary on behalf of all of Israel. The *Midrash* has God say of this "centralized" *Menorah*:

> The lightning owes its origin to the celestial fire, and it issues forth and lights up the whole world, as it says, *As for the likeness of the living creatures, their appearance was like coals of fire, burning like the appearance of torches . . . and out of the fire went forth lightning* (Ezekiel 1:13) and lit up the whole world! Do I then need your light? Why then did I tell you to give it to Me? In order to elevate you. [*Bamidbar Rabbah* 15:7–8]

Therefore the lighting of the Temple *Menorah* is a human reenactment of the kindling not only of the planetary system but also of the primordial "First Light."

According to Philo, the light (of wisdom and life-energy) emanating from God into the universe and symbolized by the planetary system – and its replica in the lamps of the *Menorah* – shines, ideally, back to God, "because the Universe," says Philo, "is constantly worshipping its Creator."[1]

THE HAMMERING OF THE GOLDEN LAMP

The *Midrash* tells us that not only was Moshe granted a higher vision into the workings of "First Light" through the mechanism of the *Menorah,* he also was given the technical specifications to construct a concrete *Menorah* on earth:

> And you shall make a candlestick of pure gold; of beaten work shall the candlestick be made, even its base, and its shaft; its cups, its knops [ornamental knobs], and its flowers shall be of one piece with it. And there shall be six branches going out of the sides of it; three branches of the candlestick out of one side of it and three branches of the candlestick out of the other side of it; three cups made like almond blossoms in one branch, a knop and a flower, and three cups made like almond-blossoms on the other branch, a knop and a flower; so for the six branches going out of the candlestick. [Exodus 25:31–34]

The original *Menorah* as shown to Moshe seems to have been a veritable Tree of Light, like the Tree of Life surrounded by flames in the Garden of Eden. If we consider the Lamp as a tree, and the flames shooting up from the tips of its branches as its blossoms or fruits, then even before oil had been deposited in its cups and flames sprung to life, the container itself had its own shine and sap, springing out of a single ingot of pure gold.

Samson Raphael Hirsch (1808–1888), nineteenth-century leader of an enlightened and humanistic brand of Orthodoxy in Germany, visualizes this "tree, completely golden, from its root-stock to its blossoms, beaten out by repeated hammerblows from one piece of solid gold" as "the archetype of Life realizing itself."[2]

Hirsch attributes the original intention that the *Menorah* be made of a single block of gold to the fact that it symbolizes the Tree of Life, bearing the kind of legendary fruit that "tastes like its root."[3]

What can the "fruit" of a nonvegetable Tree be? In the case of the *Menorah,* it is the lights themselves, as golden as the seams of precious ore mined deep in the bed of earth. In the case of the Tree of Life, the soul is the fruit that has the taste and fragrance of the "Life of all Worlds." Therefore, Hirsch says, "development from the deepest root to the highest blossom had to be of purest gold."[4]

Emerging from the heavy hammerblows of the Master of Israel, according to Hirsch, the *Menorah* is Israel and the future destiny of the Jewish Nation.

In this way, too, the making of an earthly Lamp exactly parallels the "commandment to kindle," because one is an extension of the other and both are necessary preliminaries in achieving the desired result – illumination.

Moshe, who was completely at home in the celestial spheres, found himself utterly at a loss when it came to the task of bringing that vision down and giving it substance for the benefit of the People. That job he handed over to Bezalel, a master craftsman, who used his artistic imagination to interpret God's vision entrusted to Moshe.

There is another *Midrash* that says that, as Moshe found it difficult to duplicate the celestial *Menorah,* the Creator let him have the original – "A pure candlestick came down from heaven" (*Bamidbar Rabbah* 15:10). But the real meaning of the *Menorah* and all such Lamps is the sheer earthiness of the attempt to "ground" the Light before kindling it and raising it up once more – only through the technicalities a craftsman would understand comes illumination.

The *Menorah* as Bezalel contrived it stood on a base near the veil that hung before the Holy of Holies. In the Sanctuary it formed a kind of conductor for the *Shekhinah*. It was the original Perpetual Light (*Ner Tamid*) (Exodus 27:20; Leviticus 24:2). However, the original nuance of the Hebrew does not mean "Perpetual Light" but implies a fixed routine – continual but not continuous. The lamps were lighted at dusk and burned from evening till morning (Leviticus 24:3). In the morning they were trimmed and tended by the High Priest, whose special care they were (Exodus 30:7–8). According to some, three lamps were kept burning during the day and three at night. Since the Talmud says that if the *Menorah* was extinguished "it bodes ill for the future" (*Yoma* 39b), the indications are that some kind of light was kept burning all the time.

In remembrance of this, the practice was instituted in the synagogue in the sixteenth century of kindling a *Ner Tamid* on the Eastern wall over the Ark. This constituted a single light separate from the *Menorah*.

By the time Solomon had completed his Temple in Jerusalem, there were as many as ten golden *Menorot* in the Sanctuary, five on each side (I Kings 7:49). In the center, say the Rabbis, was the *Menorah* of Moshe (*Menahot* 98b).

The seven-branched candelabrum of the Temple, like the rest of the Temple furnishings, was considered an abstract representation of certain aspects of God Himself. It was therefore forbidden to make an exact representation of it.

This prohibition, however, was completely ignored in different periods and in different cultures. The *Menorah*, a major symbol of Jewishness appears, for instance, on some of the first Jewish coins minted by King Antigonus who reigned from 40 to 37 B.C.E. And so popular did the symbol become that some scholars have suggested that as the ban only appears in the Babylonian Talmud, it did not apply to the Land of Israel.

The *Menorah* was lavishly used in ornamentation of frescoes and mosaics in the ancient synagogues of the Land of Israel. Going back to the fifth and sixth century – in Naaran near Jericho, Beth Alpha in Galilee, and Jerash in Transjordan – most mosaics and murals were covered with single and double candelabra. There the *Menorah* is depicted on both sides of the Ark. In the upper section the ark is flanked by eagles, lions, or doves. Below are one or two candelabra, together with the other ceremonial objects. At the synagogue of Hammat near Tiberias, a *Menorah* was built out of a single block of stone; the seven branches were cut in relief and there was a hollow receptacle for the lamp on each branch. In the excavations of the synagogue of Beth Alpha, the seven-branched *Menorah* has been found flanking the ark on either side, and the same motif was discovered on gold glasses in Rome.

The seven-branched candelabra finds its place as part of a group with the other sacred implements – palm branch, citrus fruit, *shofar,* Torah Scroll, circumcision knife, vial of oil, snuff dish, and incense shovel. Again as part of a group, the *Menorah* reappears in synagogue excavations in Jerash, Kfar Nahum (Capernaum), Pekiin, Gaza, Eshtemoa, and Hammat Lif. The seven-branched *Menorah* is represented flanked by birds at Priene; with a crown of victory at Ein Nabatea; with the palm branch and *shofar* at Ashdod, Gaza, and Gadara; with a vase and rosettes at Nawa; and between two rosettes in Jaffa.

We have evidence of what the *Menorah* may have looked like from these excavations of the ancient synagogues of Israel from coins, from markings on small objects and on tombs in the Jewish catacombs in Italy, and also from the representation of the *Menorah* crowning the spoils of "Jerusalem taken into captivity" depicted in bas relief on the Arch of Titus in Rome. According to the Rambam, however, this last is a distortion of the original *Menorah* of the Tabernacle and the Temple, which had straight, not crooked branches.

Ancient representations, however, unlike the base of the

Menorah on the Arch of Titus, which chiefly features monsters, show a conical stand with three animal feet of a type common in Greek and Roman candelabra from the fourth century B.C.E. down to Augustan times. The oldest representation of the *Menorah* in manuscript form – in the Codex Amiatinus (seventh to ninth century C.E.) – shows both the conical stand with three animal feet and the equal branches.

Flavius Josephus, wanting to impress the Romans with the glories of Jewish civilization, assumed that the *Menorah* had to be made of gold (Antiquities 12:238), but he was wrong. Although we know that the original *Menorah* of Moshe was fashioned out of one single piece of gold, even the candelabrum of the Temple did not always have to be made of gold. When the Maccabees rededicated the Temple in 165 B.C.E., they were unable to use the *Menorah* of gold, which had been defiled by the Syrians. At first, as we have seen in Chapter 1, pp. 45–46, it was perfectly in order for this ascetic band of warriors to make a *Menorah* of iron overlaid with tin (or wood).

In the reign of King Theodoric (ca. 500 C.E.), the Jews of Rome assembled in the synagogues of the city for Sabbaths and festivals and lighted a gilded seven-branched candelabrum. As the supreme symbol of Jewishness, the seven-branched candelabrum appears on ceremonial objects depicted in illuminated manuscripts and on tombstones until late medieval times, when the Star of David replaced it in popular esteem.

The *Menorah* remains an ornamental motif to the present day. The Warsaw Ghetto Memorial features two outsize *Menorot* flanked by lions. The candelabrum on the Arch of Titus was taken as the model for the official symbol of the State of Israel – *Judea Resurrecta*. The sculptor Benno Elkan fashioned two tree-shaped bronze *Menorot*. One stands in Westminster Abbey in London, the other near the Knesset Building in Jerusalem.

MENORAH AS ARCHETYPE

The *Menorah* prescribed by God to Moshe in the biblical book of Exodus set a precedent for all the "lights of holiness" that were to follow. As a graphic illustration of the symbolic kinship of all "lights of the commandment," there are contemporary modular *Hanukkah Menorot* that can be used as Sabbath candles, *Havdalah* candles, and so on. Ultimately, all these "lights of holiness" derive from the Temple *Menorah* and from Primordial Light.

THE REDEDICATION AND
THE REKINDLING

Hanukkah commemorates the liberation of the Jewish people from occupation by the Syrians that culminated in the rededication of the Temple in 165 B.C.E. and the rekindling of the seven-branched Temple candelabrum. Many years passed, however, before the Rabbis decided on the exact form the commemoration of these events was to take. Of all the elements that went to make up the deliverance, far more important than physical victory, was the subsequent miracle of the rekindled lights. It was to celebrate this spiritual rededication and rekindling that the Festival of *Hanukkah* was instituted and it was decided to commemorate the events with the kindling of lamps. *Hanukkah* means "Dedication," and another name for the Festival is the "Feast of Lights."

The original *Menorah* of Temple days, which miraculously burned for eight days, had only seven branches. In reenacting this event we add an extra branch. Although the *Hanukkah* lamp was obviously inspired by the seven-branched candelabrum of Temple days, it avoids duplication by the addition of an arm.

Although the prohibition against producing a copy of the Temple Lamp was never strictly kept, when it came to celebrating the rededication of the Temple, care was taken to conform with the stipulation laid down in various places in the Talmud against making an exact reproduction of any of the Temple furniture.

A man may not make a house in the form of the Temple, or a hall in the form of the Temple hall, or a court corresponding to the Temple court, or a table corresponding to the (sacred) table or a candlestick corresponding to the (sacred) candlestick, but he may

make a candlestick with five or six or eight lamps, but with seven
he should not make it. [*Menahot* 28a]

Because the *Menorah* was intended to be a reminder of, but not as
a substitute for, the original Temple Lamp, this is one of the
reasons why the *Hanukkah* lamp has eight branches. Another
reason is to symbolize the miracle of the *Hanukkah* story.

NOT BY MIGHT BUT BY MY SPIRIT

In the second century B.C.E., an infatuation with everything
Greek gripped all of the known world. The empire of Alexander
the Great was divided in three among his successors. Not content
with political domination of the many cultural minorities in his
slice of empire, Antiochus IV Epiphanes of Syria, a descendant of
the Seleucid dynasty, sought to forge them all into one people by
imposing on them a decadent Oriental version of the Greek way
of life. Paying no regard to ethnic sensibilities, Antiochus forced
the peoples of the region to break with their own customs and
religious beliefs and conform. It might have been easy for an idol
worshipper to add a few Greek gods to his pantheon, but for a
Jew who put all his faith in the One God it was not so simple.

On the 25th of *Kislev*, 167 B.C.E., Antiochus entered Jerusalem, desecrated the altar, and seized those golden holy vessels
that had not been hidden away. After stripping the Temple
façade of its golden overlay, Antiochus returned to Syria, triumphant, with his precious spoils.

Shortly afterward, he returned to Jerusalem and set fire to
the city. He broke down the age-old ritual of Temple sacrifice by
setting up shrines to idols in many small towns around the
country. The most spiritual of the sacrifices – burning incense –
was enacted, not in the Temple, but at the doors of people's
houses and on the highways. (As we shall see, after the destruction of the Temple by the Romans the Rabbis themselves effected the transfer of the *Menorah* from its central position in the
Temple, not to synagogue or communal center, but to a location
outside the door of each Jewish household.)[5]

The Syrians tore into pieces and burned Torah Scrolls

wherever they were discovered, and anyone who had one of the precious objects in his possession was put to death. Similarly, women who dared flout the king's edict and insisted on circumcising their male infants were put to death with their newborn babies hanging from their breasts. To make the Jews forget the Torah and the Jewish way of life, specific Jewish observances, such as celebration of the Sabbath and the festivals and the practice of waving the *lulav* (palm branch) and *etrog* (citron) on *Sukkot* (the Festival of Tabernacles), were prohibited on pain of death.

Syrian police compelled prominent Jewish leaders and priests to sacrifice pigflesh on the Temple altar and on the various small altars found in the marketplaces of villages throughout the country. When the soldiers arrived at the small village of Modiin in Upper Galilee, the aged priest Matityahu rejected this demand to lower the morale of his people by desecrating the altar of his hometown. With the words "Whoever is zealous for the Torah and would maintain the Covenant–follow me!" he and his five sons raised the standard of revolt and took to the hills (I Maccabees 2:27).

On his deathbed, the aged Matityahu charged his sons to be ready to give their lives for the Covenant of their forefathers. Then he listed examples of heroic endurance and fortitude among their glorious ancestors. Abraham had been ready to go into a burning furnace or to bring up his beloved son Isaac as a burnt offering to vindicate his faith. "None who put their faith in Him," he concluded, "will ever fail in their strength." He linked military glory with observance of God's Law. "Be manful and strong for Torah, for through it you will obtain renown" was his parting advice to his children (I Maccabees 2:62, 64).

Judah, the ablest of the sons, took over as general of the rising, earning himself the name of "Maccabee"–the Hammer–after his prowess in war. This name Maccabee came to be applied to all five brothers and their followers. As their fortunes changed, the family was also known as the Hasmoneans–oil magnates–either because olive oil betokened wealth or because of the "miracle of the oil." Though the Hasmoneans were priests and not of the royal line of David and of Judah, they became so popular that, against strict Jewish law, which advocated the division of spiritual and political leadership, they later became a hereditary dynasty.

As a great Jewish soldier-hero, Judah Maccabee has done wonders for the morale of the Jewish People – then and since.

His renown "reached the end of the earth." "He buckled on a breastplate like a giant, and he belted on his weapons and organized campaigns, protecting his camp with the sword. He was like a lion in his actions, and like a cub roaring for its prey. He pursued and hunted out those who disobeyed the Torah, and those who harassed his people he consumed." [I Maccabees 3:5].

The greatest difficulty the Jewish forces labored under was lack of fighters and arms. To offset this, their great leader instilled in his men the conviction that Heaven was with them. He told them that "in the sight of Heaven there was no difference between saving through many or through a few." He claimed that victory in war did not arise from the size of the force, but that "strength comes from heaven." And this strength was likely to depend on the knowledge that one was fighting a just cause. "They come against us full of violence and lawlessness, to destroy us and our wives and our children, and to plunder us, but we are fighting for our lives and laws" (I Maccabees 3:19–21).

It was this brand of valor that ultimately led the small Jewish army to victory. Judah's words echo the Prophet Zechariah's description of the oil that fueled the Temple *Menorah*: "Not by strength, nor by might, but by My spirit" (Zechariah 4:6). Here, when the Prophet speaks of oil, he is also obviously speaking of the energy and moral force necessary to keep fighting despite every setback.

Judah showed that he really believed in the superiority of quality over quantity by complying even in this emergency with the Biblical edict that anyone who had just built a house, planted a vineyard, or become engaged, or anyone who simply felt in a pacifist mood, should be allowed to go home. Thus he was left with a small but utterly fearless fighting force.

With victory, the reaction of these battle-hardened guerrillas to their return to the Jewish capital was charged with emotion. There seemed no difference between the wild mountains and forest country in which they had camped out and this heart-center of Jewish civilization. They entered Jerusalem and saw how desolate the whole city had become, and as they made their way slowly up to the Temple via Mount Zion and saw the ruins and weeds growing in the courtyards, they broke down and cried. Then they replaced the polluted altar with a new one, provided the Sanctuary with a fresh set of holy vessels, put out leaves of shewbread on the Table, and hung up a curtain. The soldiers decorated the Temple facade with golden crowns and small shields, rededicated the gates and the priests' quarters, and fitted new doors. Once again incense smoked on the altar. The rededication ceremony took place amid great popular rejoicing on the 25th of *Kislev*, 164 B.C.E., three years after the Sanctuary had been desecrated.

Only in later centuries was one detail in the rededication of the Temple enlarged upon to epitomize the real meaning of *Hanukkah.* According to the Rabbis, the real triumph of the Jewish People was enacted not on the physical field of battle over some external enemy but in the heart-center of the Nation, around the *Menorah.*

HANUKKAH LAMPS THROUGH THE AGES

The *Hanukkah* lamp takes two forms – a single vial of oil, or the whole blaze of the candelabrum. It was the spiritual force in the little vial that kept the whole eight-branched *Menorah* alight.

The eight-branched *Hanukkah* lamp is the most popular object of Jewish ceremonial art. There are more *Menorot* than any other Jewish artifact, from the large-sized standing lamp to the miniature traveling variety. Each member of the family is encouraged to have one.

The earliest *Hanukkah* lamps do not go back further than the first century C.E. and in no way differ from the simple pear-shaped Greco-Roman lamps made out of clay or red buff pottery typical of that period. The Talmud specifically mentions the use of bronze *Hanukkah* lamps, yet there are no examples of them in existence. Excavations at the synagogue of Delos, Greece, have uncovered lamps in no way different from those common in Mediterranean lands at that time. Some even display pagan borrowings such as a Minerva or a Jupiter. Those discovered in Israel bear typically Jewish emblems such as the seven-branched palm, a substitute for the forbidden likeness of the seven-branched candelabrum. Indeed, one such oil lamp has been discovered that bears the markings of the sacrosanct seven-branched *Menorah* on its surface. In Rome, as well as in Israel, similar lamps have been discovered, bearing the same Jewish insignia but otherwise not differing in any essential way from non-Jewish lamps of the time.

These lamps consisted of a spout fixed to a dish of oil, with the wick protruding over the rim of the dish. This one-wick lamp persisted for almost one thousand years. Stone and earthenware lamps of this type were used until quite recently by the Jews of Persia and Yemen. They are seldom decorated and only occasionally bear a Hebrew inscription. Their esthetic appeal lies in their functional aspects – the oil reservoir and the grooves for the wicks.

Though the original *Hanukkah* lamp usually consisted of a single wick, in the days of the Talmud these lamps sometimes consisted of two spouts "to serve two persons" and a dish of oil with the wick protruding over the rim of the dish (*Shabbat* 3b). As late as the twelfth century, Maimonides maintained that if each household lit one light every night of the festival, it had fulfilled its obligation. However, "a lamp with two wicks (would) do for two persons" (Rambam, *Mishneh Torah, Hilchot Megillah ve-Hanukkah* 4:1–3, 5–6, 8–12, 14). For those who wanted to light an additional wick for every night of the Festival, as we do today, finishing up with eight lights on the eighth night, it was originally the custom to light an array of eight separate single-wick lamps. This one-wick lamp persisted for almost one thousand years.

According to some scholars, by Greco-Roman times the simple clay oil lamp of the Mediterranean, when used as a

Hanukkah lamp, had even evolved into a many-spouted utensil with eight apertures for wicks fed by oil from a central reservoir. These lamps were made of clay, stone, and bronze. Several such lamps with seven spouts on the rim and dating back to the Middle Bronze Period have been found in Syria and in Israel, especially at Nahariyah and Tanaach. Equipped with a vertical metal stand as they supposedly were in talmudic times, they would have borne a great resemblance to the *Menorah* we know today. This type of lamp, popular during the first and second centuries C.E., was used until recently in isolated communities in Yemen and Morocco.

No actual *Hanukkah* lamp has been found dating from the period between the second century and the latter part of the Middle Ages. Although some eight-spouted pottery dishes go back to Greco-Roman times, there is no evidence that they were used for *Hanukkah* lamps. Rather, it seems that before the thirteenth century those ardent spirits who decided to light more than one wick a night used an array of separate single-wick metal vases. The first lamp to be identified by its inscription as having been used specifically for *Hanukkah* was found in Spain or southern France and dates certainly no earlier than the twelfth century.

Throughout its long history, the Temple Lamp and the *Hanukkah Menorah* to which it gave rise have been made of many different substances. A Dutch author writing in 1865 lists as many as fifteen materials out of which the *Hanukkah* lamp was made in his day – gold, silver, burnished brass, red copper, iron, tin or pewter, lead, glass, wood, bone, earthenware, coated with lead (glazing), uncoated earthenware, pomegranate rind, walnut shells and acorn shells – and he ends by informing us that onion skins and egg shells are not suitable. We know, however, that poor people often resorted to using eggshells, possibly in memory of the rabbi who used to juggle with eight eggs during the Feast of the Water Drawing on *Sukkot* of which *Hanukkah* is in part a memorial.[6]

Though the command to light the *Hanukkah Menorah* was primarily for the Jewish home, in the twelfth century it became the custom to have a candelabrum in the synagogue for the benefit of merchants and travelers. This large, free-standing candelabrum was a direct descendant of the Temple *Menorah*.

In the thirteenth century a change in the position of the *Hanukkah* lamp dictated a consequent evolution in its form. In talmudic times the *Menorah* was set outside the entrance to the home near the left doorpost and opposite the *Mezuzah*. The lamps were put on a pedestal, and in Israel and in Babylon it is possible they were placed under glass like a lantern to protect the flames from being extinguished by the bitter winter winds. At the time of the Crusades, however, the lamp was moved indoors to avoid calling attention to the Jewish home. At the same time, the old handle used to place this simple dish of oil in the doorway evolved into a trefoil or punch-hole, a simple hanging device used to suspend the multiple holder either at the entrance or near the window.

In the fourteenth century, Rabbi Menachem ben Meiri of Provence ruled that although the Talmud had prohibited *Hanukkah* lamps with light "in the round" – the separate flames blending into one indivisible glow (*Shabbat* 23b) – the multiple-holder variety was permitted "without a doubt." Once the multiple holder was suspended, a backplate evolved at the back of the punch-hole to give additional support. This "bench back-wall" lamp, though it served a particular purpose, provided both scope and pretext for the most lavish embellishment. Until modern times, most *Hanukkah* lamps among both Ashkenazic and Sephardic Jews were suspended from the wall.

There have been "bench" or backwall lamps of various types. Sometimes the containers were fashioned like vials of oil; sometimes they were made in the form of lions' heads with wicks projecting from their open mouths. Others were fashioned into an oval shell-like shape with the cups set along a rail in front of the lamp. Frequently, each cup was set on a separate bracket. Small dishes in different shapes were laid out beneath eight receptacles to collect the dripping oil.

From time immemorial, Jews have been moved by two major passions – a love for the Book and a nostalgia for the Holy Temple. Therefore the backwall *Hanukkah* lamp, ritual orna-

ment of the home, has been subject to the twin influences of both
the page of an illuminated manuscript and also that of architectural motifs reminiscent of the Temple. Sometimes, especially on
Sephardic lamps, the text from Psalm 30, "A Song of the Dedication of the House," is engraved on the lamp. Here, the House
referred to is always the Temple.

Mordecai Narkiss, the noted historian of Jewish art, says
that *Hanukkah* lamps "underwent all the adventures experienced
by their owners and were deeply influenced by the period and
environment in which they were fashioned, local influences
blending with traditional form and function."[7] Though the
architectural façades of the backwall may be reminiscent of
the Temple, they are often dominated by local features, so that
the skyline of buildings, say, of the artisan's native Spain, had a
discernible impact on the contour of the bench-type *Hanukkah*
lamps produced in that region. *Hanukkah* lamps produced in
Poland, on the other hand, resemble the marvelous wooden
synagogues of that land, rising several storeys high on top of one
another like tiers on a wedding cake. In various times and
cultures the backwall has been fashioned to look like Gothic
windows, quatrefoils, arched colonnades, arabesques, curlicues,
city walls, bridges, towers, and the characteristic contours of
Jerusalem.

The amount of ornamentation applied to *Hanukkah* lamps
in general varied with the cultural situation of the various communities. Spanish and Portuguese refugees brought their tradition of *Hanukkah* lamps to Holland, where sheet brass specimens
were hammered out and engraved. In Holland they continued to
use sheet brass as the main material of their lamps. Not surpris-
ingly, there is a strong resemblance between Moroccan lamps
and examples from Holland, because both countries were settled
by large numbers of these Spanish and Portuguese Jews who
brought with them the artistic tradition of the Sephardic world.
In North Africa, especially Morocco, Jews were fine artisans: It
has also been documented that many of these Sephardic potters
and metal-workers were women.

In the Middle Ages, *Hanukkah* lamps from that part of the
world were fashioned of stone or glazed pottery because a minor

Talmudic tractate maintains that untreated pottery (clay) is too ugly to be the material for a *Hanukkah* lamp. Hammered brass was a favorite technique and material in North Africa. In Persia it was only during the last century that the rounded type of lamp came to be made of silver. During the past 1,400 years the Persian Jewish community has experienced such poverty and persecution that the most frequent form of *Hanukkah* lamp in that country consists of simple brass cups, one added every day.

In sixteenth-century Italy, however, the *Hanukkah* lamp became increasingly more ornate, in keeping with the contemporary artistic Renaissance styles. Lamps were cast in copper, bronze, or brass. Urns, cherubs, tritons, masks, and cornucopias adorned the backwalls in conjunction with heroic figures such as that of Judith, associated in the popular imagination with the *Hanukkah* story. Various aristocratic coats of arms – a tribute to noble patrons – also decorated the backwall. In sixteenth-century Italy there was a whole series of bronze bench-type *Hanukkah* lamps in which the central *cartouche* of the backwall bore the heraldic marking of Catholic cardinals such as Cardinal Ippolito Aldobrandini, later Pope Clement VIII, whose hat is held up by cherubs. A possible explanation for this peculiar ornamentation of a Jewish religious implement is the wish of Jews who worked as business agents for the Church dignitaries to demonstrate their loyalty to their patrons. Renaissance and baroque styles merged into the rococo in the eighteenth century. In that era of the Enlightenment, some backwalls actually took on the emblems or newly acquired coats of arms of their Jewish owners.

As we have seen, there are two major categories of *Hanukkah* lamp – the candelabrum or standing lamp reminiscent of the seven-branched *Menorah* in the Temple and the bench-type with a backwall.

The base of the standing lamp evolved into a round or angular shape, often richly ornamented with biblical motifs, reliefs, and enamels. In the eighteenth century a reduced and daintier version of the standing lamp was transplanted from the synagogue into the home. Frequently this lamp was made of silver and stood on the table, and this is perhaps the most popular form of *Hanukkah* lamp we know today.

Toward the end of the Middle Ages, in response to the strictures of Jewish law (*Halakhah*), an additional feature made its appearance on both these types of lamp. While the *Menorah* of Temple times had only seven branches and the *Hanukkah* lamp had an eighth, a ninth servitor-candle (*Shammas*) was introduced at that time to attend on the other lights. The need for this new light was based on the holiness of the other eight, which existed only to be looked at and admired, but not to be put to any practical use. Thus, if there were no other light in a particular space except for the *Hanukkah* lamp – which in the Middle Ages when candles were expensive was not unlikely – it was forbidden to use the *Hanukkah* lamp to read or even to see by. The introduction of the *Shammas* not only provided an attendant to kindle the other lights, but also allowed people to work when the lamp was the only illumination. To distinguish the *Shammas* from the eight holy lights, it is usually elevated slightly above the rest.

The nine-branched standing candelabrum became a feature in most European synagogues by the fifteenth century. In the Nachmanides Synagogue in Lwow, Poland, built around 1698, the *Shammas* topped the central shaft at the same level as the other lights. In certain Sephardic cities, such as Aleppo, Syria, it was customary to have two *Shammas* lights to commemorate deliverance from local persecution.

So the *Hanukkiyah* – the modern Israeli name for the *Hanukkah* lamp – has two more lights than the Temple *Menorah* – the *Shammas* and the eighth branch of the *Hanukkah* lamp. In a sense the *Shammas,* though secular, is the holiest light, for it serves the function of the central shaft.[8] It feeds the others, just as the Upper (Divine) Light of God is the source of all *Sefirot* and as the lowest *Sefirah* (*Malkhut*) clothes even the Divine in the substance of the physical.

In Germany, *Menorot* were almost certainly made by Christians because, unlike Eastern Europe and Arabic and Mediterranean lands, Jews were not eligible for apprenticeship and had no means of learning to work with their hands.[9] From the Middle Ages to the eighteenth century, the *Judenstern* – a star-shaped lamp – was hung from the ceiling and regularly drawn down for use as a Sabbath Lamp. At least until the seventeenth century, it was removed for *Hanukkah* and, in talmudic tradition, hung near the door. German Jews also used the eight-branched standing lamp. These suffered the same fate as church bells – requisitioned to make weaponry for Germany's many wars. As a result, none exists today.

In Eastern Europe, where Jewish artisans abounded, the back-walled lamp was cast in brass or worked in filigree silver or in *repoussé*. Legs were added to the backwall lamp, which was customarily placed on the table or the windowsill. Jewish symbols such as deer, lions, eagles, other birds, Torah crowns, columns, gates, the Temple facade, and the *Menorah* itself decorated the backwall of Polish *Hanukkah* lamps. For better balance, many of the bench-type lamps, especially those from Poland, had two sockets for the *Shammas* instead of one. These had a loop on the back so that when not in use they could be hung on a wall as a decorative object.

WHAT IS *HANUKKAH*?

Hanukkah has evolved from a Temple festival into a popular family celebration. Although most synagogues hold *Hanukkah* candlelighting sessions during the festival for the benefit of passersby and the enjoyment of the community, this is only a beautiful custom and not essential according to Jewish law. In fact, any Jew who has only attended one of these public gatherings but has not participated in kindling lights in his own household – ideally, everyone should light his or her own *Hanukkah* lamp – has not fulfilled his particular obligation (*Shulkhan Arukh* 139:1–7, 9–11, 14–18). It is significant that Jewish law demands that the lights of the *Hanukkah* festival be lighted in the home, and it is the home that is the required setting for this most beautiful and popular of Jewish rituals.

One reason for this is that the eight-branched *Menorah* was conceived, not as a replacement for the seven-branched holy *Menorah* of Temple times, but as a kind of "doormarker" corresponding to the *Mezuzah* that marks the threshold of the Jewish home. Just as a synagogue does not require the "protection" of a

Mezuzah because it is already filled with holy books and Scrolls of the Torah, so it does not strictly require the amuletic protection of the *Menorah*. The reason most synagogues customarily possess at least one eight-branched *Hanukkah* lamp probably has more to do with the loss of the beloved seven-branched candelabrum of Temple days than any necessity to have a *Hanukkah* lamp.

The original position of the household *Hanukkah* lamp was at the gate of the house with the *Mezuzah* on the right doorpost and the *Menorah* on the left to balance it (*Baba Kamma* 6:6). As late as the seventeenth century, German Jews were in the habit of kindling the *Hanukkah* lamp near the door. In Tunisia, until quite recently, the *Menorah* was suspended from the doorpost opposite the *Mezuzah,* remaining there not only during the eight days of the Festival, but from *Hanukkah* until Purim—that is, the whole winter.

TO PUBLICIZE THE MIRACLE

The *Menorah* is lighted on *Hanukkah* "to publicize the miracle"— that is, to symbolize it and reiterate it for as many people as possible. The purpose of *Hanukkah* is to extend the threshold of sanctification of the Name.

In essence, light itself is a message, a form of communication. We see this from the curfew ordered in occupied lands, from the Morse code, from the first proclamation God issued to Creation. The text corresponds to light, with the *Mezuzah* containing Torah text on the right doorpost and the *Menorah* on the left.

The *Menorah* stood as a bodyguard at the opening of the door of the house—the point of innerness of the heart. Just as it shines out into the darkness, it guards the home from contamination from external influences. The position of the *Menorah* on the left shows that it equips the Jewish People for the exile and stands for the Messiah, the Son of Joseph.[10] In darkness it shines and stands firm. It shines out to the nations while guarding its inner core.

Sin crouches at the entrance to the heart. But if the heart is pure, the *Menorah* can be stationed in every window and orifice of the body so as to send a beam of illumination wherever is the gathering place of desire.

The Sephardic *Menorah* plaques read: *Joseph is a fruitful bough; even a fruitful bough by a well; whose branches run over the wall* (Genesis 49:22).

What is the tree that runs over the wall but the *Menorah* that shines out into the darkness of exile from the door, the window, from every chink. Without compromising its own essence, it gives unstinting illumination.

In *Kabbalah* there are basically two forms of meditation – that represented by the meditation on the Hebrew letters (the *Mezuzah*) and that represented by meditation on light (the *Menorah*). Probably the two are variations on the same theme.

The *Menorah* is a "sign" between God and Israel. The direction in which the *Menorah* is lighted depends on the kind of communication for which the lights are designed. Rabbi Yosef Karo[11] and the *L'vush,* R. Mordecai Yaffah, lighted the *Menorah* from opposite directions – R. Karo from right to left, the *L'vush* from left to right. Why these opposite traditions?

THE LIGHT OF *KAVANNAH*

Both R. Karo and the *L'vush* were in agreement about one thing – that the kindling of the *Menorah* was basically a message, a mode of communication. There was also no question that the orientation was in the direction of holiness and must follow Hebrew script – from right to left. The only difference was to whom was the message primarily addressed? Karo implies that the person who kindles must first deepen the light of his personal *kavannah* before he can bring it out to the world; therefore, he must light from right to left. But the *L'vush* implies that if the reason for kindling the *Hanukkah* lights is "to publicize the miracle," the communication is directed principally at "others." If the way those others see it is taken as a guide for the way to light, the person kindling will have to do so from left to right, in order to achieve a reverse mirroring effect.

Exactly the same dispute arises when it comes to *Tefillin* (phylacteries). Both Rashi and Rabbenu Tam agree that the

Tefillin of the Hand (which lies opposite the Heart) must first affect the self. The dispute arises over the *Tefillin* of the Head, in which the placement of the texts varies according to whether the command is intended primarily for the benefit of the person wearing the *Tefillin* or whether the energies induced are intended immediately to radiate outward. Again, we see the link between *Menorah* and *Tefillin,* between the direction of light and of text, both of which are designed to bring man and God closer.[12]

The Talmud stresses that the purpose of kindling the *Hanukkah* lights is as to demonstrate publicly the miracle of Divine intervention in human affairs, which is why, ideally, the lights should be placed outside the entrance to the home. If someone lives in an upper storey (in a modern apartment building), the lamp can be set on the windowsill looking out on to the street. The rabbis of talmudic days take into account the fact that it was sometimes hazardous for Jews to advertise their Jewishness. As the *Menorah* is intended as protection rather than as an invitation to disaster, in times of persecution and pogrom Jews could transfer the *Hanukkiyah* from outside to inside the front door, or even set it on a table in the interior (*Shabbat* 21b).

By the end of the period of the Men of the Great Assembly there was no authority to institute another festival for the Jewish People.[13] But because Israel spent seven days of the Festival of *Sukkot* making sacrifices for the seventy nations of the world and praying for them, another festival of national deliverance was merited (*Sifat Emet* on *Hanukkah*).

The best time to light is during dusk – that is, the whole period, about forty five minutes – from sunset until it grows dark, because this is the same time, according to the Talmud, when the gypsies kindle the little scraps of twig and wood they have collected for their fires. Why the comparison between the kindling of gypsy fires and the *Menorah*? Because there is a special sense of rightness if the time for doing holy things coincides with that for doing ordinary, natural things. At the same time of day that wandering people are gathering their twigs, stoking their meager fires over which they cook their supper, and deriving what pleasure they can from the flame before it burns down, so the Jewish People kindles the *Menorah* lights. Although we celebrate the miracle of the one day's ration of oil lasting eight days, nowadays our *Menorah* lights last only about forty-five minutes. They are as ephemeral as the gypsy fires. Candles, physical energy, and life burn out and become depleted, yet the *Menorah* lights, for the forty-five minutes that they last, give light not for our own pleasure or for our own use, but to reflect their Source in the Light of Eternity.[14]

Since the whole purpose of these lights is for people to see them, candlelighting time extends from nightfall until "there is no wayfarer left in the street" (*Shabbat* 21b) or, according to the *Shulkhan Arukh,* until the whole household has gone to bed. After then, one may still light, but without a blessing.

A modern example of flexibility in candlelighting time under unusual circumstances is found in the ruling of former Chaplain of the Israel Defense Forces, Rabbi Shlomo Goren, that soldiers at the front could kindle the *Hanukkiyah* half an hour before sunset and extinguish it immediately after sunset so as not to betray their position to the enemy. Where even this was impossible, it was up to the chaplain to reassure his men that they had been included in the candlelighting at the military base.[15]

On Friday, however, the candles for *Hanukkah* must be lighted before those of *Shabbat,* which are lighted approximately twenty minutes before sunset. Therefore the kindling of the *Hanukkah* lamp is permitted from midafternoon on. On Saturday night, *Hanukkah* candles are lighted after the *Havdalah* ceremony separating the Sabbath from weekdays.

Only in Jerusalem is there a custom of kindling the *Hanukkah* lamp in the synagogue in the morning as well as in the evening, but without making a blessing. While this does not acquit those who are unable to kindle the lights the previous evening of their obligation, it does help them keep track of the exact number they should light the following night. Also, it is argued, because light is not necessary in the morning, it will be obvious that these morning candles were lit with only the miracle in mind.

Most of the Festivals have many *mitzvot* connected with them. But on *Hanukkah* all that has to be done is to kindle the

Hanukkah lights. The lights of *Hanukkah* connect the light of Creation with the Light of Messiah. When we kindle the *Hanukkah* lights, the light of the Temple *Menorah* begins to stir and revive.

All the rituals connected with the Holy Temple were pragmatic and for the atonement and benefit of the People, but the *Menorah* is gratuitous; it shone only to testify that the *Shekhinah* rests upon Israel, that Israel has a point of attachment to God. It showed that in Israel's ardor to light lies a point of affinity with the light of the *Shekhinah*.

The *Hanukkah* lamp is on the left because even for the person who seems to have no connection with the light of the *Shekhinah* and lives in darkness, the *Hanukkah* light enlightens him.

The miracle of *Hanukkah* pierces to the essential tiny point of light within that is never obliterated. Externals may change, but inside the potential is always for the highest – a point to which one can always return, the eternal light within.

This small dot of light simply has to be brought out. By concentrating on one single command – the "commandment to kindle" – on *Hanukkah,* more than on any other holiday, we are able to fan this flame to a blaze of glory that reveals ourselves to ourselves, ourselves to the world outside.

DAS PINTELE YID: A TREE OF LIFE

Theodor Herzl, regarded as the founder of the modern state of Israel, wrote the following story about the *Menorah* shortly after attending the first Zionist Congress. Only two years before, in December 1895, his sentiments as a liberal intellectual were outraged when the Chief Rabbi Moritz Gudemann of Vienna issued the ruling that a Christmas Tree was not acceptable in a Jewish home.

The extent of Herzl's assimilation is shown by the fact that his parents, unlike the parents of his hero, celebrated the Jewish festival with a "Hanukkah Tree." What is interesting is the extent of his transformation within two years. With only minor changes, when Herzl writes about an assimilated artist who returns to the 'point' of light of Jewish identity in himself and helps it develop by sharing it with his children, he is writing about himself.

Deep in his soul, he began to feel the need to be a Jew. His circumstances were not unsatisfactory; he enjoyed an ample income and a profession that permitted him to do whatever his heart desired. For he was an artist. His Jewish origin and the faith of his fathers had long ceased to trouble him, when suddenly the old hatred came to the surface again in a new mob outcry. With many others, he believed that this flood would shortly subside. But there was no change for the better; in fact, things went from bad to worse. And every blow, even though not aimed directly at him, struck him with fresh pain, until little by little his soul became one bleeding wound. These sorrows, buried deep in his heart and silenced there, evoked thoughts of their origin and of his Judaism. He now did something he could not have done in the old days because he was then so alienated from it—he began to love this Judaism with an intense fervor.

Although he could not at first clearly justify his new yearning, it became so powerful that it crystallized from vague emotions into a definite idea that he needed to express. It was the conviction that there was only one solution for this *judennot*—the return to Judaism. He continued with characteristic persistence to develop one idea after another from his fundamental conviction. At this time, he was profoundly moved by several instances of apostasy, though his pride would not permit him to admit it. As a man and as an artist of the modern school, he had acquired many non-Jewish habits, and his study of the cultures of successive civilizations had left an indelible impression on him. How was this to be reconciled with his return to Judaism? Doubts often assailed him as to the soundness of his guiding thought—his *idée maîtresse*—as a French thinker calls it. Perhaps his generation, having grown up under the influence of alien cultures, was no longer capable of the return that Herzl perceived to be their redemption. But the new generation would be capable of it, if it were given the right direction early enough. He resolved, therefore, that his own children should be shown the proper path. They would be trained as Jews in their own home.

Hitherto he had ignored the holiday that the wonderful deeds of the Maccabees had illumined for thousands of years with the glow of miniature lights. Now, however, he made this holiday an opportunity to prepare something beautiful which should be forever commemorated in the minds of his children. In their young souls, a steadfast devotion to their ancient people would be implanted early. He bought a *Menorah,* and when he held the nine-branched candlestick in his hands for the first time, a strange mood came over him. In his father's house, the lights had once burned in his youth, now far away, and the recollection gave him a sad and tender longing for home.

The tradition was neither cold nor dead – thus it has passed through the ages, one light kindling another. Moreover, the ancient form of the *Menorah* had excited his interest. When was the primitive structure of this candlestick fashioned? Clearly the design was suggested by the tree – in the center the sturdy trunk, on right and left four branches, one below the other, in one plane, and all of equal height. A later symbolism brought with it the ninth branch, which projects in front and functions as a servant. What mystery had the generations read into this form of art, at once so simple and natural? And the artist wondered to himself if it were not possible to animate again the withered form of the *Menorah,* to water its roots as one would a tree. The mere sound of the word *Menorah,* which he now pronounced every evening to his children, gave him great pleasure. There was a lovable ring to the word when it came from the lips of little children.

On the first night the candle was lit and the origin of the holiday was explained. The wonderful incident of the lights that strangely remained burning so long, the story of the return from the Babylonian exile, the second Temple, the deeds of Maccabees – Herzl told his children all he knew. It was not very much, to be sure, but it served. When the second candle was lit, the children repeated what he had told them, and though it had all been learned from him, it seemed to him quite new and beautiful.

In the days that followed he waited keenly for the evening, which became ever brighter. Candle after candle stood in the *Menorah,* and the father mused on the little candles with his children, until his reflections became too deep to be uttered before them.

When he had resolved to return to his people and to make open acknowledgment of his return, he had only thought he would be doing the honorable and rational thing. He had never dreamed that he would find in it a gratification of his yearning for the beautiful. Yet nothing less was his good fortune. The *Menorah,* with its many lights, became a thing of beauty to inspire lofty thought. So, with his practiced hand, he drew a plan for a *Menorah* to present to his children the following year. He made free use of the motif of the right branching arms projecting right and left in one plane from the central stem. He did not feel bound by the rigidly traditional form, but created directly from nature, unconcerned by other symbolisms also seeking expression. He was in search of living beauty. Though he gave the withered branch new life, he conformed to the law, to the gentle dignity of its being. It was a tree with slender branches; its ends were molded into flower calyxes that would hold the lights.

The week passed with this absorbing labor. Then came the eighth day, when the whole row burns, even the faithful ninth, the servant that on other nights is used only for the lighting of the others. A great splendor streamed from the *Menorah.* The children's eyes glistened. But for him all this was the symbol of the rebirth of a nation. When there is but one light, all is still dark, and the solitary light looks melancholy. Soon it finds one companion, then another, and another. The darkness must retreat. The light comes first to the young and the poor–then others join them who love justice, truth, liberty, progress, humanity, and beauty. When all the candles burn, then we must all stand and rejoice over the achievements. And no office can be more blessed than that of a Servant of the Light.[16]

Three blessings are said before the candlelighting ceremony begins–the first, a blessing over the kindling of the *Hanukkah* lights; the second, giving thanks to God for performing miracles for past generations "in those days at this season." These two blessings are followed on the first night by the *Sheheheyanu,* thanking God for the miracle He has done for us personally by preserving us to live and experience *Hanukkah* "in our time." Obviously, the miracles performed "in those days" are being revived with the kindling of the lights "at this season" in our present lives.

When the lights are kindled the family stands back and admires them while singing:

> We kindle these lights to commemorate the miracles and the wonders. These lights are sacred and we are not permitted to make use of them but are only supposed to admire them so as to give thanks and praise Thy Name for Thy miracles, Thy wonders and Thy deliverances. ["Song over the kindling of the *Hanukkah* lights"]

The idea that these lights are holy and therefore "untouchable," that they are there only to be admired but not to be put to any practical use, has many interesting repercussions. For instance, it is not permissible to take light from the *Hanukkah* lamp to light any other kind of lamp or a stove, but it is permissible to light one *Hanukkah* light with another, for that is to use the holy to spread holiness. Any oil left over from the first night can be used on the second night, and so on. However, oil left over from the eighth night must be burned because once used for a religious purpose it cannot be used for anything else. The Talmud specifically states that it is forbidden to count money–even *Hanukkah gelt,* the pocket money children receive on *Hanukkah*–by the light of the *Menorah.*

For Ashkenazic Jews the candlelighting ritual concludes with a rousing hymn *Maoz Tzur* (the original "Rock of Ages"), based on a medieval German folksong. The same tune was later used for Luther's famous hymn, *Nun freut euch liebe Christen gmei"* (Now rejoice you Christian community). Sephardic Jews replace this with Psalm 30, "A Song for the Dedication of the House."

Why do we say *Hallel* (David's Songs of Praise) on *Hanukkah*

and not on *Purim* when the Jewish people were saved from
destruction? To physical threat the antidote is a feast. Therefore
there is a religious command (*mitzvah*) to eat on *Purim*. Although
there is no special obligation to feast on *Hanukkah,* lots of deli-
cious, rather fatty foods are eaten, such as *latkes* (pancakes) and
doughnuts, in memory of the miracle of the oil. But on *Hanukkah*
we celebrate a special *spiritual* affirmation, in addition to a physical deliverance, commemorated, not by a triumphal arch but by
the *Menorah*. The Greeks tried to make the Jews "forget Your
Torah and remove them from the statues of Your Will."[17] It is to
celebrate the miracle of *spiritual* resistance and survival that we
take a spiritual antidote of song and light. As we see from the
miracle of the parting of the Red Sea, song is the only adequate
response to miracle.[18]

Women also should light the *Hanukkah* lamp, not only for
themselves, but also on behalf of their households for, says the
Talmud, "they too were concerned with the miracle" (*Shulkhan
Arukh* 139). The implication is that not only did women benefit
from the miracle by being freed from oppression, but that they
helped to bring about the deliverance.

It was the devotion and self-sacrifice of women that made
possible the survival of the Jewish People throughout the vicissi-
tudes of its history. There are many legends involving female
heroism that have become connected in popular imagination
with the courage and faith of the *Hanukkah* lights – for example,
the stories of Hannah and her seven sons and Judith and Holofernes. Hannah urged each of her seven sons to submit to torture
and death rather than even appear to be worshipping idols. After
they had all been killed one by one, she went mad and threw
herself down from a roof. This is a story of martyrdom rather
than of miracle, the shadowy dark side of Jewish courage.

The connection with the *Hanukkah* story is most tenuous.
Probably tales of the tortures Jews had to endure for flouting the
antireligious edicts of the Hellenes were embellished in retrospect. Young mothers were supposed to have been hanged with
their babies for insisting on having them circumcised. According
to a medieval *piyyut* (liturgical poem) for *Hanukkah* in the Ham-
burg Miscellany, Antiochus also forbade Jewish women to

purify themselves in the ritual bath (*mikveh*) after their periods, but God supplied them with special secluded bodies of flowing water in which to immerse themselves. Possibly Hannah's seven sons were connected with the seven-branched Temple *Menorah*, or the flames of martyrdom were the reverse side of *Hanukkah* light. The real connection probably lies in the fact that for one *Hanukkah* story of Jewish bravery crowned by victory and rescue, there were thousands of cases of pogrom and massacre in which the heroism of the human spirit had to be its own reward and for which *Hanukkah* light, not *Hanukkah* victory (see Chapter 6, pp. 343–346), had to provide the necessary uplift.

In the story of Judith, heroism and piety win out on the stage of history. Some rabbis were even of the opinion that the "miracle" of *Hanukkah* was really brought about by a woman, a daughter of old Matityahu and that the captivating Judith was a heroic sister, at least in spirit, of Judah Maccabee. As the story goes in the Apocrypha, when her people were besieged by the Syrian general Holofernes, Judith, a rich and beautiful widow, encouraged them not to give in. She slipped behind enemy lines, seduced the general and his soldiers, cut off Holofernes' head while he made a halfhearted attempt to sleep with her, and returned safe to her own people with his head stuffed into her backpack.

Judith is one of the most liberated portraits of a woman in the whole of the Bible and the Apocrypha. Conventionally, as a woman, it might have seemed the only way Judith could conquer her enemy was through seduction. The narrative pays halfhearted lip service to this formula–just as Esther, and many Esthers after her, was able to save her People through her power over the heart of the non-Jewish King. Superficially, it is physical attraction, rather than her more spiritual qualities or those of Mordecai, that saves Israel. Similarly, Deborah is not able to rid herself of her enemy through conventional warfare or through any great "moral" qualities until some woman, Jael, seduces and disarms the enemy general. Although Judith, a blend of both Deborah and Jael, appears to be–at least in part–the heroine as seductress when she resorts to sex to win her objective, the impact of her character is far greater. What shines between the lines of the narrative is Judith's personality that wins her respect, not only among her own People – the Priests and leaders turn to her for advice – but also among the ranks of the enemy who hold her prisoner. The Syrians and Holofernes admire her for her spiritedness and her special gift of prayer. They feel that the fact she has come over to their side makes a difference and might draw God's favor upon them. Recognition of truly great human beings seems to cross international boundaries and hatreds. This, and not who sleeps with whom, or indeed, the execution that Judith feels obliged to carry out to save her nation, is what emerges from the Judith narrative.

The action of Judith makes *Hanukkah* a special holiday for women, who do no housework while the lights are burning and often during the entire eight-day period. In Haifa, Mothers' Day falls on *Hanukkah. Rosh Hodesh,* the first day of the month, is always a minor women's holiday because it is associated with the New Moon with which Jewish women are traditionally identified. *Rosh Hodesh Tevet,* the first day of the month of *Tevet,* which falls during the eight-day *Hanukkah* period, is therefore doubly a women's celebration because it is connected with the Moon through the symbolism of the *Menorah.* The day is also called the "New Moon of the Daughters." On that day, girls receive presents from their parents, and brides receive gifts from their fiancés.

When it comes to the old controversy with the Greeks about the relative excellence of holiness or beauty – the "holiness of beauty" or the "beauty of holiness" – the lights of *Hanukkah* expose the kernel of the conflict. These lights are holy; therefore they are not to be used but are to be regarded purely esthetically, according to the esthetics of holiness.

Jews are known on the whole as a practical people not overly given to contemplate either nature or metaphysics. For example, it is said that Rabbi Gamliel had a cup bearing the figure of the Goddess of Beauty. When his disciples questioned him about this, he replied that as far as he was concerned the cup's utility was paramount and the decoration of Aphrodite merely incidental; therefore it was permissible for him to use the cup. The *Hanukkah* lights are completely the opposite. Their sole reason for existence is their beauty.

THE BEAUTY OF HOLINESS

But what is so beautiful about these lights is that they belong to
a hidden inner realm of holiness that can shine outward into the
darkness of the public domain. Each *Hanukkah* light should be
distinct and far enough from its fellow that their flames should
not merge, thus creating the effect of a "bonfire." It is not required
that the lights of the *Hanukkah* lamp be connected to form one
lamp, but they should be uniformly arranged at the same height.

Since the purpose of the *Menorah* is to create light, an electric
Menorah cannot be used. Fuel or a wick must be present. As the
candles also signify human life in this world, the energy must
visibly diminish as the flame arises. Candles can be used or,
preferably, wicks floating in oil–something that has physical
substance to it that is consumed while the flames burn. For
humans, unlike the Burning Bush of Moshe, *are* consumed by
the spirit within them.

Said the Gerer Rebbe: "We see that a candle, a wick and oil give
forth light through diminishing. Likewise, the man who limits
his material wants to a minimum may give out spiritual light."[19]

R. Hiyya taught: They were to bring olive oil. Neither sesame oil,
nor nut oil, nor radish oil, nor almond oil, only olive oil from your
own olive tree.

R. Abin said: "This may be illustrated by the case of a king
whose legions rebelled against him. One of his own legions,
however, did not rebel against him."

Said the king: "'That legion which did not rebel against me
shall be the source from which shall be appointed commanders,
lieutenants, and military governors.'"

The Holy One, Blessed be He, reasoned in a similar man-
ner: *The olive tree brought light to the world in the days of Noah, as is
proved by the text, And the dove came in to him* (in the Ark) *in the
evening; and lo, in her mouth, an olive leaf was torn off* (Genesis 8:11).

Where did she (the Dove) obtain it?

R. Abba bar Kahana said she brought it from the Mount of

Olives, while R. Levi said she brought it from the branches of the
Land of Israel.

Said R. Berekiah: "The gates of Paradise were opened for
her and from there she brought it." [*Vayikra Rabbah* 31:10]

For the *Hanukkah Menorah,* Raba originally used poppyseed
oil as the longest-lasting, but changed to pure olive oil because it
gave the clearer flame. . . . And after him, olive oil is much the
most preferable (*Shabbat* 23a).

Considerations of beauty come into play not only with
actual lights but also in connection with the lamp. After a clay
lamp has been used once, it is stained with burned oil and looks
ugly. Therefore it was recommended that a beautiful metal lamp
be used instead (*Tur, Orah Hayyim* 873; *Shulkhan Arukh* 139).
Beauty is here assumed to be something shining and highly
polished and full of light, whereas ugliness is associated with
darkness. The Talmud says that whoever takes care to have a
beautiful *Hanukkah* lamp will have children who are scholars and
who will spread the light of Torah in the world. The Rambam
muses over this specially delightful command:

> The command to light the *Hanukkah* lamp is an exceedingly
> precious one, and one should be particularly careful to fulfill it in
> order to make known the miracle and to offer additional praise
> and thanksgiving to God for the wonders which He has wrought
> for us.[20]

Although in past ages the lighting of candles was something
of a luxury, even very poor people were required to light. "Even
he who lives on public charity," continues Maimonides, "should
borrow or sell the shirt from off his back to purchase oil and
lamps and kindle." Even more surprising, where there must be a
choice between buying wine for *Kiddush* on the Sabbath and
candles for *Hanukkah,* candles are given priority. Perhaps this is
because *Kiddush* commemorates the completion of the Creation,
whereas *Hanukkah* marks Divine intervention in human history
in a particular place, a particular time, and with a particular
people, and therefore is more concrete. Thus, in a certain sense

Hanukkah, not even mentioned in Scripture, is a holier festival than *Shabbat!*

On *Shabbat* one may not kindle fire – the candles are within the category of *"Muktsah"* – those objects that cannot be used or touched on *Shabbat.* Kindling the *Menorah* is the one *mitzvah* associated with *Hanukkah.* Although refraining from the creativity permitted on the eve of *Shabbat* – such as kindling the lights – is intrinsically important, the lights possess no special holiness in themselves. True, one may not tamper with the *Shabbat* candles, but that is only because of the holiness of *Shabbat,* not because of the holiness of the candles. Therefore we can use the *Shabbat* candles though we may not touch them, and whatever one is allowed to do on *Shabbat* can be done by their light.

The holiness of *Hanukkah,* however, is inherent in the lights, and one may not read by them or use them to see. Therefore, says the Rambam, because of the concept of *shalom bayyit* – the serene atmosphere necessary to enjoy *Shabbat* – if there is a shortage of funds, we may spend on Sabbath candles rather than on *Hanukkah* lights, because only then will we be able to enjoy *Shabbat* in a suitable atmosphere.

Certain wicks and oil that are not allowed for *Shabbat* candles are allowed on *Hanukkah.* This symbolizes the notion that even the souls that do not ascend on *Shabbat,* do so on *Hanukkah.* The essential "point" of the soul – its potential – remains intact like the small cruse of oil. All that is needed is that it spread throughout the whole human being. Through the person's joy in this point, it can provide warmth for every extremity of the body.

There is a hidden point of light in Israel that is above nature and is on the level of the eighth day. This point can spread to every action and turn everything to 'holiness.' This point – this vial of oil – always remains. The miracle is that it spreads to all seven natural *Sefirot.* The miracle is the emanation that transforms even the first day (for which there was enough oil) into the miracle of the eight. The miracle is that "First Light" that cannot be reached and looked at, and all the Perfection of the Higher World, can spread out to realms very close and intimate and dear to man.

Thirty-six "lights of holiness" are kindled during the eight days of *Hanukkah,* corresponding, it is said, with the thirty-six hours of Primordial Light Adam enjoyed in the Garden of Eden, with the thirty-six tractates of the *Mishnah,* and with the thirty-six hidden righteous men (*Tzaddikim*) whose love keeps the world in existence in every generation.

Including the ninth secular servitor-light, forty-four candles or wicks in all are lighted on each *Menorah* during the eight-day festival. For families with many children in which each child has his or her own *Hanukkiyah,* this is indeed a "Feast of Lights"!

From an esthetic point of view, it is uplifting on a dark winter's evening to pass through a neighborhood where many Jews live and see the sparkling forest of *Menorot* studding the windows. In the Middle Ages, Jews used to row through the canals of the Venice Ghetto, and when they caught sight of the *Hanukkah* lights in the windows or outside the doors of the *palazzi* reaching down into the water, they would burst forth into blessing and song.[21]

These *Menorah*-studded perspectives of *Hanukkah* are reminiscent of the descriptions of the blazing illumination cast by the numerous golden *Menorot* in the Temple during the "Rejoicing at the Place of the Water-Drawing" that was celebrated in Temple days during *Sukkot.* So intense was the blaze, says the Talmud, that "there was not a courtyard in Jerusalem that was not illuminated by (what was taking place within the Temple precincts)" (*Rosh Hashanah* 16a). Indeed, it is possible that the way we celebrate *Hanukkah* today is conditioned by nostalgia for that most joyous Temple celebration, and that in the *Hanukkah* lights we retain traces of that glow.

Another way in which the panorama of *Menorah* lights is reminiscent of rituals practiced during other seasons of the year is found in an exotic variant on the custom of *Tashlikh* as celebrated in some villages in Galicia, Poland. *Tashlikh* usually is the ceremony on the afternoon of the "Day of Judgment" (one of the names for *Rosh Hashanah*) when Jews make an expedition to a fresh flowing body of water to symbolically "throw away their sins." In the village of Bolehov the *Hasidim* used to form a procession and go to the water with lighted tapers in their hands.

At sunset they would kindle small tufts of straw and cast them onto the water. In the gathering darkness, these lighted floats drifted on the water, creating a magnificent spectacle, graphically illustrating the exorcism of sin. But this ceremony with the detached floating lights spells out something else. The person is a mere catalyst, a pool for these motes of spiritual energy to float in and out of, and the whole riverside scene is a mirror of spiritual life both inside the individual and in his or her interpersonal relationships.

There are other vistas, not directly connected with lights, that move us in the same way. In Israel, the varying levels of balconies and rooftops each bristling with leafy, fruit-laden rustic booths touches off emotion not dissimilar to that of skeins of *Menorah* lights.

During *Sukkot,* the sight of myriads of *lulavim* and *etrogim* waving in the wind like a living harvest presents a similar spectacle. The sight of a large community of people waving the Four Species (palm branch, citron, willows, and myrtles) resembles nothing less than a living field of grain swaying in the wind of a religious emotion. Although these religious "people-scapes" look best in Israel in their natural setting, they are powerful wherever they take place. The secret to their magic is in the power of individuals to mirror and affect one another within the larger perspective of "Israel" and mankind.

Jung analyzes similar images of dazzling vistas consisting of individual luminous quanta, scintillations, or points of light composing a *pointilliste* or impressionist panorama:

> [V]ast perspectives (such as the star-strewn heavens, as stars reflected in dark water, as nuggets of gold or golden sand scattered in black earth, as regatta at night, with lanterns on the dark surface of the sea.[22]

These atoms of light are a visual representation, Jung says, of the collective unconscious. No wonder they take our breath away! At the same time they portray the psyche as a multiple consciousness, a multitude of luminous particles that in their sum constitute the Self. But by plumbing deeper than the ego, they also go far beyond. By revealing the interrelationships between individuals by way of the basic few archetypes of man, they herald a heightened form of perception and a transformation of consciousness.

Although not articulated in words, this is the actual impact upon us of the *Hanukkah* lights, when far and wide we see the individual "points" of light imitating the starry sky. Then we can remember God's blessing to Abraham – "Thus shall be your seed!" (Genesis 15:5) – and see the Promise realized in these lights. For each one is the spark of a soul, and all together constitute a living entity that is the Image of God Himself.

Our relationship to *Knesset Yisrael* and Abraham's Promise is far more than merely that of children by blood relationship. All souls mirror and refract one another, leading Cordovero to say:

> In everyone there is something of his fellow man. Therefore, whoever sins, injures not only himself but also that part of himself which belongs to another.[23]

And this is the real reason for the commandment, "Love your neighbor as yourself" (Leviticus 19:18). For, says Cordovero, "the other really is he himself."[24]

The flavor of the different temperaments of Hillel and Shammai is distilled by the famous story of the convert who presented himself before Shammai and asked him to teach him the whole Torah while he was standing on one foot.[25] Shammai drove him away impatiently with his ruler. When another convert made the same request of Hillel, the latter replied with a variation upon the theme "Love your neighbor as yourself": "What you don't like, don't do to your fellow man. That is the whole Torah. All the rest is explanation. Go and study!"

When these two converts met, they discussed their experiences with each other, coming to the conclusion that "Shammai's hot temper would have driven us out of the world (to come), but Hillel's patience has brought us under the Wings of the *Shekhinah*" (*Shabbat* 31a). Hillel used to make statements such as "Be a lover of peace and pursue peace, loving your fellow-creatures, and drawing them nearer to the Torah" (*Avot* 1:12). And his whole character was a living example of his words.

It is their different relationships to their fellow man and ultimately to themselves that color even the differences between Hillel and Shammai about how many lights should be kindled each night of *Hanukkah*. Shammai said that on the first night of the Festival, eight candles should be lighted, on the second night, seven, and so on, corresponding to the number of heifers that used to be sacrificed in the Temple. But Hillel, known for his reaffirmation of the commandment to love one's neighbor, wanted to start modestly and "grow in holiness," ascending from level to level, going from one light on the first night to eight on the eighth.

The accepted practice is to follow *Bet Hillel* because it is better to "increase in sanctity" and bring more joy and light into the world.

However, Hillel and Shammai's argument as to whether the number of the lights on the *Menorah* should increase or decrease could be taken as symbolic of a deeper rift on theological and cosmological issues.

THE *MENORAH* OF THE *SEFIROT*

What happens if we shift our sights to the vertical plane, to the way God lights His *Menorah,* the *Menorah* of the *Sefirot*. [26] Here the flame travels from top to bottom, traversing not eight, but ten levels. Why ten, and not seven as in the Temple or eight as on *Hanukkah*? Because the seven *Sefirot* are those that impinge on the world of nature that we know, the eight when the Jew reaches beyond himself and strikes upon transcendence. But when God kindles, or emanates, He reaches down from the additional three abstract and transcendent *Sefirot*. In the case of the emanation of the *Sefirot,* says Rav Ashlag, "The illumination of a lower level must pass through the level above it. . . . The light never moves from the upper level but a kind of branch goes out to the lower level, just as one lights a candle with another candle the first candle losing nothing in the process."[27]

The cosmological imagery of the *Sefirot* conjured up on a vertical axis where Divine light and life are born from *Sefirah* to *Sefirah* without suffering any diminution in their origin is very similar to the picture projected horizontally and on the plane of history by the Men of the Great Assembly's practice of communicating the times of the New Moon to the communities of the Dispersion. This is similar to the relay torch race of the Greeks, where a single torch was transferred from runner to runner, except that when it comes to spiritual illumination the Light of Eternity remains inviolate while sending out reflections and branches at every side.

In the same way, light transfers from level to level. The descent of holiness, descent of the light, is only a growing process taking nothing away from the Divine Light. The first night is one, the second night is two, and so on.

Rav Ashlag's picture of the capacity of light to emanate and spread as an image for creation derives via the *Zohar* from *Midrash*. There, Moshe's capacity to ignite others with Prophecy, without losing anything himself, in the spirit rather of cooperation than competition, is compared to a candle that kindles others (*Bamidbar Rabbah* 13:20).

And what of the commandment God gave to Israel to light an earthly *Menorah* to redeem the scattered sparks of holiness dispersed throughout the world and return them to the Giver of Light, not on a horizontal plane but on a vertical plane – that is, by way of (spiritual) ascent? This is consistent with Hillel, not Shammai. Whereas Shammai's perfectionism would reduce the whole world of diversity to the One Light of the *Ein-Sof* and blot out the *Sefirot* and the *Sefirot* in the *Sefirot,* Hillel's way is to see the distinct individuality of each flame while binding all in a single *Menorah.*

The imagery of lamps falls into two categories, that of the tree or the standing candelabrum in the Temple – a whole piping system of Divine bounty imitative of the *Sefirot* – and the single hollow womblike "female" receptacle.

In the Temple, the "miracle" of *Hanukkah* began with the discovery of one small sealed cruse of virgin olive oil preserved throughout the period when the Temple had lain defiled by the

Syrian occupier. The image of the cruse has its antecedents in the containers that pour out infinite streams of oil for the poor widow in the time of Elisha, in the little jugs for which Jacob returned alone across the frightening River Jabok in his encounter with the Adversarial Angel, and in the actual form of the common oil lamp prevalent in the Middle East and the Mediterranean lands throughout most of human history.

Visually, the image presented here is of a small individual "point" fanning out into a dazzling crown of many shimmering lights. "The primal point," says the *Zohar*, "is the innermost light of a translucency, tenuity, and purity passing comprehension" (*Zohar* I:5,19b). This point or spark is the human soul which, when it is touched and kindled in the right way, can fan into a flame. It is in this way that the physical form of the *Menorah* expresses the whole flow of a spiritual aspiration.

Whereas in the more common form of *Menorah* in use today, each receptacle is placed on a horizontal plane, in some of the standing lamp *Menorot* the effect is of a vertical "Tree of Lights," as may be imagined in the *Sefirot*.

There is one flame and there is a mirage of reflected flames spiraling down and up. And this leap from the one to the many recurs in all imagery that has to do with light. For to kindle one flame (or have one child) is potentially to kindle many, for there is no such thing as keeping light within bounds. On the one hand there is the small inviolate womblike container of oil; on the other there is the bonfire of all eight lights of the *Menorah*. On the one hand there is the precious individual point of light in each human being; on the other there is the fully expanded crown (horizontal) or ladder (vertical) of the cumulative impact of holiness.

Even the form the *Hanukkah* lamp has taken over the ages and various halakhic recommendations support Hillel's view. For more than a thousand years the *Hanukkah* lamp consisted either of a single "candle dish"—the traditional womb-shaped oil lamp—or of an array of such all set out on a level. And the stipulation was that each should present a single distinct unit and not be lost in a shimmering blur of light.

Similarly, an image of what a *Sefirah* would have looked like is described in the *Idra Zutta* : "like a candle whose light sparkles and spreads to all sides and corners – and from afar there seem to be many lights but – on closer inspection there is only one candle" (*Zohar* III:288a).

Mystically, this is to follow the pathway of the *Sefirot*. In the emanation of the *Sefirot,* as we have seen, there is no death. When the Higher Light travels down the staircase of the *Sefirot* to meet the world of substance, it does not move from its highest point in *Ein-Sof.* It merely triggers off or kindles a candle on the branch or *Sefirah* adjoining it while never moving out of its place. Similarly, when Jews kindle the *Menorah,* they light a real Lamp with oil garnered from real olives, at the same time touching off reverberation after reverberation until the light reaches its Source. The earthly *Menorah* is not reabsorbed into the Divine Nothingness, and what happens on a "vertical" or spiritual plane is also what takes places "horizontally" and in our world. No level "dies" at the expense of another. The act of kindling possesses esoteric significance and is also a physical act that exists in the mundane world – we kindle oil pressed from real olives that grow on a real tree, in real soil.

And that is why Hillel encouraged the one light to blossom out into the eight. While Shammai ascends from the world of the Many to their Source in the One, Hillel recognizes the precious individuality in each tiny lamp in addition to showing how each contributes to the blazing vistas of a cosmic *Menorah.*

A PLACE OF GREAT LIGHT

There is a mandate in the Jerusalem Talmud (*Pesahim*) that "a synagogue should have great light." This recommendation stems from the verse: "I have not spoken in secret, in a place of darkness" (Isaiah 45:19). In the *Zohar* this has been interpreted to mean that the synagogue, like the Temple and the Tent tabernacle, is a microcosm and replica of the order of Creation. Just as the creation of light was God's first act, so "a synagogue should have great light" (*Zohar* III:59b–60a).

Among the few stipulations for synagogue architecture is the necessity for windows. The famous eleventh-century biblical commentator Rashi gives an illuminating explanation for the window requirement. Windows, Rashi claims, allow the supplicant to see the sky and thus inspire him with a feeling of celestial elevation in his prayers.

If possible, any obstruction to the view from the windows was to be demolished and it was recommended that the site of the synagogue be the highest point in town or by a flowing body of water. This would provide worshippers with unrestricted vistas, instilling in them, even in a limited space, the feeling of oceanic awe that Freud speaks of as the very quintessence of religious consciousness.

"A synagogue should be a place of great beauty ... wonderfully decorated, for it is an earthly copy of a heavenly prototype." (*Zohar* II:186). In the Middle Ages, Eliakim ben Joseph of Mainz summarily ordered the removal from his synagogue of the stained glass windows containing figures of lions and snakes. His younger contemporary, Ephraim ben Isaac of Regensburg, permitted murals with animal and bird motifs. Isaac ben Moses of Vienna recalled having seen paintings of birds and trees in his boyhood in the synagogue of Meissen. He felt these paintings should not be allowed because they provided a distraction during prayer and study. Rabbi Meir of Rothenburg disapproved of illuminated Hebrew books for the same reason.

THE RADIANCE OF *SHABBAT*

There is no mention of a specific commandment to kindle Sabbath lights in the Torah, whereas one of the main types of work specifically forbidden on *Shabbat* is the making of fire, symbol of all human creativity.

The Hebrew for this commandment *lo sivaeru aish,* was the touchstone of a controversy between the Pharisees – the Rabbis, who were more representative of the People, and the Sadducees – the Priests, who were completely wrapped up in hierarchy. The Sadducees took the Bible literally and translated the Hebrew: "You shall not have a fire burning in your homes over the *Shabbat*." Consequently, not only did they not kindle lamps on *Shabbat,* they made sure every fire and light was extinguished.

During God's "Day of Delight," they sat in the dark and froze. The Pharisees, however, who believed God's Written Word had to be interpreted in the light of a living Oral Tradition, took the Hebrew to mean that, though a fire cannot be kindled on the Sabbath itself, all necessary preparations ought to be made beforehand to have light and warmth throughout that Day.

Even the negative commandments stem from a positive essence. *Shabbat* is not mere cessation of labor, but a connection with labor's ultimate goal. It marks the culmination of the labors of the week, setting a seal of perfection on the Creation. Therefore the negative commandment not to light a fire on *Shabbat* itself – that is, not to continue with Creation – is not a denigration of fire but its consummation. The light and radiance of *Shabbat* are the goal of all the efforts of the six days of work. This view crystallized into the law that both *Shabbat* and the Festivals be ushered in with the kindling of lights.[28]

The rabbinical command to kindle the Sabbath lights in particular was probably a direct rebuttal of the killjoy, overly literalistic Sadducean interpretation of the law. Since the Sadducees were the priests, it is understandable that they should have wanted a monopoly on their privilege of kindling lights and transmitting spiritual benefits.

Therefore the candles lit before *Shabbat* take on additional significance. Preparation for *Shabbat* that ensures the necessary conditions of comfort is almost more important than observance of *Shabbat* itself, for only with the right preparation will *Shabbat* be celebrated as the delight it was intended to be.

The work of the Six Days is an integral part of *Shabbat* itself when carried out in this spirit of anticipation. For *Shabbat* is depicted as an eagerly expected royal guest:

> It is incumbent on every man to be very very zealous in making the Sabbath day preparations, to be prompt and diligent as a man who has heard that the Queen is coming to stay at his house, or that the bride and her entire entourage are coming to his home. What would a man do in this situation? He would rejoice greatly, and exclaim: What a great honor they do me by their coming to dwell under my roof! He would say to his servants: Arrange the

house; clean and tidy it; prepare the beds in honor of the arrival and I will go and buy the bread, meat, fish – whatever I can obtain in their honor. A man in this situation will busy himself for the preparation of the Sabbath food, even though he has a thousand servants.

Now, who is greater than the Sabbath which is both bride and Queen and who is called delightful; a thousand times more so should the master of the house himself be busy in making the preparations even though he have a hundred servants.[29]

Before *Shabbat* the house is thoroughly cleaned; people bathe and put on festive clothing. Some even purify themselves in the ritual bath in honor of the Day. A certain Rabbi Hamnuna was alleged to have been able to see angels ascending and descending on emerging from his ablutions.

The ingredients going to make up the special flavor of this Day are both physical and spiritual. Holiness is nothing rarefied. The command to "sanctify" this Day has been explained in very sensuous terms: "Sanctify the *Shabbat* with choice meals; with beautiful clothes; delight your soul with pleasure and I will reward you for this very pleasure" (*Devarim Rabbah* 3:1).

Poor people went to great lengths, even *fasting* on other days of the week to afford to buy some extra delicacy for *Shabbat,* and it was commonly believed that though everyone's annual budget was determined in Heaven from *Rosh Hashanah,* expenses for food for *Shabbat* and festivals and for the education of children went on an extra account and were free. "If he spends less on these, he is given less and if he spends more he is given more" (*Bezah* 2:16a).

The first allusion to a Sabbath lamp, which also presents us with a description of the spirit of *Shabbat* in caricature, goes back to the Roman satirist Persius (34–62 C.E.).

But when Herod's day (*Shabbat*) is come, and the lamps carrying violets are put in the greasy window and emit their unctuous clouds of smoke; and when the tail of a tuna fish floats carted around in a red dish, and a white jar is bulging with wine, you move your lips in silence and turn pale at this Sabbath of the circumcised.[30]

The earliest form of *Shabbat* light was the Mediterranean oil lamp, a clay saucer or bowl with a fold or lip in which the wick floated in oil. A more sophisticated development was the enclosed version with two lips, one for the wick and one for the oil. The only difference between this Sabbath lamp and others found in the Mediterranean region was in the Jewish motifs that sometimes decorated it. With time, these lamps became more elaborate. The folds changed into a spout; the spouts proliferated as the number of wicks increased. Sometimes this series of spouts were arranged in a row like a *Hanukkah* lamp; others formed a circular pattern. The central saucer, which was made of metal, was kept covered to prevent the oil from spilling. All week this lamp would hang close to the ceiling. For *Shabbat* it would be lowered.

These lamps varied according to their place of origin. The *Judenstern,* an example popular in Germany, was star-shaped to symbolize the messianic hope felt on this day of the Messiah, the day of rest foreshadowing the peace of the messianic era.

Oil lamps were in vogue until the eighteenth century or even later; candlesticks appeared before the seventeenth century. Sometimes candlesticks and hanging Sabbath lamps were lighted together, side by side.

By the second century C.E. it was an established practice for women to light *Shabbat* candles on behalf of the household. The lights should last at least for the duration of the Sabbath meal.

The woman covers her eyes as she lights the candles and says the blessing. Holding her hands outstretched over the flames to form a kind of barrier, she then draws them in to cover her face to avoid looking directly at the *Shekhinah* whose radiance she is drawing toward her. After the candles are lighted, everything is subtly different, the atmosphere deepened and transformed.

An instantaneous connection is established between the woman saying the blessing over the lights and the blessing of the priests in the Temple and the synagogue, traditionally a male prerogative. While the priests bless the congregation, the worshippers customarily avert their eyes from the radiance of the *Shekhinah.*

While the lights the woman has kindled are her "children," she focuses for a moment on the Source of light. At the moment of the physical kindling of the lights, she does not see them. Her concentration is elsewhere. As on *Hanukkah,* the kindling of the lights signals a pause that is applicable especially to a woman, allowing her to retreat deep into herself in imitation of God's initial act of *Tzimtzum.* Only through these few personal moments of meditation can she draw down upon herself and her family the invisible energies of the Primordial Light of *Ein-Sof.* On Friday night the Jewish home itself becomes a shrine, and the mother a channel for intercession and blessing.

In fact, on Shabbat, the mistress of the house is herself a Queen. She plays the part of the Earthly Female to the Higher Female represented by the *Shekhinah.* And as *Shabbat* is a foretaste of Heaven in this world, drawing down the *Shekhinah* Herself as a royal visitor, the separate roles on this one day tend to overlap.

But the explanations the Rabbis give for why woman was given "the commandment to kindle" are not all so complimentary. She was given this command, they say, because "man is the Lamp of the Holy One."

> As it is said: *The soul of man is the lamp of the Lord* (Proverbs 20:27). And Eve came on the scene and put out the light. Said the Holy One: "Let her have the commandment to kindle to give her the chance to reillumine the light she put out (by tempting him to disobey God and eat the forbidden fruit) (so she can bring back sparkle into the world again). That is why women are commanded to kindle the Sabbath candles" (*Bereishit Rabbah* 18:8).
>
> Said the Holy One: "If you are careful about lighting the Sabbath candles, I will give you (true) light as it is said: 'And God will be your everlasting light.' " [*Midrash Tanhuma Noah*]

The *Zohar* implies that there is a deeper reason why woman should be entrusted with the light of *Shabbat* than simply her duty to rectify the harm caused by her ancestress. The home that she governs resembles the "Tabernacle of Peace," and she is the personification of that sacred space.

> This tabernacle of peace is the Mistress of the world and the souls which are the celestial lamp abide [in Her]. Hence it is right for the woman of the house to kindle the light, because thereby she is attaching herself to her rightful place and performing her rightful function. [*Zohar* I:48b]

The mistress of the house is strengthening her family and the peace of her home by bringing out her connection with the *Shekhinah* through the kindling of the *Shabbat* candles.

We have seen that it is precisely out of the darkness and the urge for individuation that is part of the artistic "mothering" urge in God that man was created. Eve's duty to kindle lights may not be so much to atone for any guilt on her part; on the contrary, she may have introduced darkness to the world to give those lights the chance to shine. Eve had children only after she and Adam had lost Paradise. She might have found the loss of Paradise well worth such a gain!

Women are given the privilege of being the kindlers of light because they already are the life-bearers, and the gift of light is identical with the gift of life.

Though women are exempt from many of the commandments, according to rabbinic law there are three commandments for which they are specifically responsible – separation from their husbands during the menstrual cycle, separation and dedication of part of the dough when baking bread, and the kindling of the Sabbath candles.

While traditionally women stay with the lights at home, the men finish the Friday evening prayer in the synagogue by learning the passage in the *Mishnah* dealing with the kinds of substances permitted to be used in burning the Sabbath candles.

> With what may we light the Sabbath lamp, and with what may we not light it? We may not light it with a wick made of cedar-bast, uncombed flax, floss-silk, or with a wick of willow-

fiber, desert weed, or duck-weed (since such wicks burn unevenly). It may not be lighted with pitch, liquid wax, castor oil, nor with oil that must be burned and destroyed, nor with tail fat, nor with tallow. Hanum of Media says: We may use melted tallow. The sages, however, say: It is immaterial whether or not it is melted, it must not be used for the Sabbath lamp.

Oil that must be burned and destroyed may not be used for lighting on a festival. R. Ishmael says: One must not, out of respect for the Sabbath, use (ill-smelling) resin. The sages allow all kinds of oil: sesame oil, nut oil, radish oil, fish oil, gourd oil, resin, and naphtha. R. Tarfon says: We may use only olive oil for lighting the Sabbath lamp.

Nothing that comes from a tree may be used as a wick for the Sabbath lamp except flax. A wick made of a piece of cloth which one has twisted but not yet singed–R. Eliezer says that (it is still considered a part of a garment and) it is subject to the law of uncleanness; it must not be used for lighting the Sabbath lamp. But R. Akiva declares that it may.

If one puts out a light on the Sabbath because he is afraid of heathens, robbers, or an evil spirit, or for the sake of enabling a sick person to sleep, he is not guilty of breaking the Sabbath; but if he did it to spare the lamp or the oil or the wick, he is guilty.

One is required to say three things in his house on the eve of the Sabbath just before it gets dark: "Have you separated a tenth part of the food we are to eat on the Sabbath? Have you prepared the boundaries of the Sabbath? Light the lamp." [*Mishnah Shabbat* Chap. 2, pars. 1, 2, 3, 5, 7]

This is said by the men after the Friday night service before they return home to be greeted by the light of the *Shabbat* candles. It can be taken as an example of the theoretical learning of Torah matched by the actual performance of the "commandment to kindle" carried out by the women.

A passage that follows almost immediately reads, "And all your children shall be versed in God's wisdom, and great shall be the peace of your children" (Isaiah 54:13). Do not read "children" but "builders." For great will be the peace of those who love (and spread) the light of Torah (*Berakhot* 64a).

While light and blessing are pouring forth in the home, in the synagogue the men are learning about it—what is being built and strengthened in both cases are the outer walls and the inner citadel of a Sanctuary. A direct connection is established here between meticulousness with the lights and having children versed in Torah. On *Hanukkah* the Talmud also explicitly promises that the reward for making an effort to have a beautiful *Menorah* is wise and beautiful children. The lights really seem to represent the children; they are the stones and building blocks in the construction of a Sanctuary fit for the *Shekhinah* to dwell in.

TWO CANDLES AND AN ADDITIONAL SOUL

Why are two candles lit on *Shabbat?* There is a belief that then we are blessed with a *neshamah yeterah,* an additional soul or extra spirituality. When we prepare for *Shabbat,* we make ourselves ready to receive the radiance of "First Light" in its purest form—that is, we make ourselves a vessel for it. What is that vessel but an extra soul so that we do not explode into fragments from overflow of the Divine Light.

One interpretation given for God's "resting" on *Shabbat* is that then He gave the world a soul. This marked a radical change in the quality of time, bringing about a corresponding change in people. R. Judah Loew ben Bezalel of Prague (the Maharal, 1592–1609) earned the name of The Tall Rabbi because he became a head taller on *Shabbat.* The rumor arose about Rabbi Hayyim of Chernowitz that a rose blossomed on his cheek during the Sabbath. The *Midrash* comments on the words of the Creation Story in the Biblical text, "And God blessed the seventh day. . . .": "He blessed it with the light of a man's face. The light of a man's face during the week is not the same as it is on *Shabbat*"—presumably because the additional *neshamah* brings with it an extra glow.

One candle for *Shabbat* is sufficient, but two carry the appropriate symbolic balance of "observance" (active)—the masculine light – and "remembrance" (passive) – the feminine light. In addition to these "father" and "mother" candles, many families add a candle for each child.

The duplication of loaves and candles is said to stand for the masculine and feminine principles, or the positive and negative way in which the commandment to observe *Shabbat* is phrased on the two occasions in which it is mentioned in the Bible – "Keep the Sabbath" and "Remember" it. Another reason is the double ration of manna that the Israelites gathered on Fridays, the additional portion being for *Shabbat*. [31]

The reason for having two candles addresses the very purpose of *Shabbat* – to mark the climax of the complex interactions that produce Creation. God is no longer one in His world, but has projected a secondary force (the female), which results in a third and a fourth and an accelerated process of differentiation and family building. But on *Shabbat* all these forces come together in harmony. The two candles, like the portions of manna eaten by the Children of Israel in the desert, like the two loaves of bread and the two bouquets of myrtles of the old man encountered by Rabbi Shimon bar Yohai on Friday evening, stand for the two sexes and all the possibilities for growth and further creativity entailed by their interaction.

The goal of Creation, according to the Kabbalists, is to reunite the Holy One with His *Shekhinah,* who plunged deep in the abyss of matter and exile in order to be with her children. The two candles of *Shabbat* represent this desired reunion. On Friday night the feminine aspect of *Shabbat* is predominant. The theme is the Creation of the world, fertility, and giving birth – in which the whole Universe is the vessel to receive God's light, one colossal *Menorah*. The imagery of the Friday night liturgy is feminine: "And He rested on it (on her)." Of the two loaves, representing the two sexes, the lower (female) loaf is cut.

On *Shabbat* morning the mood changes and becomes masculine. The identical phrase is used, but with a change of gender: "And He rested on it (on him)." During the meal, the top (masculine) loaf is cut.

With the words "You are One and Your Name is One," the natural poles of light and dark, masculine and feminine, come together during *Shabbat* afternoon. Toward twilight, when we eat the third meal, again there is a deepening and a softening of the atmosphere as the feminine returns. The expression then used is: "And He rested on them" (a blending of the masculine and the feminine). So united are the two that there is only one loaf, and for the *Havdalah* one candle is used, composed of two plaited wicks, or two candles held together as one.

Shabbat brings the masculine and the feminine together again in the intertwinings of the *Havdalah* candle. Splitting and fusion are very much akin. As in a wedding,[32] the separation is only a precondition for union, not only between two individuals but also between the separate parts of a single psyche. By the close of *Shabbat,* the human being is made whole.

TAKING LEAVE FROM A QUEEN

The feeling at the departure of *Shabbat* resembles the terror experienced by Adam at the loss of "First Light." During *Shabbat* the *neshamah yeterah* has served as our contact with the transcendental world; with the departure of the *Shabbat* Queen we are plunged back into the sphere of darkness and separation. What do we do to strengthen ourselves against imminent deprivation but take light and fragrance and wine and all the symbols of *Shabbat* for the *Havdalah* ceremony, and comfort ourselves with "songs of the night." Just as *Shabbat* enters with light, with wine, and used to enter with spices, so it departs, like the procession for a Bride or a Queen.

The ceremony of *Havdalah* makes the distinction between light and dark, holy and secular, Israel and the Nations, *Shabbat* and the other six days of the week. Either two candles with flames touching or a single candle, composed of thin plaited strands of wax was used to symbolize separation and union at the same time. Some of the wine is expressly dripped onto the plate under the goblet and set afire with the candle. In the smoke of the burning liquor the angels can depart without being observed. Fingertips are dipped into the bowl and then passed over the eyes, an allusion to Psalm 19:9 in which God's commandments are described as "enlightening the eyes."

There is a custom of cupping the hands around the flame and gazing at the fingernails, in keeping with the belief that in Eden, Adam and Eve were completely covered with a membrane akin to this hornlike substance that emitted rays of Primordial Light. Also, the reflection of the light on the fingernails causes a shadow to appear on the palm of the hand, thus indicating the distinction "between light and darkness," which is what the *Havdalah* ceremony is about.

The *Havdalah* candle must consist of at least two strands because the blessing says: "Blessed are You Who creates the lights of the fire"—in the plural to signify the teeming multiplicity of creation.

On the first day, God created sufficient light[33] to illuminate the world until the first sunset. Then it grew dark and Adam became afraid. God then gave him two sticks with which to create fire, the plaited wicks of the *Havdalah* candle.

Because it is forbidden to kindle fire on *Shabbat,* the kindling of the *Havdalah* candle is the first labor of the week. According to some authorities it is all right to say *Havdalah* over the fire on the hearth or the stove or even a glowing coal as long as the source emits sparks. Even nonfrosted incandescent electric light would be all right, as long as the glowing filaments remain visible. Fluorescent lights, however, are not permissible.

Different explanations have been given as to why spices play a role together with the lights during the *Havdalah* ceremony. Spices are part of the armory of love, and fragrance heralds both the arrival and the departure of the beloved.

Smell has been regarded as the highest and most spiritual of the senses. In fact, the Hebrew words for the various types of soul are the same as the words for "breath." The *Shulkhan Arukh* remarks: "Let everything that has breath praise the Lord. And what is it that only the soul and not the body derives pleasure from—it is the odor of sweet fragrance."[34]

As is demonstrated by the "Soul Light" in memory of the dead, there is a very deep identification between "light" and the soul. So much so, that God's first Creation of light or a "lamp of darkness" has been interpreted as His Creation of a reservoir of souls from which all individual souls are taken.

The passage "From what can we kindle the wick," said on Friday night, corresponds to the description of the bouquet of incense offered in the Sanctuary described in an identical part of the service for *Shabbat* morning. And from the story of Rabbi Shimon bar Yohai[35] it seems likely that an early way in which it was customary to greet the *Shabbat* was with two bouquets of myrtle, rather than, or possibly together with, the two *Shabbat* candles; also representing the union of masculine and feminine. This practice of greeting the *Shabbat* Bride with myrtles (escorts of the lovers) is now defunct, but until the sixteenth century myrtles were intermingled with the spices used in honor of the Queen's Departure (*Havdalah*), thus giving the spice box its name, *hadas* (myrtle). The following is the translation of the words said over the *Havdalah* candle:

> Behold the Lord of my salvation, I will be confident and not be afraid. For the Lord is my strength and my song. O Lord, be my salvation. Joyously will you draw waters from the springs of salvation. Salvation is the Lord's. May Your blessing be upon Your People. The Lord of hosts is with us, the God of Jacob is our Stronghold. Lord of hosts, happy is the man who trusts in You. O Lord save us. May the King answer us when we call. For the Jews there was light and joy, gladness and glamor. May we have all of that! I will raise the cup of salvation and call on the name of the Lord.[36]

> Blessed art Thou O Lord our God, King of the universe, who creates the brands of the fire. Blessed are You O Lord our God, King of the universe, who divides between the holy and the secular, between light and darkness, between Israel and the Nations, between the seventh day and the six working days of the week. Blessed are You O Lord our God, who divides between holy and mundane.

> He who makes a distinction between the holy and the weekday, may He forgive our sins. Our seed and our silver may He multiply like sand on the shore or like stars in the sky. The day turns like the shadow of a palm tree. I shall call out to God

who watches over me. Says the watchman: "The morning is come and also the night."

Your integrity is like Mount Tabor. O pardon and pass over my transgressions. For who will remember what happened yesterday, or during the night watch! In the twilight, the evening of the day, and in the deep blackness of the night, I call upon You, O Lord, save me. Reveal to me the path of life; deliver me from poverty, in the period of twilight, between day and night [I cry out] O cleanse the impurity of my deeds, so that those who provoke me may not [be able to] say: "Where then is the God who created you, He who inspires you to sing songs in the night?" O God, we are like clay in Your Hand. Be as tolerant for severe offense as for the slightest lapse. Each day pours forth speech to the next day, and each night pours forth praise to the next.

He who makes a distinction between the holy and the weekday, may He forgive our sins. Our seed and our silver may He multiply like sand on the shore or like stars in the sky.[37]

The question has been raised: "Is it permitted to extinguish the *Shabbat* lights so that a sick person may get some rest?" (*Shabbat* 30a–b).

THE LAMP OF THE LIVING

The lives of David and Solomon constitute a discussion about the comparative values of the living and the dead. In the Psalms, King David said: "The dead do not praise God" (Psalm 115:17). And his son Shlomo agreed with him: "A live dog has a better life of it than a dead lion" (Ecclesiastes 9:4). When did Solomon say this? After his father died on *Shabbat,* and Solomon was able to break *Shabbat* to feed the dogs in his father's house, but could only move his father's body if he placed a loaf of bread or a small child on top of it, which would give the body some value to the living.

Life is better than death because the living can engage in the learning of Torah and performance of *mitzvot.* But one cannot desecrate the *Shabbat* to bury even the greatest person. One may, however, desecrate *Shabbat* to feed a dog.

While a patient is alive, one must do everything to prolong life even for an hour. And health should not be jeopardized to observe *Shabbat*. But this is true only as long as increased "life" is the result and not to honor the dead. That is why the rabbis say: "Better an hour of repentance and good deeds in this world than the entire life of the world to come. Therefore a man should live by the Torah and do good deeds while he still can, for once dead he will stop being so preoccupied and the Holy One will derive no praise through him" (*Avot* 4:22).

Nevertheless, Solomon said: "Let me praise the dead, for they are well out of it" (Ecclesiastes 4:2). Why did he say this? When Moshe prayed for the People of Israel in the Wilderness, he received no response, but when he entreated God to "remember Abraham, Yitzhak, and Yisrael, Your servants" (Exodus 32:13), he was immediately answered. The merit of the dead counts more than that of the living, for it is fixed in everlastingness, whereas one of the great and terrible things about living is that in a moment one can lose it all. Thus Solomon spoke only the truth when he said: "Let me praise the dead, for they are well out of it" (Ecclesiastes 4:2).

If a king of flesh and blood makes a decree, one may doubt whether it will be enforced. It might be enforced while he is alive and not after his death. But with Torah, all decrees are kept. So Solomon spoke correctly when he said: "The dead are well out of it."

David said to the Holy One: "Master of the world. Forgive me for my sin with Bathsheva."

God replied to him: "You are forgiven."

David rejoined: "Make me a sign in my lifetime."

God said to him: "In your lifetime I will not make your forgiveness public, only in the lifetime of Solomon your son."

But God said to David: "More do I enjoy one day when you sit learning Torah to the thousands of sin offerings your son Solomon will offer to Me in the future on the altar."

When Solomon built the Temple he tried to introduce the Holy Ark inside. The gates locked together (and refused to open).

Solomon said the twenty-four songs of praise and there was no response. Then he said: "Lift up your heads, O you gates, and may the eternal gates be lifted up, so that the King of Glory may enter" (Psalm 24:7). The Gates raced after him to swallow him up for presuming to use the expression "King of Glory" as a description for himself.

The Gates asked: "Who do you mean by the King of Glory?"

The King's men quickly replied: "The Lord, strong in might."

They turned away and answered: "Lift up your heads, O you Gates, and be lifted up O you hidden entranceways, so that the King of Glory may come in. Who is he, the King of Glory? The Lord of Hosts, He is the King of Glory" (Psalm 9:10). Still Solomon received no response.

But as soon as he appealed, "O Lord God, do not turn away the face of Your anointed, remember the loving actions of David Your servant" (Chronicles 6:42), he received an immediate answer.[38]

The potential holiness of the living, the possibility of rising to great heights, supersedes even *Shabbat* and the "heights" themselves. Certainly a great man who has lived a good life and passed on – to Heaven, the Next World, the World that is wholly *Shabbat* – is not as "high" in this scheme of values as even the lowest of the living, whose possibility of achieving greatness is limitless, whereas even the greatest *Tzaddik* is limited to only what he achieved in his lifetime.

When it comes to prayer, however, when one has to rely on one's merits, the achievements of even the greatest of the living are of no avail as there is no guarantee while a man is alive that he might not at the last moment sink to the bottom-most depths. On the other hand, the merits of the dead are absolutely reliable and efficacious because their value is fixed. But the flickering, pulsing lamp of *Shabbat* may not be extinguished for their sake.

THE CANDLE AND THE FLAME

It says in the Psalms: "The Commandment is a candle while the Torah is Light itself" (Proverbs 6:23). The relation of a "candle" to light is conveyed in the saying in the Talmud "What good is a candle in broad daylight!" (*Hullin* 60b). One might have thought that light itself (a torch) might be superior to any particular manifestation of the light (a candle). Yet on different occasions different means for lighting are appropriate.

Basing himself on sources in the Talmud,[39] the Maharal (R. Loew ben Bezalel) sees the torch as the light most appropriate for *Havdalah,* whereas he recommends the use of a "lamp" to bring *Shabbat* in. What is the difference between these two and why are different kinds of light supposed to be used on different occasions?[40]

It appears the Maharal selected candlelight for *Shabbat* for esthetic reasons. There is a softness, a shadowiness and a depth in the atmosphere induced by candlelight, whereas the glare of a torch can be intimidating.

But what is the Maharal's physical definition of a candle? He defines a *ner* (the root of the word *menorah*) as a dish containing a wick and oil, and for this he finds support in the Talmud:

> Raba defines a *ner*–that is, a candledish, or a lamp–in the following way: Consider a dish that is filled with oil, with many wicks placed inside of it, along the rim. If a cover is placed upon these wicks, they may each serve as a separate candle (*Shabbat* 23b).

According to a non-Jewish anthropologist, Arab and Jewish tribes of Morocco in the early twentieth century were in the habit of kindling a light or *m'nara* (surely an Arabization of *Menorah*) to drive away the *ginn* (demon), or genius of the lamp. This *m'nara* consisted of a wick in a little bowl filled with oil. So both a *ner* and a *m'nara* consisted basically of oil dishes or receptacles.

This type of light is especially appropriate for kindling on *Hanukkah* and *Shabbat,* says the Maharal, because it constitutes a perfect symbol for the human soul. The Maharal feels this to be true because for him the soul is not completely spiritual. If it is the most spiritual point in a human being, it is the most physical part of the Divine. What is the soul, in fact, asks the Maharal, but the light received by the *body* from on High, and in relation to the Highest it is a vessel or candle dish.

The Maharal felt that a candle dish, not a torch, was the most appropriate symbol for this containment of the "Light," because of its finite nature and because in itself it was a composite. Says the Maharal:

> The soul—the divine light which the body receives from above—does not directly cleave to the whole body. Although the body is especially adapted to receive the soul, nevertheless this union can only be compared to the kind of union the flame has with the oil lamp—the flame cleaves to the wick alone; not to the other components of the candle, the oil and the dish. So too the body contains a faculty, to which the soul adheres, itself acting as nothing more than a receptacle; and since the soul does not directly cleave to the entire body but only to the appropriate faculty it is similar to a lamp.[41]

The Maharal explains that just as it was only when a man's body was completed that it became a lamp or receptacle for the Divine light, so it was only when God had finished creating the physical world that it received the Divine Imprint—*Shabbat*—which is the Soul or *Form* (Body) of Creation. The Maharal has now established an implicit connection between *Shabbat* and the human soul; both are related to form and esthetics of the physical, for which the appropriate symbol is a candle.

He maintains that the wick wrapped around with wax or any solid fat, which we know as candles nowadays, became part of Jewish usage only in the Middle Ages. Influenced by Christian practice, the candles do not constitute what the Talmud regarded as appropriate. Not only do these candles not constitute proper vessels-for-the-light, but also an appropriate candle dish or *Ner* is made up of a composite, whereas these tapers are not.

This second stipulation of a certain relativity and imperfection when it comes to what constitutes his idea of a candle, fits in with his whole notion of the soul as not being entirely spiritual.

Since in our modern candles fire consumes the entire fuel

and wick as it travels down its length, this form of lighting could be said to function like a torch, signifying the purity of Divine Fire of the *Shekhinah,* rather than the human soul, he maintains. But in that case, says the Maharal, it is questionable whether they can be used for *Shabbat* since the whole idea of *Shabbat* is to demonstrate the "Divine Idea wedded to physical Creation." And if it jars to use these "candles" for *Shabbat,* it is absolutely inappropriate to use them to reenact the totally "human miracle" of the *Hanukkah Menorah.* A "torch," he implies, signifies Divine Fire which, like the Burning Bush of Moshe, was "totally ablaze and yet not extinguished," whereas the act of kindling both the *Shabbat* candles and the *Hanukkah Menorah* "represents the spiritual enkindling of the human being," whose resources are finite and whose gift is therefore more precious.

The distinction the Maharal is drawing here is between a single entity (the torch) that is composed entirely of spirit and between something made up of a composite of the spiritual with the physical. Of course, since an image is necessarily physical, a torch only approximates the idea of spirituality. Although a torch is also made up of "fuel energy," according to the Maharal's description it conveys the idea of unadulterated spirituality because it is totally given over to consumption by the flame. The lamp receptacle or candle dish, on the other hand, holds a lot back; it burns only at one point, while remaining totally earthbound, totally human. It is on its function as a receptacle, its sheer earthiness, that its definition depends. The lamp or candle dish represents the physical performance of a commandment or the bringing down to earth and grounding of the Divine Light.

"The Torah is light, and the *mitzvah* is a lamp (or a candle)" (Proverbs 6:23). The *ner* is a holder of the light of Torah. Through physical acts of *mitzvot,* the inner light of Torah shines through the body and the human personality. The *mitzvah* has the potential to "hold" the light. "Your Word is a lantern unto my feet and a light to my way" (Psalm 119:105).

When we hear great music or have a sublime experience, the feeling is one of ecstasy. How can one retain it? It is *through* the performance of physical acts, such as the Commandment to kindle and the other *mitzvot* that the *Shekhinah* Light is "held," grounded, and becomes ours.

Through the images of the torch and the candle, two forms of spirituality are being compared. On the one hand we have light itself, spirituality in its purest form, which is God, *Shekhinah,* Torah in this context, and on the other hand we have something that is touched by flame and still remains physical – the human being, the soul in the body, the Oral Law, performance of practical commandments in the physical world. All these can be subsumed under the single image of a candle.

In addition, the human soul, while it remains in the body, is not by any stretch of the imagination totally spiritual. Rather it is only a "part of God Above," the intersection between the spiritual and physical realms as symbolized by a candle. On the other hand, the soul is also part of the body – though capable of interlocking with Divine Fire it still remains attached to the physical realm. Therefore "the human spirit is God's Lamp," not light – that is, God's receptacle, His candle dish, His instrument through which He can gain entry into the physical world. Though the soul is the spiritual part of the body, to God, the human soul is the most physical part of Himself. It is His Body, His way of being realized and incarnate. And for all this a candle, and not a Torch or Fire itself, is the appropriate symbol.

The paradoxical nature of the exact "point" where soul and *Shekhinah* meet is expressed by an outright contradiction in the Maharal. "The entire world cleaves only to a small part of God's Glory," explains the Maharal. And while the "entire world" can be compared to a candle in its intermixture of matter and spirit, the precise "point" at which it intersects with "God's Glory," the torchlike part of the composite, the part that breaks into flame, is the precise place where the *Shekhinah* has taken up residence:

> As in a torch, the fire is so powerful that it affects the oil, though the oil is not attached to the fire. As it is said: *Blessed is God's Glory from its place* (Ezekiel 3:12).
>   The *Targum* explains: "The entire world is filled *with the glory*[42] of His Honor, Blessed is the Glory of the Lord from the (remote and distant) place where His *Shekhinah* dwells."[43]

After defining a candle as an image for a physical receptacle tipped by spirituality at only one point, the Maharal conjures up a reverse mirror image for God. He says the physical world, as represented by a "candle," is only attached in part to the Glory. Also that the soul only occupies a part of the body. And he says "the entire world" is filled with the light of the spirit, whereas only an infinitesimal part of God's Glory is taken up with the sum total of Creation. The question could reasonably be asked. Whose is the "part" and whose the "whole"? Most of God is infinite and unknown; only His Glory, or the *Shekhinah,* is His link with any type of human referent.

Just as what the Maharal defines as a "candle" is anything partial, here under his definition of candle is not only the human soul, but also God Himself, or at least that part of Him, known as the *Shekhinah* or the Glory, that relates at all to humanity.[44]

The reason a candle should be used to bring *Shabbat* in and a torch to see it out is clarified in the Talmud in the context of a discussion about the kind of light that should be used to search for bread crumbs before Passover.

On the evening before the *Seder* night, a candle is used to make a last-minute search for leaven.

The School of R. Ishmael taught: In the evening of the 14th of Nisan, leaven is searched for by the light of a lamp. Though there is no proof of this, there is an allusion to it, because it is said, *seven days shall there be no leaven* (in your houses) (Exodus 13:7); and it is said, "And he searched, and began at the eldest, and left at the youngest. And the cup was found (in Benjamin's sack)"; and it is said, "And it shall come to pass at that time, that I will search Jerusalem with lamps; and it is said, 'The soul of man is the lamp of the Lord, searching (all the innermost parts of the belly).' "

What is the purpose of the additional quotations?

And should you answer, this "at that time" is a statement of lenient treatment by the Merciful One, as if to say I will not search Jerusalem with the light of a torch, which gives much light, but only with the light of a lamp, the light of which is much less, so that great wrongdoing will be found out but petty wrongdoing will not be found out, then come and hear! The soul of man is the lamp of the Lord (searching, and so on).

Our Rabbis taught: One may not search either by the light of the sun or by the light of the moon, or by the light of a torch, only by the light of a lamp, because the light of a lamp is suitable for searching.

And not (by the light of) a torch? Surely Raba said, "What is the meaning of the verse, *And his brightness was as the light; he had rays coming forth from his hand: and there was the hiding of his power*" (Habakkuk 3:4). To what are the righteous comparable in the presence of the *Shekhinah?* To a lamp in the presence of a torch. And Raba also said, "(To use) a torch for *Havdalah* is the most preferred (way of performing this) duty." [*Pesahim* 7b]

It is understandable that Raba should insist that the *Havdalah* ceremony be carried out by the light of a torch. The very word *Havdalah* means distinction. During *Havdalah*, when a clearcut division is being made between forces of light and darkness, the light of the torch is appropriate. For this kind of distinction, nothing but the rigid, uncompromising light of a torch will do. Indeed, one of the technical stipulations of the *Havdalah* light is that it be powerful enough to distinguish foreign currency.

In some Hasidic and Sephardic communities, it is customary for the Bridal Procession to enter carrying lighted tapers (*Nerot Huppah*) and make a circuit seven times around the groom. Consequently, they should carry torches or brands rather than candles, because the bridegroom has to be quite clear he has the right woman, unlike Jacob, who was deceived into marrying the wrong woman.

But the form of lighting recommended to search out the last crumbs of leaven before Passover is that of lamps or of a candle, rather than of essential flame. Why is this? Why, after all the trouble family members have taken with cleaning for Passover, is the final stage of symbolically searching for leaven (a symbol also for evil) pursued only by the light of a candle even though some of the leaven might actually be overlooked because of the amount of shadow that normally accompanies candlelight? What is the special virtue of candlelight?

As far back as the Talmud the "candle" is shown to possess some qualities the torch does not:

Said R. Nahman ben Isaac: "The one can be brought into holes and chinks (in the wall), whereas the other cannot be brought into holes and chinks."

R. Zebid said: "The one (throws) its light forward, whereas the other (throws) its light behind."

R. Papa said: "Here (with a torch) one is afraid, whereas there (with a lamp) one is not afraid."

Rabina said: "The light of the one is steady, whereas that of the other is fitful." [*Pesahim* 7b]

There is an illuminating example in the *Bahir* of a setting in which the light of a candle might be more useful than sunlight for "searching out the inward parts." It may be broad daylight, but the sunlight may not penetrate into a dark backroom. There, the light of a candle or a lamp could be very useful (*Bahir,* no. 149).

What room could the *Bahir* possibly be talking about that is best illuminated by a candle but the whole of this world. What does a candle resemble, asks the Talmud, but life in this world? Just as the time a candle will stay alight is limited, so too is life in this world. The Maharal also associates this concept of finiteness with a candle when he quotes the verse, "A *mitzvah* is like a candle while the Torah is like light" (Proverbs 6:23). He explains the passage from the Talmud–

Just as a candle comes to an end, so the reward of a physical *mitzvah* eventually ceases. However, just as light is never ending, so reward for the Torah is without limit. [*Sota* 21a]

in the following way:

This world is also like a candle in that it is a corporeal body recipient of a Divine Form, like a material candle which has light (flame considered to be like a Divine Form) attached to it.[45]

But the explanation given in the Talmud, unlike the *Bahir*'s example of the dark room, is not one in which the candle exposes more to sight than the torch. On the contrary, the Talmud is saying that there are occasions when distinctions should be blurred and scrutiny not too far-reaching. Just before Passover, after all efforts have been made to get rid of leaven, the search for leaven can be undertaken with some leeway. That is why on that occasion it is appropriate to use a candle, which will not highlight all the dust in the cracks, rather than a torch, which will mercilessly expose the slightest flaw. After that, a blanket invalidation of all dust is enough and nitpicking is not required.

Apart from the particular case of the pre-Passover candle, the startling suggestion is being made here that there are occasions when the naked dazzling light of the Absolute would simply make all life–essentially made up of temporization and compromise–shrivel up and die. When the scrutiny required ought to be tempered with compassion for human frailty, the light of a candle that knows how to live with shadows is sufficient.

The implications of this intentional oversight as symbolized by the light of the candle has wider ramifications. For instance, one of the most tragic categories in which a Jew can find himself is that of being the child of an adulterous union. Through no fault of his own, this person cannot marry within the community. Where the person's stigma is well known there is no recourse, but it is not the responsibility of the community to set up blacklists and catalog personal tragedies. This is an example where the law must be publicly kept, but it is not necessary to probe too far to uphold a law whose tragic implications have put religious authorities into considerable despair throughout the centuries.

The distinction between a candle and a torch can be used to highlight the circumstances when different types of scrutiny are required. Sometimes, as with the *Havdalah* light, the division between light and shadow must be total, but sometimes, God Himself withdraws a light that sears and kills (the letter of the law) in favor of a more humane and lenient handling of the situation, as symbolized by the intentional softening and blurring of distinctions induced by the light of a candle.

"The spirit of man is the Lamp of the Lord, searching all the inward parts" (Proverbs 20:27). "And it shall come to pass at that time that I will search Jerusalem with lamps" (Zephaniah 1:12). So, when Jerusalem (or the soul) comes to be judged, God uses the weaker light of the candle dish (the human perspective) rather than the yardstick of perfection.

These two different qualities of light are also conveyed by the set of stories or *Midrashim* about the Hidden Light. "First Light" or "Hidden Light" corresponds to the "torch" that is totally dazzling, so that God mercifully "hid" it, whereas the light that grows with man as his insight deepens can be equated with candlelight.

The *Bahir* meditates on these two types of light:

> There were two (types of) light, as it is written, *Let there be light, and there was light* (Genesis 1:3). Regarding both of them it is written, *And God saw the light) that it was good* (Genesis 1:4).
>
> The Blessed Holy One took (one of these types of light) and stored it away for the righteous in the World to Come. Regarding this it is written, *How great is the good that You have hidden away for those who fear You, that You have accomplished for those who find shelter in You* (Psalm 31:20).
>
> It is furthermore written *And God saw all that He made, and behold, it was very good* (Genesis 1:21). God saw all that He had made and saw shining brilliant good.[46]
>
> He took of that good, and (gave) it to this world. This is the meaning of the verse *I have given you a doctrine of good, My Torah, do not abandon it* (Proverbs 4:2). We say that this is the treasury of the Oral Torah. [*Bahir,* nos. 146–147]

Thus, there were two forms of light corresponding to the Written Torah (given by God) and the Oral Torah (woven by the Rabbis and the Community of Israel in response to the demands of daily life). The Oral Law, categorized as feminine,[47] corresponds to "this world," whereas the Written Torah, properly understood as the Higher Torah of Revelation, has its role cast as masculine, and corresponds to the Next World. The *Bahir* continues:

> The Blessed Holy One said, "This (light) is considered part of this world, and it is the Oral Torah. If you keep it alight in this world, then you will be worthy of the World to Come, which is the good stored away for the righteous."
>
> What is (that good composed of)?

It is the force of the Blessed Holy One. It is thus written, *And the glow will be like light* (*He has rays from His hand, and His hidden force is there*) (Habbakuk 3:4). The glow that was taken from the first Light will be like (our visible) light if His children keep the Torah (the Written Law) and Commandments (the Oral Law) that I wrote to teach them. [Exodus 24:12; *Bahir*, no. 147]

The *Bahir* concludes that, when Israel occupies Herself with *mitzvot* and Torah, She is in possession of these two utterly different qualities of light – an insight that keeps pace with personal development and an overarching comprehensive vision.

Though a lamp pales by comparison with the torch of the Sun, the lamp (or humanity) has its advantages over the angels and the whole transcendent world. It is the weak vulnerable aspiring human heart that God desires and therefore it is this that beats at the core of creation.

The Maharal sees the "commandment to kindle" as very much connected with this world. Its reward, therefore, would seem to be to receive a rich portion of worldly blessings. Unfortunately, when it comes to this – worldly goods, however rich one is, death is always there to snatch everything away. But the Maharal reveals that through kindling a certain type of candle, eternity and this world can merge – by having children to pass on the light. If an individual kindles this kind of candle and encourages his children to learn, he can enjoy not only full blessing in this world, but vicariously gain an eternal hold on existence.[48]

FOR THE COMMANDMENT IS A LAMP

Rabbi Hiyya and Rabbi Jose once stayed at an inn together, and at midnight they awoke to study the Torah. The daughter of the innkeeper also awakened and lighted the lamp for them. Then, instead of leaving the room, she stayed behind, but out of sight so that she might listen to the words of the Torah. Rabbi Jose began by speaking about the verse: *For the commandment is a lamp, and the Torah is a light* (Proverbs 6:23). [*Zohar* IV: 166a–169b]

The action of the story and the content of the learning are immediately seen to correspond. The innkeeper's daughter lights a lamp for the scholar–that is, she fulfils the commandment of hospitality–and she stays to listen to the holy words and enjoy the "light" of Torah. Her action immediately equates her with the lamp that she lights.

> *For the commandment is a lamp, and the Torah is a light* (Proverbs 6:23). "This means," he said, "that whoever endeavors to keep the commandments in this world will have a lamp lighted for him in the other world through each commandment he fulfills, and he who studies the Torah will merit the Supernal Light from which that lamp is lighted. For a lamp without light has no value, and light without a lamp cannot shine, so the one has need of the other.
>
> "The religious act is necessary to prepare the lamp, and study of the Torah is necessary to light the lamp. Blessed is he who takes it in hand both with light and lamp!"[*Zohar* IV:166a]

The standard differentiation is that the Torah (masculine) stands for God or light in general and belongs to the other world, whereas the commandment (*mitzvah*) is a practical application of the Torah in this world and therefore can be represented by a Lamp (feminine). She is also the Oral Law and *Knesset Yisrael.* However, in Rabbi Jose's interpretation, the worlds are reversed while still remaining differentiated. For instance, observance of the commandment in this world will cause a "lamp to be lighted" for the person in the next. There is still a touch of "this world," a quasiphysical instrument, projected into the next world. In the spiritual world the soul has been compared to a "Lamp," still a remnant of the individual consciousness as lived in this world.

What Kabbalists say in various ways is that by using physical organs to perform God's Will here below, man weaves for himself spiritual garments or lights for a Lamp that will serve to retain him as an individual entity in the hereafter.

However, just as carrying out the commandments ensures continuation of some remnant of this world in the next, the learning of Torah already penetrates this world with the light of the world to come. The reward is not some sort of continuation of individual consciousness in the hereafter. The reward is not the "soul" as represented by the "lamp." The reward is revelation of the light of God Himself here and now.

Rabbi Jose says that both are necessary – light and lamp, Torah and its realization in daily acts, Bride and Groom.

> Another interpretation of Proverbs 6:23 is as follows:
> "The lamp of the Commandment" is the lamp of David – that is, the Oral Torah. This is like a lamp that has continually to be trimmed and attended to in order to receive light from the Written Torah. For the Oral Torah has no light in itself except that which it receives from the Written Torah, which is an actual source of illumination.
> When Rabbi Jose had spoken, he turned round and caught sight of the innkeeper's daughter standing there behind them. He continued. [*Zohar* IV:166a]

Rabbi Jose does not stop his discourse when he sees the young woman's thirst for Torah. He does not prevent her listening. On the contrary, from this point, his whole discourse is attuned to her.

> *For the commandment is a lamp.* What sort of lamp? The lamp that represents the special commandment that applies to women – the Sabbath light.[49] For although women do not have the privilege of studying the Torah, men, who do have this privilege, give that light to the lamp which it is the women's duty to kindle. To women goes the merit of preparing the lamp; to men, by the study of the Torah, the merit of supplying the light for the lamp. [*Zohar* IV:166a]

From what Rabbi Jose says here it is unclear who trims and prepares the lamp. In the story we know it was the girl. But here it seems the Torah (or the male) also helps undertake that very practical task. Here, in fact, both "prepare the lamp," the man by supplying the oil, the woman by physically setting out the candlestick.

When the woman heard these words (what the man's contribution is supposed to be), she broke into sobs. In the meantime, her father had also risen and come to join the company. Seeing his daughter in tears, he asked why she was crying. She told him what she had heard, and he too began to weep.

"Then," said Rabbi Jose to them, "is it possible your son-in-law, the husband of your daughter, is an ignorant man?"

And the innkeeper replied: "Indeed, that is so. Therefore it is that my daughter and I must constantly weep. Once I observed him leap down from a high roof just so that he could be present to hear the *kaddish* prayer with the congregation. Then the idea occurred to me to give him my daughter as a wife. This I did as soon as the congregation had left the synagogue. For I said to myself, judging from his eagerness in leaping from the roof to hear the *kaddish,* he will certainly one day become a great scholar, although at that time he was only a youth and I had never met him before. But he does not even know how to say the grace after meals. I could not even teach him to recite the *Shema!*"

Rabbi Jose said to him: "Make a change and take some other man as a husband for your daughter. Or perhaps he may have a son who will be a scholar." [*Zohar* IV:166a]

(Even among the poor, the most desirable quality a young man could bring to a prospective match was learning.)

As the couple is only engaged, Rabbi Jose sympathizes with the hard lot of father and daughter and suggests that they break off the match. However, if that is not possible, he comforts them with the possibility that if the young man is not learned, at least his future sons might be. There is no question of a daughter playing that particular role! The passing on of this type of learning usually is from father to son, and only where there is no man to play his role does it devolve upon the family of the mother.

But there is already a clue that the fiancé is not as inept as he appears. He recommended himself to the father originally, not because of his learning but because of his action – because he was even prepared to risk his life to participate in the *Kaddish.*

This is important on many counts. *Kaddish* is a mystical

prayer in which human beings have the capacity to augment God's greatness in the cosmos. It is said especially by a son on the loss of a parent. Just at the moment of greatest loss, when the world seems unutterably impoverished, God's greatness is strengthened by Israel and called in to fill the gap. (We learn later that the young man never knew his own father.) In any case, one quality the innkeeper is certain to look for in any prospective son-in-law is his readiness to say *Kaddish* for him after his death, because his daughter is considered ineligible as a woman to perform that service. So the young man's love for the *Kaddish* prayer shows a soul prepared to give up life for the sake of the "Holiness of the Name," reveals certain mystical tendencies important to the writer of the *Zohar,* and also (as we learn later) shows the loyalty of the young toward the older generation. Although the innkeeper does not yet know that the young man is an orphan, he is bound to be impressed by the great lengths to which the young man will go not to miss saying *Kaddish.*

Thus all three members of this family are people with the finest values. Rabbi Jose is especially moved by the girl's attempt to compensate for her fiancé's defects by learning Torah herself.

The young man had also by this time got up, and now leaped into the room and seated himself at the feet of the Rabbis. Rabbi Jose looked at him long and earnestly, then said: "I most certainly see that the light of the Torah will spread into the world either from this young man or from his descendants."

The young man smiled and said: "My master, may I be allowed to say a few words in your presence? At first I was too shy to speak in the presence of older people and had vowed not to speak on the Torah for two months. Today that period ends, so now that you are here I will dare to utter words of Torah." [*Zohar* IV:166a]

Then he began to expound the words, *The commandment is a lamp.*

"This," he said, "refers to the *Mishnah* in the same way as the *Torah and the commandments* (Exodus 24:12) mean the Written and Oral Law respectively."

And the Torah is a light which kindles that lamp from the

side of Primordial Light. The Primordial Light is destined to produce fruit for the world to come. And not only for the world to come, but even now every day; for this world would not be able to exist at all if it were not for this light, as it is written, *For I have said, Mercy shall be built up for ever* (Psalm 89:3).

"It was this light that the Holy One sowed in the Garden of Eden,[50] where it grew, multiplied and brought forth fruit which has nourished the world, as it is written: *A light sown for the Righteous* (Psalm 97:2).

"Only when Israel is in exile does this light cease. So how can the world be sustained at all? Therefore it says *is sown*—that is to say, continually.

"Now, from the time when the stream was cut off from the Garden, the Gardener has ceased to visit. But the light sows itself, bringing forth fruit out of itself like a Garden which brings forth without being sown, though it must be admitted that what is produced has no longer that perfection which (it) attained when the Gardener was present.

"So the significance of the words *And the Torah is a light* is that the Torah, which emanates from the region of Primordial Light, is continually being sown in the world and sends forth fruit without ceasing and the world is nourished by it.

"*The commandment is a lamp* contains the mystery of 'Keep' (the feminine negative commandments); *the Torah is a light* contains the mystery of 'Remember' (the positive, masculine commandments). And all forms one mystery of faith.

"The Sin of Adam was not healed until the time when Israel stood at Mount Sinai and received the Torah, when the Lamp and the Light (Male and Female) became united together." [*Zohar* IV:167a–168b]

The intervention of the young man with words of Torah comes as the denouement of the situation. His Torah in itself is the salvation and happy ending because it shows him to be worthy of his Bride.

Even at the moment when the young woman is forced to draw on the words of the Rabbis to sustain her family, there is never any question that she herself should come forward with anything original. She learns, she listens and takes in, but she does not actively contribute to the debate. But her fiancé, after a forced silence of two months, finally has something to say.

The young man's description of Israel in exile or of the world or the Garden without visitation from the Gardener is almost a metaphor of her plight. When there is a beautiful woman with no man for her, there the "light must sow itself." The desired union of Male and Female at Mount Sinai rights this balance of the absent male, and this also happens in the story.

And now, Masters, I may tell you that I am from Babylon, the son of Reb Saphra. Unhappily, I never had the privilege of knowing my father, so I came here to the Holy Land, and fearing lest the inhabitants of this land should be lions of wisdom and knowledge, I resolved in humility not to say one word concerning the Torah in the presence of anybody for two months. On this very day these two months are over, and I am fortunate that you came here today so that I can have your opinion on my skill in producing original words of Torah.

He finished, and Rabbi Jose lifted up his voice and wept. They all then rose and kissed the young man on the brow. Said Rabbi Jose: "Blessed is our lot that we were found worthy to come this way so that we might listen to words concerning the Ancient of Days from thy mouth, words which until today it has not been granted to us to hear."

Then they all seated themselves again, and the youth said: "Masters, as I have seen the sorrow that I have brought to this father-in-law of mine and to his daughter, who are filled with grief because I seem not to know how to recite the grace after meals, so I must tell you that until I grasp the full significance of this prayer I determine not to consummate my marriage. For although I could have been united with her without sin of any kind, yet I did not wish to deceive her or her father about myself as it was impossible to explain myself until the two months were passed."

Rabbi Jose and Rabbi Hiyya, as well as the innkeeper and

his daughter, now all wept together for joy. And Rabbi Jose said: "We pray thee, as thou hast begun, shed on us further the light of day!" (*Zohar* IV:168a).

Now day broke, and they all stood up and kissed the youth. So Rabbi Jose said: "Indeed, this is a day of joy, and we shall not depart from here until it has become a day of festivity for all the village. It will be a festivity in which the Holy One will participate."

Then they took the young woman and blessed her with many blessings; after which they bade her father prepare the house for the festivities. And all the inhabitants of that village came to the house and shared in the rejoicings. And they called her "Bride," and made merry with them the whole day.

The young man, too, contributed to their joy with words of Torah. When they were seated at the table he spoke about the following verse: *And you shall make the boards for the Tabernacle of shittim wood standing* (Exodus 27:15).

"These boards," he said, "stood round the canopy serving the Bride (the *Shekhinah*), so that the Supernal Spirit could dwell in that canopy. That is why the Bride Below (the girl being married) must have a canopy, all beautiful with decorations prepared for her, so as to honor the Bride Above (the *Shekhinah*),[51] who in turn is present and participates in the joy of our human Bride.

"For this reason the canopy should be as beautiful as possible. For, as below, so above: as the bride here below is blessed with seven blessings, so is her prototype (*Shekhinah-Malkhut*), who receives the fullness of blessing from the preceding *Sefirot*. A woman being married is called *Kallah* (bride, with the nuance of 'perfection') only after the seven blessings have been pronounced.

"Blessed is the Jewish People who are worthy to represent below that which is above."[52] [*Zohar* IV:166a–169b]

"If you keep My light, I will protect your Lamp," says Bar Kappara. "If you keep my Torah, I shall protect your life" (*Vayikra Rabbah* 31:4). But ultimately the reward for fulfilling the "commandment to kindle" must also be connected with the purpose for which the commandment was given. "The act of kindling," says the Maharal, "represents the spiritual enkindling of the human being; surely it is this route of the growth and spiritual transformation of the person that is the true reward to be received above."

KINDLING THE LAMP OF THE *NESHAMAH*

There is a commandment to "cleave to the Lord your God" (Deuteronomy 10:20). But how is it possible, the Rabbis ask, for human beings to cleave to One who is "consuming fire" (Deuteronomy 4:24). The answer given is to keep His commandments because the commandments were given to form a connection with Him. Indeed, the Hebrew word for a commandment, *mitzvah,* comes from the word for "to connect."

When one keeps the "commandment to kindle," the answer – how to cleave – dances in flame in front of our eyes. For a burning candle is the very image of passionate and all-consuming attachment and cleaving of the flame to the wick. And what is demonstrably so for these particularly attractive, particularly sensuous and visible "commandments to kindle" is also true for all the commandments.

A good way to understand the impact of the fulfillment of any commandment is to focus on this image of kindling a candle or a lamp. For the observance of any of God's commandments creates a light.

If the way of cleaving to "consuming fire" is through the commandments, it is because there is a secret correspondence between the commandments and the physical organs, as if the one were made for the other. According to Philo, the commandments have the forms and shapes of human limbs, and all the organs are made to keep the *mitzvot.* By so doing, man weaves for himself, limb by limb the spiritual "body" or garment of light with which he will arise after death.

> If a man does not want the light of his soul to be absorbed in the infinite light of God after his death and sink into it without trace, it is up to him to obtain as much merit as possible during his earthly life, for all merit is a source of Light, as the Scriptures say –

Light which never goes out. And if a man adds merit to the little spark of his soul, then his soul becomes so powerful a Light that not even the Infinite will swallow it up and it will never be absorbed.[53]

Performance of a *mitzvah* consolidates not only a spiritual foothold in this world "below" through children, but also spins a spiritual body for the soul in the next. By transmuting "flesh" into "light," the Hebrew for which in both cases is *or* with an *ayyin* or with an *aleph*, person's "light" may still be allowed to flow according to the contours of his own ego and personality while in the body.

> However many meritorious acts and good deeds a man lays up to his credit, it is for his own benefit, and not for the benefit of his son or for the benefit of his daughter. The soul knows that all the trouble it takes, it takes for itself; therefore it never has too much of meritorious acts and good deeds.
>
> R. Levi said: "It is like unto a townsman who has married a royal princess; even though he feeds her with all the dainties in the world, he does not fully discharge his obligation. Why? Because she is a royal princess. So, too, however much a man does for his soul, he does not discharge his full obligation. Why? Because it is from on high." [*Vayikra Rabbah* 4:2]

Beyond using the commandments as a way of retaining a hold on the physical world, or at least on the ego, observance is a means of transmuting man's nature and bringing him close to the Divine. And the kindling of the *Menorah* is a model of how this works. If we kindle the physical lamp – the oil from actual olives – we ourselves will be kindled.

Everyone possesses an inner power or light. Every existing thing has its light, the quintessential proof of its existence. There is a Hasidic story about the lights of two friends blending when they meet to create a third light that is the very mirror of their friendship. Light signifies not only the personality of each, but also the vitality of their friendship. If they do not refresh their relationship by meeting at least once a year, this precious third light will be extinguished.

But quite apart from the spiritual aspect of the flame, even the type of fuel burned to give us light is important as a symbol of how the soul operates in the world.

> Said the Medzibozer to his grandson, Israel, who was in the habit of moving backwards and forwards when he prayed: A wick of linen burns quietly and gives a better light than a cotton wick which burns noisily. Believe me when I say that a sincere movement of your smallest toe is sufficient to show your enthusiasm (literally, "taking fire").[54]

The "commandment to kindle" is expressed in a particular way – "to raise up lights" – as one raises up children. *Knesset Yisrael* is depicted as a mother raising up her brood of children-lights. And these are conceived with their flames streaming upward to a Divine source – like a note in music, each soul rises in the scale of light (the *Sefirot*) to its origin. And the "lamp" par excellence – the spiritual "child" that we visualize rising – is the lamp of the soul of which each individual is a caretaker and "mother."

> *The spirit of man is the Lamp of the Lord.*
> God said: *Let My lamp be in thy hand and thy lamp in My hand* (Proverbs 20:27).
> What is the lamp of God? The Torah says *Thy word is a lamp unto my feet, and a light unto my path* (Psalm 119:105). For those who study Torah give forth light wherever they may be. It is like one standing in the dark with a lamp in his hand; when he sees a stone, he does not stumble, neither does he fall over a gutter because he has a lamp in his hand.
> And it says also, *For the commandment is a lamp and the teaching is light* (Proverbs 6:23).
> Why is the teaching called "light"? Because it often happens that when one is eager to fulfil a commandment, his Evil Inclination within him dissuades him, saying: "Why do you want to perform this command and diminish your wealth? Instead of giving away to others, give it to your own children."
> But the Good Inclination says to him: "Give rather to a

good cause; for see what it says: *For the commandment is a lamp,* just as the light of the lamp is undiminished even if a million wax and tallow candles are kindled from it, so will he who gives for the fulfilment of any commandment not suffer a diminution of his possessions." From here we learn, *For the commandment is a lamp and the teaching is light* (Proverbs 6:23). [*Bereishit Rabbah* 36:3]

The image of light and the myriad lamps is one of growth and spiritual fertility that extends far beyond one's own physical children.

Why does the commandment speak of "a lamp"? Because if one performs a commandment it is as if he had kindled a light before God and as if he had revived his own soul, also called a lamp, for it says, *The spirit of man is the Lamp of the Lord* (Proverbs 20:27). [*Bereishit Rabbah* 36:3]

We attempt to help souls rise up after a death. To facilitate the ascent of the soul of a close relative, a *neshamah* or soul light is kindled on the anniversary (*Yahrzeit*) of the death, and also on the Day of Atonement, when even souls of the departed are judged anew and *Yizkor,* the Prayer for Remembrance, is said. The *Kaddish* said during the period of mourning is a parallel means of elevating the soul, through words rather than lights. The actual words are "raise up" and exalt God, but in doing so on behalf of the dead who can no longer speak for himself, the soul itself is raised.

In Israel, memorial lights are kindled on public buildings on *Holocaust Remembrance Day.* The Memorial Light can be made of any substance, but must burn for at least twenty-four hours.

The "flame" of the *Yahrzeit* light literally stands for the life and soul of the departed, and the whole act of kindling is an image of the Soul ascending and returning to Her source.

The kindling of the *Menorah* has also been taken by sources as various as R. Nachman of Bratzlav and the Christian Bible to signify the ascent of the Soul after death. The Christian gospels say clearly: "Then shall the kingdom of Heaven be likened to

Ten Virgins, that took their lamps and went to meet the Bridegroom" (Matthew 25:1).

"In the world-to-come," says *Berakhot* 17a, "men will sit with their crowns in their heads." "In" and not "on" their heads, to imply that they will no longer have free will about taking those crowns off. According to R. Nachman of Bratzlav, these crowns correspond to the seven lamps of the *Menorah*. Just as in the Temple the actual *Menorah* stood opposite the Holy of Holies, in the world to come the seven lamps (the seven parts of the Human Face) will shine "opposite the *Shekhinah*" – that is, human beings will directly reflect Divine Light.

The transformation brought on the soul by death, says Reb Nachman, is symbolized by the kindling of the *Menorah*. The Seven Lamps are the Seven Days of Feasting to celebrate the union of the lower soul with the higher soul. But the Seven Lamps are also the Seven Days of Mourning, also represented as a wedding.

Mourning is a form of wooing, Reb Nachman implies. While the survivors mourn their loss, the departed soul rises closer and closer to Her consummation, which has in it something of joy. In fact, the Seven Days of Mourning spurs the departed soul on to rise to greater and greater heights, finally arriving at "the Light of the Divine Face." This wooing, from ascent to ascent, takes seven days, until finally the soul sees God "face to face." In fact, this is why the *Sephardim* celebrate the *Hiloulah* the anniversary of the death of their greatest saints by journeying to their graves and feasting. And it is why *Hasidim* do exactly the same.

These highpoints in the calendar are far from macabre occasions. It is a Jewish – and seemingly universal – practice to kindle lights at the graveside of parents, biblical figures, and holy men. This probably springs from a deep atavism, symbolic of life in death. If it is not a single candle, but a *Menorah* that is lighted, as was the case with the Ramban's mother, the *Menorah* becomes a mother figure nursing the soul light even in the womb of the grave.

However, the soul is not likely to ascend very far after death if it does not do so while still alive. The performance of every *mitzvah,* as visibly as the "commandment to kindle" raises up a light that is itself an image of the soul ascending. For observance of the commandments sows lights above as well as lights below. While the lights below are living children, lights above are our "spiritual children" – that is, our good deeds, and the higher and higher levels of one's own soul that blossom and come alive as we realize our potential.

The human predilection is "always to scintillate upwards" (*Tanya,* pp. 78–79). Fire tends to ascend. And this constitutes a return of fire to fire, of the soul to the "reservoir of souls," the earthly *Menorah* of the human soul to the celestial *Menorah,* the "bundle and reservoir of souls," which is what the *Menorah* ultimately signifies.

Although the Maharal presented us with images in which fire seemed to desire and to some extent depend on the wick – that is, the physical substance of the light – there are other schools of thought that see it the other way round – the wick desires to be elevated by the fire, while the fire simply desires to rise and return to its Source. For example, the Gerer Rebbe reiterated the constant religious refrain that somewhere a choice must be made between worldly and spiritual goals, and that one cannot simply take the one as the expression of the other.

> The soul of Israel [which is the very heartbeat of man] is comparable to the light of the candle that intrinsically seeks to be parted from the wick in order to unite with its source above although we would thereby be extinguished. [*Tanya,* pp. 77–78]

What is being described here is simultaneously an act of kindling and a movement of ascent that corresponds to a reversed motion of the spiraling emanation of the *Sefirot.*

God fanned out the emanations in a series of *hitpashtut* (expansions). The Way of Return is through *histalkut* (contractions). To imagine this is to get some inkling of infinity and the soul. The soul is both one point of light and the whole unfurled crown of *Menorah* lights.

Interestingly, whereas Jews see the "candle" as a stand-in or figure for the soul of the departed, there is a seemingly universal belief that dying people see the light of the other world and are drawn up and fused with it.

The *Sefirot* are essentially spirals tracing the descent of Divine light and the ascent of the light of the Soul. The *Sefirot* have themselves been referred to as the "Supernal Commandments," and they too are said to be shaped according to the pattern of the human limbs.[55] Thus, if a human being keeps the commandments here below, there is a notion that he is enkindling the lamp of the *Sefirot* and preserving the very fabric of the pleroma. Conversely, neglect of the commandments not only causes the individual's "light" to be reabsorbed in the Divine, but it reverses the whole Divine movement of emanation, weakens the fabric of the *Sefirot,* and plunges the entire creation back into the abyss. According to this formulation, the *Sefirot* are instruments or lamps, kindled either by God sending light to the world, or by man sending light back to Him. On the one hand, each single *Sefirah* is a lamp; on the other, all the *Sefirot* taken as a whole are "God's Lamp."

According to the *Zohar,* there are at least two types of soul—a lower soul (feminine, *ruach*) and a higher soul (masculine, only for purposes of this interpretation *neshamah*. When the lower soul unites with the higher soul—that is, when the soul rises—"they bring forth light, but if they separate they do not give light."

When the male and female come together, they shine with a celestial light, and in their union they are designated "Lamp," *NeR* (lamp) being the abbreviation of *Neshamah-Ruach* (soul-spirit); as it says, "The lamp of the Lord is the soul of man" (Proverbs 20:27; *Zohar* III:99b).

There is a *Midrash* to the effect that we may do what we like, but our soul, *Neshamah,* here designated as feminine, faithfully reports to God about everything. What is the soul, after all, but the King's Daughter.[56] If we are married to the Princess, of course the King will know everything.

Do not wonder, "Who is telling tales about me?" It is enough to know that the one closest of all to you is also dearest to Him. That is to say, *The lamp of the Lord is the soul of man* (Proverbs 20:27). And also, His spirit is in you, as it is said: *The spirit of man*—that is to say, God's Lamp — *is that which the Lord God breathed into his nostrils the spirit of life* (Genesis 2:7). [*Pesikta Rabati* 8]

In *The Gates of Light,* Rabbi Joseph Gikatalia (1248–1325 C.E.), an early Kabbalist and a pupil of R. Abraham Abulafia, makes an enigmatic comment to the effect that through keeping the commandments man's physical limbs are so purified that God's "consuming fire" is tempered to a totally delightful light energy, "providing delight and ecstasy to those who attach themselves to it with a pure soul."

It is therefore called the Lamp of God. It is what lights the Lamp of the Soul. The soul is then attached to it, and this is its desire.[57]

A FIRE THAT CONSUMES

Gikatalia is saying that "there is a part of the Divine Light that is dangerous." It is a "consuming fire" and yet it is precisely to this quality that man is commanded to attach himself. How can this be done? By the purification of the physical, the "wild" and dangerous fiery quality of the Divine — the passion that consumes — is "tamed" and tempered to human limitation, and from fire it is transmuted into a Lamp providing illumination and delight.

The Talmud also dwells upon the vehement destructive quality of the fire that consumed the sacrifices and allegedly decimated many of the priesthood:[58] "On the altar was a divine fire that crouched like a lion" (*Yoma* 21b). The *Zohar* encapsulates this simile into a metaphor: "A lion consumed the sacrifices — fire falling from heaven."

Gikatalia sees the physical exertion of keeping the commandments as a means of purification of the physical organs themselves, making them into vessels ready to contain light rather than fire. As it says: "The *mitzvah* (performance of the physical act) is a Lamp, and Torah is light" (Proverbs 6:23).

Gikatalia is unusual in taking the "Lamp of God" (a feminine, receptacle image) to be a part of God and not something purely human.[59] Even if the "Lamp" does refer to God, unlike the extremist "torch" of Divine Fire, it must signify that part of the Divine that relates to man, because the very word "lamp" is an indication of something grounded, earthly, and nurturing.

Usually, however, the "lamp of God" is taken, as it says in the Psalm, for the human spirit. At most, when the human soul is so purified as to truly be God's image, the "Lamp" is transformed into a transpersonal human entity for the collective mirroring of the Divine.

However, it does seem to mark a point where the most spiritual part of the human and the most human part of the Divine come together. An interpretation of the second verse in Genesis, "And God's Spirit was hovering over the abyss" (Genesis 1:2), has been rendered as essentially the soul of Adam or of the Messiah (*Bereishit Rabbah* 2:4, 8:1–2; *Hagiga* 12a) or the Primordial Light of the *Menorah,* the reservoir of souls from which the individual soul was formed. Here, "Spirit of God," individual human soul, reservoir of souls, and especially the soul of Adam, soul of the Messiah come together in the form of the Menorah!

A "lamp" is a reflector or image, so the "Lamp of God" is also the "image of God"; into this category the *Sefirot* fall, said to be reflections of the Divine Light and also to be shaped according to the human limbs. Into this category also falls mankind, whose soul was created in "God's image" and declared in the Psalms to be God's Lamp.

This is a case of reflection and irradiation at all levels. Man's limbs and the commandments are the internalized *Sefirot,* creating the Human Form Divine, or God's Lamp. Similarly, the commandments themselves correspond to the human limbs and are an instrument of light energy, called in the Psalms a "Lamp," as opposed to the Light of God's Torah. As for the *Sefirot,* they also flow according to the shape of the human limbs; they are the Supernal Commandments, and also serve as a lamp. And there is a sense in which God Himself, or at least the part of Him present in the world, His *Shekhinah,* is also molded according to human lineaments and human goodness.

However, according to Gikatalia, in the same way as is true for other Kabbalists when it comes to archetypes like Original

Adam and *Knesset Yisrael,* the "Lamp of God" is not a collective human entity so much as that part of God that relates to man. In essence, these archetypes are meeting points of human and divine, reflections and mirror images. As in the story of the two friends whose lights mingled, the representation of a physically grounded Lamp whose branches reach up into the sky is a reflection of the new lamp formed by their relationship.

There is a *Midrash* in which Israel asks God about the "commandment to kindle":

> Master of the World, how can You ask us to give light to You. You surely are the Light of the World and Brightness abides with You, yet You say: "The lamp shall give light." To which the Holy One, Blessed be He, replies: "It is not because I require your service, but in order that you may give Me light, even as I give you light." [*Bamidbar Rabbah* 15:5]

The *Midrash* suggests that though God certainly does not need anything that man can do, He looks for certain forms of reciprocal behavior, "in order that you may give Me light as I give you light." And strengthening this connection is the function, not only of the *Menorah,* but also of all other commandments and religious acts.

> Bar Kappra began: "*When you light My Lamp, I shall illumine your darkness* (Psalm 18:28). Said the Holy One to man, 'Your lamp is in My Hand and My Lamp is in your hand.' That 'your lamp is in My Hand' is proved by the text, *The soul of man is the Lamp of God* (Proverbs 20:27). And how do we know that 'My Lamp is in your hand'? – *to raise up an eternal light* (Leviticus 24:2). Said the Holy One, 'If you have kindled My Lamp, I will light yours.'" [*Vayikra Rabbah* 31:4]
>
> Said Bar Kappra: "Both the Torah and the soul are compared to a lamp. The soul, as it is written, *The Lamp of the Lord is the soul of man* (Proverbs 20:27). And the Torah, as it is said: *For the Practical Command is a lamp and the Wisdom is a light*" (Proverbs 6:23).

Said the Holy One to the man: "My Lamp is in your hand and your lamp is in My Hand. 'My Lamp is in your hand' – that is the Torah. 'And your lamp is in My hand' – that is the soul. If you keep My Lamp, I shall keep your lamp. If you extinguish my lamp, I shall put out yours. How do we know this? As it is written: *Only take heed to yourself and be very careful of your life lest you forget these words*" (Deuteronomy 4:8). [*Devarim Rabbah* 4:4]

The opening statement here is startling. There is no question of an equal interchange of "light for light." The delimitations are shown quite clearly. God has Eternal Light, while man is in darkness. To the question posed recurrently in the *Midrash* as to why the "Light of the World" (or Eternal Light) should ask Israel to kindle, the answer is given here succinctly. "Because you are in darkness. It is not I that need light, but you do. And by your kindling of My light I will have the impetus to keep yours shining."

When Israel keeps the Commandments or when Israel lights the Lamp, not only is the *Shekhinah* drawn down into the world of matter, but a contrary movement is set in train by this "passive female" to actively bring redemption.

To the ever-repeated question as to why God, the "Light of all worlds," should require the kindling of the *Menorah,* the answer is that it is the duty of the Community of Israel (the Beloved) to "give light back to God, as a blind man was asked to kindle a lamp in a house for a man who guided him to it."

Out of the darkness I brought forth light; do I then need your light? I only told you to kindle lamps in order to elevate you . . .
As Israel raises on high the lighted *Menorah,* She is herself elevated. [*Bamidbar Rabbah* 15:5]

Mitzvot, such as the "commandments to kindle," are like a ladder of light let down to earth. Whoever attaches himself to it is raised up automatically, as on a pulley. By observing each commandment, Israel becomes identified with the Lamp it bears on high. So *Shekhinah-Menorah-Yisrael* are identified as they rise.

NOTES

1. Erwin R. Goodenough, *Jewish Symbols in the Greco-Roman Period* (New York: Pantheon Books, 1954), vol. 4, p. 86.

2. Samson Raphael Hirsch, *The Pentateuch,* trans. Rabbi Isaac Levy (London: Soncino Press, 1957), vol. 2, Exodus 25:31–40.

3. Ibid., vol. 4, Numbers 8:1–4.

4. Ibid.

5. See pp. 200, 204–207 and references to door placement in Chapter 5.

6. See Israel Abrahams, *Festival Studies* (London: E. Goldston, 1934), p. 149.

7. See Mordecai Narkiss, English "Introduction" in *Menorat HaHanukkah* (Jerusalem–Bezalel Museum, 1939), p. 21; also "The History of the *Hanukkah* Lamp," *Youth Aliyah Review* (Winter 1959): 279–320.

8. Rachel Bernstein Wischnitzer, "Origine de la lampe de Hanouka," in *Revue des Études Juives* 89 (1930):135–146.

9. See Mordecai Wischnitzer, *History of the Jewish Crafts and Guilds* (New York: J. David, 1965) and Therese and Mendel Metzger, *Jewish Life in the Middle Ages* (New York: Alpine Fine Arts, 1982).

10. Jewish tradition posits two Messiahs as two different forms of leadership, (1) Messiah, son of Joseph (and Rachel), a Jewish leader in exile during a time of powerlessness, and (2) the true Messiah, son of David (and Leah), sovereign ruler in his own land.

11. Kabbalist and author of the *Shulkhan Arukh,* the definitive code of Jewish law.

12. I heard this explanation from Rabbi Saul Berman of the Lincoln Square Synagogue.

13. The Great Assembly was a legislative body comprised of 120 men, *Anshe Knesset Ha-Gedolah.* It is said to have functioned during and after the Persian period in Jewish history, about 500–300 B.C.E.

14. I heard this "insight," or "*Torah,*" from Rabbi Saul Berman of the Lincoln Square Synagogue.

15. Shmuel Hacohen and Eliyahu Shragai, eds., *Ha-Nerot Hallalu, Perakim le-Hanukkah* (Israel Military Rabbinate, Israel Defense Forces) (Israel: *Tzava Haganah le-Yisrael,* 1950), p. 6.

16. Theodor Herzl, "The *Menorah*," a publication of the Zionist Organization, *Die Welt, Hanukkah* 1897, trans. from the German by Bessie London Pouzzner, *The Menorah Journal* (1915), 1:264–267.

17. Author's translation of the *Al HaNissim* prayer inserted into the *Amidah*–the Standing Prayer–during *Hanukkah*.

18. Based on the Kalever Rebbe.

19. Louis Newman, trans., *The Hasidic Anthology* (New York: Scribner's, 1938), p. 514.

20. Solomon Ganzfried and Hyman Klein trans., *The Code of Maimonides,* Book 3, *The Book of Seasons* (New Haven: Yale University Press, 1961), pp. 468–471.

21. Some Jews lived in grand style in sixteenth-century Venice. See Cecil Roth, *History of Italian Renaissance Jewry* (Philadelphia: Jewish Publication Society, 1959), and Israel Abrahams, *Jewish Life in the Middle Ages* (London: E. Goldston, 1896).

22. Carl Jung, *The Structure and Dynamics of the Psyche, Collected Works* (New York: Pantheon, 1960), vol. 8, p. 199.

23. Rabbi Moses Cordovero, *Palm Tree of Deborah*, trans. Louis Jacobs (New York: Sepher Hermon Press, 1974), p. 7.

24. Ibid.

25. Hillel and Shammai lived about 30 B.C.E.

26. From a historical perspective there is no evidence that there was such a cosmological concept as the *Sefirot* in the time of Hillel and Shammai. The first mention we have of the *Sefirot* is in the *Sefer Yetzirah,* written at the earliest in the second century. But that is not to say that the kabbalistic tradition does not go back much earlier. Also, the first extant link between the *Sefirot* and light dates back only to the twelfth century, while documentation as to the further link between the construction of the *Sefirot* and the *Menorah* goes back to the thirteenth century. Again, this is not to say that there was not a hidden oral tradition or that some manuscripts were not lost to us.

    I believe that the parable of Ten Virgins bearing Ten *Menorot* in the Christian gospels is just such an extant allusion to a very ancient tradition of Celestial Lamps as well as to their cosmological and spiritual symbolism. The reverberations between *Midrash,* Christian Scriptures, and the Kabbalists of the Middle Ages, would support this view. The *Zohar* specifically speaks of "virgins" or "young women" as "worlds," which, in the terminology of *Kabbalah* and of Hasidism, refers to *Sefirot*.

The link between Hillel and Shammai's argument over the kindling of the *Menorah* and the concept of light relayed by the *Sefirot*, however, is a voyage into imagistic fantasy on the part of the author, rather than part of any as yet historically documented scholarship.

27. Ashlag, *Ten Luminous Emanations*, vol. I, pp. 115–116.
28. With thanks to my friend Solomon Mowshowitz. The Priests were given the gift of spreading light. See *Bereishit Rabbah* 15:6 and the controversy with the Rabbis focusing on light and fire.
29. *Sefer Hasidim, Vulgata*, par. 54, quoted in Abraham Yehoshua Heschel, *The Sabbath* (New York: Farrar, Straus and Giroux, 1951), pp. 65–66.
30. Joy Ungerlieder-Mayerson and Freema Gottlieb, *Jewish Folk Art* (New York: Summit Books, 1986), p. 121.
31. My friend Micha Odenheimer told me a story of his Rebbe, Moshe Feinstein. A woman asked Reb Moshe whether she needed to light two candles. Could she not achieve the effect of two candles by placing one opposite a mirror. Reb Moshe thought for a moment and then said: "But in that case you would need four candles." The woman did not understand.

    "For the two women," he answered humorously. "You and your reflection in the mirror."
32. There is a custom, especially among *Hasidim* and *Sephardim*, to have seven lighted tapers for the Wedding procession. The Groom and his attendants circle the Bride seven times with these *Nerot Huppah* to make sure that unlike Jacob cheated of his beloved Rachel, the young man is getting married to the right woman.
33. See Chapter 3, pp. 158–159, this volume, which describes Adam's horror when the First Light vanished.
34. R. Solomon Ganzfried, *Code of Jewish Law* (*Kitzur Shulkhan Arukh*), trans. Hyman E. Goldin (New York: Hebrew Publishing Company, 1961), vol. 2, p. 24.
35. See Chapter 7, p. 394, for the ending of the story from the *Zohar* about Rabbi Shimon bar Yohai meeting the old man with two myrtles.

36. The blessing over wine is omitted here.

37. This prayer is attributed to Rabbi Isaac ibn Ghayyat, who lived in Spain in the eleventh century.

38. A paraphrased version of Joseph Heinemann's treatment of *Midrash Tanhuma* in his "The Human Soul is God's Lamp" in *Drashat B'tsibbur B' Tikufat Ha-Talmud* (Jerusalem: Mossad Bialik, 1970), pp. 52–56.

39. Raba says: "(To use) a torch for *Havdalah* (as opposed to a candle) is the preferred (way of performing this) duty" (*Pesahim* 7b).

40. Judah Loew ben Bezalel, the Maharal, *Ner Mitzvah al-Hanukkah* in *Or Hadash* (Prague original), Hebrew trans. by Freema Gottlieb (reprint: Bnai Brak, Israel, 1971), pp. 69–70.

41. Ibid.

42. The *Kavod* (Honor or Glory) became an equivalent for the *Shekhinah*. In Arabic the word *Shakhinah* means glorious.

43. The Maharal, *Ner Mitzvah,* p. 69.

44. See Chapter 8, *The Work of the Menorah,* on the notion that man is only an *incomplete* image of God, that he captures only one out of four dimensions, and that sculpture of the human form should, therefore, be permissible (pp. 429–438).

45. The Maharal, *Ner Mitzvah,* p. 69.

46. The Hebrew for "shining brilliant" is *mazhir bahir,* a reference to the two major kabbalistic texts, the *Bahir* and the *Zohar,* literally "The Brilliance" and "The Shine," both named after particular qualities of light. God saw the Torah and the Commandments, and He also saw the enlightenment to be derived from kabbalistic lore. All of these are different tonalities of light and all of them are good.

47. See "Light of the Feminine," p. 12.

48. Based on the Maharal, *Ner Mitzvah,* p. 70.

49. Not only the commandment to learn Torah, but also many of the more practical commandments are addressed to men and not to women. However, three special commandments are applicable particularly to women and are known as "women's commandments." They are separation from men during the menstrual cycle, separation of part of the dough when baking bread, and the kindling of the Sabbath lights.

50. See "Hidden Light," pp. 142, 179.

51. See Chapter 1, pp. 36–38.

52. The Jewish People and every Jewish Bride represents *Knesset Yisrael* and the *Shekhinah,* the 'Feminine' part of God.

53. Jiri Langer, *Nine Gates* (Edinburgh, Scotland: James Clarke and Co., 1961), pp. 136–137.

54. Newman, *Hasidic Anthology,* p. 328, no. 9.

55. "Whoever performs one commandment causes that power to descend upon the same commandment above . . . and he is considered as if he maintained one part of the Holy One, Blessed be He, literally." R. Menahem Recanati, Introduction, *Ta'amey ha-Mitzvot,* fol. 13c, quoted in Idel, *New Perspectives,* p. 188.

56. See this chapter, p. 260, *Vayikra Rabbah* 4:2.

57. Rabbi Joseph Gikatalia, *Gates of Light* or *Shaarey Orah,* 1, p. 14b, quoted in Aryeh Kaplan, *Meditations and Kabbalah* (New York: Samuel Weiser, 1982), p. 130.

58. For any minor lapse or impurity, the Priests died. Those who looked after the altar knew it was at risk of their lives that they enjoyed this privilege. And then there is the signal case of Nadav and Avihu, the sons of Aaron who perished for sacrificing "strange fire."

59. The *Midrash* also does the same. At one point, Israel is compared to an olive tree and God to the Lamp that will shine with Israel's oil.

FIVE

LIGHTS

OF

MAGIC

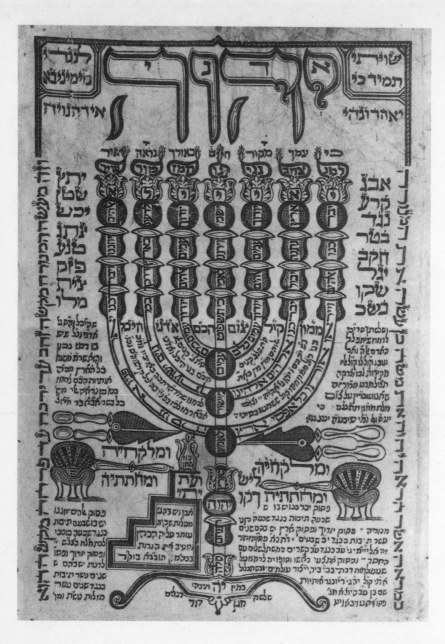

Shiviti (eighteenth-century Spain or Italy) by Abraham Alenkar. The Amulet traces the locus of Divine Light from Zion to every place on earth and the locus of prayer and *mitzvot* from every place on earth back to Jerusalem, Heaven's Gate. (*Courtesy of The Library of The Jewish Theological Seminary of America*)

Since Temple times, the *Menorah* has been popularly invested with powers human and divine. It serves as a convenient mirror or screen for the projection of various lineaments of the human body (*Adam Kadmon*), each of which is associated with a particular set of qualities. These qualities, when extended and enhanced to an infinite degree, become what we think of as godlike. From the very outset, the *Menorah* has symbolized the Providential, nurturing maternal aspects of God as embodied in the Eye and the Hand.

THE *MENORAH* AS THE EYES OF GOD

As a lighted house usually signifies someone's presence there so the *Menorah* 's light in the Temple is a sign and a conductor of God's Presence. The *Menorah* in the most human terms, was described by the Prophet Zechariah as the very "eye(s) of God" (Zechariah 4:10). According to Arabic mystics of the early Middle Ages, the "eyes" referred to are human; they are God's saints. How does God "see" in this world except through the eyes of human beings who have given their selfhood to His service. Jewish mysticism contains the same idea, only with the saints described as "Lamps."

There is an intimate connection between light and the eye that makes the description of the Temple *Menorah* as "God's eyes" very gratifying. The eye is the organ through which light is perceived and reflected, and a beam of light or even a star is often spoken of as an eye because of its impact upon the on-looker.

On the tombstone of Eusebius the Alexandrian and his wife Theodora there is a Greek inscription under an outline of a *Menorah* to the effect that this is the image of the "God who sees." Jerusalem, Zion, and the Temple are the site of the *Akedah,* the place where Abraham was prepared to sacrifice his son and where, as a reward, God promised him "I shall be seen."

Also, Jerusalem has been described as the "eye of the universe." The Land of Israel, Jerusalem, and Zion are places where the beholder is blessed with an extra dimension of "seeing," illumination, and revelation of Divine Presence.

Here we are faced with a collection of containers inside containers, which, like a set of Russian dolls, all symbolize the same thing:

> Abba Issi said in the name of Samuel the Lesser:
> The world is like a human eyeball.
> The white of the eye is the ocean surrounding the world.
> The iris is the continent,
> The pupil is Jerusalem,
> And the image in the pupil is the Holy Temple.
>
> (*Derech Eretz Zuta* 9:13, 59a)

The whole world symbolizes an eye, but Jerusalem is the pupil of the eye; the Holy Temple is the quintessence of eye, while the *Menorah* is the quintessence of a quintessence – the eye that is reflected in the pupil of the eye.

Adam was a microcosm of the world. The whole world resembles the ball of his eye (the eye reflects what is seen, so what is seen is said to resemble the eye!); the ocean that encircles the earth is like unto the white of the eye, the dry land is the iris; Jerusalem the pupil, and the Temple the image mirrored in the pupil of the eye.[1] [Here Jerusalem is not a part of objective reality but the projection of something within God, as is the whole world.]

Embryologically and anatomically, both the eye and the hand are extensions of the brain and can even be considered as exposed parts of it. Just as God sends Divine Light to us through the channels of the *Sefirot,* so, through the central nervous system, the brain issues and transmits its commands to these extremities. What the person sees not only puts him in touch with the outside world but also reveals that person's true nature.

SEEING AS A CREATIVE ACT

Ancients and Kabbalists did not regard seeing as an involuntary reflex. On the contrary, they believed the eye sent out a stream of energy similar to that of the Sun causing the object to become visible. Galen (d. 201 C.E.) held that vision was produced by rays of light emitted by the eyes. In the Renaissance, Leonardo da Vinci (d. 1519) thought that the eyes emitted a stream of light, which came into contact with the thing seen. All agreed that seeing was a creative act, in which the "seer" was at least a collaborator with the object under scrutiny. This belief, though it fell increasingly into disfavor in the rationalistic age of the eighteenth century onward, has been brought back into favor by Einsteinian atomic theory.

The analogy between the brain, the nervous system, and the human organs, and Divine Light, the Sefirotic channels, and man can be drawn even further. For just as the idea has been put forward that the brain developed after the eye to make use of information assimilated by that organ, so the Kabbalists have suggested that there is a way in which we can reverse the emanations so that our acts and the streams of light we give out can even affect and shape the Divine.

If what we see is radically affected by how we see it, if even God is molded by the way man imagines Him, the heart itself becomes a powerful instrument for evil or good. It was also believed that people became the targets of the stray thoughts and *kavannot* of others let loose and transmitted through the eye. And this was the grounds for belief in the Evil Eye.[2]

According to a *Midrash, sohera* is the name of the magic shield with which God will protect all who traffic (*soher*) in the Truth of the Torah. *Sohera* or *soheret* is also the name of the Jewel that is beyond price—Sophia, Wisdom, or Torah itself. What the *Midrash* is saying is that the Torah is both an ornament and a shield forged by The Holy One as a defense against evil both from without and from within.

R. Shimon bar Yohai topped this with the additional remark that The Holy One, Blessed be He, gave Israel at Sinai a weapon upon which the Ineffable Name was written. "Thou shalt not be afraid of the terror by night" (Psalm 91:5)—namely, Igrath, Queen of the demons (*Badmidbar Rabbah* 12:3).

The protective qualities popularly associated with the wearing of a six-pointed "Star of David" actually derive from the *Menorah*. According to legend, when King David went into battle the original *Magen David* was not shaped like a hexagram but like a *Menorah*. On it Psalm 67 was engraved in full, one verse for each branch of the candlestick.

> God be merciful to us, and bless us and cause His face to shine upon us. [Psalm 67:2]

The "Star" was not an intrinsically Jewish sign but was imposed on the People by non-Jews in Germany as late as the fourteenth century, and was intended as a badge of subjugation at the same time as the Jüdenhütte, the three-cornered "Jew's hat" became the enforced insignia of the Jewish male, as a mockery of a crown.[3]

As an abstract representation of "God's eyes" and Divine Omniscience, the Temple *Menorah* embodied certain popular beliefs. The *Midrash* states explicitly that if the Jewish People take care to kindle the *Menorah* lights, God will "preserve them from all evil things" (*Bamidbar Rabbah* 15:8).

COLORS AND AMULETS

One of the many dangers the kindling of the *Menorah* is said to guard against is the Evil Eye. Here the magic principle of *simila similibus curantur* is operative. The logic by which sympathetic magic operates is very similar to that of the most sophisticated medicine. As in the use of antibodies to provide immunity against disease, so objects meant to represent the eye – here the Temple *Menorah* or "God's Eyes" – are used as a protection against the Evil Eye. In fact, a good definition of the Evil Eye is a mirror that kills itself with its own impurity, like Medusa seeing herself in a mirror.

Belief in the Evil Eye originated in Babylon. Before that, there was also a Phoenician, Canaanite, and Carthaginian influence. The Arabic for a person with the Evil Eye is *fih l'ain* or *fih l-nefs* (like the Hebrew *nefesh,* soul), meaning "He has the breath (or the soul)," as the Eye was a manifestation of special spiritual powers. Another Arabic expression for the same dubious gift was *fih l-kelma,* "He has the word." Thus a whole nexus of connections between word and light, soul and light, and word and spirit are pinpointed.

A person may cause injury, even unintentionally, by the glance of his eye. And speech makes it worse. Among the Jews and Arabs of North Africa there are stories of how people could kill with a look. The threat of being taken over by other people's mental and spiritual world, as reflected in the eye, and not possessive jealousy, has been suggested as the real reason for the seclusion of the harem and for women wearing the veil. In Arab lands, very handsome men also used to veil their faces, especially at feasts and fairs, in order to preserve themselves from the evil eye.[4]

The idea behind use of the veil was a variation on the "Hidden Light." According to legend, "First Light" was so sensitized that it was subject to misuse by wicked people. It was also so dazzling that it could kill. This is why God hid it. In the same way, God hides the Sun in a sheath so that it will not strike out at people like a sword but allow them time for gradual acclimatization. It has been pointed out in "Song of Songs" that there is something "terrible" about "Beauty," "Fair as the Moon," "clear as the Sun," "Terrible as an army of Banners" (Song of Songs 6:10)–and that is why it is hidden.

Not only veils and sheaths, but also flashing mirrors, the color black, and a whole barrage of grotesqueries were used by the Arabs of North Africa to combat the Evil Eye. These acted as diversions, attracting to themselves the malignant look.

Hideous objects were deployed close by to divert attention from the object of desire. Thus, the skull of an animal or the black picture of a Christian–Christians were not popular with these Infidels–or a black cooking pot painted with white stripes would be posted in Arab vegetable gardens and orchards with the same function as a scarecrow. When a new house was built, a black pot was hung on the wall to distract the demons' displeasure. This is in a way similar to the Jewish practice of creating a small imperfection inside the home so as not to live in a flawless interior when the Holy Temple lies in ruins.

Some tribes in Morocco protected their girls by attaching something black to their dresses or by tying a black goat's tail to the hair of boys or by hanging a black pippin in their gardens. It was usually the custom for a bridegroom to wear a white cloak, but sometimes he wore black to guard against the Evil Eye. When the Bride was conducted to her new home, a black man sometimes led the procession so that onlookers would stare at him and divert attention from the real star of the occasion.

Colored beads and bright stones were often attached to silver Hebrew amulets. Silver coins, jewels, and semiprecious stones such as corals and pieces of carnelian, mother of pearl, and amber were believed to have amuletic properties. Blue beads hold a special fascination for *Sephardim*. I was told they represented eyes threaded together. Probably blue beads are so popular as protection because blue eyes were held to present a special threat. Arabic or Sephardic beads are reminiscent of the verse in the "Song of Songs": "You have enchanted me with one bead of your necklace" (Song of Songs 4:9).

Interestingly, the Catholic custom of "telling" a rosary

might actually be a link both with the Jewish *Atarot* and the *Sefirot*. *Sefirot* also comes from the Hebrew word "to count" or "to tell." And the *Atarah* nowadays is the name given not only to the Diadem of *Knesset Yisrael,* but also to the silver embroidered edging of the *Tallit*. At moments of intense concentration, however, the *Tallit* and the *Atarah* are drawn round the head like a crown. The *Tallit* itself symbolizes the robe of the Holy One with which He drew out the emanations of white (light) and blue (the sapphire or His Throne, after which the *Sefirot* are allegedly named). Therefore, the *Sefirot* really exist like jewels in some kind of Divine necklace linking man with Divine Light. At the same time as these beads and *kavannot* bring positive forces into the world, they also protect against negative forces.

Blue was the lucky color in the Middle East, and the color blue was enough to provide a basic form of amulet. Asurbanipal, King of Assyria, writes: "I caused brick to be baked with blue (enamel) and I placed them over the doors." So the Jewish custom of protecting the doorpost with *Mezuzot* and *Menorot* had parallels among the Assyrians.

Not only the doorposts of houses, but also the head and other parts of the body were similarly decorated. In Morocco parents used to impress a blue spot or blue lines on the forehead of their children, or tie blue ribbons in their children's hair or round their ankles, or thread bits of blue on a string, which was slung over their shoulder, to safeguard them from the Evil Eye.

Tikhelet, the blue dye of the *chilozan,* a kind of seafish, was used for the *Tzitzit*. This Jewish blue was not primarily used to guard against negative forces but as a reminder of the positive.

The Ramban (Rabbi Moshe ben Nachman, twelfth century) asks how the fringes attached to the *Tallit* help us remember the Commandments. Rejecting the notion that the spelling of the Hebrew for fringes, *Tzitzit,* can be forced into the equivalent of the 613 *mitzvot,* he says it is because of the blue thread that runs through them (Ramban on Numbers 15:37–41). Blue is special both because of its name and because of the actual impact of that color upon the senses. *Tikhelet* contains in it the word *Kol,* the All, or the fullness, perfection, and consummation of everything, the end and resting place of desire. It is also related to the Hebrew word for yearning and for Bride, *Kallah*, and a name of the *Shekhinah*.

Thus it says in the *Bahir* (no. 117) that a king had in mind to plant nine masculine palm trees in his garden, but He realized that if they all were of one sex, they would not endure. So He took the palm tree, which is long like a phallus but which bears dates with a split like the female sex organ, and He took the *etrog* (citron). In the Bible it is referred to as the "tree of Beauty" (Leviticus 23:40), the feminine representative of the festal bouquet of *Sukkot*. So in the doctrine of the *Sefirot*, was the lowest feminine Kingship formed. "And on account of her, woman was taken from man, for the higher and the lower world could not endure without the feminine." Although the preponderance of higher *Sefirot* was overweeningly male, the whole structure was not complete without the finishing touch of the feminine.[5]

In the Talmud it says on Genesis 24:1 "And the Lord had blessed Abraham with everything (*Bakol*)," that if this really were the case, then a man cannot really be said to have tasted all the most fundamental experiences this world has to offer until he sees himself reproduced in a daughter (*Baba Batra* 16b). Therefore, the Hebrew word *Bakol* (with everything) means that God blessed him with a daughter; she was the finishing touch to his happiness. Again, the Hebrew word for 'everything' is associated with the *Shekhinah* in the expression in *Baba Batra* 25a, *Shekhinah Bakol*, or the Divine Presence permeates everything (*Bahir*, nos. 51, 52).[6]

It is the Ramban's contention that the color blue is the consummation of all color and that on the horizon all shades melt into the blue and appear to be that color. This natural phenomenon of the merging of all colors in one overriding unity in the world of sensual experience is taken as an analogy for the ascent of consciousness, "leading one finally to think of Him who is on High."

Hezekiah (the king) said: "In what way does blue differ from other colors, that God should have commanded that it be inserted in the fringes?"

Because blue resembles grass, grass resembles the sea, the sea resembles the sky, the sky resembles a rainbow, a rainbow resembles a cloud, a cloud resembles the heavenly throne, and the throne resembles the divine glory; for it says, *As the appearance of the bow that is in the cloud* (Ezekiel 1:28).

He accordingly gave to those who fear Him the color of blue which resembles His own glory; as it says, *That they put with the fringe of each corner a thread of blue* (Numbers 15:38). [*Bamidbar Rabbah* 14:3]

Blue here is an aid to meditation. We are faced with a whole series of associations of the color blue, until we ascend to the Glory Itself. The Talmud interweaves the sapphire stone coloration of the Throne of Glory into the same type of meditation.

Rabbi Meir asked: "Why is blue different from all other colors?"

Because the color of the sea is blue and the Heavens resemble the sea in this respect, the Heavens again are similar in color to the Throne of Glory for it is written: *And they saw the God of Israel; and there was under His feet as it were a paved work of a sapphire stone and as it were the body of the heavens in His clearness* (Exodus 24:10). Furthermore, it is written: *And above the firmament that was over their heads was the likeness of a throne, as the appearance of a sapphire stone* (Ezekiel 1:16). [*Hullin* 89a]

Blue is the color of the feminine aspect of God that helps create the world. It is the color of the firmament, of the dividing water created on the Second Day. It is an expression of the creative act of separation stemming from the Left Feminine side of the Divine. Interestingly, the Hebrew word for "Glory" (or the *Shekhinah*)—*kavod*—means "blue" in Arabic. When the camp of the Israelites was about to set out, the *Menorah* and all its lamps were always wrapped in a cloth entirely of blue (Numbers 4:6).

Colors were used for all kinds of amulets. For example, reddish stones were used as a protection against hemorrhages and fluxes—red against red. Just as the various names of God were written down in the color of the specific *Sefirah* linked with that Name as—for instance, red for judgment, white for Love, green for Mercy, and encased in an amulet to bring down an influx of good–so they were also used to combat evil.

To combat the Evil Eye, the Arab inhabitants of Palestine often used to mark their doorposts with a square or a circle, a continuation of the custom of the Canaanites, of positioning their sexual fetishes to stand guard on the threshold. As we shall see on p. 300, not only were various motifs of eyes enlisted by Arabs and by Sephardic Jews to deflect the malignant rays raining forth from the Evil Eye, but the hand, and sometimes a combination of the eye and the hand, was called upon.

Visually the *Menorah* resembles no other human organ as much as a hand–fingers extended from the central shaft. That Sephardic Jews have settled on this resemblance is demonstrated by the fact that in the amuletic papercuts with which they protect the interiors of their homes from the Evil Eye, they alternate the image of the *Hamsa* (the amuletic figure of the Protective Hand) with that of the *Menorah*. Each branch of the *Menorah* is made up of *Serugin,* miniscule letters of special Psalms etched to form the branches of a *Menorah*. Verses stenciled on the branches include the eight lines of Psalm 67, "God cause His face to shine upon you. . . ."; the forty-two-letter name of God, and the verse; "Joseph is a fruitful bough, even a fruitful bough by a well, whose branches run over the wall" (Genesis 49:22). These amulets all serve as protection against the Evil Eye.

The *Menorah* of Moshe was tipped with almond blossom– the Hebrew for almond being *shaked,* which also means "to watch," a kind of Divine vigilance. "The Lord watches over His Word to do it" (Jeremiah 1:12). Each flower starring each branch, and each flame blossoming from each hollow serve as a kind of watchful eye for protection of the interior.

Legend has it that the staff of Aaron, which swallowed the wands of all the Egyptian magicians, also came from the almond tree. And a wand obviously is an extension of the hand.

There is a Sephardic synagogue in Jerusalem on whose walls a blend of all these motifs figures. Friezes are decorated with permutations of Divine Names drawn in the shapes of hands, seven-branched candlesticks, and long almond-shaped eyes.

It was specifically the *arms* of the *Menorah* that the Prophet Zechariah referred to as "the eyes of the Lord that wander to and fro through the ends of the earth" (Zechariah 4:10). In the *Menorah* the images of both hand and eye come together.

Rooted in Zion, the Lamp spreads light and blessing to all nations. It is said that when the *Menorah* shines it is a sign that the *Shekhinah* rests upon Israel. Just as the Sun, the Moon, and the stars are described as "signs" in the physical heavens, so the *Menorah,* a copy of the planetary system within the microcosm of the Temple and also a "feeder" of celestial light to the entire cosmos, is the quintessential sign, the "Symbol of Symbols." As such, it had to serve a creative function – transmitting light and blessing to the Jewish People and to the furthest reaches of the cosmos. It was virtually a generator of godliness in the physical world.

Similarly, the *Menorah* is both a positive sign of Divine Presence and a protection against negative forces.

> For I, saith the Lord, will be unto her a wall of fire round about, and I will be the glory in the midst of her. [Zechariah 2:9]

Pure protection and Presence from within and without, just like the *Menorah* – on the one hand God will wall Jerusalem with a barrier of fire from her enemies; on the other the same fire, become light, will be the royal identity burning in her very midst. In short, she will be sandwiched within and without by the Divine Light.

THE *TEFILLIN* AND THE *MEZUZAH*

The *Menorah* has popularly been invested with magical properties, as have other visible "signs" of Jewishness, such as *Tefillin* and the *Mezuzah*. The Gaon Sherira lumps together *Mezuzah, Tefillin,* and *Menorah* as amuletic signs to ward off evil.

According to the Talmud, *Tefillin* ward off Satan and demons, and the *Mezuzah* keeps the demons out of the house. The Greek translation of the word *Tefillin* means "amulet." Contrariwise, the Hebrew word for amulet is *kamea,* yet the same word is applied to *Tefillin.* [7]

In the Torah, the *Tefillin* and the *Mezuzah* were signs of the written Covenant between God and Israel and, as such, channels for Divine help. In both the *Tefillin* and the *Mezuzah,* there are Hebrew quotations about the Unity of God, which presumably might counter any susceptibility to believe in lesser powers.

There was a tendency to use letters and writings for magical purposes to gain control over the workings of nature or the future. So, the sixty letters making up the Blessing of the Priests (Numbers 6:24–26) were said to be sixty guardian powers protecting Israel against the terrors of the night (*Shir HaShirim Rabbah* 3:7; *Bamidbar Rabbah* 12; *Pesikta Rabbati* 5).

Use of amulets is noted without any value judgment in II Maccabees 12:40 and in *Mishnah Shabbat* 60a. But in his *Guide to the Perplexed,* the Rambam, comes out virulently against "the craziness of the amulet writers" (1:61).

> Those who inscribe the names of angels or of Holy Ones or a phrase from the Bible on a seal within it (a *Mezuzah*) come into the category of those who have no share in the life to come, for not only have these misguided ones negated the *mitzvah,* but they have also made of the great *mitzvah* extolling the Unity of God, whose Name be blessed, and His love and His service as if it were a mere *kameah* (amulet) for their own benefit, as they believe in their foolish minds. [The Rambam, *Mishneh Torah Hilhot Tefillin* 5:4]

The use of amulets is one of the many links between Sephardic Jews and *Hasidim.* Even as great a rationalist as the Rambam does not deny their efficacy and tacitly admits that they work on exactly the same principle as the *Mezuzah,* he only opposes putting something holy to profane use.

The Talmud takes a pragmatic approach to curative amulets. If they worked, they were not considered "following the Canaanites" (*Shabbat* 67a). (Here there is a tacit admission as to their ultimate source.)

The superstitious element that surrounds many of these signs frequently derives, as the Rambam himself pointed out,

from a genuinely supernatural content. The *Mezuzah* is supposed
to have powers of life and death; the Israelites were rid of a plague
of serpents by looking up at a bronze Serpent, which later stood
in the Temple courtyard. In Temple times another "light" image,
in addition to the *Menorah,* was invested with the magical qualities of an oracle.

The *Urim* and *Tummim* were apronlike garments worn by the
High Priest. These breastplates were set with twelve precious
stones engraved with the names of twelve tribes (Exodus
28:15–30; Leviticus 8:8).

The High Priest used the *Urim* and *Tummim* to ask God
questions about the outcome of certain political enterprises on
behalf of a representative of the government much as Saul asked
the help of the Witch of Endor before his final battle (Numbers
2:21; *Yoma* 7:5, I Samuel 14:18). Although the *Urim* and *Tummim*
were legitimate oracles whereas witchcraft was forbidden, natural magic was not condemned because it did not work, but
because it placed obstacles in the way of faith in God.

There are various opinions as to why the *Urim* and *Tummim*
were so-called and how they worked. The Talmud said they
were called *Urim* and *Tummim* because their message was enlightening and complete (*Yoma* 73b).

URIM AND *TUMMIN*: MEDITATION
ON THE LETTERS AND MEDITATION
ON THE LIGHTS

The *Urim* and *Tummim* combine both major forms of meditation
to be found in Judaism – meditation on the Letters and meditation
on the Lights. The oracle was brought about by rays of light
shining on the letters that made up the response; alternatively,
those letters stood out, forming themselves into the wording
(*Yoma* 73b). The face of the inquirer (the king or Head of the
Sanhedrin) was directed to the High Priest, who directed his gaze
towards the *Shekhinah.* Questions settled by the oracle included
the division of land and the conflict between Saul and David.
The oracle was no longer consulted after the end of the First
Prophets (*Sota* 9:12).

Basing himself on the Talmud (*Yoma* 73b), the Rambam says

that the names of the various Tribes were engraved on the stones of the breastplate. Miraculously, certain letters would protrude or shine out after the Oracle had been consulted, spelling out the answer to the query. According to Rashi, the *Urim* (literally, lights) consisted of a separate document bearing the Tetragrammaton (the Divine Name), ensuring that the oracle would be clear and that it would come true (Rashi on Exodus 28:30).

Ibn Ezra believed that the *Urim* and *Tummim* were symbols for the Seven Servants – that is, the Seven planets (Ibn Ezra on Exodus 28:30) – and that concentration on them was similar to an act of astrology.

Abraham Abulafia said that when the High Priest directed his consciousness to the Divine Name, he become clothed with the Holy Spirit. Then the High Priest would imagine the meaning of the letters shining in front of him and permutate his response through the power of prophecy.

He adds that in addition to symbolizing the lights of the cosmos, the *Urim* and *Tummim* represent "First Light," allowing leeway for subjective vision and for every individual's personal light. In them is signified both the light of the Torah, "as one to whom God has granted a little bit of knowledge and enlightened the eyes of his heart to see the entire world with its light," and the light of the luminaries.

Abulafia proceeds to combine imagery of the external light of the Sun and the Moon with the spiritual knowledge of Torah. He explains the meaning of the Blessing, "May God shine His face upon you" (Numbers 6:25) as an allusion to cosmography – the Sun derives its strength from 'First Light,' the Moon from the Sun – and as a metaphor for spiritual illumination. On the one hand there is 'God's Face,' His view from the standpoint of eternity or Primordial Light; on the other hand, this view contains the multitude of subjective facets or rays of light by which each one "sees what he sees."[8]

Thus, each person's perception is a fragment of "First Light"; each person's "light" by means of which everyone "sees what he sees" is a mirroring of the Divine Face – and the *Urim* and *Tummim* are an image of both the subjective and the objective view.

According to Abulafia, the *Urim* are the "glass that shines," the objective vision of the Transcendental as seen by Moshe, while the *Tummim* are the "glass that does not shine," the imaginings and nighttime visions of all other prophets and dreamers, which contain the dross of the subjective projection. The *Urim* signify the inner Form of Man, identified with the Intellect, and the *Tummim* refer to the Imagination.

There are certain magical corollaries to man's having been made in the image of God. One is that man, and indeed every object on earth, as well as being a vessel for the Divine Light, is actually a mirror and replica of it. Another is that there exists a whole train of correspondences between Above and Below. The "signs" epitomize this inherent symmetry.

The underlying idea is based on what goes on between lovers – "My Beloved is mine and I am His" – a relationship built on some point of likeness. Just as a magician takes control by making the wax image of his victim, so we allow ourselves to be appropriated by God through these outward symbols. As seen by the young Solomon Maimon, both pagan magic and *Kabbalah* have an identical purpose – to bring down the flow of Divine light. But whereas the Canaanite magicians relied on natural principles as unfolded in astrology and in the splendid rotation of the Sun, the Moon, and the stars, Jews use the letters and the commandments of the Torah to compose the spiritual inward "Work of the Sanctuary, Work of the Menorah."

Sephardic Jews mention the *Menorah* every day when they put on *Tefillin*. Before they wind on the straps of their phylacteries, binding themselves to God with the words: "And I betroth thee unto Me forever . . . ," they say a special prayer mentioning the *Menorah* as a connection between Heaven and earth, similar to the armbands they are winding round, and a veritable conduit for God's bounty to Creation through the seven *Sefirot:* "And may Your sweet oil course through the seven channels of the *Menorah,* distributing Your goodness to Your creatures. O, open Your Hand and satisfy all living with favor!"

The branches of the Temple *Menorah,* the straps of the *Tefillin* make up seven rings, binding man to God. When Jews put on *Tefillin,* or perform any command, such as the commandment

to light a *Menorah,* reverberations are set in motion on high, like
the overture and response between lovers. The impact of performing any of these acts on the *Sefirot* and the very structure of
divine cosmology has been described in much the same terms,
alluding to the overflow of bounty from a cosmic *Menorah* as that
in the passage recited when putting on *Tefillin:*

> When the Supernal Luminary watches men and sees their good
> and proper deeds, (then) in accordance with what they stir below,
> they stir above, and He opens His good storehouse and pours the
> fine oil upon His head and from thence upon His other attributes
> (*Sefirot*).[9]

The image of the Supernal Luminary (God) we have to work
with here is a cosmic *Menorah,* with the oil of abundance flowing
from above to below.

In another work of Sephardic *Kabbalah* of roughly the same
period[10] the commandment of *Tefillin* is described as crowning
the King with a Diadem or *Atarah.* In Eliezer of Worms's *Sefer
haHokmah,* God's *Tefillin* are said to be composed of the *Tefillot*
(Prayers) of Israel interwoven into a Crown that ascends to sit on
God's Head. Here and in *Kabbalah* the *Atarah* is generally the
feminine equivalent of *Keter Elyon,* the *Shekhinah,* Prayer personified, and *Knesset Yisrael.* [11]

Originally crowns consisted, not of jewels but of oil and
essential light brimming over from above for the benefit of what
lies beneath or vice versa. The essential image of crowning is oil
overflowing from *Keter* or the Crown of the Head to the other
attributes or *Sefirot.* Conversely, when Israel observes any commandment, such as *Tefillin* and especially the kindling of the
Menorah, She accepts upon Herself God's Kingdom and in doing
so, She becomes His Crown. When She prays, the Crown takes
the form of Prayers; when Jews put on *Tefillin,* each knot is a
jewel on Her *Atarah* and the *Menorah* is composed of a Crown of
Lights. Each single prayer, each candle, each knot of the *Tefillin,*
every individual soul, is a channel conducting the flow of light up
and down between *Atarah* and *Keter Elyon* (God and the People of

Israel). To chart the ebb and flow of their relationship is to trace out the shaft and branches of a cosmic vertical *Menorah*.

According to the Talmud, the eight-branched *Menorah* was originally conceived as a kind of "doormarker," corresponding to the *Mezuzah* that marks the threshold to the Jewish home, and its original placement was opposite the *Mezuzah* (*Baba Kamma* 6:6). The original correspondence between *Menorah* and *Mezuzah* is highlighted by the interpretation suggested by the minor Talmudic tractate *Soferim* of the verse from the Song of Songs: "How fair you are; and how lovely are you" (Song of Songs 7:7). "How fair you are with the *Mezuzah,* and how lovely are you with the *Hanukkah* Lamp."

The *Mezuzah* on the right doorpost (for entry) and the *Menorah* to balance it on the left (for exit) both served as guardians of the home and as proclamations of Jewish identity, one in the form of light, one in the form of a text or "Word," a special distillation of light.

HOLY SYMMETRY

In the Shabbat Bridal Song, *Lekha Dodi,* by Solomon Alkabetz of Safed (1505–1584), is the line "right and left you will spread out." Only through fixing the "signs" of *Mezuzah* and *Menorah* on the right and the left doorposts, says the Kalever Rebbe, will Israel ultimately realize the joy of the Messiah.

In Babylonian architecture, a sacred temple, ark, throne, or chariot would be flanked by two balancing entities; whether cherubim, dragons, olive trees, or lamps, they were obviously bodyguards, and there had to be two of them for symmetry.

This balance of two bodyguards required by royal personages is also preserved in Jewish iconography. Thus the Holy Ark is protected by two lions, and around Solomon's Throne were ten *Menorot,* five on one side and five on the other, probably symbolizing the Ten *Sefirot.* And even the *Menorah* itself is composed of seven branches, the Seven *Sefirot* of natural material realms, three balanced against three, with a central shaft. It is the central shaft that reaches right up to the heavenly reservoirs, while the two groups of three serve as its bodyguard, in the same way as in the week the Seventh Day is "guarded" by the three days before and the three days after *Shabbat*. The same kind of symmetry is preserved both by the hand and the eye, which come in pairs protecting the body and the face, both on the right and on the left hand side.

Just as in ancient shrines in the Near East two lamps would be placed as a kind of bodyguard outside the entrance, the *Menorah* was positioned outside the Holy of Holies "opposite to" or "as a conductor of" *Shekhinah*, and the later *Menorah* of *Hanukkah* was placed opposite the *Mezuzah* at the entrance to the Jewish home. In both cases the *Menorah* performs the function of bodyguard (or protector from external malign forces), together with some other object (the Holy Ark, or the *Mezuzah*).

An understanding of the function of the *Mezuzah* can provide an insight into some of the layers of meaning associated with the *Menorah*, with which to a certain extent it seems to correspond.

The occult powers of the *Mezuzah* go back to the Redemption from Egypt. During the last of the Ten Plagues, the Israelites were commanded to sprinkle the blood of the Paschal Lamb on their doorposts. Because the Lamb was an Egyptian deity, so the story goes, the Israelites were demonstrating their faith in God by their action. In a sense it was their own blood they were ready to sprinkle on the doorposts to their homes. Three times they sprinkled the blood, once on each doorpost and once on the lintel. Then, says the Bible, the Angel of Death "passed over" the households of those Israelites whose doorposts were marked in this way. Later, in Temple times, this threefold sprinkling was reenacted as a rite for the Paschal Sacrifice, representing the three exiles.

We can only draw upon the secret energy of the *Hanukkah* light kindled on the left through the strength of the *Mezuzah* on the right. What is the text written in the *Mezuzah*? It is the *Shema*, the Central Prayer in Judaism: "And you shall love the Lord your God with all your soul." So the *Menorah* light is the equivalent of the life-force of the soul.

Since the Angel of Death passed over the Jewish doorposts, *Mezuzot* have been popularly invested with powers over life and death. Long life is mentioned as the reward for having a correct *Mezuzah* affixed to one's door. Thus the Talmud and the *Zohar* tell us that the *Mezuzah* guards against premature death because Jewish children were saved during the Passover night. Where there is a valid *Mezuzah,* says the *Zohar,* death departs. It was customary whenever there was an epidemic or widespread catastrophe to examine whether the Hebrew letters and Divine Names in the *Mezuzah* were still intact. Solomon Luria (1510–1573) reported that "an evil spirit used to torment Rabbi Meir of Rothenburg whenever he took a nap at noon," but that after he attached a *Mezuzah* to the door of his study the evil spirit let him alone.

Isaiah Horowitz (c. 1555–c. 1630) summed up the protective powers of the *Mezuzah* this way:

> God says, I have set a guardian outside the door of My sanctuary (the Jewish home) to establish a decree for My heavenly and earthly household; while it is upon the door every destroyer and demon must flee from it.[12]

It was a commonly held kabbalistic notion – articulated, for example, by Rabbi Isaac the Blind of Provence (thirteenth century) – that the term *guardian of Israel* so commonly used in the prayers and in the psalms refers to God's Tenth feminine Kingship, the *Shekhinah,* in her capacity as *Matrona,* a word which he derives from the Aramaic *Matara* – "guard."[13]

Thus, this text of Isaiah Horowitz's might with some leeway be interpreted to the effect that it is the feminine function of the *Shekhinah* to guard God's "heavenly and earthly household" from other malign feminine influences such as Lilith and her progeny of demons.

In the First World War, Jewish soldiers carried *Mezuzot* in their pockets to deflect bullets. Silver *Mezuzot*-like fish were also used against the Evil Eye. According to Rashi, the gentile rulers in countries to which Jews were exiled were also convinced of the protective properties of the *Mezuzah* and were eager to place them over the doors of their castles and palaces.

However, it must be noted that the originality of the Israelites did not consist in the fact that they decorated their doorposts, the corners of their garments, or their persons. These were the places where the ancient Canaanites and Phoenicians used to put their totems and *Terafim*. Setting up an especially powerful force to guard the entry to one's home is logical. The only question is what to guard it with. The Israelites guarded their doorposts with signs and texts reminding them of the unity of God.

HAND SYMBOLISM

Among Jews and Arabs of Mediterranean lands, the *Hamsa* or Protective Hand, in addition to being a symbol representing the eye, is used to decorate the doorpost to drive away evil influences from the threshold of the home. In Marrakesh there was hardly a house, shop, wall, or door where the five fingers were not represented by the rough image of the hand with the out-stretched finger, five fingers united by a horizontal line, or five isolated lines, longer or shorter, occasionally dwindling into dots. The open hand looks like a capital E with five staves instead of three. In Fez, five fingers emerge from a common shaft painted with tar, red earth, henna, or blue, and an impression is made of the hands with black tar on the doors and the walls. In Libya, a woman would dip her right hand in white, blue, green, or red, and stamp her palm, fingers raised, on the wood or clay surface of the wall in front of the door to her home. In Algeria, a sculptured hand was attached to one side of the wall of the doorway, just as the *Menorah* and the *Mezuzah* were in Jewish homes. The image of the hand was a secret recipe for fumigating the door of one's home.

The oldest "hand" in existence is to be found on the caduceus on the stelae of Tanit Tene Baal, a celestial lunar goddess, consort of Baal-Hamon in Western Phoenicia. Human figures with arms extended have also been found on Phoenician and Punic monuments.

Certain basic Hand Symbolism that seems to have originated in Mesopotamia, Assyria, Canaan, Israel, and Judea has traveled a very long way from its original home. It is alleged that Israelite traders brought this symbol to North Africa in Solomonic times. What is more, although in many parts of Europe even Jewish ritual objects were fashioned by gentile artisans because Jews were barred from entry into the guilds, in Sephardic lands the position was exactly the opposite. It is likely that even the jewelery worn by Arabs was fashioned by skilled Jewish artisans who transmitted the motif of the hand from the Near and Middle East.

Scholars speculate that the basic motif emigrated via Assyria and Persia to India as the *muzra* or *mudra* (a Sanskrit seal), or possibly a seal ring and the artifact that is so imprinted; a code of basic stylized hand positions that form part of East Indian dance celebrating various episodes in the life of the Buddha; and as *sakti,* in Tantra the feminine counterpart of the god. It has been pointed out that these various meanings of the *mudra* are connected, because the basic meaning of the word is a mold or matrix used for stamping objects and a seal to make an impression on clay – and the "matrix" of a woman is where the embryo is formed.

Woman is identified with earth and the fertility of the flesh; her flesh or clay is infinitely plastic and can produce myriad shapes. But though she has to endure this unending stream of infinitely changing forms passing through her, she is not only identified as victim, but also in all fertility religions as the powerful Creator-Destroyer goddess. She is associated with not only the individual piece of clay but with Earth itself, the Archsculptor who molds and destroys and remolds as she wishes. If Woman is victim of biology, and therefore has been visualized as Fate and a force of Necessity and physical limit, when she identifies with the sexual part of her nature, she is portrayed as wielding authority over the entire physical realm. The Pali for *mudra, muddika,* derives from *mudda,* authority.

Not only does the terminology in which the *Shekhinah* is described derive from the same Near Eastern source, but when differentiated and feminized in the literature of twelfth- and thirteenth-century *Kabbalah,* She has a similar role to play as regent over the tenth lowest natural realm of substance.

An amazing kabbalistic insight on the part of the thirteenth-century mystic Rabbi David ben Yehuda he-Hasid par-

allels these Indian and Near Eastern versions of the seal and the
clay. In the *Yom Kippur* liturgy the moving comparison is made
between flesh and blood (mankind) and the raw clay in the hands
of the Potter who can form and destroy at will. Who then is the
Potter? With allowable naiveté one might have unquestionably
believed it was God. But according to R. David ben Yehuda
he-Hasid, the Potter is *Malkhut,* or the lowest kingship.

It is Her function as Potter both to make form out of the clay
substance of this world and to seal the decrees that are issued on
the closing service of the Day of Atonement (*Ne'ilah*), which is
one of Her names. We may have believed this prerogative
belonged to the Supreme Judge. What does this mean? At a
certain level we, our subconscious, we the Community of Israel,
we mankind, are both the prisoner in the dock (the Clay) and the
judge passing sentence (the Potter). In his *Book of Mirrors* (*Sefer
Mar'ot ha-Zove'ot*), R. David ben Yehuda he-Hasid writes:

> This is why (on *Ne'ilah,* the closing or literally "sealing" service
> of the Day of Atonement) we say "Seal us." Because *"Ateret"*
> ("Crown" or the "Community of Israel") ascends to the Palace of
> the King (*Binah,* Understanding or the Supernal Mother) who
> brings out the documents to be sealed. Then She receives the
> documents and brings them down with Her and seals them for
> life, namely the righteous, and the wicked for death. That is why
> we pray, "Seal us for life." We are praying before "Crown," who
> is "Seal" (*Ne'ilah*) that She seal us for life.
>
> A parable: To what may this be compared? To a king who
> came to sign decrees against his subjects. The king's viceroy
> pleaded for the subjects. Finally he (the viceroy) took the decrees
> from his hand and sealed them with the royal signet ring.[14]

Thus "Queen," *Ateret,* or *Knesset Yisrael* takes over the
weight of God's duties on *Yom Kippur.* Israel, as the symbolic
function of *Logos* among the Gnostics, is knife or cutter and an
analytical principle of ever-increased individuation. The burden
of passing sentence and sealing decrees on the Day of Atonement
is carried out by Her. According to this mystical belief, it is the

very spirit of Israel, identified with "Queen" (God's regent here below), whose hand gives pattern to substance and is the "Potter" shaping human clay waiting appraisal during that awesome Day. So, while the Collectivity of Israel stands in atonement, it is also the Collectivity of Israel, or her mirror-image reflected in God, that issues the decree with the sealing of the hand.

> She (*Knesset Yisrael*) is called the Potter; just as a potter who shapes and fashions clay vessels, making them narrow or wide on the potter's wheel, as it is written: *Like clay in the hand of the potter* [so are you in My hand, O house of Israel] (Jeremiah 18:6).[15]

Here again the association of substance with its countless possibilities of form, with some kind of implacable natural goddess whose hand or *sansara* wheel drives on relentlessly, is part of a heritage shared in common with the whole of the Near East and Far East. Only *Malkhut,* earth or the clay vessel, is a form of crystal, congealed light, or light substantialized through the process of emanation. The clay pot is capable of serving as an oil dish and as God's Lamp.

The *mudra* also resembles the *Sefirot* in that the Ten Fingers of the Hand stand for different characteristics of the Divine, and their various combinations make up the sacred pattern of Indian classical dance, later spreading to the Buddhists of China and Japan.

HAMSA

In the Near East, representations of the ten fingers of The Hand allegedly offered protection against the Evil Eye. It was the Arab custom, inherited from the Phoenicians and the Philistines and their Carthaginian descendants in North Africa, to put the hands above the head, making "fists," called the "Horns" or "Hand" of Baal, with their index and little finger stretched out as a gesture of derision to ward off the Evil Eye. Even today, in Sicily and southern Italy this gesture is considered a protection against the Evil Eye. The custom of mocking a cuckold, later adopted by the whole of the Western world by making "horns" at him on top of the head, also derives from these roots. But horns have not always signified cuckoldry. On the contrary, horns are Vessels for the oil used to crown a king, and Moshe was said to have had horns shooting forth rays of light from his face.

"There will I make a horn spring forth from David; I have prepared a lamp for Mine anointed" (Psalm 132:17). A horn of oil and a lamp are interchangeable metaphors because they are containers of oil and light. A crown consists of many horns or light rays like fingers on a hand placed above the head.

If the "hand" spread East, it also traveled West. When Moshe kept his hands raised high and Israel looked up and remembered their Father in Heaven, victory was assured: similarly the upraised thumb symbolizes life, success, victory, while the thumb pointed downward signified defeat. The "Horns of Baal" have found their way into the history of the twentieth-century via the Allies' V-sign for Victory.

The Protective Hand is called *Hamsa* in North Africa and in Arab lands after the five fingers of the hand. Subsequently, the number five itself has come to be associated with a means of combating the Evil Eye. Standing in for the hand, it figures prominently in amulets against the Evil Eye. A bean pod would be taken, consisting of five beans, or glass beads of five different colors grouped in two circular series. Or a Pentacle would be drawn consisting of a five-pointed star traced out on paper without raising the pen. Curiously, because the "Five" has so long been linked with ways to combat the Evil Eye, it is often purposely not mentioned because of the painful associations that have evolved over time. Figures containing the number five have been found on guns, pottery, trays, bags, rugs, saddlecloths, and carpets. In contemporary times, this type of artifact retains its popularity as an ornament, but its original magic character is being lost.

Hand-shaped amulets were adopted by the Arabs from the earlier inhabitants of North Africa. Metal or glass hands decorate Libyan tombs in the same way as *Menorot* decorated Jewish graves. Women wear the "Hand" as an ornament and men use them on boxes and tobacco pouches, the fingers embellished with pearls. The Bedouin in Tunisia believed that the person who held a blue glass hand carrying a candle would become invisible. Kamea or talismen were worn by Jewish children. Small flat images of the hand became popular charms. Some hands were engraved with holy names, crescents, and disks. In Fez, women hang a little silver or gold hand at each temple to provide protection. A small coral hand is a characteristic amulet of the French Midi. The Berbers wear earrings decorated with a hand in the right ear. This hand, which has six fingers, was made by Jews. This seems to indicate that just as Jews were forbidden to reproduce the seven-branched candlestick in the Temple and so produced an additional branch, they did not wish to reproduce the five fingers of the hand and therefore added a sixth finger.

Modifications of the hand, with the stipulated addition of a sixth finger, were found on Jewish houses in Alcazar. Moroccan Jews are said to have suspended their lamps from a brass hand.[16] These are both charms and decorations at the same time as they serve a functional use. The "Hand" had its positive as well as its negative aspects. It was supposed to bring luck. Not only the human hand, but also an animal paw was invested with occult powers. Perhaps this is the derivation of the lucky horseshoe.

In Tunis, Tripoli, and Spain, the gesture of stretching out the fingers of the right hand toward the person suspected of having the Evil Eye and pronouncing the phrase *Hamsa fi'ainek!* was used to throw back the evil influence emanating from the eyes. This gesture also might suggest the wish to thrust one's fingers and thumb deep into the eyes of the adversary.[17]

There is a custom in Morocco on encountering a person who supposedly has the Evil Eye to count up to ten, stretch out the middle finger of the right hand, and quickly push it forward crying out *Asra!* (Arabic for Ten, equivalent of the Hebrew *Eser*). Here the one finger stands in for all ten. Sometimes only two fingers were pointed out in agressive defense, one for each eye. In this gesture, both hand and eye come together.

Hands were also imprinted on the upper arm of Arab women in Fez, thus making an impression of hands on hands. The first gift to a fiancée was frequently a golden hand. After a Moroccan wedding, a lamb was killed, a hand soaked in blood, and an imprint made of it on the wall of the home of the newly married pair to protect them against misfortune.

In Shawia, Morocco, it was the custom when buying an animal to paint five vertical lines with henna on some wool and tie it to one of the animal's legs if it was a horse, a mule, or a donkey, or round the tail if it was a bull or a cow. Silver amulets with five knobs of colored glass represented both the eye and the hand.

RAISING THE HANDS IN HOLINESS

The Jewish religious gesture of spreading out the hands with all ten fingers extended is discussed by Rabbi Moshe Cordovero in his *Orchard of Pomegranates.* He sees this movement as representing the Ten *Sefirot,* with all ten fingers as channels for the Divine influx.[18]

This same position is used both for the receiving of the Divine influx and for its transmission. Thus prophecy, Torah leadership, and rabbinical status are passed on through the generations by means of the laying on of hands. Just as a Jewish king was anointed by pouring oil on his head and forehead and between his eyes, so intellectual and spiritual powers are passed on through the hands. A parent also blesses a child by spreading both hands over the child's forehead and reciting the verse, "May the Lord bless you and protect you, May the Lord cause His face to shine upon you" (Psalm 67:1).

The *Bahir* questions the purpose of this gesture of raising the hands and attributes it to the Ten *Sefirot.* [19]

And what is the reason for the raising of the hands and blessing them with a benediction? This is because there are ten fingers on the hands, a hint to the ten *sefirot* by which the sky and the earth were sealed. And those ten correspond to the ten commandments, and within these ten all 613 *mitzvot* are included. [*Bahir,* no. 124]

The expression "Raise up your Hands in holiness" refers to a similar gesture, whose particular power is pinpointed by the *Zohar* as residing in the human hands, which have become conductors of *Shekhinah* Light.

> There is a teaching in the name of R. Jose saying: "When the priest spreads forth his hands, it is forbidden to look at them for the reason that the *Shekhinah* is hovering over his hands. At that moment there is a whisper followed by silence through the universe. So when a King is about to join his Queen. All his attendants are agog and a whisper runs through them: Behold the King is about to meet his *matrona!*" [*Zohar* III:147b]

The raising of the hands is a gesture of joining; channels are linked by means of which the Divine influx can descend upon the person blessed. When the hands are stretched out they emit light rays through which the *Shekhinah* makes Her descent. The meeting of the Vessel and the light is the union of the physical and the spiritual. A parallel gesture among the Arabs is the *Fat'ha* ceremony, which consists of an invocation with the hands stretched out, palms turned upward and fingers extended.

The power of hand symbolism in Jewish and Arab culture derives from the fact that in cultures where human images of the Divine are totally taboo, the hand has been taken as an abstract symbol for the source of all Power and Help–God himself. When the Israelites were liberated from Egypt, the Bible refers constantly to God's "powerful Hand and outstretched arm." And on *Pesach* each year, the burned shankbone on the Plate during the *Seder* night represents both the lamb whose blood the Israelites sprinkled on the doorposts of their homes and God's arm extended to save them. In the murals of the Dura Europos synagogue in Syria (246 C.E.), the Hand of God is portrayed as a figure for God Himself. This motif reappears in the *Bet Alpha* synagogue (early sixth century C.E.) in the mosaic of the *Akedah,* the single most popular theme in Jewish iconography. There the Hand of God emerges from the clouds to save Isaac from the slaughter. The effect is of a *deus ex machina,* similar to that in the Exodus and Resurrection panels at Dura.

God's Hand – one imagines not so much His fingers but the palm of His Hand – is described in Job 12:10 as the ultimate resting place of the soul: "In His hand is the soul of every living thing and the breath of all mankind." In the Talmud the "Hand of God" is visualized as waiting to receive the human soul at death.

> This is the hand of the Holy One which is extended under the wings of the Living Creatures to receive from the Hand of the Accuser those who repent. [*Pesahim* 119:1]

Because the power of God is infinite, even His Finger is of unimaginable weight. Thus God "shows" Moshe the *Menorah* with His finger – that is, He points to it. The "Finger of God" is a monument, a phallus, a rod, a magic wand, like the wands of the Egyptian magicians that changed into snakes or like the wand of Aaron that blossomed into the flowering branch of an almond tree (the *Menorah*) and swallowed up the magicians. It is also symbolized by the scepter of King Ahasueras that was extended to save the life of Queen Esther and with her, the lives of all Israel.

The Hebrew word for Hand, in addition to its primary meaning also means *power* and *agency*. Thus, in a Medieval text, *Mi Yad'el,* a certain Rabbi Ishmael asks: *Mi Yad'el,* that is, who might be God's counselor (or right-hand man)? And then proceeds to doubt that God has need of such a thing.

To which Rabbi Akiva asks him: "But doesn't it say: 'Let us make man' (Genesis 1:26). Does not that indicate that he took counsel with the heavenly academy?" (We have seen that, according to the *Zohar,* when God said: "Let us make man," the predominating potency being brought into play was that of feminine plasticity) (*Zohar* I:22a–b).[20]

But, in the above discussion, Rabbi Nehunya ben Haqqanah takes the "hand" literally. And who actually is the hand of God? "That is to say, God has no hand . . . for everything that has a hand also has need of a hand, but God, who has no hand, has no need of a hand (that is, the aid and support of others) . . . (Every expression to the contrary, even in the Torah itself, being only by way of metaphor.) . . . And just as He has no hand, so He has no other limb."[21]

However, although in an absolute sense God may have no physical organs (because He has no need of them), in the world as we know it – the natural realm of *Malkhut* – He does indeed have a Hand; He does have a Body; He has us as limbs and channels for *Shekhinah* Light.

THE HAND OF MIRIAM AND THE HAND OF GOD

The "Protective Hand" has been called by the Arabs the "Hand of Fatima" or the "Hand of Aisha"; Christians refer to it as the "Hand of Mary," and Jews, the "Hand of Miriam." Each of the monotheistic religions called it after a heroine of their faith. But its oldest derivation seems to have been Jewish, although it may go back much earlier to a goddess of Canaan.[22]

What is the significance of this amulet that it was named after these heroines of the monotheistic faiths? The source is most likely Jewish, because only in Judaism are we faced in the same story with another two candidates to whom the hand could have been attributed. If there is a hero in the whole episode of the Exodus from Egypt it is God Himself. The deliverance was brought about "not by an angel, not by an intermediary" but by God Himself. And the "Hand of God," as we have seen is a constant characterization of the means of salvation. Why then "the Hand of Miriam"?

The "Hand" had come to represent not merely God's Omnipotence, but His Providence and intervention, "Grace from Above" viewed as a typically nurturing and feminine characteristic. The way Grace works is exemplified in the saving action not of Miriam, but of the Egyptian Princess.

In fact it was the Hand, not of Miriam but of the Egyptian Princess, that was gifted with the almost supernatural power to save the future infant redeemer of Israel.

The Princess's Father had just passed an edict, so the Bible tells us, that the Jewish People were to be annihilated by throwing all Hebrew baby boys into the Nile. Women without men, without male fighters, did not count, and could therefore be allowed to live to swell the ranks of the all-powerful Egyptians. Little did Pharaoh suspect that this shifting alliance of women worked two ways and that his own daughter would voluntarily secede and join her forces with those of his enemy.

When the Princess went out with her maidens to bathe, she saw a cradle bobbing about on the waters. She was standing some distance away, so she sent her maid–the Hebrew word is *amah*–to fetch the cradle. When she opened it, she discovered an unmistakeably Jewish baby boy, one of her Father's intended victims. Miriam, sister of Moshe, had hidden herself and waited to see what would happen to the child. Seeing the Princess smiling at him, she gained the courage to come out of her nearby hiding place and offer her services as a nurse.

That is the story in the Bible. But Rashi has a different interpretation. He plays with the word *amah* which, in addition to meaning "maid," also means "arm," "armslength," and "cubit," named after the span of an arm.

Immediately she saw the cradle, the Princess guessed what it might contain. Although she was standing too far away, genuine kindness prompted her to reach out. She did not send a maid. Princess though she was, her immediate reaction was to stretch out her hand. From the normal length of an arm, her reach was extended until she was able to lift the future redeemer of Israel out of the reed bed.

This is exactly how the "Hand" of God works in the world, through the agency of His "maid," through the investment of human energy furnished by human hands. And in the human hand is seen the Hand of God–that is, even miracles can only be brought about through the initial investment of human effort.

The Rabbis asked why did Batiah reach out in the first place? She knew that, by the laws of nature, she could not possibly reach it. The answer is that she did not think. She acted instinctively.

Batiah wanted to help so much that she forgot her limitations. Desperate, she stretched out her hand, and through this act transcended the bounds of the possible, thus becoming transformed from the daughter of Pharaoh (any fertility goddess in the

Near East or India) into the "daughter of the supernatural." At the moment she stretched out her hand, her name was changed from "Daughter of Pharaoh" to Batiah "Daughter of God."

In recognition of her act, the man who was to lead the People out of Egypt became her child, the child of the daughter of the tyrant. The Hebrew name the baby's parents gave him was forgotten. The name that has survived thousands of years is the one given him by Pharaoh's daughter. Moshe is not a Hebrew name. It is ancient Egyptian, meaning "drawn from the reed bed." Out of chaos and the darkness of inchoate substance, she drew out the light.

The name of this tyrant's daughter is unique in the Bible. Moshe, unlike the demigods and heroes of other nations, was fully human, but the Egyptian woman who raised him is said to have crossed the boundaries between human and divine. She is Batiah, "Daughter of God," according to the *Midrash,* because she did not surrender to the limits of nature. When it came her time to leave this world, she, like Elijah, did not suffer death but ascended physically to Heaven.

Her act makes her transcend her origins at one bound. She is "Daughter of God"; she loses all personality and is immediately subsumed under the *Shekhinah.*

It is said that the *Shekhinah* never descends below ten hand-widths from above the earth, and it is said that the *Menorah* should be no more than three handwidths high. In between the two are seven handwidths of untraversed territory. How, then, do Divine and human ever meet?

God's Light descends lower than the stipulated measure because human effort—the stretching out of the hand of the Egyptian Princess to save the ark containing the Baby Moshe—has transcended the Seven Natural *Sefirot* at one bound and touched the realm of miracle. The *Shekhinah* descends to the same degree the human spirit animates Herself in Her effort to ascend. Only in this way can human and divine impinge.

By a miracle that extended the forces of nature, the Hand of the Egyptian Princess became the saving Hand of God. When Moshe was born, says the *Midrash,* his parents' home was filled with light. Which light? The light of Torah, the Revelation that was to come to the world through him. And what did the Egyptian Princess pluck from the reeds of the Nile but the Light of the Torah enclosed in a little ark.

As with the miracle of the Lamp on *Hanukkah,* God's plan is to wrest that little light out of the darkness of Egypt, the complete dependence on inexorable physical law out of the River Nile. The Talmud stresses that lighting is as public demonstration of the miracle that sometimes God does intervene in human affairs. At first, even when the Hasmoneans did not have enough oil to keep the Lamp burning, they did not hesitate but kindled it anyway. And that initial gesture caused the light to shine and shine. Just as Elisha ordered the poor widow to pour her last cruse of oil into as many vessels as she could borrow, the act of pouring–and the hand signifies action–was itself a Vessel for God's infinite oil to pour and pour.

The single Hebrew word for miracle, symbol, and an army ensign or flag is *ness,* perhaps because a miracle is only the revelation and public demonstration of the secret miraculous nature of reality. And on *Hanukkah* the purpose of lighting is to bring out this essence, to reveal the miraculous in nature. The Menorah is a sign–in Hebrew, *ot.* Because *ness* also means ensign or flag (something that is lifted up), a *Menorah,* too, is God's ensign because He asked Israel to raise up lights. "And when you lift up the lamps of the Menorah. . . " (Numbers 8:2). It is up to man to bring out the burning vision of the miraculous that actually exists within nature, just as the Princess "lifted up" the Light from the reeds by extending her arm.

Ultimately, the extended hand is that of God, but it works through human beings. For example, when the children of Israel "looked up" and saw the Hands of Moshe propped up by Joshua and Caleb, they thought of their Father in Heaven and were victorious (*Rosh Hashanah* 3:8). Here the hand was extended on the vertical, from earth to Heaven, while the axis traversed by the hand of the Egyptian Princess was horizontal.

It was specifically the arms of the *Menorah* that Zechariah referred to as "the eyes of the Lord which wander to and fro through the ends of the earth" (Zachariah 4:10). So the *Menorah* is not simply a vertical link between Heaven and earth, Heaven and Israel, but is also a horizontal, channeling light and blessing to all nations from one end of the world to the other. Though the *Menorah's* extensions – arms or eyes – are "on Her head," forming a kind of antlered headpiece or crown, they can also be visualized as tubers, feelers, one-eyed tentacles of Divine vigilance and care.

Starting from the Holy Land, which the Bible says "from the beginning of the year till the end of the year" is the lodestar of "God's eyes"; from the *Menorah* in Jerusalem; and from the Temple, these arms or tentacles feel their way from one end of the world to the other, embracing all of Creation in streamers of Divine Energy and serving as channels back to the *Shaar Hasha-mayim* (the Gate of Heaven).[23] From here, the "light" of Israel and of mankind is transmitted collectively back to the Creator.

The *Midrash* asks why we should continue to pray facing Jerusalem after the Temple has been destroyed. Does God pay any special attention to that ruined space when the *Shekhinah* has gone into exile with *Knesset Yisrael?* The answer is given with typical ambivalence:

> One text says, *And mine eyes and My heart shall be there perpetually* (I Kings 9:3), while another says, *I will go and return to My Place* (Hosea 5:15). [*Shir HaShirim Rabbah* 4:4–9]

According to the last text, while the *Shekhinah* is with Israel, God has gone partially into retreat.[24] But according to the first text, His "eyes" and His "heart" are centered on Zion. How can these contradictions be resolved?

ORIENTATION OF THE HEART

The *Midrash* explains the logistics of how personal *kavannah* (concentration) in prayer can affect the mechanism of Divine Energy Above and Below in the following way:

> A man should concentrate his mind on the Holy of Holies.
>
> R. Hiyya the Great and R. Simeon b. Halafta say: It means, the Holy of Holies here below.
>
> R. Phineas said: "I will harmonize your two statements; it

means the celestial Holy of Holies which is directly opposite the Holy of Holies here below; and so it is written, The place (*makom*) *O Lord, which Thou hast made for Thee to dwell in* (Exodus 15:17); as though to say, exactly opposite (*mekuwan*) Thy dwelling place, namely, the Sanctuary above." [*Shir HaShirim Rabbah* 4:4–9]

When Israel is in exile, the prayer of every Jew flows east to Jerusalem, where it forms a reservoir, a female entity of Prayer that then enters the Gate of Heaven, rising up to crown Her Creator. So the line of orientation is drawn, first, horizontally eastward to Jerusalem, and only after is it drawn vertically, from earth heavenward to the "Jerusalem-Above."

This is how Yehuda Halevi in his famous "Ode" describes Zion's geographical position in relation to the *Shekhinah:*

> There the *Shekhinah* is your nextdoor neighbor
> and your Maker
> Has opened up your gates
> Opposite the Gates of Heaven.
> Sun, Moon and stars were not luminaries for you.
> But the 'Glory' alone was your light

Zion houses the *Shekhinah* and Zion's Gates adjoin the Gates of Heaven in the same sense that the *Menorah* also stands opposite to, or is the conductor of, *Shekhinah*. The two doorposts – the Gates of Zion and the Gates of Heaven – stand opposite one another and in some sense they correspond.

After the destruction of the Temple, the *Shekhinah* found a home in every Jewish house, which in itself constituted a "sanctuary-in-little" wherever it might be. Nevertheless, the *Mishnah* ruled that in the Diaspora, when a Jew prayed, he should direct his face toward the Holy Land; in the Holy Land, he should direct it towards Jerusalem; in Jerusalem, toward the Temple; in the Temple, toward the Holy of Holies.

"If one is located to the east of the Temple, one should turn westward; if west, eastward; if south, northward; if north, southward. Thus should all Jews wherever they are direct their prayers toward one single place" (*Berakhot* 30a). For Jerusalem, say the Rabbis, is the elevation toward which all mouths turn. However, they concede, because God is everywhere, if one is blind, one may pray in any direction, as long as one directs one's heart towards Jerusalem.

As a reminder of this "orientation of the heart," it is customary to hang an artistic plaque on the eastern wall of every home pointing straight in the direction of Jerusalem.

This wallmarker, which Ashkenazic Jews call a *Mizrach,* is essentially the opposite of the blank space frequently left on the wall facing the entrance to synagogue or home as a reminder of the·destruction of the Holy Temple. Instead of duplicating the destruction of the Temple by breaking something in our domestic environment, we add a positive link with Zion and prepare for the rebuilding of the Temple by sending out our prayers in an easterly direction to greet Her in advance.

The term *Mizrach* applies properly to the cities to the west of Jerusalem, where Jews during prayer turn due east. Thus, excavations of ancient synagogues west of Israel (Miletus, Aegina, Priene) face east, as did the ancient Egyptian synagogues mentioned by Josephus (*Apion* 2:10). Synagogues north of Jerusalem and west of the Jordan, such as Beth Alpha, Capernaum, Hammath, and Chorazin, all face south, whereas those east of the Jordan River, ed-Dikkeh, Umm al-Qanatir, Jerash, and Dura Europos, all face west; the remains of the synagogue at Masada in the south face northwest to Jerusalem.

The emotional primacy of an eastern orientation is evoked by the poem of Yehuda Halevi written during the Crusades:

> My heart is in the East,
> And I in the uttermost west. . . .

The word *Mizrach* originally meant "to arise" or "to shine," from the verse beginning "From the rising (or the shining) of the sun to the setting down thereof, may the Name of the Lord be praised" (Psalm 113:3). If east is the direction of Jerusalem, it is also the direction of sunrise. Even *Mizrach,* the Hebrew for "East," means the shining of the Sun.

It is paradoxical that, precisely among the Oriental commu-

nities where it is most widespread, the *Mizrach* (Eastern orienta-
tion-marker) is known either as a *Shiviti* plaque or, simply, as a
Menorah, because of the seven-branched candelabrum frequently
depicted on it in its Sephardic manifestation.

This *Shiviti* or *Menorah* served as a physical focus for spiritual
energies directed toward God and as channels for reception of the
Divine influx of bounty directed toward man. If the *Shiviti*
expressed the idea of: "I place (*Shiviti,* in Hebrew) the Lord before
me always" (Psalm 16:8), the reality is that the Hebrew letters of
the Divine Name (the "Lord," in the verse) are depicted physically in large upon the plaque as an object of focus and concentration; the *Menorah,* also frequently placed at the plaque's center,
is an ideogram of the same deployment of spiritual force. In the
center of these Sephardic *Menorot,* the *Hamsa* or Protective Hand
varies with the *Menorah* in taking pride of place. In point of fact,
the entire plaque serves as a Hand pointing in the direction of
Zion. Little wonder, then, that the light in Jerusalem is not like
that experienced elsewhere!

So, the "Quest for the Orient" is not located purely on any
geographical map, but is itself the threshold to a realm beyond
nature. If blessing is transferred by the laying on of hands, then
its course is charted in a similar way to the kabbalistic theory of
the emanation of light whereby sources of illumination and
renewal radiate towards us in direct proportion to the hands that
stretch out to receive them. Our consciousness (Eyes) and capacity (Hands) trace out the true lineaments of the Lamp of God.

NOTES

1. Ginzberg, *Legends,* pp. 49–50; *Derekh Eretz Zuta* is included among
   The Minor Tractates of the Talmud, Massektot Ketannot, trans. the
   Reverend Dr. A. Cohen (London: Soncino Press, 1900), vol. 2, pp.
   591–592.
2. F. T. Elworthy, *The Evil Eye* (London: Murray, 1895).
3. Gershom Scholem, "The Star of David-History of a Symbol" in
   The Messianic Idea in Judaism (New York: Schocken Books, 1971),
   pp. 257–281. See also M. Grunwald, on *Magen David,* in *Jewish
   Encyclopaedia,* vol. 3, p. 202. The "star" was adopted by Christians

as a symbol of Messianism and incorporated into churches long before Jews used it. The hexagram is Aryan German in origin. The "star" is not included among Erwin Goodenough's *Jewish Symbols* and was not a motif in Temple architecture. Only one verse in Isaiah "And a Star shall step forth from Jacob . . ." tempted Christians to seize this particular poetic imagery, and magnify it into a symbol. Children and the Jewish People are compared to *stars*, but not to some heroic "star."

4. Edward Westermarck, *Ritual and Belief in Morocco* (London: Macmillan, 1926), p. 427.
5. See Scholem, *Origins,* pp. 172–173.
6. Ibid., pp. 87–88.
7. "She used to fasten *kamiot* (phylacteries) on his arm" (*Bekhorot* 30b).
8. Moshe Idel quoting Abraham Abulafia, *Shomer Mitzvah* Ms. Paris BN 853, fol. 56b–57a, in Idel's *The Mystical Experience in Abraham Abulafia,* p. 106.
9. Ibn Gabbai, *Tol'at Yaakov,* fol. 49a in *New Perspectives,* p. 177.
10. Idel points out this link between *Tefillin* and the *Atarah* made in the anonymous thirteenth-century manuscript *Sefer ha-Yihud* Ms. Milano-Ambrosiana 62, fol. 114b. See Idel's *New Perspectives,* p. 374 n. 209.
11. Both together go to form twin *"Atarot."* See Numbers 32:3 and Matt, *Book of Mirrors,* p. 27, for the following excerpt:

     > You must realize: *Atarot alludes to two crowns: the upper crown and the lower crown. For just as He is called Keter Elyon'* so *Malkhut* is called *Ateret,* which means *crown.* When *Ateret Yisrael* joins Herself with *Keter Elyon* and rises up to *Ein-Sof,* they are called *Atarot.*

12. Isaiah Horowitz, *Shne Luhot ha-Brit* (*Shelah*) 1, 187a, 19 (*Hullin*), quoted in Joshua Trachtenberg, *Jewish Magic and Superstition* (New York: Behrman House, 1939), p. 146. See also Solomon Luria, *Amude Shlomo, Semag* 11, 23.
13. See Scholem, *Origins,* p. 299.
14. Matt, *Book of Mirrors,* p. 28.
15. Ibid., p. 29.
16. Edward Westermarck, *Ritual and Belief in Morocco,* p. 453.
17. Ibid., p. 446.
18. Rabbi Moses Cordovero, *Pardes Rimmonim* 15:3.
19. The *Sefirot* here refer to the listing of the ten dimensions of the

cosmos found in the *Sefer Yetzirah* (Book of Creation). These dimensions are up, down, east, west, north, south, beginning, end, good, and evil.

20. See also Chapter 3, pp. 148–150.
21. *Mi Yad'el,* from the *Sod ha-Gadol,* 232, quoted in Scholem, *Origins,* p. 121, n. 124.
22. See p. 296.
23. *Shaar Hashamayim,* the Gate of Heaven, that is Jerusalem and the Temple site in Jacob's dream.
24. See p. 55.

SIX

LIGHT

OUT

OF

DARKNESS

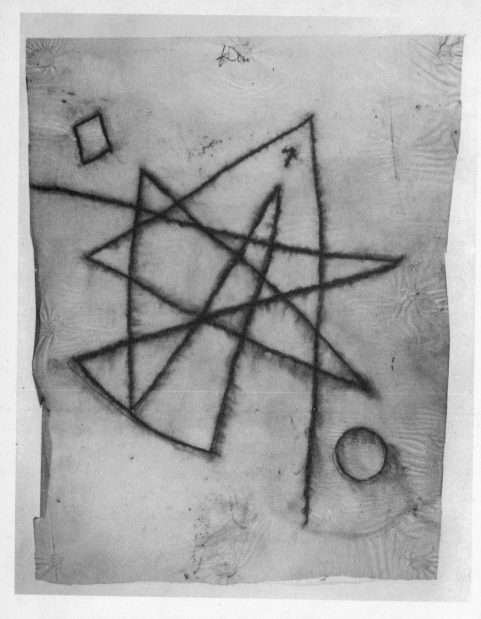

Forced Emigration by Paul Klee. "Come and see how beloved are Israel before the Holy One, for wherever they were exiled, the Divine Presence accompanied them (*Megillah* 29a)—even as far as the crematoria. (*1934. Pen, 17 × 12½" Rötel-drawing detail paper, signed above in the middle. Private coll. CH Paul Klee Foundation, Bern. Copyright © 1989 by COSMOPRESS, Geneva*)

When is the time to say the Evening Prayer? The *Shulkhan Arukh* decrees that the Evening Prayer should be said at night. Night means when it is completely dark and when at least three small stars cluster together—about forty-five minutes after sunset.

SONGS OF THE NIGHT

Tradition has it that the three Patriarchs instituted the Morning, Afternoon, and Evening Prayers. Yet we are told that Jacob, originator of the Evening Prayer, prayed when the sky was still light. Also the Ari[1] and his followers upheld the practice of our Father Jacob of praying before darkness had really set in. What lies behind these diverse practices?

The Three Prayers stand respectively for the First, Second, and Third Temples. Two of these came into existence and were destroyed, the third has yet to be built. At present, the majority of *Knesset Yisrael* is still in exile. The Evening Prayer stands for the rebuilding of the third Temple, and it is *Knesset Yisrael*'s "prayer-in-darkness," Her faith in suffering and "songs in the night," that will actually help to initiate that dawn. Therefore the appropriate time for saying the Evening Prayer now is when it is dark.

However, Father Jacob was different. Though he lived more than two thousand years ago, he was in touch with redemption. He had already "seen" it. The author of the *Zohar,* literally the "Radiance," and other great Kabbalists were also in touch with that light. But for the majority who cannot yet see this light, this prayer – their "songs in the night" – should be said when it is quite dark.

What is the equivalent of the "songs of the night" mentioned in the Psalms? According to the Rabbis it is learning. They say that the reward of one who learns at night is very great. The *Zohar* says that when the Torah is studied by night, "a little thread of (the) Hidden Light steals down and plays upon them that are absorbed in their study" (*Zohar* IV:149a). Darkness has a special quality. On the one hand, because there are fewer distractions, night lends itself to a depth of concentration that is not possible in daylight. On the other hand, precisely because of this special atmosphere, yearnings for all kinds of passionate diversions are aroused at night. To concentrate and channel them is a real victory. Therefore the light that can emerge can be so much deeper.

It says in the *Zohar* that the great art of man is to be able to mine deep below the surface meaning of Torah and transmute darkness to light, refurbishing the obscurity of the apparent meaning of the text into all the colors of the rainbow.

During the night of exile and suffering and "absence of God," such "songs of the night" are like a young child's whistling in the dark to keep up his spirits.

Thus the degree of light or darkness necessary for prayer is measured by different types of perception. The one who lives in the light beyond appearances and can already see the Redemption can say the Evening Prayer while it is light. But those enmeshed in their particular situation, must pray out of how they feel; they must pray out of darkness, and there is a particular poignancy in these "songs in the night."

R. Hiyya taught in a Baraita: (We are told in the first three verses of Genesis that) at the very beginning of the earth's creation the Holy One envisioned the Temple built, destroyed, and rebuilt. *In the beginning God created the heaven and the earth* (Genesis 1:1) – the Temple built. *And the earth was without form and desolate* (Genesis 1:2) – the Temple destroyed. *And God said; Let there be light, and there was light* (Genesis 1:3) – the Temple completely rebuilt in the time-to-come. [*Pesikta de Rav Kahana* 5, ed. Mandelbaum, pp. 340–341]

If fire break out and catch in thorns, so that it consumes stacks of corn . . . he that kindled the fire shall surely make restitution (Exodus 22:6). Said the Holy One Blessed be He: "I must pay for the fire I have kindled. I ignited the fire in Zion, as it is said: *And He kindled a fire in Zion, and it ate up her foundations* (Lamentations 4:11). *But in the future I will be unto her, says the Lord, a wall of fire round about and a glory will I be in her midst* (Zechariah 2:7). [*Sefer Aggadah* I:150–151]

AMIDST RUINS

Once Rabbi Gamliel, Rabbi Elazar ben Azayiah, Rabbi Yehoshua and Rabbi Akiva were going up to Jerusalem.

When they reached the Mount Tsophim (from where they saw the destruction of the holy city) they rent their garments.

When they reached the Temple Mount they saw a fox running out of the ruins of what was once the Holy of Holies. They all burst out crying, but Rabbi Akiva smiled.

"Why are you smiling?" asked his companions.

"Why are you crying?" retorted Rabbi Akiva.

"Why should we not cry?" was their answer. "The Holy of Holies is so desolate that foxes are running in it."

"For this very reason," declared Rabbi Akiva, "was I smiling. Since I see the words of the prophets being fulfilled:

Therefore shall Zion for your sake be ploughed as a field and Jerusalem shall become heaps (Micah 3:12), *so that foxes walk upon it* (Jeremiah 4:2).

"[This convinces me] that the consoling prophesy of Zechariah (8:4-5) shall also soon be fulfilled: *There shall old men and old
women sit once more in the broad places of Jerusalem . . . and . . . the city
shall be full of boys and girls playing in the broad places thereof.*"
      Thereupon they all exclaimed:
      "Akiva, thou hast comforted us! Akiva, thou hast com-
forted us!"[2] [*Aichah Rabbah* 5:18; *Devarim Rabbah* 1:5; *Makkot* 24a]

      Rabbi Akiva's laughter can only be explained in the context
of the laughter of the Almighty. As it says, *He who sits in the
Heavens will laugh* (Psalm 2:4).

Jerusalem is built with turrets *(talpiot):* Hiyya ben R. Bun said: "It
means that what was once beauty has been turned into a ruin.
Said The Holy One, Blessed be He: 'It is I who made it a ruin in
this world; it is I who will make it a thing of beauty in the world
to come.'" [*Shir HaShirim Rabbah* 14:4-9]

      God has a different perspective from man – and that is why
He can laugh. People also can laugh, sometimes from hindsight
or when their present circumstances are illuminated by a future
perspective. That is how Rabbi Akiva, who obtained his insight
into the future from the Prophets, could afford to laugh.
      As for Sarah, she laughed for the first time out of delighted
embarrassment when she bore a son after she had already gone
beyond a woman's normal years of childbearing. This child was
called Yitzhak (after her laughter) because she said "God has
made me into a laughing stock, for everyone who hears about me
will laugh" (Genesis 21:6). Hers was a laughter of embarrassment
combined with disbelief – quite the opposite of the laughter of
Akiva.
      There was another occasion when Sarah laughed, rivaling
the faith of Rabbi Akiva. But this was not the earthly Sarah as
she was when she was alive. It was Abraham's idealized picture
of her in the eulogy he sang for her after her death. Then he
imagined her laughing as she never had laughed when she was
alive, and he composed a love song for her describing what he
saw.

The "Woman of Valor," according to the *Midrash,* is the first Jewish love song. Abraham sang it to Sarah, but she never heard it because he sang it not *to* her but *for* her, after she had passed away. What line shines out in this eulogy? – "Her lamp does not go out at night." Instead of simply drawing the picture of the thrifty housewife who cannot stop working day or night – someone like Martha in the Christian Bible who bustled and was a self-righteous and disruptive presence – Abraham's portrait of Sarah takes on an entirely new meaning in the context of these "songs of the night."

SARAH: THE CENTRAL SHAFT OF LIGHT OF THE *MENORAH*

According to the Greek Jewish philosopher Philo (born about 15–10 B.C.E.), Sarah is the name of the central shaft of the *Menorah,* – the Eternal Light that, like the Watcher of Israel, neither slumbers nor sleeps, but feeds a multitude of "children-lights."[3] ("Thus shall be your seed!" God promised Abraham, showing him graphically the innumerable stars in the sky. "Thus shall you make it!" said God to Moshe, pointing out to him the multicolored lights of the *Menorah.*) A possible connection between Sarah and Eternal Light lies in her name, which means "Princess." The original promise the angels made about her to Abraham was that she would be "Mother of nations; kings of peoples would come from her" (Genesis 17:16). And it is because of Sarah's role as Mother and Queen that she stands in for the *Sefirah* of *Malkhut* where the *Shekhinah* holds sway. Therefore, Sarah-Princess is a Primal Mother image identified with the *Shekhinah* who followed Her children into exile.

But think of Sarah, the woman in her actual situation and how she died. Her role was seemingly unheroic. God ordered Abraham, the Father, who had suffered no pregnancy, no labor pains, who had other children with other wives, to make his heroic sacrifice of an heir. Sarah was not asked. The presumption must have been that the demand would have been beyond her.

Abraham never had the heart to tell her what God and he had in mind for her son. But a messenger carried her the news. It must have seemed to her that laughter had turned to bitter mockery in the end. After she had resigned herself to the fact that she was too old to have children, God was mocking at her by giving her Yitzhak, only to take him from her.

There are *Midrashim* that say Sarah's life ended with the news of Yitzhak's alleged sacrifice. Before she could hear that God had actually intervened to save the boy's life, she died of a broken heart, no angel having bothered to inform her her son had been saved.

As far as this mother was concerned, her only son was dead, and there was nothing after that. Like countless other future Sarahs–for "Sarah" was the contemptuous collective label foisted on all Jewish women by the Nazis–she died in doubt and darkness, not knowing what had happened to those dearest to her. For her, even her son's name becomes an additional irony. Yitzhak–"He will laugh." Yitzhak–"He who sits in Heaven will laugh."

To Sarah, Abraham sings an eternal love song, for he knows that God intervened to save her son, and that in his children by Sarah "all the nations of the world will be blessed." He sings and tries to comfort her with a different perspective on the death of her son, he who knows that Yitzhak survived. "She has no fear of the snow for her household. She laughs at what threats the future may bear" (Proverbs 31:10–31).

In Abraham's idealized portrait of her, Sarah possesses a healing laughter that can exult beyond the tragedy of the moment–through exile and the sacrifice of the first of many of her children she is still able to reach toward a consolation not offered to the actual woman in her own lifetime. "The daughters (the nations) rise up and call her happy. She laughs at the time to come."

"Her light does not go out by night." In the night of the *Akedah,* "God will see" (Genesis 17:1); in the flames of the Destruction of the Temple, the deeper night of exile, pogrom and crematoria, "her light will not go out." So Sarah, the woman who died bewildered and bereaved, becomes merged with the *Shekhinah* Light that shines beyond more than two thousand centuries of suffering.

"Her lamp does not go out at night." Exile and darkness in themselves are lamps because, like the earth, they contain buried treasure and the seeds of blessing, the conditions that bring about the germination of renewal.

The flames of the *Akedah* made of the sacrificial site a place alight with "seeing" and illumination of Divine encounter. Mount Moriah, the place "where I shall be seen," became Mount Zion, the site of the Jerusalem Temple. But all the light of all revelations and visitations of Divine Presence that would attend on the Temple in Jerusalem throughout history are considered as nothing by God compared with the precious fire of the *Akedah* of Yitzhak. What was the special quality of the wood and the brand Abraham brought to the sacrifice? Was it not rather Abraham and Yitzhak's inner fire, their ardent determination and readiness to sacrifice life, or that which was even more precious, to fulfil God's will. It surely was this attitude of father and son, rather than any actual flames, that invited the light of Divine Presence to return to Mount Zion throughout the generations and still makes God consider Himself eternally indebted to this pair.

The *Hanukkah* lights symbolize the readiness to sacrifice oneself for the holiness that is the essence of Israel. It is as if each one of us were Elisha's little cruse of oil, ready to be poured and give all riches without stint.

And it came to pass on the day that Moses had made an end of setting up the tabernacle . . . that the princes of Israel . . . offered. And after that: Speak unto Aaron, and say unto him: When thou lightest the lamps. This bears on what Scripture says: *O fear the Lord, ye His holy ones; for there is no want to them that fear Him* (Psalm 24:10). You find that eleven tribes brought offerings, and the tribe of Ephraim brought an offering; in fact, all the princes brought offerings except the prince of Levi. Who was the prince of Levi? It was Aaron; for it says, *And thou shalt write Aaron's name upon the rod of Levi* (Numbers 17:18). Now Aaron did not bring an offering with the other princes, and so he thought: Woe is me! Perhaps it is on my account that the Holy One, blessed be He, does not accept the tribe of Levi? The Holy One therefore said to Moses: "Go and tell Aaron: Do not be afraid! You have in store for you an

honor greater than this! For this reason it says, Speak unto Aaron,
and say unto him; when thou lightest the lamps, the offerings
shall remain in force only as long as the Temple stands, but the
lamps shall always Give light in front of the candlestick, and all
the blessings with which I have charged you to bless My children
shall never be abolished." [*Bamidbar Rabbah* 15:6]

When God's Palace was in existence, the Priests kept the
Menorot trimmed for a continual ceremony of coronation and
dedication, but after the Palace was burned down what was the
point of a Crown? Maiden Zion, the *Shekhinah* Queen, stripped
of her jewels and of her finery, hair disheveled and clad in
garments of mourning, followed her children weeping into captivity, and the *Menorah* lighted their way.

THE LIGHT IN EXILE

The Destruction of the Temple delivered Israel from death. God
was so consumed with anger that He directed a flame against the
nation. An angel deflected this wrath against the Temple. Rather
than destroy human lives, God was induced to deflect His anger
on to stones and clay. The Temple was destroyed, not the
People, but the spirit of the Temple and the spirit of the People
remained untouched. Destruction by fire of the walls of the
Temple was enough, while the *Shekhinah,* the light within,
accompanied the People into exile.

With the destruction of the Temple, the lights in the house
were not put out but became stronger than ever. The whole
House was surrounded by fire so that the walls became pa-
per-thin and burned to ash. The light itself emerged from the
house and led the way for the Jewish People like a beacon into
exile. Meanwhile, the crown contracted and receded into itself,
the fire burned out, and the Palace became a charred ruin. According to legend, the Golden *Menorah* itself went into hiding.

According to Jeremiah (5:19), all the gold vessels of the
Sanctuary, including the *Menorot,* were carried off into captivity
by the Chaldeans. There is another legend, however, that when

the Temple was about to be destroyed by the Babylonians, the original *Menorah* was hidden away; but when Cyrus restored the Temple treasures, the return of the *Menorot* are not mentioned.

When the Romans held sway, Pompey saw Herod's Golden *Menorah* when he stormed the Temple in 63 B.C.E., but he left it untouched, as did Crassus who plundered the rest of the sanctuary ten years later.[4]

When the Romans destroyed the Second Temple in 70 C.E., the *Menorah* vanished. Flavius Josephus claims that two priests handed him two golden *Menorot* during the siege, but no mention is made of what happened to them or whether one of them was in fact the original *Menorah* of Moshe.

One of the few tantalizing clues left us as to what happened to the original *Menorah* can be found in the representation of the Roman triumph of "Judea led into captivity." Among the spoils born back to Rome by the Jewish prisoners, the seven-branched *Menorah* has pride of place. The Arch of Titus was known as the Arch of the Seven-Branched Lampstand.[5] In the Middle Ages the Arch was incorporated into the fortifications of Rome. As a result, the side-pillars were damaged, and the attic had to be restored in the nineteenth century.

According to Josephus, Vespasian had the *Menorah* deposited in a special Peace Temple erected after the Jewish War.[6] After the Peace Temple was burned in 190 C.E., most of the treasures escaped destruction. The Peace Temple was rebuilt some years later, and destroyed again by an earthquake or by lightning in 408 C.E. After this succession of calamities, a number of treasures were saved and exhibited in the vicinity.[7]

In the introduction to his history of the Gothic wars, the Byzantine historian Procopius of Caesarea (sixth century C.E.) reports that the "treasures of the Jews" were captured by the Vandals after the Sack of Rome in 455 C.E., and taken to Carthage in North Africa. From there they were removed in triumph by Belisarius and taken to Byzantium, where they were hidden in the Imperial palace at Constantinople.[8] The learned Emperor Constantine Porphyrogenitus (905–959) of the Eastern Roman Empire reports that the Imperial Palace of his day contained a "Dome of the Seven-Branched Candlestick" and that occasionally the candlestick was taken out, lighted, and paraded in solemn procession through the streets.[9]

After the Sack of Constantinople in 1204 during the Fourth Crusade, all further mention of any such candlestick vanishes, except for a legend that a high official at the court of Justinian was warned by a Jew that the "treasures of the Jews" should not be kept at Byzantium as they had already brought bad luck to Rome and Carthage. The Emperor then hastily had them sent back to Jerusalem, where they were deposited in a church. The *Midrash* has it that the original *Menorah* would remain hidden until the Messianic redemption.

During the Babylonian exile, the Divine Presence accompanied the People into exile:

> Thus saith the Lord God: Although I have removed them far off among the nations, and although I have scattered them among the countries, yet have I been to them as a little sanctuary in the countries to which they are come. [Ezekiel 11:16]

Here God is saying that although the Jewish People have been dispersed and distanced from their own ground (or container) and their Temple has been destroyed, He Himself has become like a living Temple to them. He is the "ground" in which they can find roots even in exile. Thus the exile is only from the physical container; in a sense, the conditions of exile bring the People closer than ever to the Divine Presence.

> Come and see how beloved are Israel before the Holy One, Blessed be He, for wherever they were exiled, the Divine Presence was with them. [*Megillah* 29a]

Hanukkah commemorates an event in which the Jewish People took destiny into their hands and fought back. Through millennia of exile, powerlessness, and subjugation under foreign yokes, the light of the *Menorah* shines, speaking of the valor and unquenchable fighting faith that makes for national revival.

"SANCTIFICATION OF THE NAME"

In the hindsight of victory, there is a tendency to forget that the time of the First *Hanukkah* was one of the first eras of persecution and martyrdom that were to become so commonplace in Jewish history:

> They shed innocent blood around the altar, And polluted the sanctuary.
>> Because of them the inhabitants of Jerusalem fled.
>> She became a dwelling place of foreigners.
>> And foreign she became to her own blood.
>> And her children forsook her.
>> Her sanctuary was laid waste like a wilderness.
>> Her feasts were turned into sadness,
>> Her sabbaths into a reproach,
>> Her honor into contempt.
>> As great as had been her glory
>> By so much was her dishonor increased,
>> And her high renown was turned into sadness.
>
> (I Maccabees 1:37–40)

As the Syrian officers went from town to town pressing everyone into conformity with Greek mores, many died a martyr's death rather than betray their faith. The case of the aged Eleazar, a "man of noble countenance," is an illustration of the passive type of heroism for which some Jews have been known throughout the ages. When faced with the option of eating swine's flesh and an agonizing death, not only did Eleazar go without resistance to the slaughter, but he almost volunteered for the role.

The officers responsible for staging the public ordeal, old acquaintances of Eleazar's, offered to save his life by letting him secretly substitute ritually clean (kosher) meat for the pig if he would keep up a public pretense of conforming. In this way he could save his life by not publicly flouting the king's edict, while not eating anything that would violate his conscience. To their civilized conscience, this seemed an ideal solution, but not to the heroic Eleazar. For him, more important than the prohibition against eating nonkosher meat – a mandate that could be set aside when it came to the saving of life – was the underlying principle of the necessity for a public vindication of faith, a concept known as "Sanctification of the Name."

To uphold *this* principle it was necessary to face death rather than neglect even the most minor of Jewish customs. If Eleazar had complied with the officers' demands, he would not have been infringing Jewish ritual observance. But the mass of ordinary Jews would have been misled into believing he had, and the seeming collapse of so venerable and respected a leader would have eroded their morale. So, rather than undermine their faith, Eleazar preferred to die. While undergoing torture, the old man cried out: "The Lord, who has holy knowledge, understands that although I might have been freed from death I endure cruel pains in my body from scourging and suffer this gladly in my soul, because I fear Him." In the classical tradition, Eleazar, by his death, became a hero and a role model, leaving behind him an example of nobility and a memorial of virtue to the young and to the body of his nation. Translated into the Jewish idiom, this is an example of the "Sanctification of the Name."

The Jewish People has been blessed with a superfluity of martyrs like Eleazar throughout a long history of religious persecution. It is paradoxical that Christianity sees in the dynamic faith (martyrdom) of heroes like Eleazar and Hannah and her seven sons a symbol of the triumphant course of the Church Militant. For Jews however, perhaps as a contrast to the suffering of their actual experience, the military exploits of Matityahu and his five sons and the heroic story of Judith hold far greater appeal.

In this *Hanukkah* story, certainly God's masculine saving might and power to do miracles are not vindicated – not the assertive "masculine" courage of a Judah Maccabee or a Judith, but the "feminine" passive devotion and fortitude of Eleazar and of Hannah and her children.

The Jewish notion of "Sanctification of the Name" and the Christian concept of martyrdom share much in common. The Greek *martyr* means "witness." The idea is to bear witness or provide the evidence for God's rule in the world which, because it is far from visible, can only be demonstrated in the lives, acts, and sometimes in the deaths of those who take it on faith. The idea is to "see" (or believe) and to bear witness for what one sees. Just as the site of the *Akedah* was chosen as the Temple site—a "place where I shall be seen"—so the *Menorah* within the Temple has been called the "image of the One who sees."[10] Here the silent invisible watcher and witness is God Himself.

We can only draw upon the secret power of the *Hanukkah* Light on the left through the strength of the *Mezuzah* on the right. Inside the *Mezuzah* is the portion of the *Shema* in which it says you must "love the Lord with all your soul, even to the giving up of your soul." And it is through the strength of such sacrifice as this that the *Hanukkah* lights draw down salvation (The Kalever Rebbe).

In a world of persecution and martyrdom, this joyous Mother-image of the *Menorah* with Her multitude of children-lights is somewhat of a paradox. In Christian iconography, the *Menorah* surrounded by two olive trees—in the Jewish conception, either the separate powers of the Kingship and the High Priesthood, or the Two Messiahs, the Messiah in Exile and the Messiah from the royal line of David—has been transposed into a burning cross on either side of which two felons are crucified, witnesses to the "Death of God." They have taken an image of triumph celebrating God's visible Rule (the *Menorah*) and transposed it into the very symbol of agony and suffering.

In different situations and with different temperaments, heroism can take either an active or a passive form. Taken together the active/passive spirit of the dedication of a Judith and of a Hannah, Mother of the Seven, became the very spirit embodied in the seven-branched candelabra.

At that time the lighting of the *Menorah* "to publicize" the miracle became synonymous with the urge for the "Sanctification of the Name," which too often could only take place through martyrdom.

The sheer femaleness of the *Menorah* Light links it with the destiny of a Sarah, of a Hannah, of a Judith. Though women normally are exempt from commands that are circumscribed by time, because of the feminine spirit that became synonymous with the *Menorah* Light, because the *Menorah* is in essence a woman-image, and the role every particular woman plays is a substitute for the *Shekhinah,* not only can women kindle their own *Menorot,* they can also light for their families and for their communities (*Shulkhan Arukh* 139).

The two Hannahs come to vindicate the ignominious, tragic, and subordinate role of Sarah. The destiny of the first Hannah is a happy one. When Hannah has a child, her reaction is to burst out into song rather than into laughter. Hers is a song of thanks to God, and it is out of an overflow of gratitude and joyous dedication that she, and not her husband, offers him for Temple service.

The story of the second Hannah is more somber even than that of Sarah. While Abraham was prepared to offer one son – Sarah's only one, not his, and without even informing her – the second Hannah witnessed the martyrdom of seven sons *with no Divine intervention.* Her role is far more representative of what Jewish women have experienced throughout the millennia.

In one version of the story of the martyrdom of Hannah and her seven sons, after the Mother encourages each of her children to face torture and death rather than worship idols, she is left with her youngest, a babe in arms. The King allows her to give her youngest child a last embrace. As she suckles him, she tells him that when he arrives in the world-to-come he must relay the following message to Father Abraham: "Tell Abraham that, while he was ready to give one son, I have given seven, that his was a test, but mine was in earnest." When the last child died, Hannah, crazed with grief, threw herself off the roof. Then, so the *Aggadata* says, a Heavenly Voice, literally the "Daughter of a Voice," was heard softly to lament: "A happy mother of children!" (Psalm 113:9).

Was this the soft sarcasm of the feminine, helpless aspect of the Deity, completely out of control in a universe gone mad, or did Hannah's departing spirit in her agony become one with the collective anguish of *Knesset Yisrael?*

After the destruction of the Temple, God's Sovereignty was no longer evident in the world and the justice of Divine rule seemed to have been withheld or contracted into some inner recess. No longer did the kindling of the *Menorah* represent a visible act of Crowning in the physical world; from being an implement in His Service, it took on esoteric and apocalyptic significance. The Jewish People, stripped of all visible manifestations of sovereignty that the *Menorah* had symbolized until that point, added an eighth branch to its candelabrum, signifying the vindication that would crown human effort in the world-to-come and in the Messianic future that would take place at the end of history.

The *Menorah* was now depicted as living in dark containers such as caves, the stomach of a fish, graves, the womb. During the Roman era the *Menorah* was reproduced in gold placed between two layers of glass in glass bottles and flung into Jewish graves like messages in a bottle cast into the Ocean—asking Death to restore and crown identity.

The *Sifre Devarim* says that the image of the *Menorah* is appropriate for graves.[11] For instance, on the stone of Eusebius the Alexandrian and his wife Theodora in Almyra, there is an engraving of a lampstand, with the words "Image of God Who Sees" underneath it, an allusion to the Prophet Zechariah's comparison of its branches to God's "eyes" (Zechariah 4:10). In tombstones from Venosa there are Hebrew inscriptions and a lampstand. The Hebrew speaks of a God "of fire" and of the burning bush that burns but is not consumed, as a symbol of the Deity.

The *Menorah* motif was scratched on tombstones and placed among pagan emblems in the cemetery of the Vigna Randannini Catacomb in Rome. Bronze and ceramic oil lamps also discovered in these catacombs bore the image of the *Menorah* on their surface, as did amulets, seals, rings, and cornelians. The *Menorah* motif appeared on tombstones until late medieval times, when the Star of David replaced it in popular esteem.

In Roman times, a head of a deceased person struck on a shield or a medallion born by two winged victories in the gentile sarcophagi was replaced by a representation of the seven-branched *Menorah*. As a decorative motif in funerary art, the *Menorah,* even though it was a mark of Jewishness, was held aloft by pagan figures such as victories, two Bacchi, and representations of the seasons. Nevertheless, the fact that the *Menorah* replaced what would have been the face of the deceased in the case of a non-Jew makes it a thoroughly Jewish innovation. Thus, on the threshold of death, the *Menorah* vindicated simultaneously the fact of Jewishness and the individual soul and personality, the "face" of the deceased, and by so doing stood at once for the hope of personal resurrection and for the redemption of Zion.

While a lamp or candle dish may represent the individual soul, the *Menorah,* as a complex system, is a place where all identities merge, the "bundle of life" and the collective reservoir of souls personified as a feminine entity.

When the Ramban was very old, he called his students and told them: "All my days I thought I would see the comfort of Zion and go up to Jerusalem joyfully with the whole of Israel. And behold I have grown old. In a little while it will be my turn to leave the world and redemption is far off. How can I leave the world when Jerusalem is still desolate? Therefore, my beloved students, let me take my leave from you and go up to the Holy Land. I will mourn there at the graves of our holy ancestors. And I will build up a Jewish settlement in Jerusalem which will be the start of the redemption. For only if I do these two things can I die in peace."

When the students heard the words of their holy Teacher they did not know what to say. If he left them, who would light up their eyes with words of Torah? They stood around his chair and kept quiet. Then they started crying. He said to them: "Why do you cry when my soul rejoices to come to the land of prophecy and holiness? If you have a request, tell me what it is. Perhaps I shall be able to fulfill it before I leave on my travels." One of his students raised his head and said: "Master, you are going to the Holy Land, the Land of the Fathers and the angels and the holy prophets. May God lengthen your days. However, when you are called to the divine court, we won't know that you have departed from the world and we won't mourn for you. That is why we are sad."

His friends chorused tearfully after him: "You will die in a far country and we won't know a thing."

He said to them: "The Torah I have taught you will light

your way if you learn it with perfect heart. Then when the day comes that my soul returns to God, you will know and pray for me."

They said: "How shall we know?"

He said to them: "On the seventh of every month, one of you will go out to the old cemetery in Gerona to visit my mother's grave. On the day of my passing he will see a *Menorah* sprouting seven branches, with the middle light burning. Then he will know that the light has been kindled for my soul which has departed from the world."

The Master took his leave from his pupils. Each one drew near him and kissed his hand while he blessed them and kissed them on their head. After that he went out in a wagon, with the whole community of Gerona accompanying him with tears.

Months and years passed by and on the seventh of every month one of his students went to stand by the grave of the mother of their Rebbe. Nothing stopped them, neither rain nor wind nor cold nor drought.

But in the third year, in the month of Adar, on the seventh day of the month–the day when Moshe Rabbenu (Moses our Teacher) was born and died, may peace be with him–a student was standing by the woman's grave when the sun set and its ray fell on the grave, and where it fell a *Menorah* of gold stood with seven branches and the middle lamp was burning. The student fell on his face.

When his spirit returned, he rose to his feet and ran to the city. He rent his garments and his hands struck his head. All who saw him knew what had happened, and the students rent their garments and made a great mourning and a funeral and all the people prayed for the soul of their great Teacher who rose to eternity via the Holy Land.[12]

In North Africa, strange phenomena of light were connected with dead saints. In Dukkala, *ignis fatuus* in a desert place are taken as a sign that an unknown saint had died there. In the Riff, trees connected with saints were seen shining at night.

> On the one hand it is the supreme destiny of the *Tzaddik* to become the perfect image (that is, mirror) of God. And on the other: Man's perfected image [which he lost with Primordial Light] will be restored in the future world.

> Since the human soul is likened to a lamp; as it says, *the spirit of man is the lamp of the Lord* (Proverbs 20:27), and it says *When thou raisest the lamps* (that is, the souls), the *Menorah* also is a pointer to Resurrection. It is the metallic, lustrous, man-made equivalent of the Tree of Life.[13]

WHY THE *MENORAH* GREW AN EIGHTH BRANCH

All the time the Temple was standing, only seven of the branches of the *Menorah* were lighted by human hand. After the Destruction, the Jewish People, stripped of all visible sign of sovereignty that the Temple *Menorah* represented, added an extra branch to its *Menorah*. This was an esoteric act rather like the custom of kindling a *Neshamah* Light for the soul of the dead.

When a person dies, the whole world cries out at the enormity of the act that has been perpetrated. The body dies and the soul seems also to have vanished – it is as if the presence of the person is no more. How can finitude and infinitude both be leveled at one blow? It is as if God Himself were killed. When a human being dies, it is very hard to believe in God. The whole world is constricted. And that is precisely when Jews say the "Mourners' Kaddish," proclaiming their belief in the magnitude of the Infinite even when they suffer seemingly irreparable loss. Then, too, we kindle the *Neshamah* Light.

Paradoxically, it is just at the moment of the disappearance of the light of the human soul, that God can be felt most closely. One can almost hear the gentle brush of the *Shekhinah's* wings. That is why, according to Rashi, after the death of Rachel, the *Shekhinah* set up house in Jacob's heart.

Only physically, mathematically, does the person disap-

pear. For every disappearance, every death, we light a candle of
Presence. Similarly, the kindling of the eighth branch of the
Menorah evokes the memory of the kindling of the vanished
Temple *Menorah* and the *Shekhinah* that was present there.

When one single human being suffers, what does the *Shekhinah* say: "My head hurts! O, my head, my head!" (just like the
child who died and was later resurrected by Elisha [II Kings
4:19]).

God waits to be activated by human activity. There is a
correlation between emotional processes below and on high. We
have already seen that human grief "causes tears to be shed on
high."[14]

> Whenever Israel is enslaved, the *Shekhinah* is enslaved with them,
> as it is said, *And they saw the God of Israel, and under His feet there was
> the paved work of sapphire* (Exodus 24:10). But after they were
> redeemed what does it say? *And the likeness of the very heaven for
> clearness* (Exodus 24:10).[15]

While Israel was still enslaved, under the feet of the
Shekhinah were the bricks of enslavement (*livnat hasappir*), with a
play on the word *levenim*—the bricks the children of Israel made
when slaves in Egypt); but when they were redeemed, the
condition of the *Shekhinah* was transformed to *"the likeness of the
very heaven for clearness."*[16]

The *Shekhinah* shares the pain of exile (*Sanhedrin* 46a).[17] It
was during Israel's pains of exile that the Divine Presence (God's
yearning to dwell on earth) and *Knesset Yisrael* (Israel's supreme
yearning for the Divine Presence) coalesced into a (feminized)
Shekhinah.

In the days of exile and humiliation when the Jew had no
permanent home, he was able to say: "A wife, she is his home."
For she followed him faithfully into exile "in a land that was not
sown" and there she gave him shelter. So the *Shekhinah* acted
collectively for the whole of Israel. As indispensable and ungla-
morous as an aging and plain-faced mother, She stumbled around
after Israel like a collapsible Temple-in-little, a domesticated
"cloud of glory."

The lighting of the *Menorah* in the Jewish home during the
winter Festival of *Hanukkah* is an act of crowning, after the

Temple and all symbols of Israel's sovereignty had been destroyed.

The *Menorah* opposite the Holy of Holies in the Temple on Mount Zion in Jerusalem is like a set of Russian dolls, a collapsible Temple-in-little, a container within a container within a container . . . of Divine Light.

THE DIALECTIC OF LIGHT

The Temple, like the luminaries of the Sun and the Moon, like the space of creation, like Israel, like the human being, was a colossal lamp or container-of-the-Light, the function of which was to give light to the world.

It is a property of light to radiate outward. (From Zion shall go forth Teaching, out to the four corners of the world.) And yet also there is contrary movement toward incarnation and containment of vital forces. So there is a dialectic of movement—from out in, and from in out.

God's light was contained within Him. He projected it on the backdrop of Creation. Then it was as if He "poured" light into the natural containers of the Sun and the Moon. Then He breathed a living soul into man, whose body again was seen as a "receptacle" for Divine light. Then again He poured light into the Sanctuary, the Land of Israel, Jerusalem . . . and then again the container was unable to hold the powerful forces within; it exploded (or was burned by the Babylonians and the Romans) and light itself once more went out to the world.

The kabbalistic concept of the Smashing of the Vessels and the Scattering of the Sparks again celebrates the fragmentation and disintegration that is only a preliminary toward a movement outward that will bring about the possibility of a higher form of coming together. When do the vessels break? When there is an excess of light and the vessel can no longer contain it.

A plate is broken when the *Tanaim* or "conditions" for the contract are legalized before the wedding ceremony and the bridegroom breaks a glass under the wedding canopy as a reminder that the loss of the Temple is felt just at the moment of union. The real Breaking of the Vessel in this context must refer to the hymen and the breaking of the vessel (hymen) symbolizes both the scattering of the seed and the deeper union of the couple.

One is tempted to compare the necessary blow administered to complete happiness before the union of man and wife — the similar imperfection included in the architectural construction of the Jewish home ever since the destruction of the Temple — to the prohibition against making a fully rounded sculpture of the human body unless it contained some imperfection. All three stipulations say that human love and the full human figure cannot be perfect or godlike, although within a Temple context they may.

The shivering fragments of these household "vessels" as a preliminary to a wedding are a reminder of the Destruction of the Temple, one colossal Vessel of Light, and ultimately derive their power from the legend of the original Fragmentation or breaking of the vessels that produced our present alienated world.[18]

Every union also implies fragmentation and separation from the single intense flame that existed before. Paradise is given up in favor of reproduction, the family, and the miracle of the renewal of the life process.

This alternation between the forces of containment and those of dispersion parallels the shifts from Diaspora to Return that the People of Israel have experienced throughout history. Seen in this light, exile is as necessary as homeland, presenting an opportunity for development. God's bestowal of Darkness, as well as His bestowal of Light, serves His purpose in the world. (*Pesikta de Rav Kahana, Piske* 21, ed. Mandelbaum, p. 236).

Because the farther the light travels from its source the dimmer it becomes, darkness, paradoxically, is often an indication of a light so powerful that it is invisible to the eyes. This kind of darkness, far from being a negation of light is that Hidden Treasure that God concealed when He created the world — the darkness that contains all color. Even the effect of darkness is to reveal what otherwise would be invisible.

"I saw that light gained an additional luster from darkness" (Ecclesiastes 2:13). A higher quality of light comes from darkness, through the transformation of darkness to light.[19]

Said Reb Nachman: "When you are far from the light, you

can see it; when the light shines from afar, we can see it with our eyes open. But when it comes closer, you find it hard to look at head on." When what you love comes as close as the heart, you must close your eyes. And this is why, when Jews say the *Shema* and reach the passage, "Blessed be the name of His Glorious Kingdom (the *Sefirah* of *Malkhut,* or the *Shekhinah*), forever and ever" we close our eyes to feel the Glory of the Name.

Children are born with closed eyes as if they have just seen something glorious. When one kisses someone one loves one closes one's eyes. This is a way of seeing that is deeper than light.

The Sun drives away the Dark, so it is not such a great light. The Moon is better, because she can shine in darkness, but the Real Light is the light you cannot see. The real light, "The Soul of Man, is the Lord's Light."

Sometimes, precisely the lack of physical light is conducive to an inner illumination. The *Midrash* says God caused the sun to set early so that He could speak secretly to Jacob.

> It may be likened to the friend of a king who visited him at stipulated times; and . . . he gave an order for his sake: Extinguish the lamps and lights that I may converse with my friend in secret.
>
> In the same way, The Holy One, Blessed be He, caused the sun to set before its time and spoke with our father Jacob in secret. [*Kohelet Rabbah* 3:14]
>
> R. Hanina observed: "The Holy One, blessed be He, said: 'In the eyes which you possess there is white and black, and you cannot see with the white but only with the black. Now if in your eyes that contain black and white parts you can only see through the black (because God willed it so), shall the Holy One . . . who is all light (and has given sight to man), need light from you?' "
>
> Another comment on the text: In front of the candlestick. A mortal obtains light for a lamp from a burning lamp. Can he, however, obtain light for a lamp out of the darkness? Yet (of God) it says, *And darkness was on the face of the deep* (Genesis 1:2); and what is written after that? *And God said: Let there be light* (Genesis

1:3). Out of the darkness I brought light; do I then need your light? I only told you to kindle lamps in order to elevate you *(la'alot)*. This is the significance of the expression *To cause a lamp to burn (leha'alot) continually* (Exodus 27:20). [*Bamidbar Rabbah* 15:7]

R. Berekiah said: "Consider the eyeball; it is not through the white of it that one sees, but through the black. Says the Holy One Blessed be He: 'If I created light for you out of the darkness, do I need your light?' But as the Torah says: The Lord was pleased for His righteousness sake to magnify the Torah and make it beautiful."

R. Berekiah made another observation: "It says, *Now the earth was unformed and void, and darkness was upon the face of the deep*" (Genesis 1:2). What is written after this? *And God said: Let there be light* (Genesis 1:3). [*Vayikra Rabbah* 31:8–9]

And that is the movement of "traveling light"–to go from in out and vice versa, from God Himself to emanate outward in the *Sefirot* of Creation, from the *Sefirot* of Creation to pour into the lamps of the Sun and the Moon, from the Sun and the Moon to flow into the soul-receptacles of the Patriarchs and the *Tzaddikim,* from the *Tzaddikim* to pour into the lamp receptacle of Temple and Temple *Menorah,* from the Temple to radiate outward to all the nations; after the destruction of the Temple walls to move outward with the Jewish People into the exile and inward into a hidden retreat; from the Temple in Jerusalem to move into the *Hanukkah* lamp of the Jewish home, from the Jewish home to shine outward to the left of the entrance, training its beam into the darkness of exile–and from all these varied movements to gain a renewal.

The *Menorah* stood as a bodyguard at the opening of the door of the house–the point of innerness of the heart. Just as it shines out into the darkness, it guards the home from contamination from external influences. The position of the *Menorah* shows that it equips the Jewish People for the exile and stands for the Messiah, the Son of Joseph. In darkness it shines and stands firm. It shines out to the nations while guarding its inward core.

Sin crouches at the entrance to the heart. But if the heart is pure, the *Menorah* can be stationed in every window and orifice of the body to send a beam of illumination to the gathering place of desire.

The Sephardic *Menorah* plaques read: "Joseph is a fruitful bough; even a fruitful bough by a well; whose branches run over the wall" (Genesis 49:22).

What is the tree that runs over the wall but the *Menorah* that shines out into the darkness of exile from the door, the window, from every chink, without compromising its own essence, it gives unstinting illumination.

When the Romans came to take away R. Hanina ben Teradion to burn him to death for teaching Torah despite their prohibition, they found him in the very act of reading Torah. As they took him, his daughter clung to him crying and he asked her why. She answered: "I weep for the Torah that is to be burned with you." He answered: "The Torah is fire, and no fire can burn fire itself." They seized him and wrapped him in the Scroll of the Torah, heaped faggots around him, and kindled the pyre. In the moment of his agony, his disciples asked him: "Our Teacher, what do you see?" He replied: "I see the parchment consumed by fire, but the letters of the Scriptures are flying upward." [*Avodah Zarah* 18a]

By the Fire

A flame burns on the hearth.
The stove warms up
As the Rebbe teaches the little children
the Aleph Beth.

Remember dear children, what you are learning here.
Repeat it again and again:
Komets-aleph-o.

When you grow older you will understand
How many tears are contained in these letters
And how much weeping.

As you grow weary dragging through the exile
You will draw strength from these Jewish letters.
Just look at them!

Mark M. Warshawsky (1840–1907)

This lullaby was used as a ghetto song during the Nazi Holocaust: "At the ghetto wall a fire burns, the surveillance is keen."

In the early 1960s, a clandestine song made the rounds in the Soviet Union: "Even should they beat you or throw you on the pyre, repeat *komets-aleph-o*." Among the initiated *komets-aleph-o* was, in fact, a mystical vocalization to induce communion with God.

At all times and at every moment – but especially in moments a man spends in solitude and inactivity, or when he lies on his bed unable to sleep – he should imagine a large and terrible fire blazing before him, reaching up to the sky. And he, a human being, should imagine himself overcoming his natural instinct for self-preservation and hurling himself into the flames for the glory of God. The merciful God looks upon purposeful determination (*kavannah*) as being equal to deeds.

A man must never be idle but must continually fulfil God's holiest commandment, *I shall be sanctified in the hearts of the sons of Israel* (Leviticus 22:32) – sanctified through their self-sacrifice at least in thought. A man must have the same thought in mind at mealtimes and during sexual intercourse. Whenever he experiences bodily delight, he must say with heart and mouth that he would feel a far greater sweetness, a much more lovely delight than this sensual one, if he were allowed to offer his life for God. He must prove to himself that to die for the glory of God would be sweeter to him than any other delight.[20]

Rabbi Shneor Zalman of Liadi, the first Lubavitcher Rebbe, says that even the sinners of Israel, or rather, precisely the sinners of Israel have an attachment to the Divine Light that defies understanding and their own reasoning. How is this so?

A Jew in every aspect of his being is permeated through and through with the Light of Divine Wisdom (*Hokhmah*), the first of the emanations, and his reason is informed with that light. But in those who consciously transgress and go after worldly pleasure "this faculty of *Hokhmah* is in exile – like the exile of the *Shekhinah* Herself" (*Tanya,* pp. 115–117). Nevertheless, neither in the *Shekhinah,* nor in the defaulting Jew, has the Divine Light departed. It is only in retreat. "Therefore this love of the divine soul, whose desire and wish is to unite with God . . . is called hidden love for it is hidden and veiled, in the case of the transgressors of Israel" (*Tanya,* pp. 115–117). But the root of the divine soul, though dormant and unconscious, remains.

> [However] in a test of faith (such as martyrdom) that transcends knowledge, touching the very soul . . . [the sinner is inspired] . . . without any reasoning, or knowledge, or intelligence . . . that may be comprehended by him . . . [to withstand the test, to prevail over the prohibitions and pleasures of this world, in which before, at a lesser cost, he indulged himself] and to choose God as his portion and lot, yielding to Him his soul in order to sanctify His Name. [*Tanya,* pp. 115–117]

What is the explanation of this *volte-face?* The *Tanya* (Rabbi Shneor Zalman of Liadi) stresses that what is being tested here is not worldly appetite for pleasure, but unconscious faith that is rooted in the highest wisdom, namely, the faculty of *Hokhmah* of the divine soul. Then all the "husks" (the minor sensual yearnings and distractions) are made null and void. They vanish, as though they had never been the presence of God Himself. So it is written "As wax melts before Fire, so shall evil be dissolved" (*Tanya,* pp. 115–117).

> The force of the Divine light of the blessed *Ein-Sof* that is clothed in the soul's Wisdom is great and powerful enough to banish and repel the husks and evil forces so that they cannot even touch its garments, namely, the thought, speech, and action, of faith in the one God. . . . This is called "the fear that is contained in love" – the natural love of the divine soul that is found in all Jews, the

intrinsic desire and will of which is to be attached to its origin and source in the light of the Endless [instinctively recoiling] "from touching even the fringe of the outer garments" [namely, speech, act, etc.] of idolatry. [*Tanya,* p. 118]

The *Zohar* says:

The souls of Israel have been hewn from the Holy *Menorah,* as it is written, *The spirit of man is God's Lamp* (Proverbs 20:27). Now once this lamp has been kindled from the supernatural Torah, the light upon it never ceases for an instant like the flame of a wick that is never still for an instant. [*Zohar* V:218b]

While some religious Jews were at prayer, the Nazis made a surprise raid on the Kracow synagogue. Pointing their guns at them, they ordered them to file past the *Sefer Torah* and spit at it. Finally, all did so. Some assimilated Jews were dragged in from the neighborhood and were forced to do the same. Their religion of enlightenment–they regarded the Torah as primitive–was even more offended by having to spit. To them it was like being required to celebrate the black mass. But finally all religious and all "enlightened" people complied. Only one notorious bandit refused: "I have done many things in my life," said he, "But this I shall not do!" The Nazis shot him immediately, but they shot those who groveled also.[21] This is that Hand that was not stretched out to save.

In the Nazi death camps, Jews did their utmost to light a *Menorah* and celebrate *Hanukkah.* In Bergen-Belsen the first day of *Hanukkah* fell one day after the holders of Peruvian passports had been shot. Those left alive still determined to celebrate *Hanukkah.* The men saved the fat from their food rations as "oil" and the women picked threads out of their tattered garments and twisted them into makeshift wicks. The magnificent candelabrum itself was made out of the precious half of a potato. Dreidels for the dozen children left alive in the camp were made out of wooden shoes. In Barrack Ten the Blazhever Rebbe, a survivor of the Peruvian shooting, conducted the ceremony. On reaching the third blessing, "Who has kept us in life and preserved us and enabled us to reach this time," he broke into sobs. He had lost everyone dear to him—his wife, his only daughter, his son-in-law, and his grandchild. Then he continued to sing *Maoz Tsur*, proclaiming faith in God, the rock of our salvation. Regaining his composure, he began to speak about the verse, "He who wrought miracles for our fathers in days of old!"

"Is it not strange to thank God for miracles He wrought for our ancestors long ago, while He seemingly performs none for us in our tragic plight?" In answer to his own question he said: "By kindling this *Hanukkah* candle, we are identifying ourselves with the Jewish people everywhere. We may be certain that no matter what may befall us as individuals, the Jews as a people will with the help of God outlive (this evil) and emerge triumphant in the end."[22]

"In those days at this time." The miracle of *Hanukkah* happened at a certain point in history. At that point in history the Jews were able to throw off the yoke of the superior forces of the Syrian Empire and liberate Jerusalem and the Temple. Physical survival and rescue, however, are commonplace happenings in the life of the Jewish People, in a history in which catastrophe and deliverance alternate. This tussle for life has been going on for thousands of years. Sometimes "miraculous" rescue has come, as for Yitzhak during the *Akedah*. Sometimes physical salvation has been denied, as with Rabbi Akiva or Hannah and her seven sons. But on *Hanukkah* it was the miracle of the lights that made the Rabbis seize on this particular occasion in history and make it a symbol of transcendence and spiritual victory for generations to come.

"In days past and in our own time." *Hanukkah* is an annual event. Our response is twofold. For the miracle of *Hanukkah* that transcends time, our reaction is to sing songs of praise. But about our own personal situation, we need to be both honest and realistic and pour out our hearts to God about it.

The light of the *Shekhinah* in the Temple is only a remnant of the fire of self-sacrifice of the *Akedah* of Yitzhak that laid a foundation for God's House on Mount Moriah, the place where "I will be seen."[23]

"In days past and in our own time." The miracle of *Hanukkah* is renewed every year. The realm of the miraculous is both above time and nature and also hidden within it. The very root of time and nature have a hidden link with a Higher Source where everything takes place simultaneously.

"These lights are holy," we say on *Hanukkah*. Says the Ramban: "The World exists only because of the *Hanukkah* Lights." Even in the most adverse conditions, "in our own time," even in days of darkness and exile and questioning, we see reflected the miracle that is beyond time.

On the Festival of Tabernacles (*Sukkot*) we say, "For everything there is a time and a season."

On *Hanukkah* we say, "In those days at this season."

The Festival of *Hanukkah* is essentially a "postponed Festival of Tabernacles" in a more wintry and despairing season. For many years before it became the custom to remember the miracle of the renewed Light of *Hanukkah* by ourselves kindling lamps, *Hanukkah* was celebrated by the brandishing of the palm branch of the Festival of *Sukkot*. The Festival of Tabernacles came into existence to celebrate the Dedication of the Sanctuary in the time of Moshe and again in the time of Solomon. Before *Rosh Hashanah* or *Yom Kippur* had taken on their present importance, they all were part of the Festive "season" of the Dedication of the Temple that took place in the fall. This Festival was celebrated, not only by the waving of the *lulav*, but also by the kindling of *Menorot*.

Both the Dedication of the Altar and the Dedication of the Sanctuary were celebrated with fire and light, and were also compared to a coronation. Then when in the time of the *Hanukkah* story the Hasmoneans rededicated the Temple, the first thing they did was to celebrate a delayed *Sukkot*.

The light that burst forth on *Hanukkah* was already present in the Sanctuary and before Creation.

KINDLING THE HIDDEN LIGHT

The importance of the "commandment to kindle" is to find the Hidden Light through those little temporary physical candles. This Hidden Light is not so much the light that God has saved for us in some world that transcends this one, but the light that He has hidden in this world. What we really would like is to recognize the hidden candles when they are indeed hidden!

Although the *Hanukkah* lights last only about thirty to forty-five minutes, by kindling contact is made with millions of generations of Jews who have lighted *Menorot,* going back to the actual Hasmoneans who were fortunate enough to experience in person the "great salvation and visitation" of the miracle of the oil.[24] By kindling we connect back to the "First Light" that preceded the Creation, and forward to the Lights of the Messianic Redemption.

Each year, whatever our circumstances these little lights bring us comfort. Out of the mundane they speak of heroism and nobility; they are evidence that the *Shekhinah* rests upon Israel and that in each one of us there is the potential to aspire to something higher.

Why do we celebrate *Purim* by feasting and *Hanukkah* by light and song? Both *Purim* and *Hanukkah* were occasions when the physical life of the Jewish People was saved en masse, but whereas on *Purim* we feast to celebrate the physical deliverance, on *Hanukkah* we sing the *Hallel* because of the spiritual victory of the lights. This is expressed as "praise and acknowledgment." We say *Hallel* for the good, praising God for the timeless light that shines through our immediate situation. At the same time we realistically acknowledge the challenges faced in the here-and-now and try to understand these as also deriving from the same Source. . . . And we try to unify the two perspectives!

Just as we can never look into someone's eyes, or indeed into our own reflection, without seeing an image of a person mirrored in the pupil, so the memories evoked by these lights kindle the person who sees them so that his whole being radiates like a Lamp.

But why do we light eight branches on the *Menorah?* To correspond with the eight days of the miracle. However, another question can be asked. Why is the miracle considered as having lasted eight days when in fact there was enough oil for one day, and only seven days were miraculous. Among the many answers given to this is that the true miracle was not that the oil did not run out, but that the Maccabees bothered to light the *Menorah* in the first place.

> The very fact that they did not despair to light the lamps even the first day, despite the knowledge that they would be unable on the morrow to fulfil the Torah's command to light a perpetual lamp was in itself a miracle, a miracle which enables the people of Israel to endure through all generations and every exile. Had they always tried to surmise what the future held in store for them they would long since have lost the capacity to survive.[25]

Although *Hanukkah* commemorates the "miracles and the mighty deeds" of God and the heroic Maccabees, there are other less popular stories associated with *Hanukkah* that have to do with a similar spiritual fortitude not crowned with success. The stories of the first martyrs form a more sober relief to the triumph of good of the *Hanukkah* story itself.

Hanukkah commemorates an event in which the Jewish People took destiny into their hands and fought back. Through millennia of exile, powerlessness, and subjugation to a foreign yoke, the light of the *Menorah* shines, speaking of the valor and unquenchable fighting faith that makes for spiritual rebirth.

IN DAYS GONE BY AND IN OUR OWN TIME

S. B. Unsdorfer spent much of the Second World War in various types of concentration camps. In the camp of Nieder-Orschel he was able to keep a diary in which he entered the Hebrew dates and festivals. One day in December 1943, he was delighted to discover that *Hanukkah* was only a few days off. To boost the morale of his fellow prisoners, he decided to kindle some kind of light for the festival occasion. The following is my retelling of an episode in his memoir, *The Yellow Star,* [26] which describes his attempt to celebrate *Hanukkah.*

The five ring leaders and archconspirators had to surmount two major challenges: somehow, and from somewhere, they had to find oil in the factory with which to light, and they also had to think of a place where the lighted wick would not be seen.

Their next task was to smuggle a few drops into their barracks in time for the first night of *Hanukkah.* They knew, of course, that Jewish law did not compel them to risk their lives to fulfil a commandment. But they were in such great spiritual and physical distress that they wanted to rise above the misery of their situation by imbuing it with the heroic spirit and self-sacrifice demonstrated by their ancestors. "(They) felt that a little *Hanukkah* light would warm (their) starving souls and inspire (them) with the hope, faith, and courage to keep going through (that) long, grim, and icy winter."[27]

Each of the five conspirators was given a task. One had to steal the oil; another to hide it; another to light it under his bunk. The main difficulty, of course, as during the First *Hanukkah,* was to obtain some of the precious oil in the first place. One of these five latterday Maccabees convinced the hated *Meister* Meyer (the work superintendent) that his machine would work better if oiled regularly every morning. With his approval, it was arranged that a small can of fine machine oil be kept in the tool box to which they had access. *Meister* Meyer agreed, so there was no longer the problem of where to hide it.

On Monday evening after rollcall, while everyone was having their long awaited dinner consisting of a meager portion of hot but tasteless soup, Unsdorfer busied himself under the bunk preparing his *Menorah.* He put the oil in the empty half of a shoe polish tin, took a few threads from his thin blanket, and made them into a wick. When everything was ready he quickly joined the table to eat his dinner before inviting all his friends to the ceremony. Suddenly, as he was eating his soup, he remembered they had forgotten matches.

Hungry as they were, everyone was ordered to leave a little soup, which was then bartered in the next room for a cigarette. This was "presented" to Joseph, the chef, in exchange for a box of matches, with no questions asked.

After dinner Unsdorfer made the blessings over the tiny makeshift *Menorah.* The inmates of the camp, both religious and nonreligious Jews, crowded around the flickering flame and joined in the singing; all were filled with a similar emotion. The songs were powerful reminders of how they had celebrated this festival in happier circumstances. In the small flame, images of their homes and faces of vanished parents, brothers and sisters, wives and children were reflected. For a moment, they were victims no more but simply Jews performing their religious obligations as Jews do everywhere.

A roar of *Achtung* brought their minds back to reality. The Nazi sublieutenant—referred to as "The Dog"—and his Alsatian hound were making one of their surprise visits, looking for any excuse to pounce. Suddenly the man sniffed suspiciously. He had smelled the oil.

The little *Hanukkah* light flickered on the ground, but the author could not afford to make any kind of suspicious movement to stamp it out. "The Dog" and his Alsatian began to parade along the bunks toward him. The Nazi could not help noticing the deathly pallor of the faces around him. He was certain something was wrong. Nearer he came and there seemed to be no hope, when suddenly the sirens began to wail that an air raid was in progress. Within seconds all lights in the camp were switched off automatically, and the author was able to put out the *Hanukkah* candle.

> This was the sign, the miracle of *Hanukkah,* the recognition of our struggle against the temptations of our affliction. We had been helped by God, even in this forsaken little camp at Nieder-Orschel.

> Outside in the ice-cold, star-studded night, with the heavy drone of Allied bombers over our heads, I kept on muttering the traditional blessing to the God who wrought miracles for His people in days gone by and in our own time.[28]

THE SOUL AS GOD'S LAMP

Sometimes it was impossible to find any kind of *Menorah* to kindle. While in hiding, one child traced the beloved outline of the *Menorah* on a frosted windowpane.

On the verge of stepping into the crematoria, the victims were consoled that their inability to light was not a sin: Who needs oil and wicks? Every Jew is a candle. *The soul of man is the Lamp of the Lord* (Proverbs 27:20).

In the soul of every Jew there is a cruse of oil sealed with the Divine Word and reserved for a time of need. When the time comes the cruse opens, shaken by the holy command, and the treasured light is kindled in every Jewish soul, and the flame, the divine flame, begins to rise.[29]

And God said: *Let there be Light . . . And Darkness was on the face of the waters* (Genesis 1:3). When darkness (suffering and negation) are over everything then God says, *Let there be Light*. [Shlomo Carlebach][30]

Our rabbis learn: It is a question whether twilight belongs to the day or the night. There is a question whether it belongs completely to the day or completely to the night. And when is twilight? At sunset, all the time that there is a red glow towards the east, when the lower part of the sky has dimmed but not the upper part, that is twilight. When the upper part of the sky becomes as dim as the lower, then it's night. In the words of R. Judah: "R. Nehemiah says: 'Twilight lasts long enough for a man to walk half a mile after sunset.'" R. Jose says: "Twilight is like the twinkling of an eye. The Day goes and Night comes and it's impossible to grasp the exact moment." [*Shabbat* 34]

"Day unto day uttereth speech, and night unto night revealeth knowledge" (Psalm 19:3). How did Moshe know the difference between day and night when he was up on Mount Sinai for a period of forty days and forty nights, if both day and night are bright before God?

When Moshe learned Torah, he knew it was Night; when he studied *Mishnah* (Oral Torah) he knew it was Day. When he saw the Sun offer homage to God he knew it was Night, and when he saw the Moon come and offer homage he knew it was Day.

R. Pinchas said in the name of R. Abba: "The angel appointed for prayer waits until the last community in Israel has finished praying; then he makes of all of them a crown for the Holy One. That is why we say: 'One day's praise flows into the next day.'" [*Midrash Tehillim* on Psalm 19:7]

Another interpretation of *Day unto day uttereth speech, and night unto night revealeth knowledge* (Psalm 19:3). When the elders of Israel come together to proclaim a leap-year, they take time from the day and give it to the night and they take time from the night and give it to the day.

Now they borrow, the one from the other, in trust, and yield, the one to the other, in trust; and none hears any speech between them because they do not quarrel as men do who will neither borrow nor pay except before witnesses, and except in court. For of the day and the night, it is said: *There is no speech, there are no words, neither are their voices heard* (Psalm 19:4). [*Midrash Tehillim* on Psalm 19:3–4]

What is twilight? Says R. Tanhuma: "It is like a drop of blood on the edge of a sword. The drop is divided on both sides of the blade. That is what twilight is like." [Jerusalem Talmud, *Berakhot* 81, *Sefer Aggadah* II:597]

Said R. Hanina: "Whoever would like to know the measure R. Nehemiah sets on twilight should imagine the sun resting on the peak of the Carmel shooting down and dipping in the sea and rising up—that is the measure of R. Nehemiah." [*Shabbat* 35; Jerusalem Talmud, *Berakhot* 81, *Sefer Aggadah* II:597]

R. Samuel ben Nahman said: "[The three services] correspond to the three changes in the day. In the evening a man should say: 'May it be Your will, O Lord my God, that You will take me out from darkness to light.' And in the morning he must say: 'I give thanks to You, O Lord my God, that You have taken me out from darkness to light.' And in the afternoon a man must say: 'May it be Your will, O Lord my God, that in the same way as You have given me the privilege of seeing the sun rising up so You should let me deserve to see it set.'" [*Bereishit Rabbah* 68:9]

In the night, even though it is night, there is the light of the moon and the stars and the planets to mitigate the terror of the darkness. But when is it really dark? Just before dawn. The Moon goes into her chamber; so do the stars and the planets – and there is no greater darkness than at that time. And just then the Holy One, Blessed be He, answers the world and its fullness, bringing up the dawn from the midst of the darkness and illuminating the world.

As for the Dawn, just at the time when Her light is about to break forth, at first she surfaces bit by bit, and only afterward does She explode outward; and after that the light multiplies fast; and after that She increases in full force. [*Sefer Aggadah* II:596; *Yoma* 28]

Rabbi Elazar ben Azayiah said: See, I am like a man of 70 and yet I did not merit to speak about the Exodus of Egypt during the night until Ben Zoma explained it. As it is said: *So that you should remember the day of your going out of Egypt all the days of your life* (Deuteronomy 17:3). *The days of your life:* that actually refers to the days. *All the days of your life:* This refers to the nights as well.

And the Sages say: *The days of your life:* That refers to this world. *All the days of your life:* This actually helps to bring closer the Messianic era." [Passover *Haggadah* for the Seder Night]

At 18 Rabbi Elazar was the Head of the Great Assembly. His head turned white like a 70 year old in a single night so that he could be respected as an "elder." He was brilliant, but he lacked one thing – the suffering and experience that went with age. To his youthful logic it seemed inconsistent that the Exodus from Egypt should be mentioned at night, that is, during times of suffering we could still talk of deliverance and the miracle of the Redemption from Egypt (Egypt being equated with darkness and nighttime). When Ben Zoma, who was really old, explained it to Elazar from his experience, only then did he understood that to *speak* of redemption in times of suffering and darkness, to visualize it, actually helps *bring about* redemption.

It is told of R. Hiyya and R. Shimon that they walked in the valley of Arbela early in the morning and saw the dawn breaking on the horizon. Thereupon, R. Hiyya said: "So too is Israel's redemption. At first it will be visible only slightly, then it will shine forth more brightly, and only afterwards will it break forth in all its glory." [*Shir HaShirim Rabbah* 6:10]

The *Menorah* is this hope of ultimate redemption. It is *"the shining light that shineth more and more until the perfect day"* (Proverbs 4:18).

NOTES

1. Rabbi Isaac Luria (the Ari) was a sixteenth-century Kabbalist.
2. Rabbi Dr. Wolf Gottlieb, *From Days of Old* (*Mi 'Mei Kedem*): *Stories and Sayings from Talmud and Midrash* (London: Central Council of Jewish Religious Education of the United Kingdom, 1948), pp. 68–69.
3. See Chapter 5, p. 295.
4. *Antiquities* 14.4–7.1, Tacitus, *History* 5.9 quoted in L. Yarden, *The Tree of Light* (Ithaca, NY: Cornell University Press, 1971), p. 4.
5. See L. Yarden, *The Tree of Light,* p. 7.
6. Ibid.
7. Ibid.
8. Seventh-century Jewish apocalyptic work, *The Wars of King Messiah.* See Yarden, p. 7.
9. J. H. Levy, "A Note on the Face of the Sacred Vessels of the Second Temple," in *Kedem* (1945) 11:123; A. Jellinek, *Beth ha-Midrash* 11:60; Constantinople Porphyrogenitis *De Ceremoniis* 1, 1, 5ff.; *Corpus scriptorum historiae byzantinae,* ed. B. C. Niehbur (Bonn, 1848).
10. See p. 278.
11. Morton Smith, "The Image of God," *Bulletin of the John Rylands Library* 40 (Manchester, England, Sept. 1957).
12. Asher Barash, *The Golden Candelabrum* (Tel Aviv: Masadah Press, 1943), p. 353.
13. Based on material in Morton Smith, "The Image of God," *Bulletin* 40:497–512. See also Ginzberg, *Legends,* vol. 5, pp. 112–113; *Pesikta Rabbati* 8:29b; Zechariah 4:2.
14. Chaim Vital, *Ez ha-Da'at Tov,* pt. 2 (Jerusalem 1982), 5b, quoted in Idel, *New Perspectives,* p. 198.

15. *Mekhilta de Rabbi Ishmael,* ed. and trans. Frank Lauterbach in Max Kadushin, *A Conceptual Approach to the Mekhilta,* pt. 2 (New York, 1969), p. 113, quoted in Idel, *New Perspectives,* p. 225.
16. Idel, p. 225.
17. See Rabbi Dr. Wolf Gottlieb, *Bim'ai Kedem,* pp. 85, 93.
18. Based on an "insight" or a "Torah" told to me by Micha Odenheimer.
19. *Bosi l'Gani,* p. 13.
20. From the "Delights of Elimelech" in "The Fifth Gate" in Jiri Langer, *Nine Gates,* pp. 135–136.
21. Retelling by this author of an incident in Thomas Keneally, *Schindler's List* (New York: Simon & Schuster, 1982), pp. 60–61.
22. Philip Alstat, "Lights Are Kindled in Bergen-Belsen," *American Examiner–Jewish Week* 30 Nov.–6 Dec. 1972, p. 21, quoted in Goodman, *Hanukkah Anthology,* pp. 186–187.
23. Based on the Kalever Rebbe.
24. Ibid.
25. Eliyahu Kitov, *The Book of Our Heritage,* trans. Nathan Bulman (Jerusalem: 1968), pp. 286–288, in Goodman, *Hanukkah Anthology,* p. 280.
26. S. B. Unsdorfer, *The Yellow Star* (New York: Thomas Yoseloff, 1961).
27. Ibid., p. 149.
28. Ibid., p. 353.
29. Goodman, *Hanukkah Anthology,* pp. 186–187.
30. A Shlomo Carlebach "Torah" (insight) that he gave to me during a Sunday brunch taped discussion on Light.

SEVEN

OUT

OF

THE

DEPTHS

A Yeshiva Student in Pre-Holocaust Poland by Roman Vishniac. Through *Da'at,* a synthesizing awareness, the highest ideals of both Western (Greek) and Jewish beauty come together. This Elijah factor can reconcile masculine and feminine, light and darkness, the Tree of Knowledge (*Shekhinah*) with the Tree of Life, the yearning for God and God Himself. (*Photograph. Copyright © 1988 by Dr. Roman Vishniac*)

The "nether regions," we are told, is the real home of the *Shekhinah* (*Bereishit Rabbah* 19:7). Her physical environment below is often represented by the female image of the "cave," and there are many statements in the Talmud that are not particularly complimentary to Woman, who is equated with darkness and with physical life.

THE INNERMOST RETREAT OF THE
SHEKHINAH

There is a series of Jewish "cave" stories, however, that, through the varied interplay of light and shadow, project a much more positive attitude to this world, to the Feminine, and to the adventure of personal individuation and growth. All of these must be set against that central parable of light and spirituality, Plato's "Myth of the Cave."

To Plato the cave represents the prison house of this world of illusion; outside is the Sun of Truth, of objectivity, and spiritual reality that for him make up The Good. Between these two realms is the play of varying nuances of light and shadow on the wall of the cave. And before any of the prisoners is released, they must slowly become acclimatized to the dazzle of absolute brightness that for so long has been concealed from them.

Plato's account is virulently anti-this-world. He compares the horizontal journey of stepping out of the Cave to the vertical pilgrimage of ascent of the soul.[1] Anyone who attains a vision of the Good, says Plato, will be extremely loath to return to the cave or "to occupy themselves with the affairs of men"; ever after, their souls "will feel the upward urge and the yearning for that sojourn above."

The most interesting and complex Jewish "cave" story centers on the figure of Rabbi Shimon bar Yohai. To Rabbi Shimon, one of the most important teachers of the *Mishnah* in the second century, has been ascribed authorship of the *Zohar,* the principal book of the *Kabbalah,* allegedly put into manuscript form by Moses de Leon (ca. 1280). Rabbi Shimon once insulted the civilization of the occupying Roman forces and as a result was sentenced to death. Forced to flee, he went into hiding in a cave buried in the sand near Meron in Upper Galilee. It is not too far-fetched to think that the *Zohar,* the key book of the *Kabbalah* attributed to him, crystallized precisely in the gloom and discomfort he was forced to undergo during his protracted stay in the cave.

After twelve years Elijah, harbinger of redemption, stands at the entrance to the cave to inform Rabbi Shimon and his son Rabbi Eliezer that times have changed and that they can safely emerge. But the fanaticism of their persecutors has by then eaten into their very souls, and so they have entirely lost touch with the world. At first the pair had taken refuge in the House of Study and been fed by Rabbi Shimon's wife. But in the cave they were entirely cut off from women, living on wild carobs and a stream of water, with no company but each other. When, at Elijah's urging they emerged and saw people going about their usual ploughing and sowing, Rabbi Shimon exclaimed: "These people are forsaking everlasting life. . . .!" "Wherever their glance fell," says the Talmud, "was burnt to a cinder" (*Shabbat* 33).

Then a heavenly Voice pronounced: "If you only came out to destroy My world—back to your lair!"

Until the advent of Elijah, the tale of Rabbi Shimon represents a totally true-to-life account of a historic episode. But no sooner does this mythic character put in an appearance than Rabbi Shimon is transformed into nothing less than a living weapon. Wherever his glance falls, a fire flares up and scorches out of existence that patch of secular reality.

How objective was this destruction on the part of the bemused Rabbi Shimon? Like the inmates of Plato's Cave, he must have experienced great trauma in adapting to the world of the light. It is conceivable Rabbi Shimon's eyes were so dimmed by his stay in the cave that wherever he looked glittered as if it were burning. Whatever he saw only served to enrage him even more.

His fanaticism is symbolized by the advent of Elijah, a figure who, in his biblical career, had a special affinity with fire. When the King sends two sets of officers with fifty men apiece to arrest the Prophet, they are incinerated by "Divine fire" at Elijah's request. A fanatical searing Divinity breaks loose, manifesting itself in a series of mass immolations.

This passionate destructive quality, identified only by association with God's prophet, is in fact an aspect of God Himself or of His *Shekhinah*. For just as Elijah "consumed" the royal officers, God deals with His most beloved servants for even the smallest lapse. The Levites who carried the Holy Ark were especially subject to plague at the slightest moral lapse. . . .

Again when their time is up, a Heavenly Voice [alias the *Shekhinah*] bids the Rabbis "Get out of your cave!"

They go out and linger at the entrance. They have become accustomed to the underworld of fire and darkness and are reluctant to meet the natural sunlight of this world. If it took Rabbi Shimon and Rabbi Eliezer thirteen years to make the transition from fire to light, it has taken God millennia.

Although the writers of the *Midrash* give us many hints of the notion, it is not until the work of the Kabbalists from the thirteenth century on that light was explicitly pinpointed as the perfect image for God.

In the Bible God more aptly refers to Himself as a "consuming Fire," prone to devour either Israel or Israel's enemies at the slightest provocation. What is the peculiar quality of fire attributed to the Divine? Apart from passion, when fire is mentioned in connection with God, it is usually in context of anger and jealous possessiveness.

> For a fire is kindled in Mine anger, and shall burn until the lowest hell . . . and shall set on fire the foundations of the earth. [Deuteronomy 2:21]

> And when the People complained, it displeased the Lord: and the Lord heard it; and His anger was kindled; and the fire of the Lord burnt among them, and consumed them. [Numbers 11:1]

> Take heed unto yourselves lest ye forget the covenant of the Lord your God. For the Lord thy God is a consuming fire, even a jealous God. [Deuteronomy 4:23-4]

THE FIRE OF MYSTICAL UNION

Fire is not an indication solely of anger, but sometimes also of sheer intensity verging on ecstasy, as when the People could not bear to hear God enunciate the Ten Commandments because the fire was too much for them. Fire, in "light" terms, was also simply an indication of the unmitigated brilliance of the Glory, as when Moshe went up on Mount Sinai. "And the sight of the Glory of the Lord was like devouring fire on the top of the mount in the sight of the children of Israel" (Exodus 24:17).

Not only God's Glory, but also His Torah is composed of fire.

> The Lord came from Sinai; he shined forth from Mount Paran, and He came with ten thousand saints; from His right hand went a fiery law for them. [Deuteronomy 33:2]

From a modern standpoint, God's quality of Fire lacks the ethical dimension simply because it is neither personal nor humane. On the other hand, although fire is not necessarily benign, the kind of consummation it offers is that of the ecstasy of spirit and annihilation of self.

This "fire" in its pure form is found in the story of the sons of Aaron, who carried "strange fire" into the "Holy of Holies" when this was not part of the ritual (Leviticus 10:1). A Divine Fire, the very fire they had brought in their censers, shot forth and consumed them. Why did they act so impetuously, and for what crime did God kill them?

The only explanation for this turn of events is provided by Moshe's partial consolation to his brother: "By those who are close to Me, I shall be sanctified and in front of the People I will be glorified!" (Leviticus 10:3). The greater the intimacy the greater the threat. Nadav and Avihu knew what they were risking when they entered the Holy of Holies without being asked. Their action is reminiscent of that of Queen Esther, who went before a human king without being invited. If Ahasueras had not stretched out his scepter to receive her, his bodyguard would have chopped off her head. Death was the normal penalty for such a breach of etiquette. However, she only entered the King's presence to save the lives of her People, and not out of a personal whim. Nadav and Avihu entered the Holy of Holies out of spiritual hedonism because they wanted to experience the utmost ecstasy by fusing their souls with the Divine. They were prepared that the very fire they presented would consume them, and died in the quest for pure ecstasy and self-dissolution.

A rationalist like Gershom Scholem would have us believe that in Judaism there is an unsurpassable gulf between Creator and Creature, so that the notion of losing oneself in union with the Divine does not exist. The imagery of fire used by Jewish mysticism as far back as Biblical days and the story of Nadav and Avihu contained in the Torah itself is enough to show that Scholem was wrong. While there was a tendency for the very dominant rationalist mainstream in Jewish thinking to dwell on the unsurpassable gulf between Man and God, experientialists simply flung themselves across it. One may say this "death wish" was not very Jewish – the Bible does criticize Nadav and Avihu's bringing "strange fire" into the Holy of Holies. Nevertheless, the personal consummation they experienced was the one they desired, that of mystical union as demonstrated by the imagery of fire.

The death they invited upon themselves is only a graphic dramatization of the later Hasidic yearning for *Deveikut* (absolute union with the Divine). The imagery in which the experience of self-surrender is described, Moshe Idel has pointed out, is similar to the consumption of the spark by fire and the dissolution of a drop of water by the ocean. The graphic language in which both the Kabbalists of the thirteenth century and the *Hasidim* of the eighteenth century describe this experience of mystical union can leave no doubt that the annihilation of self is as much part of the Jewish mystical experience as it is of any other. Rabbi Shneor Zalman of Liadi (the first Lubavitcher Rebbe) compares the cleaving of the soul to "Divine Fire" with the act of swallowing in which food is absorbed into the body of the person ingesting it. Despite the terror that attends this whole description, it also is fraught with a passion, sweetness, and pleasure, that suggests that the act of swallowing described in relation to the upper portion of the body is only an image for the act of intercourse.

> [W]hen man cleaves to God, it is extremely delightful for Him, and very sweet, so much so that He will swallow it into His heart, and so on, as the bodily throat swallows. And this is the true cleaving, as he becomes one substance with God into whom he was swallowed, without being separate (from him) to be considered as a distinct entity at all. That is the meaning (of the verse) *And you shall cleave to Him* – (to cleave) literally.[2]

Already five centuries earlier, Rabbi Isaac of Acre had extended the comparison of spiritual fusion of soul and the Divine, with physiological processes of eating and of sex, to include the Temple sacrifice.

He identifies the soul with the burnt offering consumed by the Fire.[3] When the Temple was in existence, sacrifice (the Hebrew for which means *closeness*) was a means of approaching and coming closer to God. But the real sacrifice, for which the animal was only a civilized substitute, was the human being bringing the offering. Subjectively, when an individual brought an offering, it was himself, his own life, his blood that was streaming on the altar and being elevated by Divine consumption.

Sacrifice may be a way of serving God that has fallen into disrepute because modern thinkers would like not to grant the mysterious spiritual component in the most physical acts. In his *Light of the Eyes,* Rabbi Isaac of Acre illustrates how just such primitive and physical a rite as animal sacrifice, like sex, helps in the maintenance of civilization. It is because of the drive toward spiritual fusion, the element of fire.

A certain sage asked his colleague about the subject of the (Temple) sacrifices, and said: "How is it possible that a matter as disgusting as the burning of fat and the sprinkling of blood, with the smell of the skin, and hair of the burnt offering which is completely consumed, should be a matter by which the world is sustained, that it should be a cause for unification above and for blessing and for the sustaining of all that exists?"

He answered: "I will tell you a parable, as to what this resembles. A child is born and is left alone when he is little, and he sustains himself with herbs and water, and he grows up and it happens that he comes within the habitation of human beings, and one day he saw a man coupling with his wife. He began to mock them and say: What is this foolish person doing?"

They said to him: "You see this act; it is that which sustains the world, or without this the world would not exist."

He said to them: "How is it possible that from such filth and dirt there should be the cause for this good and beautiful and praiseworthy world? And it is nevertheless true – and understand this."[4]

The physical process of metabolizing food has become the paradigm in Hasidism for the possibility of transforming the human being and his animal drives into "divine fire." When a man – or the best example of a man, the *Tzaddik* – takes in food with a pure intention, sparks are extracted as he digests that are then elevated to a higher state. (From being part of the vegetable or animal kingdom, they become man.)

Similarly, with man himself, his spiritual element is brought near for Divine consumption, and the spark of soul in the human being literally becomes divine. Thus, "when you raise the lamps" means "when you offer yourself, your physicality," "when you and your ego become the burnt offering," this very sacrifice will be a cleaving of fire with fire, as the soul buries her light in the Divine. And though the physical sacrifices are no more, this type of burnt offering in man's inner Temple is continually acceptable.

The story is told of Abraham that when the angels visited him in the guise of wayfarers, he immediately went to the herd to find a calf and prepare a meal for his visitors. The calf escaped and Abraham followed it in hot pursuit. The calf fled into a cave from the innermost recess of which light was streaming forth (*Vayikra Rabbah* 31:4).

Hard as he found it to tear himself away from the seductive vision of the Glory, he was able to return to the world to attend to the needs of his guests. In order to fulfill the mandates of hospitality, he, unlike Nadav and Avihu, gave up his own spiritual yearnings and returned to the world outside the cave and to his social responsibilities.

In the discussion by the commentators of how Nadav and Avihu "sinned" in their supreme sacrifice of themselves, one suggestion is that they had not yet been stabilized by marriage. They had nothing to draw them back to life. All their passion went into their offering and they died in the moment of Divine Union, giving the world or their responsibilities no thought.

SACRIFICE AND THE COVENANT

It is said that the relationship between man and woman is basically Fire. If they direct their lives together in one way, the Fire of the *Shekhinah* rests between them; if not, they will then be consumed by "alien fire" (the passion of Nadav and Avihu).

According to the *Midrash Tanhuma,* the couple died because "they entered (the Holy of Holies) without their clothes." The thirteenth-century mystic, R. David ben Yehuda he-Hasid expands upon this with the explanation that because they had not carried out their obligations vis-à-vis the Covenant–that is, to marry and have children–the articles of Divine clothing that observance of these commands would have covered, were missing at their time of entry into the Holy of Holies. Interestingly, he says that the "part" of the Divine that swallowed them was "Fire on high, *Malkhut,* who is called Fire" (the Feminine part of God).[5]

The death of Rabbi Akiva contrasts completely with that of Nadav and Avihu. While they sought martyrdom by extinguishing their souls in the Divine Fire, he had martyrdom thrust upon him. And even in his greatest agony, he did not try to lessen his sufferings by preempting death. He was one of the Four alleged to have entered Paradise while still alive, and the only one to return unscathed. When he was surrounded by the mounting flames, he could have found a way out of his agony, had he so chosen. But as much as he longed for a quick release, even more precious to him was each last moment of a life in which, until his very last breath, he could continue to keep God's commandments.

> If he had wanted to, he could have strengthened the love and awe in his heart and caused his soul to cleave to his root so as to bring about the integration of the light of his higher soul in *Ein-Sof.* [Then] his higher soul would certainly have departed from him and ascended upwards . . . and had he been willing to do that, he would have separated from his agonies. [That is, he would no longer have felt the physical flame leaping about him as his higher soul was consumed in the light of *Ein-Sof.*] But, out of his will and desire to perform the commandment ["And you shall live by them," that is, the commandments], he maintained his soul within him and carried on suffering.[6]

For Rabbi Akiva, the fulfillment of the commandments in this world was more important than the ideal of mystical union with God. He was therefore unwilling to speed up the end of his physical life and his union with the Divine, even though performance of the commandment to "Sanctify the Name" was a living agony. As a result, not only did he achieve the ultimate union, but he elevated the physical world in which he lingered.

Paradoxically, his giving the proper value to each moment of life and not rushing into the consummation that underlay his fulfillment of all commands was his best guarantee of ultimately achieving the goal, whereas the singlemindedness of Nadav and Avihu brought about the opposite effect. If their desire was a swift consummation and self-obliteration in the Divine Fire, the result was, at least in the religious imagination of the Jewish People, that they had to return in a whole chain of future lives to rectify what they had hastily left undone. Their individual human light did not go out, but neither had they won for themselves a final resting place in the Beyond. They had to come back again and again until they had acquired enough merit to keep their souls alight in the next world.

According to some opinions, only the soul has to undergo metempsychosis to make a *tikkun* or reparation for something left undone in a past life. The prime example of this is someone who has died childless or who has committed some sexual offense either by commission or by omission. This slight to the Covenant must be made good.

Since both Nadav and Avihu died childless and unmarried, their offense, as well as being a sin against the Covenant, was a "slight" against Woman also. Their desire was totally to sever their connection with the physical, with which Woman was equated, to obliterate their own lower animal (female) soul (*nefesh*) in favor of their Divine soul (*neshamah*), as represented by the Higher Feminine. So, while they gave up Woman completely, it was only to identify more strongly with the more spiritual feminine part of themselves that only God could fulfill. They may consciously have been giving up relations with Woman as the Other only because theirs was a homosexual relationship to start with. In their attitude to God, they wanted to make themselves into the censers of the fire they carried, to act the part of pure Vessel, notably a woman's role. And in relation to each other, they were totally fused and indistinguishable. So much so, that because they both died in the same desire and as part of the same consummation, their souls are said to have merged to return as Pinchas, their nephew and Aaron's grandson, who championed the sexual honor of the Jewish People and vindicated the Covenant. Pinchas, in turn, came back as Elijah, who had to pick up the threads of reparation.

But because none of these people had children, they had to return again and again to be their own children, so to speak. Finally, Elijah had an ersatz child, the boy he resurrected through an act more intimate than sex or giving birth. But even this was a symbolic child. No wonder, then, that Elijah is pictured in the *Zohar* as a catalyst figure. He brings the "King" and the "Queen" together, The Holy One, Blessed be He, and the *Shekhinah*. He is present at the entry of every Jewish boy baby into the Covenant. All this he can do because his celibacy – an unfashionable notion in contemporary attitudes and in contemporary mainstream Judaism – makes him fallow ground for God's Spirit.

THE FIRE OF ELIJAH

The fire that Elijah plays with to such dramatic and destructive effect is also part of his character. A discrepancy has been pointed out between the historical account of Elijah given in the book of Kings and the idea of Elijah conjured up in the imagination of Israel throughout the centuries.

Nevertheless, despite the zeal and ardor, frequently finding outlet in destruction, that are his distinguishing marks, even in his lifetime, Elijah is no stranger to the giving and the sustaining of life. If Elijah has no pity on the king's soldiers whom he incinerated when they came to arrest him, he has great empathy for ordinary unsophisticated people like the widow of Zarapeth who, according to some accounts, was not a Jew.

According to the Talmud, it is Elijah and not God who was responsible for sentencing the Jews and the peoples of the surrounding area to famine and drought. But when faced with the suffering of one simple woman and her child about to die of starvation, Elijah is affected powerfully and ready to bring about miracles for the sake of these individuals.

The Prophet bids her to mix her last handful of meal with her last drop of oil, and share this final meal she is preparing for her son and herself with him. If she shares her limited rations with him, the Prophet implies, his virtue will stand her in good stead. Her physical resources will be blessed and become unlimited, and she and her son will live on them until all Israel is rescued from famine by the coming of the rainy season. A glimpse of the suffering of the woman who has befriended him is enough. Perhaps the entire People received rain because the Widow of Zarapeth taught God's Prophet what the poor have to endure when God sends His mass punishments upon the world.

If God is apt to answer His Prophet with "fire from Heaven" (I Kings 18:24), He also has delivered over to him the key to His treasure house of rain. With Elijah's prayer – and prayer is the equivalent of water, a feminine form of light-energy – the drought ends and the People have food to live on.

The miracle Elijah accomplishes here is in a hidden form – the revival of the dead. Elijah changes Heaven's decree from death to life. And rain for an agricultural people is life. The body dies because there is a limit to physical resources. A machine can work so long and no longer. By commanding the poor widow to share her last morsel with him, and then make her handful of meal and small cruse of oil last for an unstipulated number of days (of which the eight days of *Hanukkah* are symbolic) until relief comes, Elijah is revealing the mystery of the incarnation of spirit within physicality. He is reviving the dead.

THE "DOUBLE PORTION" OF ELISHA

Before Elijah dies, his disciple Elisha asks for a "double portion" of his Master's spirit (II Kings 2:9). By this he means that at the moment of death, some "sparks" from his Master's soul should migrate to him. In the repetition of the story with Elisha as the protagonist, what transpires is doubly clear. One of the wives of the "sons of the Prophets" comes to Elisha and says that she has lost her husband (Elisha's disciple) and become so poor that creditors want to take her two sons into slavery. Elisha then asks her what she has in the house. She says that all she has is a jug of oil. He tells her to borrow as many vessels as she can from her neighbors. Then she should shut the door behind her so that nobody will see the miracle about to take place. When she starts pouring, the single jug of oil will pour and pour and fill all the vessels she has prepared. Only when there are no more vessels left will the oil cease.

An entire tradition of *Kabbalah* involving vessels may have been based on this miracle of Elisha.[7] All that must be provided is the container (the *Menorah*) – and light will shine and shine. This miracle contains the very heart of the miracle of *Hanukkah* – oil enough for one day that lasted for eight. A certain amount of respect is paid to physical law in that, according to the *Zohar*, blessing rests only on something that already exists. The poor widow only had enough oil, says the *Zohar*, to anoint a fingertip, but that was enough to fill all receptacles.

In the account of the widow of Zarapeth, part of the physical preparation necessary is moral. The poor woman must extend herself and share her limited means (the Vessel), for the miracle to begin to work. Similarly with the wife of the "disciple of the Prophets," the commentators explain that her husband Ovadiah had saved the lives of one hundred of his fellow "sons of the Prophets" from the wrath of the idolatrous Jezebel by hiding them in a cave and sustaining them and illuminating their hideout with oil-lamps that were never permitted to go out. After his death, Ovadiah's charitable acts returned to him again with the miracle of the jug of oil performed for the benefit of his widow and children. "He lends to the Lord who is charitable to the poor" (Psalm 19:17).

From this we learn that what is subject to finite physical law is the vessel or the instrument, and that there is a spiritual fuel that in itself is unlimited. It is to this that the Prophet Zechariah alludes when, in describing the oil piped through the golden channels of the *Menorah,* he suddenly proclaims, "Not by strength, nor by might, but by My spirit" (Zechariah 4:6). It is this that the oil represents.

The widow of Zarapeth then left the Prophet and did as he said. When there were no more empty vessels to fill, she asked her sons to bring her broken vessels because she reasoned that

God, who could fill what was empty, also could mend what was broken. (This could refer to people as well as vessels.) After every possible type of container was filled, the oil stopped. According to some commentators, the oil went up in price. Then the woman asked the Prophet what to do next. He told her to sell as much oil as she needed to pay off her creditors. Then she was still left with enough oil to live comfortably with her children for a long time.

In the Elijah version of this story, the oil and the meal last many days until the rains bring a natural salvation and relief to the entire People. According to the Midrashic embroidery of the Elisha version, the woman and her children can live on what remains of the oil "until the Resurrection" (*Bereishit Rabbah* 35:3). Clearly in the mind of the writers of the *Midrash*, the "day of rainfall" is equated with the "day of the resurrection of the dead."[8]

There is no suggestion either in the biblical text or in the *Midrash* that this woman and her children actually live on until the Resurrection. It seems that the story itself is haunted by the single motif of resurrection and renewal of the juices of life. The *Midrash* has Ovadiah's widow go out to the cemetery and revive her dead husband. Finally, it is the "kindness of the dead that lives on," the oil lamps that were not to be extinguished even in the darkness of the graves and the caves, that induce Elisha to listen to her. Since Adam and Eve, caves have always been suitable places for burial. Both caves and graves can be taken as symbols of the womb.

The miracle of the oil is the resurrection of the physical. In the story of Elijah, the incident is directly followed by the death and resurrection of the poor widow's son, whereas in the case of Elisha, the miracle of the oil is followed by the resurrection of the son of another woman, apparently unrelated to Ovadiah's widow. But the sequence in both stories suggests that the multiplication of physical resources—as symbolized by the expansion of the oil, the miracle of emanation, defying physical limit—hints at the resurrection of the dead. With the return of the rains, the earth itself streams with new life. The movement is from death to rebirth. Thus in the miracle of Creation lies the germination of the Resurrection.

Into Elijah's hands was entrusted the Key to Rain and the Key to Resurrection, both tapping into the hidden channels of renewed blessing and vitality.

In the Elijah version of the Resurrection story, after the poor widow and her boy have been saved from starvation, the child still falls ill and dies. Quite irrationally, the widow turns on her benefactor and blames him for her misfortune. He as good as killed the child, she says. Does she have any right to say that? Did the fact that he provided her with food once give her a lifetime guarantee and place him in her debt forever? She blames her "man of God," not simply for his lack of involvement in the subsequent death of the child whose life he had saved, but somehow, through his very lack of involvement, for having helped to bring it about. "What have you got against me, O man of God, that you come to me to remind me of my iniquity and to slay my son" (I Kings 17:18). She says he killed her son. Obviously he didn't. Yet on a deeper level, perhaps he did. He certainly does not feel entirely free of responsibility.

Logically one might think his debt to her for her hospitality was amply paid off, and that the fact of the child's falling sick has nothing at all to do with the episode about the magical increase of dwindling resources. But the emotional truth is otherwise. And from what follows we see that Elijah does not think her denunciation of him unjustified, or that she has no more claim on him because her child died of natural causes.

What was the purpose of the miracle of the oil and the meal if not to save life? When resources that have been consumed are renewed, what is this but the realization of the potential for regeneration latent in the physical. For what is Creation if it does not contain within itself forces for renewal!

The truth is that once someone does a favor, a personal bond is established between him and his beneficiary and he cannot simply walk away uncaring when the beneficiary is swept away by another calamity. And if that is true of a human benefactor, how much more is it true of God. Once God created man in all his weakness and vulnerability, He simply has no right – this is the logical sequel of the woman's argument – at some later time to allow decay and misfortune to catch up with him.

Immediately Elijah turns to God and blames Him. Not the man of God but God himself killed the child. Why? The woman has said it herself. Any small share of guilt she might possess – not more, and probably far less than that of any other more fortunate person who did not lose an only child – was exposed by proximity to Elijah's fire. And this, Elijah simply cannot bear. Elijah knows the nature of what possesses him. He turns on God and accuses Him of outright evil: "As well as wreaking havoc in general, will you also do evil to this woman with whom I stay by killing her son?" (I Kings 17:20). He has reached the stage where he wants to be able to live with ordinary people without having to fear they will shrivel to a cinder by contact with his holiness.

THE FETUS AND THE *MENORAH*

Elijah's appeal to God to save the son of the woman who has provided him with shelter is echoed in the petulant childish tones of Jonah appealing to Heaven that a beloved cucumber, under whose shadow he found shelter from the scorching sun, should not shrivel up and die. Both these spiritual men learn sympathy for others from a contact with the outside world in which their comfort is at stake. The lesson this teaches us is just how vulnerable and childishly dependent upon the physical even a Prophet can be. Only from our own suffering can we appreciate what others endure. Therefore the initial link with the "other" need not even be human. If only by being confronted with one poor widow who has shared her last bit of food with him could Elijah appreciate the terrible implications of his edict that there be no rain for three years in all the territories adjoining the Holy Land, Jonah learned human empathy from a vegetable. In both stories, God plays a double hand. On the one hand, He is the savage God of Fire who answers Elijah's prayer to consume his enemies, the God who, in the story of Jonah, is prepared to sink a whole ship because of the sins of one individual. On the other hand, He prepares physical circumstances in such a way that from them the Prophet will grow in sympathy and bring about a commensurate mellowing in the way the Divine intervenes in human affairs.

While Elijah is faced with the difficult mission of calling Israel to repentance from worshipping the idols of neighboring countries, Jonah is confronted with the unpleasant task of inviting Israel's enemies of his day to repent. With his prophetic insight, Jonah knew that the enemies would comply, whereas God's Chosen People posed a far more perplexing task, and he resented that. Ungenerously, he was reluctant to fulfill his mission because he suspected he might be too successful. Instead of traveling to Nineveh, he tries to escape, only to be caught in a storm at sea. The storm gets worse and threatens to engulf the ship. While passengers and crew pray to their gods, Jonah sleeps, totally callous and indifferent to the fate of his fellow passengers or himself. He is approached by the captain, who asks him to pray to his God because that might make the crucial difference. Finally, as the waves get stronger, lots are cast to discover who is at fault. Naturally, Jonah is chosen. Jonah then admits that the God of heaven, "Maker of both the sea and the dryland" is in full pursuit of him. The storm and the danger to the entire passengers and crew are the result of God's hounding of one individual. Get rid of him, the captain orders, and the waves subside. With great reluctance, the crew complies (Jonah 1:16).

Jonah is saved from drowning by being swallowed by a whale, which for him is both a haven and a prison. The whale – like the ship and the ocean, like the gourd that resembles a tabernacle, and like the cave – is an example of feminine space.

From the six days of creation, the Lord had prepared a great fish to swallow up Jonah.

Rabbi Tarphon said: "That fish was specially appointed from the six days (of Creation) to swallow up Jonah, as it is said, *And the Lord had prepared a great fish to swallow up Jonah* (Jonah 2:1). He entered its mouth just as a man enters a great synagogue and stood (inside). The two eyes of the fish were like windows of glass giving light to Jonah."

Rabbi Meir said: "One pearl was suspended inside the belly of the fish and it gave illumination to Jonah, like the Sun which shines its utmost at noon and it showed Jonah all that was in the sea and in the depths, as it is said, *Light is sown for the righteous*." [*Bereishit Rabbah* 31:11]

In addition to the pearl that served as a lamp for Jonah in the body of the whale, the *Midrash* tells of a pearl that gave light to Noah and his companions in the Ark in the midst of the Flood. Jonah has regressed so far into his own unconscious that he finds himself in the womb again. What was the pearl that provided him with illumination but the *Menorah,* or the light of the human soul. Much the same is said of the fetus in its mother's womb. The fetus sits under the light of a *Menorah* learning the whole Torah until its time comes to be born. Then it is expelled roughly from this most comfortable place on earth as Jonah was from the whale. An angel strikes the fetus on the forehead and all the glorious knowledge of God it has known goes into retreat. The umbilical cord with its collective unconscious (the whale) has been severed, and the fetus develops its separate reality.

> Rabbi Simlai delivered the following discourse: "What does an embryo resemble when it is in the bowels of its mother? Folded writing tablets.
> "A light burns over its head and it sees from one end of the world to the other, as it is said, *When his lamp shined above my head, and by his light I walked through darkness* (Job 29:3). And do not be astonished at this, for a person sleeping here (in Babylonia) might see a dream in Spain and there is no time during which a man enjoys greater happiness than in those days.
> "It is also taught the complete Torah." [*Mishnah Avot* 3:7]

In the Jonah story the Prophet experiences spiritual rebirth after his stage of regression and escapism in the innards of the ship and the sea monster. He cries out to God to save him and he submits to pursuing the next step of his mission. En route, he learns from the cucumber to appreciate the value of the most insignificant organism. Obviously he was not sorry for the cucumber but for himself and his creature comforts, just as more subtly Elijah could only feel for the widow because she had befriended him. But this self-regard, when brought to consciousness, extends itself from relationship with green plants, with people who do good to us, and opens us to an appreciation of the feelings of other people in general.

After contemplating Jonah's grief for a vegetable, God addresses him: "If you are so sorry about the destruction of the cucumber you had no hand in sowing, don't you think I should care even more about the obliteration of a great civilization filled with 'human beings who do not know to distinguish between their right hand and their left'" (Jonah 4:11).

Here God, far from pronouncing a hasty collective judgment, excuses the gentile population *en masse* for simplicity and lack of knowledge of right and wrong. In addition, the incident of the withered cucumber is used, as is that of the dead child in the Elijah story, to pinpoint a crucial transition in Jonah's spiritual journey.

Jonah's encounter with the whale and the cucumber was no accident, but preordained. It actually says in the text that God had a whale ready to swallow Jonah (Jonah 1:17). God "prepares" this big fish especially for him both as a shelter and as a second womb; he is to be saved from the physical danger of storm at sea and to be provided with an environment for spiritual rebirth. Similarly with the cucumber, God lets it spring up on purpose to shield Jonah from the scorching sun, only to take it away and hear his complaint. And the same with Elijah. It is God who tells the Prophet first that he will be sustained by the widow of Zarapeth. Then it is God who slays the son of his benefactor so that the Prophet could begin to ask the questions that all humans ask. The widow and Elijah's cave, the ship Jonah sailed in, the whale and the cucumber—all were milestones in the personal development of the Prophet, each "stage" marking a further transition in his journey of spiritual resurrection.

THE DAY OF RAIN AND THE DAY OF RESURRECTION

The miracle of resurrection takes place behind sealed doors. Elijah lays the child on his bed and stretches out on top of him. Eye to eye, mouth to mouth, he prays for God to restore the child's soul to him.

Nowhere in the account is it actually stated that the child has died. What is said is that his soul (or breath) has deserted him. What Elijah prays to God for is that the breath should find its center within the body once more. When the child revives, Elijah places him securely back in the arms of his mother, who sees this act as a living proof her guest is indeed a man of God.

In the Elijah versions, both the story of the preservation from famine and that of the resurrection concern the same woman, but they are neatly divided as themes for two different tales. In the Elisha recapitulation, the events appear to happen to two different women, but it is obvious the themes overlap. In the story about Ovadiah's widow, this overlapping is only seen clearly in the *Midrash* and in rabbinical explanation. Ovadiah's widow appealed 265 times to the Prophet without being heard, until she went to the cemetery and called on her husband, as it were, reviving him from the dead. Finally, it was Ovadiah's virtue and his kindness to the "sons of the Prophets" while he was alive that made Elisha answer her appeal and perform a miracle that would allow her and her child to have a means of livelihood. So in this tale, Elisha agrees only to save life in order to perform a vicarious kind of resurrection on behalf of his disciple Ovadiah.

Thus one might think that the two themes of physical maintenance and of resurrection are entirely separate—but the opposite is true. The two stories, though separate, manage to reflect upon each other. It is as if the Elisha stories each contain a plot and a subplot. If physical plenty (the miracle of the oil) is the dominant theme in the story of Ovadiah's widow, then resurrection is hinted at subliminally throughout. In the story of the Shunamite, the two themes overlap in the one text.

This story falls into two parts. The first is about fertility; the second centers on resurrection. So in the short span of a single tale, a story about the miracle of birth changes into one about the resurrection of the dead.

The Shunamite, a "woman of distinction," suggests to her husband that the upper storey of their home be walled over to create a small self-contained studio for the Prophet, so that whenever he passes by he will have somewhere to stay undis- turbed. She has the room furnished very simply. A bed, a table, a chair, and a lamp will provide for his basic needs. This little room is intended as a replica of the Sanctuary, so that the Man of God can comfortably commune with the *Shekhinah*. The table is the altar, the lamp the *Menorah,* and the bed the Holy of Holies.

Acting on the assumption that the Shunamite woman has done this out of self-interest, Elisha is prepared to do her a favor in return for her hospitality. But when he asks her what she would like, she replies modestly that she lives among her people and does not need any special favors from the great. The Prophet is rather disconcerted because now he really is in her debt. Then his disciple Gehazi, who understands the woman's situation better, informs Elisha that his benefactress is childless. Elisha then promises her that, like Sarah, "at this season" the following year she will embrace a child.

The Shunamite's reaction to the Prophet's promise is not one of outright gratitude. The woman entreats the Prophet: "No, my Lord. O Man of God, Do not fail your maidservant!" (II Kings 4:16).

She had given up hope of having a child. If the man of God were to set her hoping and nothing came of it, the torture would be too hard to endure. She preferred he take back his promise rather than disappoint her.

She is not of the stoical school of those who thank God: "If You had redeemed us from slavery but had left us to die in the desert, it would have been enough for us!"[9]

She did not ask for anything in the first place. She gives freely without expecting anything in return; she even gives him a last chance to take back his promises rather than deceive her finally. But she begs him to spare her the ultimate torment – that she should be pregnant for nine months, go through labor, bear her child, embrace and suckle him, only to have him die! Better not to taste such a joy, she warns the Prophet, than to have it snatched away from her.

And her suspicions are not without foundation. For the disillusionment she fears is exactly what happens every day.

How could she have expected him to treat her like Ovadiah's widow and let her enjoy her reward "until the Resurrection of the dead"!

Elisha's blessing, which he promised would find fruition "at this season next year," is reminiscent both of an earlier and a subsequent miracle. The language is exactly the same as that of other birth stories—Sarah and Manoah's wife, the mother of Samson, are also promised they will have children "at this self-same season next year." And very similar language but with a different time frame—"at that time during this season"—is used for the miracle of *Hanukkah*. But in the case of *Hanukkah*, we look back to a past miracle rather than forward to what is yet to come. While the natural fruitfulness of the body and the land can be equated with "the Day of Rain," the miracle of *Hanukkah*, looking beyond any reasonably to-be-hoped-for future, can be subsumed under "the Day of the Resurrection."

THE SEASON OF LIGHT THAT TRANSCENDS TIME

Although it is true that when the inmates of a concentration camp celebrated the miracle of the oil of *Hanukkah* "at that time in this season," they were commemorating something long past; yet symbolically that is not entirely accurate. For the language "at this season" is cyclical, resurrecting what is only apparently past. As terrible as the situation of the concentration camp inmates appeared to be, like Abraham's idealized Sarah whose "light did not go out by night," they were able to link themselves not only to the past, but to the recurring miracle of light that transcends time.

The story of Elisha and the Shunamite woman is made up of two parts. When Elisha "grants" his benefactress a child in the first place, this is the equivalent of the miracle of the oil. It is a miracle of the extension of physical resources. The second part is the resurrection story itself.

Many years pass. The child is no longer a baby. He goes out to join his father with the reapers. One day he has a stroke and cries out "My head! My head!" and collapses. His father orders a servant to carry him to his mother. This is described with the utmost poignancy. The child sits on her knees until noon, then dies.

The Mother bears her son's body up to the small cell she has built for the Prophet, lays him out on Elisha's bed, and closes the door behind her. She tells no one, not even her husband, not even the man of God's servant, that the boy is dead. She believes that God can do anything, including bring her child back from the dead. What she does not believe is that she deserves the laws of nature to be publicly set aside for her sake. So she covers up the death, tells no one, and rides out to meet Elisha. When the Prophet sees her at a distance, he sends his attendant Gehazi to find out what is the matter. She is willing to confide in nobody, however, except the Man of God himself. So she puts him off with some pretext, tells him she is fine, and continues to ride on until she comes up to the Prophet and breaks down at his feet. Gehazi tries to push the importunate woman away but Elisha orders him to let her be; he realizes she is overwrought for good reason.

She does not say what has happened, but what she does say is enough: "Did I ask a son from my lord? Didn't I say: 'Do not mislead me'" (II Kings 2:4). This leaves Elisha in little doubt as to what has happened.

THE BREATH OF LIFE

He sends Gehazi with his staff to revive the child, but nothing happens until he shuts himself up in the room alone with the boy. Like Elijah, he lies on the boy's body, mouth to mouth and eye to eye, and administers a form of artificial respiration, literally breathing his own life into the boy to restore the connection between the inert body and the "Reservoir of Souls."

Although Elijah strove all his life to uphold a patriarchal culture against the matriarchal goddess cult of a Jezebel, and in so doing appears to present an uncompromisingly masculine stance, his special ability to resurrect a child may indicate a secret wish on his part to become a mother. For what does his position crouching over the inert body of a child really describe? It is far more intimate an entanglement than any father usually achieves with his child. It reminds us of intercourse between the male and the female, but instead of the male inserting his penis into the vagina and ejaculating sperm, the Prophet's mouth breathes breath and spirit into the ready made body of a child. The action of God's creation of man as described in Genesis, and this description of the Prophet's revival of the child, contain in them motifs both of love making and the pangs of labor. And both differ from these normal human acts in that in both cases the body, or vessel, is presented ready made, and then God (or the Prophet) breathes into them "the breath of life."

The three different Hebrew words for "soul" – *nefesh, ruah,* and *neshamah* – denote various types of breath. This suggests that ancient Israelite mystical practice may have included a yogic breathing technique similar to the type employed by Elijah– Elisha to resurrect the dead. It is as if the inert little body were some kind of passive musical instrument or an aeolian harp awaiting Prophetic inspiration; the body is a vessel, a channel or pipe for the life that flows through it, waiting to be reactivated by the breath of the Prophet. Especially in the case of Elisha, in a sense Elijah's "spiritual son," the Prophet closely imitates God's creation of man. "And He breathed into his nostrils the breath of life; and man became a living soul" (Genesis 2:7).

In *Kabbalah,* the soul is sometimes described as itself being made up of various components – sometimes three, sometimes five – stretching out accordion fashion from heaven to earth. To resurrect the dead, the Prophet must master these types of breath, draw upon that "Reservoir of Souls" that upholds all the rest, and restart the carousel of light and of life moving between above and below.

In the Cave at Horeb, Elijah discovered that God was to be found not in the storm, not in the earthquake nor in the fire, but "in a still small voice" (I Kings 19:9–1). The element that brings about resurrection and can revive the life-force is a mere breath, the Hebrew for *soul,* expressed as voice and language, the partic- ular faculty that distinguishes the lowest *Sefirah* of *Malkhut.* Each of the Seven Natural *Sefirot* is represented by one of the Seven Organs of the Face. "Queen" is epitomized by the "mouth." The Hebrew for the double portion requested by Elisha is a *double mouth.* And this is why Elijah lay and breathed into the dead child "mouth to mouth," so that the flow of air should reenter his body.

In the spirit of *Kabbalah,* what the Prophet is bringing together in reconnecting higher and lower worlds is the union of the "King and the Queen," The Holy One, Blessed be He, and His *Shekhinah.* And in this coupling the Prophet plays the part of the "in-between"; reuniting the male and the female, he plays the part of neither, or a bit of both. In addition to symbolizing the more ethereal part of breath – having cut his connection from his own vegetable earthly animal soul (*nefesh,* female) – he connects his *ruah* – his intermediary spirit with the Divine. Elijah also represents one of the organs of the human body – the phallus, the sign of the Covenant itself, which, according to a mystical tradition is not the property of the male, as one might suppose, but of the female who has proprietory rights in it; and in the case of Elijah, he, as phallus, belongs in the service of the *Shekhinah.*

TRANSFORMATION

These stories of birth, sustenance, and regeneration delineate an Elijah–Elisha far different than the "Angry Prophet" who simply devours opposition with the fire of his zeal. Here the "mothering" forces of creation and of nurturing back into life are brought into play, rather than those of destruction. Elijah can embody within himself an aggression and an ardor that mellow into enlightenment over centuries of metempsychosis only because the process has already begun in his own lifetime.

In biblical Judaism, unlike daughter religions, miracles do not play a major role. Powers of resurrection come naturally to Elijah, however, only because he is involved in the even more miraculous and all but impossible process of the transformation of his own human nature. The primary material he works with are the opposites of fire and light, aggression and acceptance within himself, but the resolution he strives for goes far beyond the limits of his own personal life.

The method by which the personal life is translated into history may be by the biological transmission of character traits through the generations, by transmigration of souls, or by the transfiguration of the individual personality into an archetype with which succeeding generations can identify. However, the ironic interweave of forces set in motion by human beings does not stop with death, but lives on in different guises.

Elijah succeeded in transforming the more cruel parts of his personality in his own lifetime, and suggestions of his triumph are found in the historical account of his death in the biblical text. What is more, his apotheosis succeeded his moments of deepest despair.

Elijah had just reached the epitome of his career. He had been vindicated by Divine Fire before the eyes of king and people, the false priests had been slaughtered, and the rains brought the People relief. Even the King had shown signs of repentance. Then his triumph crumbled. The heathen queen Jezebel, the true power behind the throne, threatened him with bloody revenge for the slaughter of her priests. Again he had to flee from Jezebel's infatuated husband. Elijah is bitter and he is utterly exhausted. All his resources are depleted. His finest victory has turned into his greatest defeat. In the desert he experiences what amounts to a psychic breakdown. His whole life amounts to nothing but a failure, and he prays for death. He journeys for forty days and nights to Horeb to relive as an individual the Revelation of Sinai in the place where it was enacted.

At Sinai, he shelters in a cave in the mountain itself when God addresses him:

And (the Lord) said: Go forth (from thy cave), and stand upon the mount before the Lord. [I Kings 19:11]

The setting here is a forerunner of a future occasion when not God but Elijah stands at the entrance to the cave and tells Rabbi Shimon that his time of incarceration is over and he is now free to leave his cave. The same setting is also a precursor to the incident immediately following, when not Elijah but the *Shekhinah* bids Rabbi Shimon "Return to his lair!" because he is destroying Her world. The movement out of the cave is one demanding a depth and breadth of humanity and self-acceptance by Elijah for which he is not ready yet.

The whole setting of the cave and the mountain exactly duplicates that of the Giving of the Torah on Mount Sinai, when the bond between God and Israel was formalized by the Covenant of marriage. That was a public event marked by thunder and lightning when God spoke to the People "out of the fire" (Deuteronomy 5:5). By the time we reach the isolated figure of Elijah within his cave, the idea of the Divine has become more internalized and God has decided as a consequence to cut down on the pyrotechnic effects. It was fine to use them to instill awe in ordinary people, but for Elijah they were nothing new. He needed to be convinced that gentleness might carry sway.

In a scene that is a perfect reenactment of the occasion when Moshe was instructed to squeeze into the cleft of a rock (also the starting point of the entrance to a cave) so that God's Glory could pass by, God "passes by" on this occasion also (Exodus 33:19–21).

> And a great strong wind rent the mountains and broke in pieces the rocks before the Lord; and the Lord was not in the wind; and after the wind an earthquake; but the Lord was not in the earthquake.
>
> And after the earthquake, a fire, but the Lord was not in the fire; and after the fire, a still small voice.
>
> And it was so, that when Elijah heard it, that he wrapped himself in his mantle, and went out, and stood in the entering in of the cave. And behold there came a voice unto him and said: "What doest thou here, Elijah?" [I Kings 19:11–13]

If God enticed Elijah to Horeb to remind him of the merit Israel had amassed by accepting the Torah; or if, aware that Israel's observance of the covenant was not perfect, He was anticipating a recapitulation of the pleasure He experienced when, after the Sin of the Golden Calf, Moshe sprang to His People's defense, He was sadly disappointed.

Elijah's stance is both like and unlike that of his great

predecessor Moshe. After the People spontaneously accepted the Torah, and a few of the Ten Commandments were uttered to the accompaniment of lightning and fire from the top of Mount Sinai, Moshe stayed on the mountain for forty days to receive the whole of the Law on behalf of the People. His disappearance made them look for something tangible to adhere to and led to their fashioning the Golden Calf. After having come closer to the Divine than any other People, they had sunk so low that God was prepared to destroy them all. But first he tells Moshe to look down and see what his People have done. What does their Leader do? Taking the brunt of God's anger upon himself, he spontaneously shatters the Two Tablets of Stone on which the Covenant was inscribed. The situation is so threatening, something has to be destroyed. Better stone should perish than human flesh. It is as if, with the Covenant destroyed, vengeance will have been exorcised and the human beings allowed to escape. And Moshe cares about individual people as well as for the abstract Glory of the Covenant. The way the *Midrash* puts it is that by shattering the Tablets, Moshe has destroyed Israel's marriage contract with God; therefore, although Israel's whole status is depreciated, she cannot be condemned for adultery.

Before his transformation, Elijah, faced with the same choices, would have upheld the dignity of the Covenant at all costs even if it meant having Israel burned for adultery.

The *Midrash* points out that while God makes a pretense of demoting Moshe and holding him responsible for those in his charge—"Go, get thee down; for thy people hath dealt corruptly"—with Elijah He openly invites him to "go up" and open the case for the defense. At that time Elijah was not ready to gratify God so much!

Addressed in such deceptively dulcet and sympathetic tones after a long period of having been persecuted and hounded as a fugitive, Elijah breaks down. Eagerly he pours out his sense of injustice and his complaints against Israel:

> I have been very zealous for the Lord God of Hosts. [I Kings 19:14]

Although the whole function of a Prophet is to act as a Counsel for the Defense on behalf of the People, and certainly not to waste energy defending himself against them, at this juncture Elijah has nothing good to say about Israel. He speaks as if he were the last decent person left on earth.

For the children of Israel have forsaken Thy covenant . . .
And I, even I only, am left. [I Kings 19:14]

Elijah is beset by a tremendous feeling of isolation. He is like the survivor of a holocaust stranded on a desert island. The whole burden of preserving the Covenant, he believes, rests on him alone.

THE COVENANT OF PEACE

Some rabbinic interpretations view Elijah as a reincarnation of the ideal of Covenant loyalty embodied in Pinchas, the Israelite leader in the time of Moses who was so incensed at the sight of a Prince of Israel openly embracing a Midianite princess that he shafted both of them instantaneously on his spear. In piercing both lovers as traitors to the erotic bond between God and Israel, both arm and spear became symbolic of one huge phallus of the Covenant. The prodigiousness of Pinchas's feat provides an example of a decisiveness of action almost more rapid than the havoc wreaked by fire in the story of Elijah and the soldiers or in the account of Rabbi Shimon and the peasants. His spear, like flame, streaks forward as the living extension of his wrath. Pinchas, like Elijah, is described as "very zealous" for his God. For his instantaneous reflexes, Pinchas received the reward of God's eternal covenant of peace, of which Elijah, as his spiritual heir, feels he is left as sole defender.

But peace may not seem exactly a fitting reward for the bloodshed for which Pinchas was responsible. It does appear rather incongruous that such a display of destructiveness should have been allotted so fine a reward. Indeed, there is an opinion that God gave Pinchas His "covenant of peace" to compensate for his fanaticism and to make harmony out of what inherently were totally opposing characteristics.[10]

However, this "gift" from God to His champion may have been double-edged. God's "eternal covenant of Peace," for such a hot-blood as Pinchas, must have been hard to bear. The reward may have been intended as a learning experience. Pinchas was not to be allowed to rest in "peace" until he achieved "wholeness" (the other meaning for *Shalom*, Hebrew for "peace") until he had learned the quality of humanity. God's eternal covenant of peace is a peace that has to be worked through or forged throughout eons of Jewish suffering. God doomed Pinchas to come back to life again and again in various guises to learn more tolerance. In the working out of his destiny, Elijah was only his first and his major reincarnation.

Yet Pinchas may not have been as cruel as it appears. In himself he already contained the two poles of stern judgment and of love. From a superficial point of view, Pinchas seems to have been one of those religious enthusiasts who, while full of zeal for God, lack the basic human sympathies. This may not have been so in fact.

When Pinchas took instant action in piercing both lovers through, he was staving off a greater threat that might have engulfed the People. The dynamic is like the swing of a pendulum, his cruelty actually serving to deflect the greater wrath of God and to arouse His compassion. In fact, God volunteers the information to Moshe that Pinchas's main motivation was not only love for the Divine, but the urgent need to save Israel from the Divine vengeance that the flagrant shamelessness of the licentious couple openly invited. God Himself is good enough to explain the mechanism of what is going on to Moshe for future reference:

> Pinchas has turned away my anger against the Children of Israel. Because he has been zealous for My sake in their midst. I Myself need not consume (them) out of jealousy.
> [Numbers 25:10–13]

Pinchas's prompt action has in effect saved God's "face," thus deflecting the tremendous force of His wrath from Israel.

The godly zeal of a Pinchas or an Elijah, cruel as they may seem, does provide a humane service in that it is a substitute for God's own "jealousy" against His People. At a certain point, says the *Midrash,* when God wanted to destroy the Jewish People, the Archangel Michael turned his sword against the Temple, and the lives of individual human beings were spared. Even the Destruction of the Temple, sad as it was, ultimately was rooted in love, because it staved off a worse cataclysm.

The *Midrash* compares God's rage to that a King may feel when his son is about to be beaten. Terrified, the whole court hears His Majesty cry out: "Let me alone! Let me alone that I may get at him!" No one dares enter to intercede until the boy's tutor realizes the incongruity of it all. For the King is alone. He thinks to himself: "If the king is alone with his son in the room, why does he say: Let me alone! This must mean the opposite, that His Majesty wishes someone actually would intervene!" (based on *Shemot Rabbah* 42:9).

God may be Omnipotent, Omniscient, and All-Transcendent, but in order to enter into relationship with Man He has temporarily waived these prerogatives. It is expected that the Prophet, the *Tzaddik,* or the Leader, as representative of Israel and of the human end of the Covenant, will to some extent manipulate the Divine psyche to show its better Self. There is a tacit understanding between God and anyone He chooses to appoint as leader that it is the latter's role to convert fire to light and take away God's heat against people.[11] For instance, when a human being is moved to act as champion on God's behalf, God can be induced to exhibit a change of heart and move away from His Throne of Judgment to His Throne of Mercy. The *Tzaddik* or Prophet must sometimes accuse Israel to give God the opportunity He desires to defend them, and sometimes he must defend them so eloquently as to convince God of the justice of their cause. In either case, as God takes great pains to point out to Moshe, he must play upon the stops of the Divine mechanism in such a way as to elicit a humane response.

Moshe may, in fact, be considered Israel's greatest Prophet, not primarily because of the quality of his prophetic vision, but because he lived up to this role the best. Moshe goes to every subtle length to intercede for Israel. Not only does he directly take their side, he also plays devil's advocate. When he accuses Israel, God rushes to their defense. As the *Midrash* puts it: "When He blew hot, Moshe blew cold, and vice versa." That is, Moshe deliberately blamed Israel for some slight failing in order to have God spring up in their defense. The dialogue between God and His alter ego, the Prophet, was like a seesaw. All prophets and intermediaries to a lesser extent serve the same function. In fact, the *Midrash*'s explanation for the intimacy between God and Moshe – "Face to face He spoke with Him" – is not that Moshe enjoyed any special personal intimacy with God apart from his role as Israel's leader, but that God made a pact with Moshe that "two angry faces should not pour hot water into one beverage. When one poured hot water, the other would pour cold" (*Shemot Rabbah* 45:2–3).

After the Sin of the Golden Calf, Moshe, pretending to be furious with Israel, leaves the camp as a deliberate gesture aimed not so much at the People as at God. When God bids him return and become reconciled with them, he cannot resist turning on Him in triumph: "See, Thou art not able to remove Thy love from them even a little while" (*Shemot Rabbah* 45:2).

Elijah's repetition of the wanderings of Moshe and of Israel in the wilderness of Horeb prior to receiving the Torah marked the beginning of his transformation.

> God found in Elijah's time no man more pious than he, but when he accused the Israelites he angered Him.
>
> He let him fall asleep (in the desert) and let him see Moshe beseeching God for forty days to forgive the sin of the Golden Calf. And God said to him [Elijah]: "You should do the same and remember that the Israelites received the Torah at Horeb." [*Zohar Hadash* 23b]

A basic stratagem to which Moshe resorted was to fall back on the essential component of the Covenant – the merit of the Fathers. He will not agree to be God's chosen and start off a "New Israel" while the original Israel is destroyed. Instead, he is prepared to sacrifice himself if God will forgive them.

Essentially, God's Covenant with Israel is not dependent on their merits but on the Promise He made to their forefathers. In his defense, Moshe takes ample advantage of this. It is the tactic God also expects of Elijah, and is resentful when He does not get it. For Elijah, on the one occasion God entices him to Sinai to speak on Israel's behalf, only seeks to justify himself, and he abandons their defense completely. By thinking of himself as the only person left loyal to the covenant, he forgets what the Covenant consists of – the accumulated merit of the forefathers on behalf of a collectivity, whose merit can prevail.

THE FOUR RABBIS IN SEARCH OF THE ULTIMATE

There is a cave story in the *Zohar* that is a jewel in itself. Four rabbis hear a "Divine Voice" (the *Shekhinah*) ring out from a cave: "Lamps shall give light from the lampstand." These four are surely the famous four rabbis of Midrashic lore who penetrated Paradise in quest of the ultimate, only one of whom, Rabbi Akiva, came back with body and soul and mind intact.

> Our Rabbis taught: Four men entered the Garden – namely, Ben Azzai and Ben Zoma, Aher and R. Akiva.
>
> R. Akiva said to them: "When you arrive at the stones of pure marble, say not, Water, water! For it is said: *He that speaks falsehood shall not be established before My eyes*" (Psalm 101:7).
>
> Ben Azzai cast a look and died. Of him Scripture says: *Precious in the sight of the Lord is the death of His saints* (Psalm 116:15).
>
> Ben Zoma looked and went mad. Of him Scripture says: *Have you found honey? Eat only so much as is sufficient for you, lest you be filled therewith, and vomit it out* (Proverbs 25:16).
>
> Aher mutilated the shoots.
>
> R. Akiva departed unhurt. [*Hagiga* 14b]

What was the advice Rabbi Akiva gave his friends?

> [In your speculation on the origin of the cosmos,] when you come to considering the 'foundation stone' [that is, the

> *Shekhinah,* or God's Presence in the world], do not say that
> there was water above and water below [both for the
> celestial and the terrestrial beings]. Because it is written, *'He
> that speaks falsely shall not be established before My eyes '* (Psalm
> 101:7).[12]

What Rabbi Akiva is saying is completely enigmatic, except for
the picture it presents. The Rabbis' Vision of Paradise was one of
a stone shimmering rather like a mirror and reflecting both the
Divine and the human world. This substance, like Fire in the case
of Nadav and Avihu, but made of the cooler ingredients of water
and light, could have an extreme effect: it is the Pearl beyond
price, the stone which, on seeing Rachel (the *Shekhinah*) Jacob
removed from the well to let the waters of fruitfulness flow free.
At the sight of this Pearl, one of the four died of ecstasy, rather in
the spirit of Othello: "If t'were now to die, twere now to be most
happy!" Another, Aher, not only became a heretic, but also
"mutilated the shoots" – that is, harmed the young disciples by
spreading heresies. Unlike Elijah, who found living in two ex-
tremes a strain, Ben Zoma went mad; he inhabited the next
world even while he was in this one. There is an amusing
anecdote that describes him in this state of absolute bliss when he
hardly belonged any more to the world of the living. For him it
was quite clear that the difference between the next world and
this one was barely a handswidth.

> It once happened that Simeon ben Zoma was standing wrapped
> in speculation, when R. Joshua passed and greeted him once and
> a second time, without his answering him. At the third time he
> answered him in confusion.
> "What means this, Ben Zoma!" exclaimed R. Joshua.
> "I was contemplating the Creation (and have come to the
> conclusion) that between the upper and the nether waters there is
> but two or three fingerbreadths," he answered. "For it is not
> written here, and the spirit of God blew, but hovered, like a bird
> flying and flapping with its wings, its wings barely touching (the
> nest over which it hovers)."

Thereupon R. Joshua turned to his disciples and remarked to them, "The son of Zoma has gone."

Only a few days elapsed and the son of Zoma was in his eternal home. [*Bereishit Rabbah* 2:4]

The sequel to the tale of the four rabbis continues in the *Zohar*. In the cave, the four rabbis hear a voice issuing the following ultimatum: "Lights shall give light from the lampstand!"

Here the Community of Israel (a female image) receives the light while the Supernal Mother is crowned, and all the lamps are illumined from her. [*Zohar* V:150a]

This coronation of *Knesset Yisrael* and of the nurturing maternal aspect of the Divine is enacted by the kindling of a *Menorah* in a cave, symbolic of feminine space, and there is an obvious metaphor for the womb or for the unconscious from which the light of creativity can emerge. In the *Midrash* about the fetus and the *Menorah,* as in this passage of the *Zohar,* illumination is to be had precisely within feminine space. In this way Jewish images of the feminine (the cave) are entirely unlike the Greek. In Plato, the cave is a prison, while in the *Zohar* and the *Midrash* it provides the best conditions for illumination.

The prime example of a mystic who witnessed the splendor of the *Shekhinah* in a cave was Moshe. He was told by God to stand sheltering in the cleft of a rock from where he was able to view the Glory. Yet the *Midrash* expands upon the scene as if it were part of some interior landscape, comparing their interchange to the unceasing murmur of the sea against the rocks of a cave, or like the air continually passing through a conch shell.

You find sometimes *And the Lord spoke unto Moshe . . .* and *And Moshe spoke unto the Lord.* It can be compared to a cave situated by the seashore into which the sea once penetrated, and having filled it, never departed, but was always flowing in and out of it. So it was that the Lord spoke unto Moshe and Moshe said unto the Lord. [*Shemot Rabbah* 45:3]

The cave, we have seen, is the last retreat of the *Shekhinah,* an amphitheater of feminine Space, the receptacle of Divine Light. By comparing the greatest leader of *Knesset Yisrael* to a cave, he is metamorphosed into a feminine vessel open to divinity. The cave, in fact, is both this world of darkness and also a container of *Menorot,* both Temple and Paradise, grave and womb.

Little wonder, then, that Rabbi Shimon and Rabbi Eliezer find it hard to leave this second womb to venture out into the "real" world again. What convinced them to do so, and what consolation were they able to derive from the fact that they had?

> They saw a hunter laying his snares for birds and spreading his traps. When the two Jewish mystics heard the "Daughter of a Voice" whisper; "Reprieve! Reprieve!," the bird went free. But when they heard the Voice whisper: "His time's up!," the bird was trapped and taken.
>
> Rabbi Shimon said: "There is Providence even in the fall of a sparrow. If this is true of a bird, how much more so of a human being!"
>
> They left the Cave. [*Shabbat* 33]

In this hallucinatory episode, the victims are depicted as "birds," an image of the holy *hayyot,* the highest part of the human soul (*Tikkunei Zohar* 23a). Not only does the "Daughter of a Voice" represent the *Shekhinah,* the hunter is also Her representative or messenger in that he carries out Her wishes. But if Elijah can be viewed in one sense as the hunter in the Talmud story, he is known, not only as the "guardian of the birds" (*Tikkunei Zohar* 23a), but himself is also a bird, longing for self-transformation (*Midrash Tehillim* on Psalm 8:7). Also, the *Shekhinah* seen in the story of Ben Zoma, is frequently represented as a bird. Subject and object, fate and victim are all part of the "still small voice" that whispers to the rabbis and brushes them with Her wings.

Just as the voice veers from mercy to judgment, so Father and Son represent these same perilous swings of mood. And just as hunter and bird are different aspects of the *Shekhinah,* Rabbi Shimon and Rabbi Eliezer also are differentiated parts of Elijah, expressive of the same double mode of dealing with reality.

Wherever the young man looked, shriveled at his glance; wherever the older man looked was healed and restored to life.

Said Rabbi Shimon to his [ardent] young son: "The world has more than enough with the pair of us!" [*Shabbat* 33]

What he sees of the ambivalent cruelty of nature, enables Rabbi Shimon finally to acknowledge how terrible is his own brand of fanaticism.

What has Rabbi Shimon – and Rabbi Eliezer, who is only the younger, more fiery and uncompromising part of himself – got against Roman civilization? Why do they prefer to live as outcasts, supporting themselves on spring water and wild carobs, rather than compromise with the system laid down by Roman society? What is Rabbi Shimon's argument with human civilization in general and with the simple agrarian life of his own people?

As a disciple of Rabbi Akiva, Rabbi Shimon was not by nature an ascetic, unworldly individual. Like his great teacher, he loved the Land of Israel and was a political activist and supporter of the messianic *Bar Kokhba*. [13] In modern terms, he was a political activist who tried to bring about the rebirth of a Jewish state in History. His dislike of the specifically Roman amenities – roads, bridges, baths, etc. – was on the grounds that they only played into the interests of the colonial power. The Romans were trying to build up the land to exploit and dominate it more thoroughly.

But even if he had come to terms with the *Pax Romana* as an equitable enough form of living to serve as the backdrop for an internal religious life, he might have considered luxury and physical comfort to be at the expense of spirituality. He is known to have told his students who wanted to leave the Land of Israel to make their fortune that he could make the hills and valleys of Israel flow with gold, but it would be at the expense of their reward in the next world (*Shemot Rabbah* 52; *Yalkut* on Proverbs 31).

Certainly this unworldly attitude must have grown on him when he lived cut off from society in a cave. So much so, that his dislike of the Roman *civitas* extended itself to an intolerance for the luxuries of city life in general. The longer he was isolated in the cave, the more he devalued any involvement in the mechanics of human existence. The ploughing and sowing that so incensed him is basic to the simplest type of survival. He was opposed to exactly the same cycle of birth, breeding, and dying against which the Buddhists rail.

After living with the radiance of the *Shekhinah* and the splendors that inspired the *Zohar* for twelve years, his alienation from civilization is scarcely surprising. So the *Shekhinah*–or at least the *Shekhinah* in voice form–appears in order to teach him a lesson. He is bidden "not to destroy My world!"

His return to the cave is described as an enforced punishment, not a delight. The fact that this second sentence lasted twelve months is telling, for traditionally twelve months is the length of the stay of the wicked in the underworld. Just as the Nazarite has to bring a sin-offering when he returns to normal life, so Rabbi Shimon, must atone for germinating in himself the seeds of a destructive fanaticism. His additional twelve months' sentence must have been far harder to bear than the whole of the previous twelve years in which there was an objective danger to his life from the Roman government. Freedom was at hand, yet he was forced to live apart from human society.

The time of their release from the cave is the eve of *Shabbat*, just before sunset. They see an old man in a great hurry. He is holding two bundles of myrtles in his hands.

"What are those for?" they ask him.
"They are in honor of the Sabbath," they are informed.
"Would one bundle not be enough?"
"One is for *remember*, and the other for *observe* (the masculine and feminine way of celebrating the Sabbath)."
    "See how beloved God's commandments are to Israel!" exclaims Rabbi Shimon to his son.
    "Immediately their minds are set at rest." [Based on *Shabbat* 33]

The 'fire' that destroys those who misuse their energies by devoting them solely to temporal pursuits is transfigured into the radiance of those who direct all the forces of this world and of the six days of the week into providing candles for *Shabbat*. (The two bundles of myrtles with which *Shabbat* is greeted were later transformed into the two *Shabbat* candles.) But why are there two candles?

A TWOFOLD BOUQUET

The whole week the ordinary people work and sow and plough. But to prepare for *Shabbat* they pick beautiful sweet-smelling plants, mystically symbolic of the coming together of lovers – the world of immanence with that of Transcendence. After the husband returns home from synagogue on Friday night, he picks up these two bunches of myrtles, standing for Bride and Groom. Each bouquet consists of three twigs. In all, he has in front of him the six days of the working week. He walks round the table as one makes a circuit round a Wedding Canopy, welcoming the Seventh Day, the crown of the labor of every working Jew, that turns him or her into a King or Queen for a day. Therefore, one light is for the masculine and the other light for the feminine; one is for transcendental reality and the other for the reality of this world; one is for the pure fire that burned on the altar and the other for the gentle illumination of the *Menorah* lamp. And both are necessary if fire is to change to light and growth.

The brilliance that Rabbi Shimon saw inside the cave was emitted by the *Menorah* which, when kindled by *Knesset Yisrael* below, results in the crowning of the Supernal Mother in the higher world. Israel's performance of a simple ritual – the commandment to light – brings about the union of a double bouquet. Inside the cave and outside the cave, there is no difference; the same form of illumination suffuses both.

The pair were able to leave the innermost retreat of the *Shekhinah* – their own unconscious drives – because for them the Land of Israel and the cave had become the same place.

In these stories, the cave is a subliminal alert to an inherently mystical content. The cave in this story of Rabbi Shimon is reminiscent of Plato's myth. With Plato it is clear that the cave, the fire, and the shadows cast by the fire in the cave are all illusions, and that the outside world of sunlight is reality. But Rabbi Shimon needs a second spell in the cave to learn the same lesson. At first, the fire issuing from the cave is detrimental to the comings and goings of life. But in the Talmud, the world of the Sun is the real world of everyday life, whereas in Plato it is an image for transcendence. Rabbi Shimon's acceptance of the potential spiritual content of everyday living and illusion goes beyond anything suggested in the Platonic myth.

In the *Zohar,* the talmudic tale of Rabbi Shimon is repeated but breaks off with the entrance of Elijah. After that the account concludes with the information that both Rabbi Shimon and Rabbi Eliezer were visited by Elijah twice daily and initiated into the Prophetic mysteries (*Zohar Hadash* 59c; *Tikkunei ha-Zohar* 1a). This instruction – or revelation (*Giluy Eliahu*) – that forms the basis of the *Zohar* and of the *Kabbalah* continues after the pair are finally allowed to leave the cave and return to the real world.

The frequent reappearances of Elijah to administer instruction during the wanderings of Rabbi Shimon and his son and disciples throughout the Holy Land form the setting for the *Zohar.* Thus a bridge is created between the esoteric womblike retreat of the cave and the economic and political "masculine" arena of the public domain, and no dichotomy is sensed between the two. While the fiery youth (Rabbi Eliezer) continues to exemplify the uncompromising sternness appropriate to the cave – the quality of stern judgment in *Kabbalah* is stereotypically feminine – the father (Rabbi Shimon) shows more tolerance of the world as he finds it; his vision heals what the other consumes. For both of them, fire mellows and becomes enlightenment. This illumination continues to thrive during their journeys back and forth throughout the the Holy Land, crystallizing in an illumination that permeates the pages of the *Zohar* eleven centuries later.

There is an addendum to this story of Rabbi Shimon and Rabbi Eliezer. According to a more realistic account of their exit from the cave after the strictures against them had been relaxed, they were quite happy where they were. For thirteen years they subsisted on a diet of carobs and figs, and lived in conditions of such discomfort that they had sores all over their body. For all his asceticism, it was the son who suggested that they take the opportunity to heal themselves by bathing in the hot springs of Tiberias. Instead of inveighing against Roman baths, both men felt so good afterward that they wished to show their gratitude to the citizens of Tiberias. They set up a stall in the market and sold their wares to the people at a discount. According to another version of the story, they purified the place from defilement by the dead – Herod had built Tiberias on a graveyard. But in both versions, rather than scorning life in the community, they showed a positive and responsible attitude toward the benefits received from the city (*Esther Rabbah* 3:7–9).

Rabbi Shimon was subsequently buried in a cave in Meron, possibly the very one in which he lived and meditated for thirteen years. Not so Elijah. No grave received Elijah's body. If in life Elijah exemplifies God's own transmutation from fire to light, in his individual ascent, too, the identical elements of fire and storm and whirlwind that he worked with contribute to his spiritual transformation. Then, borne up in a Chariot of Fire, his body itself, says the *Zohar,* became light.

> When the human soul leaves the body so as to go to the other (heavenly) world, it cannot enter there until it has received another body made of light. This we know from Elijah; he had two bodies – in one he appeared before men, in another before the holy angels. [*Zohar* III:88b]

According to the *Zohar,* every *Tzaddik* has two souls, one on earth and one in heaven. Therefore the Chariot of Fire that descended to claim the earthly Elijah was his own "body of light" or heavenly *neshamah* (*Zohar* I:59b). On the one hand he is the earthly Elijah; on the other he has been transformed into the angel Sandalphon, so called because his "sandal" is placed "on earth and yet (his body) reaches into the sky" (*Hagiga* 13b). In the Talmud, Sandalphon is characterized as "a pillar standing on the earth and reaching up to the *hayyot,*" Ezekiel's "living creatures," the highest, most spiritual part of the soul who "run back and forth" between heaven and earth while supporting the Chariot of the Divine throne" (Ezekiel 1:14).

He (Sandalphon) stands behind the chariot of the divine throne and braids crowns for God. [*Zohar* I:167b; *Hagiga* 13b]

He receives the prayers of the Jewish People and twists them into wreaths (crowns) for God. [*Avodah Zarah* 3b]

In doing so, he is duplicating the mission of *Shekhinah* -Rachel, the Feminine Figure of Prayer who presents the Prayers of *Knesset Yisrael* and Mankind to God in the form of a crown. But, in fact, Sandalphon's role in the Divine cosmology is to unite the *Shekhinah* with The Holy One, Blessed be He, by acting as best man. The *Shekhinah,* who is the very personification of Prayer, is borne up by him and he acts as her messenger. According to R. Meir Ibn Gabbai, Sandalphon represents the potential unity of the lowest emanation of the *Shekhinah* with transcendence.[14] But although Elijah is also taken as a personification of the phallus, he himself does not participate in the union of King and Queen; he only helps to array them for the Wedding.

ELIJAH AS SPIRITUAL CHILD OF RACHEL

There are various discussions among the commentators as to Elijah's antecedents. From which Matriarch did he descend? Some say he comes from Gilead in the Tribe of Gad, and therefore must be a child of Leah. Some say that as he is constantly referred to as a priest, he must come from Levi, also a descendant of Leah. There is a *Midrash* that says that while the rabbis were arguing about this, Elijah himself turned up with the answer:

Sirs, why do you debate about me? (he wanted to know). I am a descendant of Rachel! [*Bereishit Rabbah* 71:9; *Seder Eliyah Rabbah,* p. 97]

As a priest he was genetically a descendant of Leah, but spiritually he was Rachel's child, inheriting some of her unique characteristics and mission in history.

Elijah, like Rachel, has the gift to turn away the natural

forces of destruction and shame God into compassion. He too is
an intercessory figure, ready to wrest living children from death
itself. In life he seems to have lacked certain humane traits, yet
his sleeplessness throughout the generations amply makes up for
that. And his concentration on reviving the dead child is maternal and nurturing, corresponding to Rachel's pangs of child-
birth that are not yet completed.

The human figures of Rachel and Elijah are alike in that any
moral flaws they may have exhibited only enhance their appeal
to the heart and to the imagination. It is precisely from such
flawed aspiring human nature that redemption is worked out.

In all the Elijah tales celebrating the Prophet's reappearances, he is a figure of mercy and hope. Elijah, son of Aaron
(lover of peace) stands for positive human relationships. He is a
defender of the rights of the individual, and is entirely opposed to
the principle of aggression and exclusiveness that he sometimes
embodied in life. He appears in many guises—as an old man, as
an Arab (*Berakhot* 6b), as a horseman (*Shabbat* 109b), as a Roman
official (*Ta'anit* 21a; *Sanhedrin* 109a; *Avodah Zarah* 17b), and once
as a harlot (*Avodah Zarah* 18b). He defends those innocently
accused (*Berakhot* 58b; *Ta'anit* 21a; *Avodah Zarah* 18b), cures a rabbi
of a toothache, and brings a man and his wife together. He helps
the poor, whether Jew or non-Jew (*Ketubot* 61a; *Nedarim* 50a; *Baba
Metzia* 14b), and even sells himself as a slave to save a family from
destitution.[15]

By talmudic times, Elijah had even developed a sense of
humor and playfulness and had opened his mind to more than
one viewpoint—qualities utterly foreign to his former, solemn
one-sided fanaticism. There is a talmudic saying that when the
Angel of Death enters a town, the dogs sniff him out and bark,
but when Elijah makes his presence felt, the dogs roll on their
backs and begin to play (*Baba Kamma* 16b). This is scarcely the
Elijah whose self-pity staged a role for him bordering on that of
the misanthrope rather than tragic protagonist.

There is a story that a rabbi once came upon Elijah in the
marketplace of a large town. He inquired who among the crowd
would enter Paradise. Elijah pointed out a prison warder who
was passing by. The man had secretly tried to lighten the burden

of the prisoners in his charge. Elijah then gestured to two clowns who cheered people up and brought them closer together (*Ta'anit* 22a).

Throughout his many appearances, Elijah retains his initial fire. That is why his benign presence is invoked and a special chair of honor is set aside for him at the ceremony of circumcision, which involves the spilling of a few drops of the infant's blood. On the *Seder* night, too, Elijah is allotted a special cup of wine. At a key point in the service, we open the doors for the poor, the wanderer, and for the advent of the miraculous, and the wine in the Cup of Elijah appears to diminish at that moment. Surely Elijah has participated as guest of honor at the *Seder* table and drunk from the cup.

Elijah, associated with fire and light, also participates in the *Havdalah* ceremony, which terminates the Sabbath and distinguishes between light and darkness. Allegedly he reappears during every form of pogrom and persecution of the Jewish People – he was seen in the death camps; he went into the crematoria.

After Elijah's exit from the cave, and throughout history, as we observe in his relationship to the poor and virtuous people of his time, he has undergone a complete character change – from an intolerant fanatic on God's behalf, to a harbinger of physical blessing and rescue.

Elijah's final manifestation, according to the Prophet Malachi, will come both as light and as fire. For he will usher in the Day of Judgment, when the guilty will be consumed by burning, whereas for good people the Sun of Righteousness will arise with healing in its wings (Malachi 3:19–20).

But the *Tikkun* (Redemption) Elijah initiates is not only that of historical Messianism; as we have seen, he is also a living demonstration of the concept of personal redemption. The type of integration he brings to bear is that of a higher intuition, reconciling seeming contradictions that clash only when they are separated from the whole.

There is a belief that before Adam's sin, he did not possess the kind of gross material body that we know; his was a "subtle inner" body of light, and the whole physical world was more ethereal and luminous, composed of pure intellect, to match. That is why the *Shekhinah,* before Adam sinned, represented the Tree of Knowledge; only after the connection between the Tree of Knowledge and the Tree of Life was severed, did Knowledge change to a purely sensual, physiological type of knowing. There is still a belief, for example, that a king has two bodies, one his individual physical body, the other an abstract glorious representation of his nation. So Adam, before he sinned, had one abstract body of light that represented all mankind without fragmentation and in total harmony, and Elijah is gifted with the art of restoring that pattern. In himself he redeems Adam's sin by reconciling knowledge and life, the Fear of God and His Love.

For ultimately the deepest rifts that must be healed are internal. On this, R. Nachman of Bratzlav says:

> It is essential that there be peace among man's qualities—that is, he is not divided in his qualities and his experiences. And the *Tzaddikim* are called "covenant of wholeness." For when God appointed Pinchas (one of Elijah's previous incarnations) as priest, He said: *Behold I give you My covenant of wholeness* (Numbers 25:12).
>
> And the individual points in which one may differ from another are also branches of the *Tzaddik,* who has within him the general viewpoint of the Jewish People.[16]

The same Elijah, who in the Bible said he alone stood for the Covenant point of view that the Jewish People had abandoned, is taken by Reb Nachman as a spokesman for the "general viewpoint of Israel." This consensus, far from being monolithic, contains scope for difference and individuality, and in this harmony of the individual and the community, it is compared to a Tree. Elijah is the prototype of the *Tzaddik* because he possesses the essential breadth of vision to reintegrate the various "branches."

As Elijah becomes more humane, so does the face God presents to the world. In the biblical story of Elijah there is a sense in which God is beginning a lesson that continues to this day—how to bring redemption to the world by expanding the individual's horizon of enlightenment.

It seems that it took many lifetimes for Elijah to completely master this spiritual technique. His way of *Tikkun* was one that started in his lifetime and is at work even now.

The "fire" of Elijah is Rabbi Shimon's fire, and the "fire" of all forced to undergo severe mental turmoil.

Allegedly, in his own lifetime, Elijah taught mysteries of Divine encounter in the "schools of the sons of the Prophets," and these ultimately crystallized into the tradition of *Kabbalah*. For many of the Kabbalists thousands of years later, including Rabbi Shimon, Elijah was a special mentor figure who initiated them into the secrets of Jewish mysticism and was a mediator between them and the Divine.

From talmudic days, as in the story of R. Shimon, Elijah appears in dreams to many rabbis to shed light on some problem or inner preoccupation. He became the crystallization of the resolution of their struggle. From this we learn that there was something archetypal in Elijah. Every man has in him a glimmering of Elijah. This process started in the historical tale in the Bible, when Elijah leaves his mantle to Elisha on his ascent in the Chariot. Elijah has no children, and the young Elisha is the student who will carry on his mission. Elisha, on the other hand, has a completely different nature than Elijah. He is not naturally ascetic; he is affectionate, and kisses his father and mother before leaving to follow the Master. But when Elijah is about to die, the young man begs for a "double portion of Elijah's spirit." His Teacher replies to this by saying that Elisha will know his request has been granted "if you see me, when I am taken from you" (II Kings 2:9–10).

R. Nachman of Bratzlav says of this verse that since Elisha was a witness to the scene of the Chariot of Fire at the very moment when his teacher became an archetype (or was swept away in the Chariot), the student "received a heavenly portion of his master's spirit."[17]

THE ELIJAH FACTOR

What do the Kabbalists mean when they say Elijah had two bodies? What does it mean when it says that on *Shabbat* we are gifted with an additional soul? And what does it mean to say that Elisha was heir to a twofold legacy?

This dualism is only to pinpoint the capacity for self-transformation. There is the self, and there is the potential. A Jew's possessing an additional soul on *Shabbat* means that his state of being on *Shabbat* is not like his state of being on any other day of the week, and that he is capable of self-transformation. And if Elijah is said to have had two bodies, a body like any other individual, and a "body of light," what this means is simply that he was in touch with the potential of his own soul. His "body of light" was his soul, which was part of the primordial splendor of *Adam Kadmon* before the sin—a time when man's body is said to have been made of light or of finer stuff than the crude clay it was metamorphosed into after alienation had set in. At that time, body and soul were made of the same crystalline *Shekhinah* radiance. This "body of light" was retained by Elijah and was detected by his disciple as a "chariot of fire" during his apotheosis. Because of Elisha's capacity to see this miracle, he was gifted with a "double portion" of his master's spirit.

Apparently, not only "fire" but also "soul" or "light" is catching; our very bodies are composed of energies waiting to be ignited. And not only Elisha, but everyone who is aware of this light and fire contains within him a portion of the "Elijah factor."[18]

The Elijah factor consists of a blend of hope and intuition, constituting "an intimation of Good." A "spark of Elijah" comes to a person at the moment before his knowledge is extended—just as Elisha saw the Chariot of Fire a split second before the Spirit descended upon him. The next moment, intuition changes from divination to reality as knowledge is extended and filled with vitality. With the development of one's spiritual personality, we are led from ascent to ascent, and at each step in the extension of awareness, we have to reckon with a deepening acquaintance with the Elijah factor. The radical difference between Hasidism and *Kabbalah* is that with *Kabbalah* we are dealing with external cosmology—there was only one *Tzimtzum*, whereas with Hasidism we are dealing with the inner workings of the individual in which we move from *Tzimtzum* to *Tzimtzum*, from ascent to ascent, in an infinite progression of spiritual development.

In this Hasidic worldview, the Elijah factor is present at all times and in every man. R. Menahem Nahum of Tchernobyl says about the verse; "Behold, I send you Elijah the prophet," that "I send" means now, at the present time, every hour the Elijah factor is sent to every man before "the day of the Lord."[19]

About the verse, "Behold, I give him (Pinchas) My covenant of wholeness" (Numbers 25:12), R. Menahem stresses again that Elijah is always present in everyone.

> All the passionate striving of those who serve God is caused by the Elijah factor. He proclaims all that is whole . . . the union of thought and speech . . . and after this there comes the Messiah aspect.
>
> And the result is [that] wherever there is unity this means shalom (peace, wholeness) . . . and that is possible only through Elijah and . . . he is always present before this union is achieved, and the unity is called the "coming of the day of the Lord."[20]

R. Menahem identifies the phenomenon and even defines its sex, which the Elijah of biblical times certainly might not have appreciated.

> Every awakening of the soul, the female spring of water, is in everyone as the Elijah factor . . . that is why one says: "Elijah has revealed himself to someone," for this factor is hidden within every human being.[21]

If, according to R. Menahem, the Elijah factor is feminine, his son, R. Mordecai of Tchernobyl, reiterates the basic femininity of the archetype. About the verse, "Who makes the clouds Your chariot" (Psalm 104:3), he says:

> The cloudy densities of this world that obscure the infinite divine light . . . how can one tear this cloudiness apart?
>
> This (can happen) through the passionate longing for God,

which every Jew has by nature and from birth, and this is called "Elijah"; this is the secret of the female (spring of) water that man awakens in himself; his longing for the Creator.[22]

So while Elijah fought against the descent into the world of pure physicality as exemplified by the goddess cult of Jezebel, he himself epitomized the stereotypically feminine longing for God, the "descending light," symbolized by rain or water. Little wonder that in his hands, says the *Midrash,* God entrusted the Key to Rain and the Key to Dew. What is water or rain, in this interplay of imagery, but prayer, as it says: "Pour out your heart like water, directly opposite to God" (Lamentations 2:19). But how can a man, and such a masculine fiery presence as Elijah, symbolize the feminine?

In the same way as the feminine, in some manifestations, can take over certain stereotypically "masculine" characteristics. We have seen that the *Shekhinah* herself can be individuated into different *Tzaddikim.*

When Moshe ascended Mount Sinai, he had to enter into the Rain Cloud, interpreted as the *Shekhinah.* In the case of both Moshe and Elijah, their *anima* or their yearning for God is delimited as female. According to R. Jacob Joseph of Polonnoye – and he was not the first to say so[23] – both Elijah and Moshe are "hidden in every Jew." This must mean also that the feminine spiritual yearning they embody is an integral part of the psyche.

The reintegration that the Elijah factor can bring about is that between masculine and feminine aspects of the person, the conscious and the unconscious, between spirit and body, between generations, and between the yearning for God and God Himself.

On the Psalm, "O send out Thy light and Thy truth" (Psalm 43:3), the *Midrash* equates Elijah, Son of Aaron (characterized as the lover of Peace), with the light, and the Messiah, son of David, with truth (*Midrash Tehillim* on Psalm 43:1). By this might be understood that light is a kind of intuition, whereas truth is its realization. Light is the flash of illumination that lights up some scene. Truth is the landscape that is there in actuality. The fact is that the flash of light precedes by a split second any coherent image of what the scene might be. Although the illumination lights up the world, there is a moment when it is everything and there is no other reality. And that is what is meant by the *Giluy Eliahu*, the "glimmer" or "revelation" of Elijah.

NOTES

1. Plato *Republic*, p. 111.
2. Rabbi Shneor Zalman of Liadi, commentary to the *Nefilat Apayim* prayer in his *Siddur*, quoted in Idel, *New Perspectives*, p. 70.
3. See Idel, *New Perspectives*, pp. 70–71.
4. Quoted in Idel, *Abulafia*, p. 203.
5. Matt, *Book of Mirrors*, p. 34.
6. Rabbi Alexander Sonder of Komarno, *Zikhrot Devarim* (1814), in a passage pointed out by Moshe Idel in a seminar on Hasidism given at the Jewish Theological Seminary of America, Summer 1987.
7. See Chapter 8, "The Work of the *Menorah*."
8. "The day of rain is like the day of the resurrection of the dead" (*Berakhot* 31a; *Ta'anit* 71; *Bereishit Rabbah* 13:4).
9. The Passover *Haggadah*.
10. Rabbi N. Z. J. Volozhin, *Humash Ha'amek Davar*, vol. 4, p. 11a (225).
11. According to my beloved Teacher, Dr. Yochanan Muffs, Professor of Bible at the Jewish Theological Seminary of America.
12. A. Altmann, "Gnostic Themes in Rabbinic Cosmology," p. 26.
13. The revolt against the Romans of Bar Kokhba (Son of a Star) took place in 135 C.E.
14. Rabbi Meir Ibn Gabbai, *Avodat ha-Kodesh, Sefer ha-Yihud*, chap. 16.
15. Rabbi Nissim ben Jacob, *Hibbor Yateh Me-ha-Yeshuah*, pp. 58 ff.
16. R. Nachman of Bratzlav, *Likkutei Moharan*, pp. 100, 104.
17. Ibid., p. 81b.
18. R. Menahem Nahum of Tchernobyl, *Sefer Meor Enayim*, p. 135.
19. Ibid., pp. 69, 135.
20. Ibid., pp. 166–167.
21. Ibid., p. 135.
22. R. Mordecai of Tchernobyl, *Likkutei Torah*, p. 47a.
23. Rabbi Jacob Joseph of Polonnoye, *Toldot Yaakov Yosef*, p. 39b.

EIGHT

WORK

OF

THE

MENORAH

The Luminous Menorah by Marilyn Charnas. "And this is the work of the *Menorah*, which the Holy One showed to him (Moshe) with His Hand" (*Sefer Aggadah* I:65). (*Courtesy of Marilyn Charnas*)

Aɴᴅ this is the work of the *Menorah*. Said the Holy One: "I shall make it for you and show you directly."

What did God do? He showed him white fire, red fire, black fire, and green fire, and from them He made the *Menorah*, its goblets, its knops, its flowers, and its six coronas, and He said to him: *This is the work of the Menorah, which the Holy One showed to him with His hand. [Sefer Aggadah I:65, no. 72]*

If light was God's first creation, why did God require man's cooperation in the kindling of Lamps? And if God Himself is light—and by His opening remarks in Genesis He merely drew out and objectified a part of Himself—what need is there for artificial or man-made forms of lighting? Why all this emphasis on the preparation, kindling, and making of *Menorot?*

According to the *Zohar*, the first light God created was a "Lamp of Darkness"—the Hebrew evoking not so much the image of a receptacle as that of a burning coal or a scintillating ember, or even an atom supercharged with elemental force.

409

MOSHE'S IMPOSSIBLE TASK

The light God created in the beginning was not only the quintessence of pure creativity and life-energy, but also a gratuitous
piece of self-expression on His part and the first work of art. This
was the *Menorah* He showed to Moshe, ordering him to reproduce it on a human scale. But Moshe found this task entirely
beyond his scope. What did God show him that was so incred-
ibly difficult?

Moshe had a longstanding history with burning lumps of
coal. There is a *Midrash* to the effect that when he was a baby
adopted by the Egyptian Princess, Pharaoh dreamed that one day
this child would take away his Crown. As he loved his daughter
very much, he did not immediately order the baby to be killed,
but decided to have him put to the test instead. On the infant's
right the Royal Crown was arrayed in full pomp on a purple
cushion. On the left he set out a censer where, on a bed of coals,
there lay one large scintillating ember smoldering with jewels of
many-colored fire.

"If the child goes for the Crown," said the King, "that will
show that, young as he is, he knows what he is doing and is after
my throne, and I shall have him put to death. But if he goes for
the shiny piece of coal, then he is just a foolish child who likes to
play and we will let him live."[1]

Both Crown and Burning Coal were dangled in front of the
baby to attract his attention. Quite naturally, the baby stretched
out his hand. He went directly for the Crown.

But then, says the *Midrash,* an angel deflected his hand
toward the ember. As soon as he touched the flame, he cried out,
quickly putting his burned finger to his mouth and burning his
tongue as well. Ever after, says the *Midrash,* Moshe talked with a
speech impediment.

As we have seen, the twelfth-century Kabbalist Rabbi Isaac
the Blind[2] uses the image of the Burning Coal as an image for
Creation and emanation of the *Sefirot:*

Their end is (found) in their beginning: just as many threads come
out of the burning coal, which is one, since the flame cannot

stand by itself, but only by means of one thing; for all the things (that is, *Sefirot*), and all the attributes, which seem as if they are separate, are not separate (at all) since all (of them) are one, as their) beginning is, which unites everything in one word.[3]

After seeing what *Burning Coal* signifies in kabbalistic sources – either the *Ein-Sof* (God Himself) or the whole complex of creation stemming from the multicolored emanations of the *Sefirot* – and realizing that *Keter* (Crown) refers also to the Highest *Sefirah*, which is associated with God, but not with the emanated world, this *Midrash* takes on an additional depth. This is Moshe making his personal choice between the overriding unity of *Keter* (God Himself), the world of multiplicity (the spiral of the *Sefirot* bringing Divine Light down to this world) and being a Jewish political leader.

An angel had to come and deflect Moshe from the Crown, which was his real goal, to the Burning Coal where the pain of all creativity begins. The baby touched this Coal and wailed a healthy cry that saved his life.

Perhaps it was not only Pharaoh who was testing the baby, but God also. When this *Midrash* is read together with *Kabbalah*, the character of God that emerges is not totally sympathetic. As in the later biblical story of Zipporah circumcising her baby and preempting the Angel of Death himself, it seems that there is a dangerous killer quality in the Divine that somehow has to be deflected or placated. If not for the pain of circumcision, if not for the pain of the Burning Coal against the tongue of the infant Moses, these innocent children really would have been struck down.

Perhaps it is not so much a question of destructiveness and cruelty as one of intensity. Divine Light is overdazzling. The "Divine Word" burns Moshe's mouth and gives him a permanent speech impediment. For how can he express in ordinary language that One inexpressible Word. What burns within him is a vision that he cannot reduce to the dimensions of the physical.

Moshe our Teacher seems to have been a prey to several fits of anxiety. When God told him to build Him a Sanctuary, he came up against a tremendous inner block; when God instructed him on the fashioning of the *Menorah*–showing it to him patiently again and again–he found it impossible to reproduce:

> By three things was Moshe baffled: he could not grasp [the complicated instruments for] constructing the Tabernacle; the making of the candlestick; and the mystery of the Moon's changes. God indicated each of the three with His finger, so to speak, to Moshe, saying of the candlestick: *This is the work of the Menorah* (Numbers 8:4). And of the Moon's changes: *The beginning of the month shall fall* at this stage of the renewal of the Moon. [*Pesikta Rabbati,* trans. Braude, p. 335]

Moshe's difficulty in understanding the architecture of the Sanctuary, the construction of the *Menorah,* and the cycles of the Moon–which also means the mechanism of the Jewish calendar–reflects his temperament. He was by nature a person who would opt for the transcendental light of *Keter,* rather than for the colored sparks of the Burning Coal. That is, he was essentially a mystic, not a pragmatist, nor a craftsman, nor a political leader.

Every time it says that "Moshe found it difficult" we are dealing with the challenge of "bringing down" to earth, grounding, and containing something spiritual and supernal in a physical receptacle.

For example, when God said to Moshe, "Make Me a tabernacle," Moshe might have supposed that it would have been sufficient for him to set up four poles and spread a tabernacle over them like a wedding canopy, but God wanted a far more elaborate affair:

> But the Holy One, blessed be He, did not do so. He took Him up on High, and showed him (the) red fire, green fire, white fire, and black fire (of the *Menorah*), and said to him, "Make Me something resembling this."
>
> He said before Him: "Sovereign of the Universe, and whence shall I get black or red or green or white fire?"
>
> He said to him, *After their pattern, which is being shown thee in the mount* (Exodus 25:40). [*Shir HaShirim* 3:11]

If Moshe found constructing the Sanctuary difficult, he found fashioning the *Menorah* even harder, as if the *Menorah* were the quintessence of the Tabernacle.[4]

Another explanation of the expression "when you light":
You find that Moshe experienced more difficulty in understanding the construction of the candlestick than he did in that of all the other vessels of the Tabernacle, until the Holy One, blessed be He, showed it to Him with His finger. *And this is the work of the candlestick. Of beaten work (mikshah) of gold shall it be made* (Numbers 8:4). *Mikshah Mahkashah* [how difficult] it is to make; for Moshe was greatly perplexed by it. [*Bamidbar Rabbah* 15:4]

Aware of Moshe's difficulty, what did God do to simplify his task? He showed him what the *Menorah* looked like with His finger or with His whole Hand, and He etched its contours in colored lights against the darkness. What does it mean that God showed him the *Menorah* with His finger or even with His hand? The finger or the whole Hand is the act of showing and unraveling the multicolored veils of the *Shekhinah*.

The immediate question that springs to mind in connection with this command to "build Me a Sanctuary" and kindle *Menorot* is the difference between human and Divine art.

In the *Midrash on Psalms,* we hear about the limitations under which the human artist labors as compared with His Creator:

And who is a Rock (Tzur) except our God? (Psalm 18:26). Hannah also said: *Neither is there any rock (Tzur) like our God* (I Samuel 2:2).
Do not read *Neither is there any rock* but *Neither is there any artist (Tzayyar) like our God.*
The artist—he cannot paint unless he has many pigments, white, and black, and green, and red, and other hues: but the Holy One, blessed be He—He makes an embryo out of a drop of white and out of a drop of red. [*Midrash on Psalms,* Psalm 18:26, trans. Braude, p. 257]

It is paradoxical that, as the Psalms point out, God's greatness is found in His "humility," in the creative power invested in

the design of infinitesimally tiny "worlds within worlds," – that
is, the infinite range and uniqueness of His Creations. It was an
invitation to become a partner in this higher type of artistic
endeavor that underlies God's command to *Moshe* to reproduce a
celestial *Menorah.*

But Moshe, who was impatient with details and whose
vision pierced through all the colors and fantasies of ordinary
dreams to a transcendent reality, found the task before him
impossible.

What did God do? He showed him the *Menorah* in graphics.
He showed it to him with many detailed visual effects, etching it
out for him in multicolored lights that filled up the entire sky. Just
as the Torah says God spoke with Moshe "face to face," so His
communication came "face to face." The *Midrash* says He
showed it to Moshe directly. How? He pointed it out to him
"with His finger" or "with His whole Hand." And both God's
"finger" and His entire Hand could be said to refer to the Glory of
the emanations.

According to one particular *Midrash* a different solution was
found for the grown *Moshe* than for the infant menaced by the
Egyptian Pharaoh. While the baby's hand was deflected from the
transcendent Crown to the "Burning Coal" of human art, one
Midrash says that, because Moshe did not like counterfeits, God
let him have the original: God "sent down a *Menorah* from
Heaven." This is an act of direct Divine intervention, without
any kind of intermediary.

> R. Levi son of Rabbi says: "A pure candlestick came down from
> heaven."
>
> Seeing that he found [the task] difficult, the Holy One
> Blessed be He, said to Moshe: "Take a talent of gold, cast it into
> the furnace and take it out again, and the candlestick will assume
> shape *of itself* . . . as it says, *its cups, its knops, and its flowers shall
> emerge out of it*" (Exodus 25:31).
>
> Moshe smote with a hammer and the candlestick took
> shape of its own accord. Moshe took the talent and cast it into the
> fire and said: "Sovereign of the Universe! Behold, the talent is in
> the fire. Do Thou as Thou wilt!"

Thereupon the candlestick came out completely formed. For this reason it is written, *According to the pattern which the Lord hath shown Moshe, so he made the candlestick* (Numbers 8:4). It is not written in this verse, "So Moshe made the candlestick," but *So he made,* the subject being unspecified. Who then made it? The Holy One, Blessed be He. [*Bamidbar Rabbah* 15:4]

There is a notion that the first two Temples were built by man, but that the third will emerge ready-made all fiery-golden and new minted from the Flame. According to this idea, God owes this to Israel, after all the fires with which He has destroyed previous man-made Temples and after the crematoria He has allowed to swallow His children. And according to this particular *Midrash,* the first *Menorah* came down ready-made by God the same way.

ART, IMAGINATION, AND BEZALEL, THE MASTER CRAFTSMAN

But among the various solutions found to circumvent Moshe's incapacity for *Menorah* making was the intervention of an inter-mediary—not an angel but the next best thing, an artist standing in the wings and ready to make God's idea a viable reality.

With Bezalel the Master Craftsman the larger question of the place of art and the imagination in religious life arises. Not by having achieved any level of holiness comparable to that of Moshe, but purely through artistic inspiration and technical skill of an artist, was Bezalel "filled with the spirit of God."

With Moshe, art and images did not play any role. He enjoyed the most direct encounter with God that has ever been given to a human being. He saw God "face to face," like the Smaller Face reflecting the Larger, like a reflection in water, as a man sees his friend. He had no use for dreams, images, visions by night. No wonder he found it impossible to translate what he saw into the form of an earthly *Menorah.* And no wonder he was taken aback at Bezalel's skill.

"How could you do it?" he marvels at Bezalel. "God showed it to me so clearly again and again and I couldn't reproduce it. And you . . . you weren't even there. What did you see?"

> Twice he (Moshe) ascended Mount Sinai to receive instructions from God, and twice he forgot the instructions on his descent. The third time, God took a *Menorah* of fire and showed him every detail of it and yet Moshe found it hard to form a clear conception of the *Menorah*. So he told Bezalel, and the latter immediately constructed it.
>
> When Bezalel had no difficulty in executing it, Moshe cried out in amazement: "To me it was shown ever so many times by the Holy One, blessed be He; yet I found it hard to make, and you who did not see it constructed it out of your own intelligence. Bezalel! Surely you must have been standing in the shadow of God (*bezal El*) when the Holy One . . . showed me how to make it!" [*Bamidbar Rabbah* 15:10]

Enter the Artist into world literature, that shadowy onlooker standing in the wings, nothing by himself, yet able to create worlds!

So much do the Rabbis read into a name that they say Bezalel was given the task of being the Architect of God's Temple because he was called Bezalel, which means "in the shadow of God." God prescribed and he was the mechanical shadow who executed.

Moshe had the highest vision of the Divine. But not everyone can express what he sees, and it lies within the special power of art to go beyond the limits of rational human intelligence and immediately connect with a higher source.

In differentiating the various properties of reason and imagination, the great twentieth-century thinker Rabbi Abraham Isaac Kuk delineates imagination also as a "shadow," exactly the same word as used by the *Midrash* in analyzing the artistry of Bezalel. The question is, says Rav Kuk, a shadow of what?

Although insubstantial and nothing in itself, the Imagination can be the "shadow" and instrument of a Higher Source to which normal powers of reason cannot attain. It can also make that lofty abstraction come alive as part of the sensuous pulse of the physical life.[5]

The "Previous" Lubavitcher Rebbe said much the same thing about the superior kind of truth that can be conveyed by a story or a *Midrash* as opposed to a law or a fact.

> There is a wisdom that is hidden by nature but which is revealed by means of riddles and parables. This is the wisdom of Solomon. . . . The stories of the Torah contain secrets and sublime mysteries much more than the laws. However, these [secrets] are not at all recognizable. The essence of their light is a sealed secret and the only way it is revealed is through hiding and concealment.[6]

The stories about Moshe's creative block and Bezalel's skill as artist illustrate the different dimensions of spirituality and esthetics. A vision to which the lonely saint can only aspire at moments can be handed down to a people by means of the plastic arts. And not only can art bring down the highest insights; like prayer, it can also be a channel of ascent for objects in the physical world.

But in the world of the *Midrash,* Bezalel's artistic skill was seen as linked to his gifts as a magician and an exponent of *Kabbalah.*

> Said R. Yehuda, "Bezalel knew how to smelt (or permutate) the letters with which heaven and earth were created." [*Berakhot* 55a on Exodus 35:30]

Through his skill in *Kabbalah,* Bezalel was able to tap into the forces that brought the world into being. With these forces he built the Tabernacle in the form of a microcosm. But is this esoteric gift for manipulating the Hebrew letters and the forces contained in them itself also purely technical? Or does it only work when allied to special qualities of character?

In the world in general it has become evident that there is not necessarily a correlation between beauty and goodness. Until the World Wars that overturned the twentieth-century dreams of human progress, there was at least a possibility that art might reflect the aspirations of humanity. But now, however uplifting German music and culture may be, with every note there is an undertone of betrayal. The more beautiful it is, the more humanity has been betrayed. We can never forget how the same culture that produced these flights of human spirit was also responsible for mass murder. So that nowadays, any connection between art and human aspiration is fortuitous. At its most serious, art presents a reflection of the absurdity of the human condition.

But at the time that Bezalel designed plans for the Holy Temple and for the *Menorah,* he fashioned a microcosm of the world as he saw it as a means for the elevation of the original. In his very name, Bezalel, there is a hint that his skill did not rest on purely technical excellence – *tzel* (shadow) is connected to the same Hebrew root as *tzelem* (image). And what is the true image of God but the human being, for whom art is a prime means of self-expression and of understanding his world. Bezalel was said to have been gifted with "wisdom of heart" and certain qualities of heart and of humanity that made him the ideal architect of God's plan for humanity. Indeed, his goal in fashioning the Temple and the *Menorah* was not just to build a fine building and a beautiful lamp, but to bring out the Divine Image in man.

In the twentieth century, Rav Kuk was impressed with the artistic powers of Rembrandt because he saw in them a deep human quality. Perhaps it shows a certain innocent idealism on the part of Rav Kuk, rather than Rembrandt, but Kuk, who could not believe that such an effect could have been produced by purely technical skill, attributed to it an ethical dimension.

In an interview with the London *Jewish Chronicle* in 1935, Rav Kuk said that he used to spend many hours visiting the Rembrandts at the National Gallery in London. Then he tells the story of the "Hidden Light" – "that pellucid serene perfect luminosity" – that was saved up for the *Tzaddikim* in the time to come. Rav Kuk was absolutely convinced this was the same light that possessed Rembrandt in his paintings.[7]

When he speaks of *Tzaddikim,* Rav Kuk is not talking about geniuses, charismatic presences, or people possessed only by a certain kind of technical brilliance, or even endowed with certain secret magical powers. He is talking about qualities of integrity and sheer human goodness that are part of the natural birthright of any human being and that anyone can attain. Only when technical power is joined with goodness would anybody be capable of seeing and rendering "first light," Rav Kuk was convinced.

THE BAN AGAINST MAKING IMAGES

In a speech Rav Kuk gave at the opening of the Bezalel Art Gallery in Israel, he compares two contrasting attitudes to art in Judaism.

> On the one hand – *You shall not make me gods of silver, neither shall you make yourselves gods of* gold (Exodus 20:20). *You shall make yourself no molten gods* (Exodus 34:17). *You shall not make for yourself any carved idol* (Exodus 20:4).
>
> And on the other hand –"See the Lord has called by name Bezalel the son of Uri, the son of Hur, of the tribe of Judah; and he has filled him with the spirit of God, in wisdom, in understanding, and in knowledge, and in all manner of workmanship; and to contrive works of art, to work in gold, and in silver, and in brass, and in the cutting of stones, to set them, and in carving of wood, to make all manner of artistic work. And he put in his heart that he may teach, both he, and Aholi'av, the son of Achisamakh of the tribe of Dan. Them he has filled with the wisdom of heart, to do all manner of work, of the engraver, and of the craftsman, and of the embroiderer, in blue and in purple, in scarlet, and in fine linen, and of the weaver, even of them that do any work, and of those that devise artistic work" (Exodus 35:30–35).[8]

How to resolve these two contradictory views of human artistry – on the one hand art is idolatry, on the other hand it is divinely inspired? Rav Kuk says that the one danger of art and beauty is that too easily they can be made into gods rather than servants. The claims of art tend to exceed all bounds:

> Our nation has always related in a positive and pleasant way to the artistic beauty manifest in the creative works made with human hands but (our respect for art) is also limited. We are cautious of excess. We will never sell ourselves to one particular idea (such as art for art, or idealization of beauty) to the extent that we drown in its depth, to the extent that we lose the capacity to give ourselves a limit and to put a boundary to the extent of its authority. Indeed, the limit of those things which are inherently good and ennobled is small, soft, delicate and beautiful *set about with roses* (Song of Songs 7:3). [*Sanhedrin* 376a]

When Rav Kuk says, "Even through a hedge of roses they make no breach" (*Sanhedrin* 376a), he means that art, like any natural part of human life, is good and valuable. The question is only one of measure and limit (essentially a Greek criterion for beauty, in any case). The difficulty arises when any part sets itself up as sole arbiter over the rest of life. (Only when the Moon wanted to be the sole wearer of the Crown was She demoted.)

Rav Kuk then says that social and cultural context play a major role in deciding how severely the restrictions on artistic expression mentioned in the Ten Commandments are taken. In eras when paganism and idolatry were rampant, Jewish expression labored under an extreme form of restriction to combat the enemy, but in times when the conflict was not so clearcut, the various prohibitions were relaxed.

He then takes his audience through the various comments on particular types of art that were permissible or prohibited.

> Although the verse, "You shall not make for yourself a sculptured image or any likeness of what is in the heavens above" (Exodus 20:4), has been understood as a wholesale ban on all sculpture and painting, in fact the Talmud forbids only sculpture of the whole three-dimensional human body, while sculptures of animals, and paintings of human or animal forms are allowed.[9]

He then states categorically: "The whole realm of adornment, ornamentation, beautification and painting is permitted with one small limitation, which only places a slight restriction and does minimal harm to art or craftmanship."

> All visages are allowed, save the face of man (*Rosh Hashanah* 24b). In fact, only the sculpture of a complete human face (is prohibited) and there are ways of understanding this (by which even this prohibition may be circumvented), such as the use of a non-Jewish apprentice in the final stage. What is left then is only a small limitation, intended to remind the nation of Israel of a root principle, to abhor and not put up with those pictures specifically characteristic of idolatry, whether of the pagan world of past or present or of the Christian world.[10]

Freeplay of the imagination and of art should be restricted, according to Rav Kuk, only to combat distorted values. But in less decadent times, these prohibitions could be relaxed, since their prime intention was to stress values, such as monotheism, for which the Jewish People stand – not to cut them off from what is a natural part of human life and human expression.

The case *for* Jewish art rests on the minute description of the images and figures in the Temple, and the most severe case *against* it is contained in the Ten Commandments housed in the Holy of Holies within that Temple.

Astoundingly, the Holy Temple boasted of expensive and glorious "this-worldly" furniture, and the holy vessels were decorated not only with patterns based on geometrical and floral shapes, but with figures of animals, birds, and even naked human beings.

In the Temple of Solomon a bronze serpent was incorporated, and in the Temple enclosure there was a large basin – the "Sea of Bronze" supported by twelve bronze oxen (II Chronicles 4:3–5). There were small ewers resting on chariots with figures of cherubim and lions. The woodwork of the Temple was richly carved with animal and vegetable imagery such as palm trees and winged creatures. The royal throne of Solomon also had a lion

THE LAMP OF GOD

sculpted at either arm and twelve lions ramped about the six steps leading to the royal seat (II Chronicles 9:17–19).

"Visages" or *Parzufin* of nonhuman creatures were allowed, notes the Jerusalem Talmud, and were to be found in the Temple itself (*Avodah Zarah* 42c). But from the Biblical text and from the observations of Philo it seems that even the two cherubim standing guard over the Holy of Holies wore faces that were very human indeed! (I Kings 6:23–35). It looks as though the cherubim under whose wings the *Shekhinah* nestled consisted of a naked boy and girl. Equally surprising are the apocalyptic murals envisioned for a restored Temple by the Prophet Ezekiel. These were to be decorated with

> Cherubim and palm trees . . . and every cherub had two faces; so that there was the face of a man toward the palm tree on the one side, and the face of a young lion toward the palm tree on the other side. [Ezekiel 4:18–20]

So much for the proscription of the representation of animal or human forms!

A skilled apologist such as Josephus found it difficult to explain the discrepancy between Temple art and the Second Commandment. He was so hard put that he charges Solomon with senility:

> As he (Solomon) advanced in age and his reason became in time too feeble to recollect the customs of his own country, he sinned and went astray in the observance of the laws, namely, when he made the image of the bronze bulls that supported the molten sea and the image of the lions around his own throne, for it was impious to make them.[11]

In the biblical text, not only is there no suggestion of "impiety" in the fashioning of such objects, but we read that they were Divinely prescribed. In the Ten Commandments we find the words:

> You shalt not make for yourself a sculptured image, or any likeness of what is in the heavens above, or on the earth below, or in the waters under the earth. [Exodus 20:4]

In the repetition of the Decalogue in Deuteronomy, the prohibition is even more clearly spelled out. It is forbidden to make

> [T]he form of a man or a woman, the form of any beast on earth, the form of any winged bird that flies in the sky; the form of anything that creeps on the ground, the form of any fish that is in the waters below the earth. [Deuteronomy 4:16–18]

With whatever suspicion the illustration of any particular object in Creation was regarded, the strictest prohibition concerned any attempt to make a representation of God Himself:

> The Lord spoke to you out of the fire, you heard the sound of words, but perceived no shape – nothing but a voice. For your own sake, therefore, be most careful – since you saw no shape when the Lord your God spoke to you at Horeb out of the fire – not to act wickedly and make for yourselves a sculptured image in any likeness whatever. [Deuteronomy 4:12,15–16]

In this case, fashioning the image of an animal, an insect, or a fish is not merely wrong because one has made an image of that particular object, but because of the larger implication of trying to represent God. And that is at the root of why it is forbidden.

Authoritative interpretations of the prohibition against image-making contained in the Second Commandment explain that it had to be taken in juxtaposition with the following verse: "You shall not bow down to them or serve them" (Exodus 20:5). That is, images of natural objects were forbidden only when used for idol-worship. Motifs drawn from the vegetable world were considered entirely innocuous objects for representation. The higher up the model to be copied stood in the echelons of creation, however, the more suspect it became, presumably because it would more likely be a rival to the Deity. Thus, there was a very strong bias against the representation of animals or humans, especially in three-dimensional forms like sculpture, which would give an additionally lifelike appearance.

The anomaly of Temple art as described in the biblical books of Kings and Chronicles implies one of two things. Either it set up a precedent for a whole tradition of Jewish art, or what was prescribed as mandatory within the context of Temple worship might be considered forbidden outside that context.

Discovery of the existence in antiquity of a flourishing tradition of synagogue art that contained representations of both human and animal forms may give credence to the former view. After Judea had finally lost its independence – when iconoclasm was no longer associated with the Temple and its invisibly enshrined deity, and with the civil fight for freedom – human and animal imagery filtered into Jewish religious life. In the third century, animal and human figurative art on synagogue murals was widely tolerated, and by the fourth century some rabbis withdrew objections that had been voiced in previous generations to mosaic pavements.

This change in attitude toward mosaics was especially noteworthy because it questioned another biblical prohibition. Leviticus 26:1 states that it is expressly forbidden to "set up a figured stone" for purposes of worship. That is why Rav (third century C.E.), when leading the *Yom Kippur* service in Babylonia, did not prostrate himself on the ground. The floor of the synagogue was paved with stones, which was only allowed in the Temple. *Targum Pseudo Yonatan,* an Aramaic paraphrase of the Bible, defines the distinctions made:

> A figured stone you shall not put down on the ground to worship it, but a colonnade with pictures and likenesses you may have in your synagogue, but not to worship it. [*Targum Pseudo Yonatan* on Leviticus 26:1]

In other words, wall paintings, though not mosaics, were allowed. The Jerusalem Talmud is on record for saying that certain artistic techniques are acceptable in some periods and cultural circumstances and not in others:

> In the days of Rabbi Yochanan they began to paint on the walls, and he did not prevent them. In the days of Rabbi Abun they

began to make designs on mosaics, and they did not prevent them. [*Avodah Zarah* 4a]

The Babylonian Talmud quietly observes:

The practice of man is that he draws a picture on a wall, although he cannot instill it with a spirit and breath and entrails and organs. [*Berakhot* 10a; *Shabbat* 149a]

Drawing the human figure is a natural inclination from childhood on, and a complete ban upon such an activity would be as absurd as outlawing laughter. The Talmud is so accepting of this instinctive tendency only because it is very rational about the natural limits of art. The very limitations of the artist give him a certain license. He can outline the contours of the image, but he "cannot give it life." He can only create the illusion, like a child playing at being grownup, but he cannot create the real thing. Thus, awareness of art's limits and weaknesses paved the way for a greater liberalism in artistic expression that extended even to representations of the human form. What is forbidden is to produce a complete three-dimensional picture of a human being. A sculpture with an imperfection of any kind is permitted. Because man has limited capacities for creating, the picture he produces is necessarily incomplete and can be no serious competition with his Creator. Therefore there is room to permit it.

The *Midrash* reflects in a similar vein upon the ineptitude of human artistry compared with the Divine:

Neither is there any artist (tzayyar) *like our God*

The artist–he cannot draw in darkness; but the Holy One, blessed be He–He can draw any figure in darkness; as it is said *My frame was made in darkness, and curiously wrought in the deepest parts of the earth* (Psalm 139:15).

Similarly, the Midrash says that man cannot write on water, whereas God traces the intricate design of an entire underwater world.

The artist—he can make nothing at all except by hard work; but the Holy One, blessed be He—He makes things by the mere breath of a word, as when God Said: *Let there be light* (Genesis 1:3).

The artist—he cannot draw a figure all at once, only little by little; but the Holy One, blessed be He—He makes a figure, all of it, in one stroke, as is said, *He is One who forms all* [at once] (Jeremiah 10:16).

The artist—the creation of his hands does not eat, but he eats; the Holy One, blessed be He—His creatures eat, but He does not eat; no, more. He gives creatures what they eat.

The artist—he dies, but the creation of his hands endures; the Holy One, Blessed be He, His creature dies, but He lives forever and ever and ever. [*Midrash on Psalms,* Psalm 18:26, trans. Braude, p. 258].

After the death of the artist, there is a postscript. For even in the time of the *Midrash* it seems that the position of an artist was a very tenuous one, and he had to be his own publicity agent in order to keep on supporting himself in his craft.

The mortal—he praises the creation of his hands, he sells it and makes his living by it; but the Holy One, blessed be He—His creature praises Him, and he provides it with a living, as is said: *The eyes of all wait upon Thee, and Thou givest them their food in due season* (Psalms 145:15). [*Midrash on Psalms,* Psalm 18:26, trans. Braude, p. 258.]

The outcome of all these meditations is the obvious one drawn also by the Talmud—that while God can instill the breath of life in His work of art, man cannot!

The mortal—when he makes a figure, he cannot put spirit, breath, entrails, and bowels into it; but the Holy One, blessed be He—He makes the figure of an embryo within its mother, and then puts spirit, and breath, and entrails and bowels into it. Of this it is written *Bless the Lord, O my soul; and all that is within me, bless His Holy Name* (Psalm 103:1). And so it is said, *Who is an artist besides our God?* (Psalm 18:26) [*Midrash on Psalms,* Psalm 18:26, trans. Braude, p. 258]

Image making is absurd because the images are not alive. The Psalmist says:

> Their gods are of silver and gold, the work of human artistry. They have mouths, but they cannot speak, eyes but they cannot see, ears but they cannot hear, noses but they cannot smell. They have hands but they cannot feel, feet but they cannot walk; nor can they make a sound with their throat. May those who make them become like them, whoever trusts in them! [Psalm 115:4–7]

It seems that the ancient world believed, with some inner rationale, that if one made something or helped to bring it in to being, one was necessarily its superior and could dominate it. Thus parents who existed before their children had authority over them, and God, as First Cause, was superior to His Creation. Not only that, but in a long chain of causes and emanations, the earlier was superior to the later, cause superior to effect. The image that springs to mind is of an impression made from an impression of an original mold. The pressure grows fainter with each application. In such a world view, for someone to worship his "child," his work of art, was patently absurd. Here lies the true humility of Moshe in his unwillingness to express the vision of a transcendental *Menorah* or Sanctuary. What he produces will necessarily be lower than himself. If he brings the *Shekhinah* down to earth, there is a sense in which he will be higher than She, and he found that difficult to accept. If we take the *Midrash* of the king who wanted a self-portrait, Moshe's reply reads like a common belief about the nature of the artist: "Am I a god, that I should be able to reproduce it!" (*Shemot Rabbah* 35:5–6). To reproduce the Divine Image would require a god at least!

Until modern times it was believed that the aim of the artist was to realistically portray or copy some external object. If the artist were successful, then the work of art would closely resemble its original. In primitive eras, when art and magic were intertwined, it was thought that the artist, by dominating the image, also gained access to power over the original, and that by injuring the image, the original might also be affected.

By pointing out the inefficacy of these images the Psalmist is also exposing the weaknesses of those who uphold them, as well as highlighting the real likeness that exists between artist and work. Just as in living together, pets and domestic partners come to resemble their owners and spouses, the reverse is also true. The Psalmist says the human being slowly becomes as deaf and dumb, mute and impotent as the images he produces.

In early times, making an image of any natural object had an obviously idolatrous implication. During the Classical era, a rather Platonic rationale was argued by Philo for the ban on representational art. What Philo objected to was not merely the imitation of natural forms, but the filling of the world with man-made images, which have the ultimate effect of distorting the soul of those who made them. He denounced them this way:

> Those who filled the habitable world with images and human figures and the other works of human hands, fashioned by the craftsmanship of painting and sculpture which have wrought great mischief on the life of mankind. For these idolators cut away the most excellent support of the soul, the right conception of the Ever-Living God.[12]

The Psalmist and Philo agree that the making of images, by distorting reality, blunts the "soul" of the artist.

During the talmudic discussion on forbidden images, some of the Rabbis interpret the verse "Ye shall not make with me" (Exodus 20:23) to mean that not only is it forbidden to make an image of God (and therefore also of man), but that it is also not permitted to make a likeness of any of God's attendants in the Heavens (the Sun, the Moon, and the zodiac). But Abaye, one of the talmudic Sages, restricted this prohibition to include only those of God's "attendants" of whom it was possible to make copies ("like them," out of the same) materials. As it would be impossible to duplicate the Sun and the Moon with exactly the same materials God used, it might be permissible to make models of them. However, when it came to making a model of these prototypes contained within the sacred enclosure of the Temple – that is, a model of either the Temple itself or of any of its furniture, including the *Menorah* – that was forbidden in any material.

> A man may not make a house in the form of the Temple, or a hall in the form of the Temple hall, or a court corresponding to the Temple court, or a table corresponding to the (sacred) table or a candlestick corresponding to the (sacred) candlestick. [*Menahot* 28b][13]

In the same discussion about duplicating the image of the *Menorah,* Abaye raises the question of whether it is permitted to delineate the human face and the human body. Abaye is the most permissive of any of the Sages before or since. He quotes the consensus of the Talmud interpreters that "all portraits are allowed, save the portrait of a man," only to question it. He is saying that the only real ban is against making a complete image of God. In Ezekiel, God is described as being four-dimensional (as opposed to the normal three dimensions of a human being). These four dimensions Ezekiel terms *four faces* (Ezekiel 1:10), only one of which relates at all to humanity. Therefore, according to Ezekiel's description, says Abaye, making an image of the human face alone should be permitted, because it forms a partial image of God and could not possibly be taken as a multidimensional and fully fleshed out portrait (*Menahot* 29b).

Interestingly, Abaye's liberal attitude to portraiture of the human face and body is misquoted by one of his disciples:

> R. Huna, the son of R. Idi, replied: From a discourse of Abaye I learnt: "*Ye shall not make with me*" (implies), ye shall not make Me. (And since man was made in God's image [Genesis 1:27], it is also not permitted to reproduce the human face.) [*Avodah Zarah* 43a–b]

According to what Abaye actually said, portrayal of the human face and figure should have been allowed because man himself was so partial and incomplete an Image of his Maker. Because representations of the human form were necessarily defective in that essential component – life – they could not rightly be considered blasphemy. On the one hand, man is made in God's likeness; on the other, whereas man is a part, God is all, and in that "all" lies the crucial difference. Whereas man has one face, God has an infinite number of faces. Whereas man changes and is finite, God is infinite and Absolute.

Man is a part of God Above. The *Midrash* compares God to a Rock or a Mountain, and the human soul to a stone because although both are made of the same substance, and God in Himself comprises everything, the human soul is only a fragment of that Rock.

Whereas Abaye in talmudic times sees the portrait of a human being as a very incomplete one-dimensional image of God, the *Zohar* takes art more seriously and therefore judges it as a commensurately graver threat:

> The graving and painting of all forms is permitted except the human figure.
>
> Said Rabbi Isaac: "The reason is, because when a human figure is represented in sculpture and/or painting, it is not only the body which is fashioned in the image of the person, but, as it were, the wholeness of the man is being reproduced, his inner form—namely, his spirit as well as his bodily form."
>
> Said Rabbi Judah: This accords with the popular saying, "As the breath of the craftsman, so the shape of his vessel." [*Zohar* III:85b–86c]

Here, the greatest of all compliments is being paid to art—that it can render the spirit.

ART AND THE SOUL OF ITS CREATOR

To lend support to the claim that one can capture the life as well as the external form of a model, a claim that the Psalms, the *Midrash,* and the Talmud dispute, the *Zohar* quotes a popular proverb that says something entirely different. The proverb picks up the link, not between the form of the work of art and the soul of its subject, but between the form of the work of art and the soul of the artist who produced it!

The question is, which artist is being alluded to in the popular proverb and what shape does his vessel take? As in glassblowing, the artistic process described is one in which the artifact takes on the very pattern of the craftsman's breath. A completely "Greek" concept – here, as in Plato – the "form" of the work of art and its "soul" are identical. Only here the "idea" is dictated by the divine breath or the light that is being dispensed. If we take the quotation simply as it stands, the popular saying affords a contemporary commentary on human art in general. More than anything else, a work of art reflects the soul and psyche of its creator. The quality of the image is dictated by the psychological state of the person who conceived it. No matter if Van Gogh is painting a chair, a naked woman, or even himself, he is always and only painting himself.

In the proverb's context in the *Zohar,* however, the craftsman under discussion obviously is the Supreme Artist, and His most consummate Creation is the Soul of Man. According to Genesis, it was with His own breath that He inspired man with soul and life-force. The human soul – the Hebrew word for which is *neshamah,* "breath" – is the supreme Vessel that acquires its shape from God's inspiration. The comment made about the human soul is also made about the creation of light itself.

The only effort required for God to create the world was the command "Let there be light" (see chapter 1, p. 5). With the merest breath, the *heh* of the feminine ending, He created the world. Therefore, because both light and the human soul were formed by the Divine Breath, both are spiritual variations on the same theme, and in the deepest sense both correspond.

What is really meant by "Primordial Light" or the Celestial *Menorah* is the reservoir of light and spirituality from which individual souls are taken. The *Zohar* takes as the real goal of art something infinitely greater than mere depiction of external form. In doing so it presents a radically different view of the capacities of the artist from that upheld by some talmudic authorities. According to them, human art is faced with certain rational limits; it cannot render a complete portrait either of God or man and can only delineate man's physical outline. According to the *Zohar* it is possible for the artist to render the soul of his subject, to express and expose and put at risk his own soul, and also to attain and convey some knowledge of God Himself. Also according to the *Zohar,* human art overlaps dramatically with the realm of magic and of Divine creativity.

The borderline between the realms of man and of the gods in the ancient world was not clearcut. And the Serpent's reading of Genesis paints a portrait of a Creator who does not want to share such Divine prerogatives as Knowledge of Good and Evil, the ability to create life, and immortality with any of His creatures. All the Serpent's arguments to Eve produce a case against God rather than against man that has not entirely been dispelled by subsequent events–unless one is reminded that God was generous enough to create man in His image in the first place.

In light of the previous passage from the *Zohar* (III:85b–86c), it seems that the proscription against creation of images, especially of human images in the Second Commandment, also stems from an extension of the first prohibition in the Garden of Eden. The ban against making images of god or man and the ban against eating of the fruit of forbidden knowledge are both extensions of human presumption into the sphere of Divine creativity. The kind of secret knowledge in question is the art of usurping the function of God by creating life. It is interesting to note that Rabbi Loew of Prague is alleged to have succeeded at this task, with one defect–his *Golem* lacked a soul.

However, such commands as "Build Me a Sanctuary" and "Let light shine from the Lampstand" do a great deal to compensate for that restriction on human creativity and thirst for knowledge. It has been said that the *Menorah* is the "fixing" of the Tree of Knowledge. The *Menorah,* image of human potential realized to its fullest capacity in which light meets Lamp and God meets man on man's homeground, is God's apology for the claustrophobic barriers of Eden.

On the one hand, man is forbidden to make images; on the other, when it comes to Temple worship, he is commanded to make images and kindle *Menorot.* But another kind of artistry that man is invited to undertake shows that far from resenting human pretensions to creativity, in the appropriate context God welcomes and even requires them.

> Another explanation of *And thou shalt make the boards for the tabernacle.* R. Abin said: "It can be compared to a king who possessed a beautiful appearance, and gave instructions to a member of his household to make a bust exactly like him."
>
> "But your majesty" – exclaimed the other – "How can I possibly make one *exactly* like you?"
>
> The king replied: "You do the best with the colors at your disposal, and then I shall complete the picture with My Glory."
>
> This is what God said to Moshe: *And see that thou make them after their pattern* (Exodus 25:40).
>
> Moshe answered: "Lord of the Universe! Am I a God that I should be able to make one exactly like it?"
>
> The divine reply was: "If thou wilt make below a replica of that which is above, I will desert My heavenly assembly and will cause My *Shekhinah* to dwell among you below."[*Shemot Rabbah* 35:5–6]

The royal commission in this *Midrash* is for man to create the "image of God," that is, his own psyche, in which all animal, vegetable, and mineral surrealist images are contained.

Essentially, the internal work upon the soul is the real "work of the Sanctuary," the "work of the *Menorah.*" Although it may be taboo to make a full physical image of a human being because he is an imitation of the Divine, this is only so because God actually wants him to fashion that image in its truest sense. God does not begrudge man the creativity of the gods; on the contrary, to fashion the Divine image is actually what He *requires* him to do. God does not want man to make a "fixed" image of God – that is, an idol – because He wants man's "image of God" to keep pace with his own spiritual progression. For what is the "image of God," after all, but man's gradually dawning awareness of Him. And that must be continually made and remade.

God is not only inviting man to "remake" his own soul; he is also begging Him to "make" God's as well:

> *If you walk in My statutes and keep My commands,* then you will create with them.
>
> Whoever performs the commandments of the Torah and walks in its ways is regarded as if he makes Him above. The Holy One, Blessed be He says: "(It is) as if he had made Me." [*Vayikra Rabbah* 35:6]

> *Whoever keeps My commandments, I regard him as if he has made Me* (Psalm 119:126); as it is written "It is a time to make God," literally.[14]

Many of the "Thou shalt nots," far from being particularly negative, exist only to highlight the positive. And precisely the image it is forbidden to make in one context (outside the Temple), it is God's supreme desire that we fashion within it. The very language used for the prohibition against image making – "Thou shalt not make with Me" (Exodus 20:23), which the Talmud said referred to "God's attendants," the Sun and the Moon in the Heavens and the *Menorah* in the Temple – is used again in the *Midrash* in urgently recommending a particular style of image making. The whole purpose of the creation is that man should "create with them" (the commandments standing for the Divine attendants); the goal is for man to be creative also to the utmost of his ability, and that he should make the grandest image of all, the Image of God (that is, the Soul) out of the physical substance of reality. So, although it may be forbidden to make plastic images of God, this is only because to carve out God Himself into the bedrock of creation is the very purpose of life. And if, in keeping with the *Midrash,* we "do our best with all the colors at [our] disposal," then "God will complete the picture with His Glory" (*Shemot Rabbah* 35:5–6).

One meaning of *mitzvah* is to *link;* another is to *sculpt* or to *hew.* It is as if the Commandments themselves are the chisels with which man will perfect not only his own soul, but God's image or "Statue" in the world; with each practical commandment that is kept by each physical organ, the "image of God" is hewn and chipped out of the bedrock of the physical. By using his own organs in God's service, the individual is carving out at once the "Human Form Divine" of mankind, the "image of God," and also, in effect, carving out the various dimensions and facets of God's spiritual body.

The indifferent God of the Buddhists who transcends all human pain and suffering is not dissimilar to the *Ein-Sof,* the Unknown God beyond our comprehension. But this God is so beyond everything that He is not even interesting. What is interesting is the "Face" He shows to Man, some unknown urge that propelled Him toward Creation and toward relationship. How God appears in the human world – the "Name of God," His outline – is what is of interest.

According to Rabbi Isaac Luria, after the Breaking of the original Vessels or *Sefirot,* their light was fragmented and buried in husks or *klippot* of evil. By carrying out the Torah with his physical organs (allegedly numbering 613 to correspond with the 613 *mitzvot*), man reintegrates these fragments or *Parzufin* of Primordial Light and helps bring about a *Tikkun* or reintegration of the various faces of the Divine.[15]

Here God is visualized as having 613 faces and not, as in Ezekiel, a mere four. On the one hand, He is One; on the other, in His relationship with the rich and diverse creation He has produced, He is infinitely versatile in His manifestations:

> Because the Holy One appeared to Israel at the Red Sea as a mighty man waging war and appeared to them at Sinai as a Master who teaches the lesson of the day and then repeatedly goes over with his pupils what they have been taught, and appeared to them in the days of Daniel as an elder teaching Torah and in the days of Solomon appeared to them as a young man, the Holy One said to Israel: "Come to no false conclusion because you see Me in many guises, for I am He who was with you at the Red Sea and I am He who is with you at Sinai: I am the Lord your God."

The fact is, R. Hiyya bar Abba said, that He appeared to them in a guise appropriate to each and every place and time. At the Red Sea He appeared to them as a mighty man waging their wars; at Sinai He appeared to them as a Teacher, as one who stands upright in awe when teaching Torah; in the days of Daniel, He appeared to them as an elder teaching Torah, for the Torah is at its best when it comes from the mouths of old men; in the days of Solomon He appeared to them as a young man in keeping with the youthful spirit of Solomon's generation—*His aspect is like Lebanon, young as the cedars* (Song of Songs 5:15). At Sinai, then, appropriately, He appeared to them as a Teacher teaching Torah: *I am the Lord thy God.* [*Pesikta de Rav Kahana, Piske* 12:24, trans. Braude, pp. 248–250]

Another comment on *I am the Lord thy God,* R. Hanina bar Papa said: "The Holy One appeared to Israel with a stern face, with an equable face, with a friendly face, with a joyous face.

"With a severe face appropriate for the teaching of Scripture—when a man teaches Torah to his son, he must impress upon him his own awe of Torah; with an equable face appropriate for the teaching of *Mishnah;* with a friendly face appropriate for the teaching of Talmud; with a joyous face appropriate for the teaching of *Aggadah* (the story part of the Talmud)."

Therefore, the Holy One said to them: "Though you see Me in all these guises, (I am the One), *I am the Lord thy God.*"

R. Levi said: "The Holy One appeared to them as though He were a statue with faces on every side, so that though a thousand men might be looking at the statue, they would be led to believe that it was looking at each one of them. So, too, when the Holy One spoke, each and every person in Israel could say, 'The Divine Word is speaking to me.'"

"Note that Scripture does not say, 'I am your God,' but *I am the Lord your God* (your very own God). Moreover, said R. Jose bar R. Hanina, the Divine Word spoke to each and every person according to his particular capacity. And do not wonder at this. For when manna came down for Israel, each and every person tasted it in keeping with his own capacity—infants in keeping with their capacity, young men in keeping with their capacity, and old men in keeping with their capacity. Infants in keeping with their capacity: like the taste of milk that an infant sucks from his mother's breast, so was the taste of manna to every infant, for it is said: 'Its taste was like the taste of the milk that an infant sucks from his mother's breast, so was the taste of manna to every infant,' for it is said *Its taste was like the taste of rich cream* (Numbers 11:8); young men according to their capacity, for of the manna they ate it is said, *My bread also which I gave thee, bread, and oil, and honey* (Ezekiel 16:19); and old men according to their capacity, as is said of the manna they ate *the taste of it was like wafers made with honey* (Exodus 16:31).

"Now if each and every person was enabled to taste the manna according to his particular capacity, how much more and more was each and every person enabled according to his particular capacity to hear the Divine Word. Thus David said: *The voice of the Lord is in its strength* (Psalm 29:4)–not 'The voice of the Lord in His strength' but *The voice of the Lord in its strength*–that is, in its strength to make itself heard and understood according to the capacity of each and every person who listens to the Divine Word. Therefore, the Holy One said: 'Do not be misled because you hear many voices. Know that I am He who is one and the same: *I am the Lord your God.*'" [*Pesikta de Rav Kahana, Piske* 12:25, trans. Braude, pp. 248–250]

Here the "Face" of God and the "Divine Word"–the Torah–are interchangeable as the way God addresses and appears to man. And this "way" is manifold. Images for this Unity-in-Multiplicity of God and His manifestations, or of the Torah and Her many interpretations, are those of a jewel with many facets and rays, a Burning Coal with many sparks, the *Menorah* with many individual lights and eyes, and the Statue with a Thousand Faces.

Craftsmanlike metaphors of hewing and chiseling are applied in particular to the Torah which, it is noted, "was engraved on tablets of precious stone that are exceedingly strong and resistant and can hammer and change other material but cannot themselves be changed by them."

"Is not My Word like fire, says the Lord, and like a hammer

that breaks the rock in pieces" (Jeremiah 23:29). This means that just as the hammer splits the rock into many fragments, so may one verse be split into many meanings (*Sanhedrin* 34a).

This verse ends by saying precisely the opposite of what it seems to start out with. It starts as if God's Word is rigid and absolute and crushes all the variety of life. But the way the Rabbis interpret it is that the Divine Word has capacity for maximum flexibility and is as rich and diverse as life itself.

> *And God spoke to Moses face to face* (Exodus 33:11). The Holy One said to Moshe, "Moshe, let us, you and I, explain the various facets of the law." [*Bereishit Rabbah* 63b]

Each irradiation or facet of the jewel or candle of the *Menorah* is the limited perspective of an individual human being. Although where actual sculpture is concerned, it is forbidden to make a multidimensional image of a man or a complete image of God—if that were possible, in the spiritual realm this is precisely the aim—to transcend one's own limited perspective and achieve as complete a vision of the celestial *Menorah* as possible.

VISUALIZATION AND THE SPIRITUAL LIFE

One type of image making that forms part of this bent for inner *Menorah* making is that of visualization. Although there certainly is no outright commandment to meditate by focusing on purely mental images (or "Hidden Candles"), for some temperaments this method seems to make a very valuable contribution to their spiritual life, with incalculable rewards.

> When a person is upright and righteous, he can meditate with appropriate thoughts, and ascend through the level of the transcendental. He must unify the levels of his soul to rest themselves in each other. It then becomes like a single *Menorah* made of different parts joined together.[16]

Many of the Kabbalists "ascended" (and came back to the mundane world) through the practice of various techniques of meditation and visualization connected with light. In general, the way of contemplation was to focus on light itself. For example, one could imagine the soul as a point of light drawing continually closer to its Divine Source[17] or one could imagine the light of the *Shekhinah* flowing all around and oneself sitting surrounded by light.[18]

Centuries later, the *Maggid* of Mezeritch repeated Azikri's esoteric technique for the masses of ordinary Jews. In order to offer proper prayer, he recommended, one must feel oneself totally encompassed in the light of the spirit.[19] Another method, recommended by Moses de Leon, was to visualize the movement of the *Sefirot* by watching the patterns of light and color flickering in front of one's closed eyes[20] (*Zohar* I:42a; *Zohar Hadash* 39d). Or, de Leon suggested, one might take so simple an item as a dish of water (the equivalent of a candle dish or a Lamp, filled with water, not oil) and watch the light dancing on its surface, similar to the dynamism of the *Sefirot*.[21]

Rabbi Azriel of Gerona sees visualization as an aid to understanding. When the "questioner" asks about the nature of the *Sefirot,* the answer given is that although they were created *ex nihilo,* like every function of the psyche they are illusions; as in color (or in light waves), however, the useful fiction lies in their dynamic:

But, by embellishing substance with imagination, we can liken the first power to the concealed light. The second power (can be likened) to the light which contains every color. This light is like *tekhelet,* the essence (*takhilit*) of all colors in which there is no known hue. The third power (can be compared) to green light. The fourth power can be likened to white light. The fifth power can be likened to red light. The sixth power is composed of whiteness and scarlet. The seventh power is the power of scarlet tending towards whiteness. The eighth power is the power of whiteness tending toward scarlet. The ninth power is composed of whiteness and scarlet and scarlet tending towards whiteness and whiteness tending towards scarlet. The tenth power is composed of every color.[22]

According to Cordovero, "the main reason why the *Sefirot* were created was to provide a ladder upon which one could climb to the highest spiritual levels."[23]

A good image for what the Kabbalists intended by the *Sefirot* was a ladder or spiral staircase down which Divine Light came to man and by means of which he could rise. These *Sefirot* were seen not only as a part of the external cosmos, but also as an internal part of man himself. It was as if everyone walked about with ladders on their heads, their various potentials of soul scaling all the *Sefirot*. For some unfortunate human beings, it often seems even their lowest soul is not contained in their body or their physical life as they actually live it, but is latent, suspended at some distance over their head. But, in general, the soul is the one point of light in a human being that connects him to something higher, reaching up to his higher soul that belongs within the Divine ambience.

The question might be asked, what role can visualization, whether of lights and lamps or letters and names serve on such a "realistic" path as that of Judaism. Cordovero explains exactly why it is important to focus on certain abstractions such as the *Sefirot*. Visualization, he says, directly affects one's powers of motivation. But how can something totally imaginary matter? Is it not self-indulgent to concentrate on an inner imaginary image, to the possible detraction of a world of moral endeavor? Is not the whole thing a futile exercise in autohypnosis? And even if there is some subjective value, what influence can it bring to bear upon external reality?

Judaism may present a picture of a very practical way of life, dealing with tangible acts. But in fact it has always been agreed that a *mitzvah* is made up of two equally important parts – the *mas'aseh*, the ultimate action or result in physical terms, and the *kavannah*, or intention of the person carrying out that act. There are many differing opinions as to which component is decisive. While there are many behaviorists who hold the nonsentimental view that even in retrospect certain types of action will affect the spiritual quality of the person undertaking them—"What was at first not purely for the sake of Heaven will become so"—all are agreed that the intention with which an objective is accomplished plays a major role. Some hold even that "intention is identical to action," in cases where success in achieving the final result is not up to the person concerned.

A technique such as visualization, then, even if it is not included in any list of ritual obligations, can play a crucial role in the spiritual life. And not only in its effect upon attitudes; but also practically it can have effects. Visualization of a completed physical action or of a rounded-off image—the Vessel—sometimes can help to achieve realization.

One may imagine that when, for lack of a lamp, a child in a hideout in Nazi-occupied Europe traced the beloved features of the *Menorah* on a frosted windowpane—although no physical light was ignited—certain energies were set in motion that in turn triggered higher and higher forces, until they touched the Highest Point of all.

According to Cordovero, we can be motivated by what we imagine, and this may have an impact not only upon us but even upon God Himself. Cordovero does not say exactly that the Absolute aspect of God will be changed by something as illusory as a color, a fiction, an imagining. What will be moved is the "Divine Countenance" He shows to man. Cordovero writes that through meditating on the colors and the Names of every individual *Sefirah*, the *Neshamah* can ascend the ladder of the Sefirotic system back to the Source.

> One may transmit the influence of a given *Sefirah* by meditation upon the color that represents its essential quality. Thus, to spread around one an atmosphere of serenity, one may meditate on white and write God's Name in white lettering and wear garments of that color.
>
> Colors that are visible to the eye or which are depicted in the mind can have an effect on the spiritual, even though the colors themselves are physical.

The *Nefesh* (lower soul) can motivate the *Ruach* (middle spirit), and the *Ruach* in turn motivates the *Neshamah* (upper soul). The *Neshamah* then ascends from one essence to the next until it reaches its source. It can then be motivated by what it imagines.

Thus (the thoughts) are like a mirror to the (Divine) Countenance. The thoughts transmitted to the Source of the *Neshamah,* the Countenance, can (be made to) appear red. It then transmits (an influence associated with the color) red (back to this Source). All influence on the Lower Face is the result of human action.[24]

A movement of ascent and of upward reflection is traced here by Cordovero. The lower soul is affected by the color of the visualization, which moves the soul one rung up–until the whole scale of notes are struck, right up to the soul rooted in the collective human reflection of the Divine, the Small Face. But on the road of ascent, the roles are reversed; the Divine Countenance itself becomes a mirror reflecting images from below. This notion lies at the root of theurgical *Kabbalah,* which boldly states that human action can influence the cosmos and God Himself.

Therefore, when we say that man is made in the image of God, we mean that, just as a lover is an image of his love, just as Moshe saw God "face to face" as a kind of reflection, just as the souls of two friends reflect each other like an image in water, man, by shaping his own character ("the work of the *Menorah*"), "makes" God Himself, or at least His relationship with Him. And although there is of course no outright commandment to kindle these imaginary and hidden candles, visualization techniques can exert incalculable power over the human soul, its spiritual orientation (*kavannah*), and over an aspect of God Himself.

If the point of the commandment to light a *Menorah* is to find through this small ritual the hidden candles in this world[25] – to celebrate God's Light especially where He seems most absent – then the technique of visualization can be of the utmost benefit.

The opportunities for creativity here are at their most radical. From a passive role of Creature and Taker, by keeping the

Commandments *Knesset Yisrael* not only perfects Her own Soul, but nurtures God into physical reality and, in a sense, according to various interpretations, not only in *Kabbalah,* but even in very ancient *Midrashim,* they "make God."

Man is made in the image of God, and human art has been described as the "shadow" of the Divine Light. In his capacity as artist, Bezalel is the "shadow of God," but there is a sense in which the Creator, as supreme Artist, dwells in the shadow of the world. He, too, "sees all, yet is unseen" (*Bamidbar Rabbah* 12:3), standing in the wings and letting the *dramatis personae* play out their parts. In the shadow-puppet play of this world, humanity is the ideal form, of which God is the reflection. That is why God requires certain actions – prayer, kindling of *Menorot* – so that He becomes active in this world.

The "Work of the *Menorah*" consists in preparing a physical grounding or Vessel for the Divine Light. On another dimension, it acts to reverse the dynamic by elevating the *Menorah.*

What is the miracle connected with the *Menorah* and what is the work for which this miracle is the reward? The miracle was that God required Israel to light in the first place:

Another exposition of the expression, *When thou lightest.* This bears on the Scriptural text, *Even the darkness is not too dark for Thee, but the night shineth as the day; the darkness is even as the light* (Psalm 139:12). Yet to us He says, *When thou lightest!*

To what may the matter be compared? To a king who had a friend. The king said to him: "I want you to know that I am doing you the honor of dining with you. Go then and make preparations for me."

His friend went and prepared a cheap couch, a cheap candlestick, and a cheap table. When the king arrived there came with him ministers who encompassed him on this side and that, and a golden candlestick preceded him.

His friend, seeing all this pomp, felt ashamed and put away all that he had prepared for him, as it was all common.

Said the king to him: "Did I not tell you that I would dine with you? Why did you not prepare anything for me?"

THE LAMP OF GOD

His friend answered him: "Beholding all the pomp that accompanied you, I felt ashamed, and put away all that I had prepared for you, because they were cheap utensils."

"By your life!" said the king to him, "I shall discard all the utensils that I have brought, and for love of you I shall use none but yours!"

So in our case. The Holy One, blessed be He, is all light; as it says, *And the light dwelleth with Him* (Daniel 11:22), yet He said to Israel: *Prepare for Me a candlestick and lamps.*

What do we find written in this connection? *Let them make Me a sanctuary, that I may dwell among them* (Exodus 25:8); *And thou shalt make a candlestick of pure gold* (Exodus 25:31). And when they had completed everything, then the *Shekhinah* came. [A variation on *Bamidbar Rabbah* 15:8]

Of all creatures, man was chosen to continue the illumination that God set in motion during the Creation. Man is the means through which all creatures adhere to God. In the Greek concept of the relationship between God and man, Prometheus had to steal fire from Heaven, whereas in Judaism God commands man to perform the "commandment to kindle."

When the Temple stood, it was like an actual powerhouse of life and light to the world. By kindling the *Menorah,* light and life were drawn to its farthest extremities. The *Menorah* bears witness that the *Shekhinah* rests on Israel and through Israel on the entire world. All is a preparation and a vessel for this "resting." If the right preparations for a suitable Vessel are made, new life will be drawn afresh from God every day from our higher root and everything will be renewed from above. Only when the appropriate preparations are made down below, can the Vessel receive the illumination from its roots.

The *Hanukkah* Light is a quintessence – it contains the potential to raise everything to its Highest Root. The "Work of the *Menorah*" consists of bringing the light down to earth.

It is written, *The righteous shall inherit the land and dwell therein forever* (Psalm 37:29): then what are the wicked to do – are they to range in the air?

What it means is that the wicked do not permit the *Shekhinah* to dwell on earth. [They have no spiritual ballast or sense of gravity.] [*Bereishit Rabbah* 19:6-7]

The true "Work of the *Menorah*" is to bring out the hidden potential of the soul so that it becomes a Lamp in which the *Shekhinah* can dwell. What is required is for a receptacle, a Sanctuary, a *Menorah* to be prepared out of the material world.

Only when the human spirit becomes God's Lamp or instrument, will Divine Light shine in on the world.

So that you should have a desire for the work of Your hands (Job 14:15). In four things did God desire (the assistance of) the work of His hands.

These are the four things: God supports His world, for it says, *I have made and I will bear; yea, I will carry, and will deliver* (Isaiah 46:4). Yet He commanded the sons of *Kohath* (a Levite family) to carry it [the Ark] for it says, *But the sons of Kohath bore them upon their shoulders* (Numbers 7:9).

A proof that God, as it were, supports them can be deduced from the fact that when they came to the Jordan and were not able to cross, God carried them across. R. Berekiah said: The Ark bore those that carried it; it was not the priests who carried it, but rather it bore them.

Again, God guards His world; as it says, *Behold, He that keepeth Israel doth neither slumber nor sleep. The Lord is thy keeper* (Psalm 101:4), yet He commanded Israel to keep Him.

Further, God gives light to the world, for it is written, *And the earth did shine with His glory* (Ezekiel 43:2), yet did He command Israel *that they bring unto thee pure olive oil beaten for the light*–thus, *Thou wouldest have a desire for the work of Thy hands* (Job 14:15). [*Shemot Rabbah* 36:4]

In each case God desires Israel to do what He actually does Himself. One might think that because He is perfectly capable of doing these things, such as illuminating the world, why ask another to do them for Him. The answer is desire itself. God desires to create, not an object, but a relationship with a being who himself creates and kindles. But the effort, as far as the human being is concerned, is simply to prepare the vessel—and then the wick simply takes fire!

> *When you raise up the lights.* It does not say "when you kindle them" because the flame rose up of itself. There was a step below the *Menorah* on which the priest stood, constantly trimming the wick until the flame rose by itself. [Rashi on Numbers 8:2]

The Riziner explained the verse "But all the children of Israel had light in their dwellings" (Ezekiel 10:23) in the following way. "In addition to residing in the Tabernacle, God resides in the community of Israel as light lives in a lamp. The Clouds of Glory did not cover only the centralized Tabernacle, but a snippet hovered over the dwelling of each and every individual in Israel, filling their homes with light. Each one of us possesses a Holy Spark, which in the right circumstances can shine with *Shekhinah* Light."

"And I shall dwell in their midst." The *Shekhinah* did not only dwell in the Temple, but in each individual member of *Knesset Yisrael*. There is a sanctuary-in-little, a miniature Temple, and a *Menorah* light in every single Jew. Nowadays this single "point" of purity is concealed. But when the Temple was standing, it was visible. Now, although the Sanctuary is hidden deep within, it can be found by searching with lamps. We seek it in every heart and soul. The Lamp is the deepest potential of the soul that can be brought out by means of observance of the Commandments. The Lamp forged by observance of the *Mitzvot* guides the search through the inner parts of the human being to the central "point" where the Sanctuary is hidden in the Jerusalem-of-the-Heart.

THE *MENORAH* MAKER

A young man left his father's house and spent a long time in foreign lands living among strangers. Some time later he returned home, boasting that while he had been away he had learned a rare and marvelous craft—how to make a candelabrum with unrivaled skill. He asked his father to gather together all the *Menorah* makers in the country so that he could show off his talent.

His father did what he asked. He invited all the greatest *Menorah* makers in the land to view the finer points of the skill his son had learned while living among strangers. When they were all assembled, the young man took out the *Menorah* he had made. But all the craftsmen found it to be extraordinarily ugly. The boy's father went and begged them to tell him the truth. So they were compelled to tell him their real opinion. Meanwhile, the son kept boasting: "Don't you realize what skill goes into my work?"

Then his father told him that the *Menorah* makers did not find his *Menorah* beautiful at all. And the son replied: "But that is exactly the point: I have shown them all what is wrong with themselves. In this *Menorah* you can see the defects of each of the craftsmen in our hometown."

"Don't you see that in the eyes of one man, one part of the *Menorah* is ugly, whereas he finds another part beautiful. To another craftsman, the part that seemed ugly to his friend appeared wondrously beautiful to him. What is ugly in the eyes of one is beautiful in the eyes of another.

"The truth is, I made this *Menorah* solely out of defects to show other *Menorah* makers that each person has a defect and does not by himself possess perfection. And if I have the power to do that, I can also do the opposite. I can make the *Menorah* as it should be made."[26]

"And I will dwell in your midst." This dwelling of the light in the *Menorah* Lamp is to be taken literally—in your vitals, in your guts, in the most sensuous and animal part of your being. All these 613 organs, by observance of physical commandments, will come together to compose a Lamp, a Vessel overflowing with light.[27] However, if it is up to man to act to create God and sustain Him in the physical world, the "Work of the *Menorah*," although it is internal, also has relevance for the external physical world and for the collective human psyche. The true artistry involved is the art of living–what to do with each object of experience, to extract the sparks of light hidden even in darkness and in material existence.

The Baal Shem Tov compares this enterprise to that instituted by a king who dropped a gem from his ring to give his favorite son a clue as to his whereabouts. So God shed sparks of holiness in the treasure hunt that was to lead to finding Him.

"There are sparks of holiness in everything, and it is they which constitute the spiritual life."[28]

Hasidism, like animism, is concerned with the "innerness" of each object and experience, because not only every human being but also animals, flowers and plants, and stones, minerals, and inorganic matter are represented as possessing a soul or a "spark" that reflects the Divine Presence.

> The holy sparks yearn to cleave unto man's intellect. It is the duty of man to restore the holy sparks to their Source. By this act a man may enter the palace of the Source of Sources.[29]

Here, man or the *Tzaddik* is compared to a medieval knight who, in redeeming stray sparks of the light of the *Shekhinah,* is rescuing a beautiful Princess.

The first "Lamp" that God created was the first beautiful work of art. What was it really but a mirror reflecting back the light of *Ein-Sof.* It was the essence of the soul, a mirror for the Light of the Endless. It is this that, above all, we are required to keep polished and shining, and anything less than it–an alienation rather than a greater affirmation of the soul of man, anything that is frozen matter rather than quickening spirit, life-denying rather than life-enhancing as a way of ascent–is often seen as an idolatrous image.

When, as Aristotle points out, the work of art is not a step farther away from the Divine, but is in fact a beckoning toward it, then it is taken as a means to rise.

THE LIGHT OF THE "FACE-TO-FACE"

What does it mean to kindle the *Menorah?* To kindle the *Menorah* is to become like Moshe, the Lover of God who saw Him Face to

Face. Said Rabbi Shneor Zalman of Liadi (the first Lubavitcher Rebbe):

> The seven lamps (of the Temple *Menorah*) are seven days, the seven days of gradual penetration leading up to the consummation of the state of "face-to-face."
>
> The Divine Light is both all-encompassing and all-penetrating. God pierces with His transcendent light to the innermost part, the hidden treasure of the soul. And by lighting the Seven Lamps, we internalize the Transcendent All-Encompassing eyes.
>
> Kindling of the *Menorah* brings about a "lightening" of God's Presence, which in turn kindles and enraptures the Heart, so that the flame of the Heart continually ascends as an unceasing sacrifice to the Creator of light. How can this state be achieved? By sanctifying the seven organs of the Face signified by the seven branches of the *Menorah,* one "rouses the Divine flow" and makes the whole Face a mirror for that light.
>
> When all parts of the face, ears, mouth, eyes, and nose are sanctified they become receptacles for the channel of the "face-to-face" encounter. Then the seven parts of the Face—the seven Lamps of the *Menorah,* are kindled opposite the *Shekhinah,* as conductors for the *Shekhinah.* [30]

The greatest light that God prepared for the righteous is not an external illumination, but the radiance that is emitted by that human being's own goodness and sweetness of disposition.

"A man's wisdom lights up his face" (Ecclesiastes 8:1). The light on a Man's Face is the closest we know of God, followed closely by the light of Jerusalem.

> Said R. Eliezer: "Even for the sake of one *Tzaddik* (good person) the world was created. As it is said: *And God saw the light that it was good.* And 'good' does not mean anything but the goodness to be found in a good person. As it is said: *Say of the righteous, 'O how Good!'*" [*Yalkut Shimoni* 1:5]

Light and *man* and *The Good* are interchangeable terms, for the sake of which the World was created. What is the power of the *Tzaddik*? His goodness. And what is the essential light? The good in human nature.

Only when God produced "First Light" did He say, "How good!" What was "First Light" but the collectivity of human spirituality, as symbolized by the *Menorah* or the reflected Image of God. All humanity together mirror the Ten *Sefirot* and thus have the power to elicit from God the light of redemption.

All individuals also reflect in themselves the sum total of humanity and have *potentially* equal power. But the *Tzaddik possesses* it in fact. Thus, on the Festival of *Sukkot* there are seven invited guests – seven *Tzaddikim* standing for the seven days, Abraham, Isaac, Jacob, Joseph, Moses, Aaron, and David. These also stand for stages in which the *Shekhinah* approaches or recedes from our physical world. The sources speak of seven or ten Lamps, or *Tzaddikim*, who stage by stage bring Redemption. In the mirroring of this gradual process of redemption in the individual, we have the seven canopies. And the same Divine arithmetic is symbolized in music, in the chords of David's harp.

How many chords should there have been in the harp upon which the Levites played? R. Judah said: "There were seven chords in the harp, as may be inferred from the text, *Fullness of (soba) joy in Thy presence, sweet melodies in Thy right hand; In Thy Presence is fullness of joy, bliss in Thy right hand* (Psalm 16:11). Do not read *soba* but *sheva* (seven joys). Each chord is a separate joy.

"Similarly David says, *On a harp with seven chords do I praise Thee, because of Thy righteous ordinances* (Psalm 119:164). In the days of the Messiah it will be made of eight chords; for so in fact says David in the melody, *For the Leader; with string-music; on the Sheminith* – eight-stringed instrument (Psalm 6:1). In the time to come it will be made of ten strings; for it says, *O God, I will sing a new song unto Thee, upon a psaltery of ten strings* (Psalm 149:9)." [*Bamidbar Rabbah* 15:11]

What are these ten strings but ten *Sefirot*.

Rabbah in the name of R. Johanan further states: "The Holy One will make seven canopies for every righteous man; for it is said, *And the Lord will create over the whole habitation of Mount Zion, and over her assemblies, a cloud of smoke by day, and the shining of a flaming fire by night; for over all the glory shall be a canopy* (Isaiah 4:5). This teaches that the Holy One will make everyone a canopy coresponding to his glory."

Why is smoke required in a canopy? R. Hanina said, "Because whosoever is niggardly toward the scholars in this world will have his eyes filled with smoke in the world to come." Why is fire required in a canopy? R. Hanina said, "This teaches that each one will be burned by reason of (his envy of the superior) canopy of his friend. Alas, for such shame! Alas, for such reproach!" [*Nezikin* 11; *Baba Batra* 75a]

Who were the Ten Lights of the *Sefirot*? They were the ten *Tzaddikim* who give light to our world. All the *Sefirot* go to make up the light of the Image of God, the light of Man's Soul, and the Saints are demonstrations of the human soul in perfection. Says the Riziner, "The Hasidic Rebbes were the Lights of the world, rejoicing over the Giver of Light (God) and singing a song at the command of the light."[31]

According to a Sufi mystic, the seven Lamps of the *Menorah,* described as the seven "eyes of God" wandering about the whole earth, are seven saints who have given up their own subjective egos and let God see with their eyes.

R. Shimon bar Yohai says: "The faces of the *Tzaddikim* in the world-to-come appear as seven joys: as the sun and as the moon, as the firmament, as the stars, and as the lightnings and as lilies and as the *Menorah* of the Temple. Why do we learn 'as the sun and as the moon'? Because it is said: *Beautiful as the Moon, clear as the sun* (Song of Songs 6:10). Where 'as the firmament'? Because it is said: *And these who are wise shall shine as the glory of the firmament* (Daniel 12:3). Where 'as the stars'? Because it is said: *And those who turn many to righteousness shall be as the stars* (Daniel 12:3). Where 'as the lightnings'? Because it is said: *They shall dart as the lightnings* (Nahum 2:5). Where 'as lilies'? Because it is said: *For him who triumphs together with lilies* (Psalm 80:1). Where 'as the *Menorah* of the Temple'? Because it is said: '*And there are two olive trees beside it, one on the right of the bowl and the other on its left*' " (Zechariah 4:3). [*Sifre Devarim* 10]

The soul has been called a lamp: "The human soul is the lamp of God" (Proverbs 27:20) and the *Menorah* is the reservoir of souls. The *Menorah* is seen as the true image of God in the world, the human soul, the quintessence of the soul of Humanity, the reservoir of individual human souls. If the human soul is God's Lamp, then the *Menorah* is the image par excellence of the Divine (*Shekhinah*) transmitted through humanity (*Megillah* 21b).

The seven Lamps are seven levels of Divine Service. Aaron was given the task of kindling the *Menorah* because he is one of the seven shepherds who draw the Divine beasts to the reservoir of souls and he attracts a strong and fierce love for God.[32]

JERUSALEM IN THE TIME-TO-COME

The *Menorah* is the image of values shared between God and Israel. And ultimately the "rescue" of the fragmented sparks of the *Menorah* of the individual psyche and the various facets of the external world will lead to the redemption not only of the *Shekhinah* but also of Zion:

Rabbi said in the name of R. Johanan: "Jerusalem of the world to come will not be like Jerusalem of the present world. (To) Jerusalem of the present world, anyone who wishes goes up, but to that [the Jerusalem] of the world to come only those invited will go." [*Nezikin* 11; *Baba Batra* 75b]

R. Aha began his discourse with the verse, *I am the Lord, that is My name . . . And My glory I do not give to any creature created later* (Isaiah 42:8).
     The Holy One continues: *Neither do I endow anything tangible with the radiance of that glory which is Mine alone* (Isaiah 42:8). In all the creation which followed upon My creation of light there is

only one tangible thing that I endow with the radiance of My glory, even though from time to time you ascribe such radiance to other tangible things. Whom alone do I endow with the radiance of My glory? Zion: *Arise, shine, for the light which is thine alone is come* (Isaiah 60:1). [*Pesikta de Rav Kahana, Piske* 21, trans. Braude, pp. 338–339]

The *Menorah* is the complete picture of Jerusalem in the time-to-come.

(Because) you have made a candlestick for Me, I will cause it to shine for you seven-fold in the Messianic Age. Then, the *Midrash* continues, the Temple will rise up again, and the golden *Menorah* be restored to its place "to gladden Jerusalem." [*Bamidbar Rabbah* 15:10]

If you will be careful to light the lamps before Me I shall cause a great light to shine upon you in the Messianic era. Accordingly it says, *Arise, shine, for thy light is come. . . . And nations shall walk at thy light, and kings at the brightness of thy rising* (Isaiah 60:3). [*Bamidbar Rabbah* 15:2]

(It is written): *And I will make thy pinnacles of kadkod* (Isaiah 54:12). R. Samuel ben Nahmani said: "There is a dispute (as to the meaning of this word) between two angels in heaven–Gabriel and Michael. Others say: '(The dispute is between) two Amoraim in the West. (*Palestine*, which is west of Babylon, where the Babylonian Talmud was composed.)' One says: '(*Kadkod* means) onyx; and the others say, jasper.' The Holy One, blessed be He, said unto them: 'Let it be as this one (says) and as that one. (Let it be as both say. Let the pinnacles of Jerusalem be of onyx and of jasper.)'"

And thy gates of carbuncles (Isaiah 54:12) (is to be understood) as R. Johanan (explained) when he (once) sat and gave an exposition: "The Holy One will in time to come bring precious stones and pearls which are thirty (cubits) by thirty and will cut out from them (openings) ten (cubits) by thirty and will set them up in the gates of Jerusalem."

A certain student jeered at him: "(Jewels) of the size of a dove's egg are not to be found; are (jewels) of such a size to be

found?" After a time, his ship sailed out to sea (where) he saw
ministering angels engaged in cutting precious stones and pearls
which were thirty (cubits) by twenty. He said unto them: "For
whom are these?" They replied that the Holy One would in time
to come set them up in the gates of Jerusalem. (When) he came
(again) before R. Johanan he said unto him: "Expound, O my
master; it is becoming for you to expound; as you said, so have I
seen." He replied unto him: "*Raca* [Empty One], had you not
seen, would not you have believed? You are (then) sneering at the
words of the Sages!" He set his eyes on him and (the student)
turned into a heap of bones. [*Berakhot* 58a; *Shabbat* 34a; *Sanhedrin*
100a]

And I will lead you *komamiyut,* R. Meir says: "(It means) two
hundred cubits; twice the height of Adam (Adam's height originally extended from earth to heaven or from one end of the earth
to another, but after his sin was reduced to a mere one hundred
cubits.)" R. Judah says: "A hundred cubits; corresponding to the
(height of the) temple and its walls." For it is said: *We whose sons
are as plants grown up in their youth; whose daughters are as corner-
pillars carved after the fashion of the Temple* (Psalm 144:12). [*Nezikin*
11; *Baba Batra* 75a]

For with Thee is the fountain of life; in Thy light do we see light (Psalm
36:10). R. Johanan and Resh Lakish both made comments on this
verse, R. Johanan one and Resh Lakish two.

In his one comment, R. Johanan said: "The verse may be
understood using the parable of a man who was walking along
the road as the sun was setting. Someone came along and lighted
a lamp for him, and it went out. Then another came and lighted
a lamp for him, which also went out. Thereupon the man said:
'From now on I shall wait for the light of morning.'"

So, too, Israel said to the Holy One: "Master of Universes,
we made one lamp for Thee in the days of Moses, and it is now
extinguished.[33] We made ten in the days of Solomon, and they
also are no more. From now on we shall wait for Thy light: *In Thy
light do we (hope to) see light*" (Isaiah 60:1).[34]

Resh Lakish made two comments: To begin with, he said,
the verse may be illustrated by a parable of a king who had a

son. When the king invited guests to his palace, he said to his son: "My son, do you wish to dine with the guests?" The son replied: "No." The king then asked: "And with whom do you wish to dine?" The son replied: "Only with you."

Likewise the Holy One said to Israel: "My children, do you wish to dine with the nations?" They replied immediately: "Master of Universes. Even if the nations' portions are both tasty and generous, we have no wish for them. What do we want? Tasty and generous portions that come from Thee."

Resh Lakish's other comment: "The verse may be illustrated by a parable of a king who had a daughter. There came a man who asked for her hand in marriage, but he was not worthy of her. There came another who asked for her hand in marriage, and he too was not worthy of her. But when there came yet another who proved worthy of her and asked for her hand in marriage, the king said (to his daughter what a father usually says to a girl when she becomes engaged): "Rise, give light, for the light of your life has come." [*Pesikta de Rav Kahana, Piske* 21, trans. Braude, p. 339]

If the *Menorah* is an image of the *Shekhinah,* then it, like the Moon, is also the Jewish symbol of Beauty:

Like a shining lamp on the holy lampstand, so is a beautiful face on a stately figure. [*Ben Sira* 26:17]

Both the *Menorah* and the Tree (especially the olive tree) are an image of the *Tzaddik,* or the perfect image of a man. Why? The Tree is not so much the image of a man—any man, in his individual life—but the line, movement, and sap of the Tree are a picture of the force of the *Tzaddik,* as a whole piping system from God to man of Divine energies of life and death and regeneration.

He shall be like the tree planted by the dividing courses of the waters (that is, the rivers of Paradise. [Psalm 1:3]

And he shall be like a tree planted by the course of waters, which gives its fruit in the right time, and whose foliage does not wither and all that he does prospers. [Psalm 1:3]

The Paradise of the Lord is the tree of life, which are His saints. [*Berakhot* 1:2c]

The (*Tzaddik*) just will become like the *Menorah*. [*Pesikta de Rav Kahana* 28, ed. Buber; *Vayikra Rabbah* 30:2]

His (Israel's) beauty (in the world to come) will be like the olive tree. [*Targum* on Hosea 14:7]

The Tree (a vegetable *Menorah* or system of *Sefirot*) is greater than the individual; it is a whole refining ecological process whereby man, and even that part of the "Image of God" reflected in man, can develop and be progressively transformed:

R. Aha said: "Israel is likened to an olive tree – a leafy olive tree, fair with goodly fruit (Jeremiah 11:16). And the Holy One is likened to a lamp – *the lamp of the Lord is the spirit of man* (Proverbs 20:27). What use is made of oil? It is put into a lamp, and then the two together give light as though they were one. Hence the Holy One will say to Israel: 'My children, since My light is your light, and your light is My light, let us go together – you and I – and give light to Zion: *Arise, give light, for thy light has come.'*" (Isaiah 60:1). [*Pesikta de Rav Kahana, Piske* 21, trans. Braude, p. 340]

R. Hoshaia said in the name of R. Aphes: "Jerusalem is destined to become a beacon for the nations of the earth, and they will walk in her light. The proof is in the verse, *And nations shall walk at thy light,* etc." [*Pesikta de Rav Kahana, Piske* 21, trans. Braude, p. 340]

If light was God's first creation, and God Himself is Light, He nevertheless needs attentive furbishing and embellishing of the *Menorot* for His Light to shine through both in Jerusalem and in the Jerusalem of the human soul.

R. Judah said in the name of R. Zeira and R. Johanan said in the name of R. Shimon bar Yohai: "Great is the merit of maintaining the needy, since it causes the resurrection of the dead to come before its time. The woman of Zarapeth, because she maintained

Elijah, was rewarded by having her son brought to life. The Shunamite, because she gave food to Elisha, was rewarded by having her son brought to life." [*Shir HaShirim Rabbah* 11:5]

From here it seems that physical preparation of the Vessel invites the miraculous. But another rabbi embroiders on this comment by saying that these women did not even provide the physical.

Elijah used to take even his own lamps and his own wicks from place to place so as not to trouble other people. [*Shir HaShirim Rabbaah* 11:5]

To cap this, R. Judah says that when it came to it, he did not eat of the woman of Zarapeth's food, but she ate of his. She only had a crumb to eat; he blessed it, so it multiplied. What did she do to deserve having her child brought back from death. That "she gave him a good welcome and waited on him" was enough!

Only the proper attentiveness and preparation is required for the spirit to return, only the preparation of lamps, for light to spring up of itself.

NOTES

1. Author's retelling of a variant on *Shemot Rabbah* 1:26 in which *Keter* and a "gold vessel" are telescoped into one.
2. In Aramaic, Rabbi Isaac's name is *Saggi-Nehor*, "full of light." The whole term *Saggi-Nehor* has come to mean a euphemism—clothing a grim meaning in fine language—but with Rabbi Isaac it was the opposite. He was so full of light that he was described as "blind," as Isaac was said to have been blinded not only by the flames of the sacrifice of which he was almost a part, but by the glory of the *Shekhinah* that appeared to him on that occasion. Some types of darkness or blindness are indications of an excess of light.

   Rabbi Isaac the Blind was the son of Rabbi Abraham ben David of Posquières (the RaBaD, c. 1120–1198), the spiritual leader of Provence Jewry. He and his son were links in a chain of Kabbalists in Provence.

3. R. Isaac the Blind, *Commentary on Sefer Yetzirah,* quoted in Idel, *New Perspectives,* p. 137.

4. "R. Yohanan bar Nappaha explained that Moshe heard God say, 'Let them make Me a Sanctuary.' Immediately he became very worried about how God could be confined within the four walls of a Tabernacle. But the Holy One reassured him: 'I shall descend and contract My *Shekhinah* between (the planks of the Tabernacle) down below.'" Raphael Patai, *The Hebrew Goddess* (New York: Behrman House, 1978), p. 111.

5. Rav Kuk's view of art was obviously based on a combination of the views of Plato and Aristotle. The greatest religious thinkers have been wary of artists and poets in a world of pure truth and justice. Plato would have had poets banished from his Republic because their songs have power to corrupt and cloud the soul. Artistic imagery is seen as lying "imitations" of an imitation. And yet, both Plato and Aristotle saw that the artistic imagination could represent a higher truth than the illusory world of reality. See Abraham Isaac Kuk, *Lights of Holiness* [*Orot Ha-Kodesh*] (Jerusalem: Mossad Harav Kuk, 1938).

6. *Bosi l'Gani,* p. 70.

7. *Jewish Chronicle* (London: 13 September, 1935).

8. Rav Abraham Isaac Kuk, Public Affairs letter 24, "Selected Letters," in *Igrot ha-Re'iyah, Igrot* 158, trans. Tzvi Feldman (Israel: Maale Adumin, 1986), pp. 190–198.

9. Ibid.

10. Ibid.

11. *Antiquities,* 5.3, 7.5.

12. Philo, *The Decalogue,* tr. F. H. Colson (Cambridge, MA: Harvard University Press, 1937), vol. 7, pp. 39–41.

13. "*Ye shall not make with me* (Exodus 20:23), which we interpret, *Ye shall not make the likeness of my attendants.*" Abaye replied: "The Torah forbade only those attendants of which it is possible to make copies ('like them,' out of the same or other materials); as it has been taught: A man may not make a house in the form of the Temple, or a hall in the form of the Temple hall, or a court corresponding to the Temple court, or a table corresponding to the (sacred) table or a candlestick corresponding to the (sacred) candlestick, but he may make one (*Rosh Hashanah* 24b) with five or six or eight lamps, but with seven he should not make, even of

other metals (since a candlestick of other metal besides gold was used in the Temple when gold was too expensive)" (*Menahot* 5:29). R. Jose ben Judah said: "He should not make one even of wood, this being the way in which the kings of the house of the Hasmoneans made it (when they first recaptured the Temple from the Syrians, and were still too poor to provide a gold candlestick)." They said to him: "Can you adduce this as a proof? The spits (the unadorned branches of the candlestick) were of iron and they overlaid them with tin. When they grew richer they made them of silver. When they grew richer still, they made them of gold." [*Rosh Hashanah* 24a–b]

14. See Idel, *New Perspectives,* p. 187.

15. Based on Aryeh Kaplan, *Meditations and Kabbalah* (New York: Samuel Weiser, 1982), pp. 210–211.

16. Ibid., p. 182.

17. Ashlag, *Emanations,* vol. I, p. 78.

18. Eliezer Azikri, thirteenth-century Kabbalist, quoted in "*Deveikut,* or Communion With God," in Scholem, *Messianic Idea,* p. 207.

19. S. A. Horodetzky, *Torat ha-Maggid Mezeritch we-Sichotav* 23.5 (Berlin, 1923) quoted in Newman, *Hasidic Anthology,* p. 159.

20. Both Moses de Leon and the *Zohar* reflect on the dynamism of the *Sefirot* through focusing on the motion of the eye when it is closed, generating inner light and color.

21. Moses de Leon compares contemplation to "the light emerging from the shaking of the water in a dish, since that light shines in one place and immediately leaves it and it returns and shines in another place. When man already thinks that he has already grasped this light, it immediately flees from this place and returns to appear again in another place and man runs after it to comprehend it, but he does not comprehend . . . so is it in this place which is the beginning of the emanations." (Unknown work of de Leon, identified in Gershom Scholem, *Eine unbekannte mystische Schrift des Mose de Leon, Monatschrift für Geschichte und Wissenschaft des Judentums* [1927], 71:109–123, quoted in Idel, *New Perspectives,* pp. 140–141, 342 n. 230.)

"And if you will take a dish with water to the eye of the sun, and you will shake it, you will see on the wall the splendor of the mirrors which are shining, they run and return and no one is able to fix them, because of the speed of their movement to and fro."

(Moses de Leon, *Shekel Hakodesh* [London: 1911], p. 113, quoted in Idel, *New Perspectives,* p. 140.)

22. Rabbi Azriel of Gerona, "Explanation of the Ten *Sefirot,*" in Meir Ibn Gabbai's *Sefer Derekh Emunah,* quoted in *The Early Kabbalah,* ed. Joseph Dan (New York: Paulist Press, 1986), p. 94.
23. Ramak (R. Moshe Cordovero), *Pardes Rimmonim, Meditations and Kabbalah,* trans. Aryeh Kaplan (New York: Weiser, 1982).
24. Cordovero, *Orchard of Pomegranates,* p. 32. The "Large Face" is the Ancient of Days. The "Small Face" is the son, the reflection of the "Ancient of Days," the "Impatient One," the *Zeir Anpin,* the angry face of reality and suffering, the developing God, Bridegroom of the *Shekhinah,* just as man is the image of God, just as a lover is an image of his love, just as Moshe saw God "face-to-face," just as *Yisrael,* literally, the "Prince of God," is the witness and bearer to God's Name in the world, a *Menorah* testifying to His Presence.
25. See Chapters 4 and 6.
26. Author's retelling of a story by R. Nachman of Bratzlav.
27. *Sifat Emet,* based on the *Kedushat Levi.*
28. Newman, *Hasidic Anthology,* p. 173.
29. Ibid., pp. 35–42.
30. Based on Rabbi Shneor Zalman of Liadi, *Likkutei Torah* on *Beha'alotekha* (New York: Ozar Hasidim, 1965).
31. Newman, *Hasidic Anthology,* p. 55.
32. R. Shneor Zalman of Liadi, *Likkutei Torah* on *Beha'alotekha.*
33. This is an example of synechdoche, the part taken as representative of the whole. In fact, the Temple was one huge *Menorah* casting a beacon of light for all nations in the world.
34. This seems to imply that the *Menorah* of the third Temple will be kindled by God. See p. 415.

GLOSSARY

Adam Kadmon: Primordial man, the connection between God's Unknown Essence (*Ein-Sof*) and the primordial space or *Tzimtzum*; in the Lurianic system, a realm above the four worlds of *Atzilut, Beri'ah, Yetzirah,* and *Asiyah.*

Aggadata: Homiletic expositions of the Talmud.

Akedah: The "binding" of Isaac, signifying Abraham's readiness to sacrifice his son at God's command.

Al ha-Nissim: Insertion in the "Standing Prayer" and in Grace after Meals, thanking God for miracles experienced during *Purim* and *Hanukkah.*

Aliyah: Ascent of the soul and of the *Shekhinah* to God; also, a Jew's return to Israel.

Amidah: The Eighteen Blessings recited three times a day while standing; after the *Shema*, possibly the most important prayer in Judaism.

Amora: Rabbi responsible for the *Gemara,* the last literary layer of the Talmud, 200–550 C.E.

Anshe Knesset ha-Gedolah: Men of the Great Assembly, consisting of 120 members; judicial body of the second Temple.

Arikh Anpin (the "Long Face"): "The Long-suffering One," referring to *Keter,* or God Himself.

Asiyah: The World of Making; the lowest of the four worlds between the *Ein-Sof* and our earthly cosmos, according to Cordovero and the Kabbalists of Safed; a post-Zoharic concept.

Atarah: Diadem, a name for the Community of Israel; the silver braiding of the *Tallit.*

Atzilut: The World of Emanation, the highest transcendental world above the worlds of creation, formation, and making—*Beri'ah, Yetzirah,* and *Asiyah.*

Baal Shem Tov (Besht) (ca. 1700–1760): Founder of modern Hasidism.

Bahir: The Book of Illumination, attributed to Rabbi Nehunia ben HaKahana (first century), but written probably during the twelfth century.

Bat Kol (the daughter of a voice): Divine inspiration or the voice of the *Shekhinah*; earliest feminine usage for the *Shekhinah* in *Midrash.*

Batiah (daughter of God): Name of the Egyptian Princess who saved Moses as a baby and who married Solomon; also a name of the *Shekhinah.*

Bet: Second letter of the Hebrew alphabet.

Bet ha-Mikdash: The Holy Temple.

Bikkurim: First fruits brought on the festival of *Shavuot*; name of a tractate in the Talmud.

Binah (Understanding): The third *Sefirah*, the Supernal Mother; God's feminine aspect in the realm of transcendence located at the top of the left column of the *Sefirotic* tree.

Birkat ha-Hammah: The Blessing of the Sun, said every cycle of 28 years.

Breaking of the Vessels (*Shivirat ha-kelim*): Disruption of the channels between God and creation.

Chilozan: Fish that gives a blue dye, used in the fringes of the *Tallit*.

Curtain: The means by which the Queen (*Malkhut*) has shut herself off from the Divine Light to reverse the process of emanation.

Deveikut: Attachment or communion with God.

Diaspora: Greek term for *dispersion*, referring to Jews and Jewish communities outside the Land of Israel.

Ein-Sof: God's Infinite and Unknown Essence.

Elul: The sixth month of the Hebrew year preceding the Days of Awe.

Elohim: The aspect of God signifying stern judgment; the feminine attribute of limitation.

Etrog: Citron, orblike fruit used with the palm branch on *Sukkot*; also signifies feminine beauty.

Evil Eye: The destructive power of the eye of a jealous person.

Gehinnom (Valley of Hinnom): A valley near Jerusalem; Jewish name for Hell.

Hamsa: Amuletic hand prevalent among Arabs and Jews in North Africa and Mediterranean lands.

Gelt: Spending money given to children on *Hanukkah*.

Gemara: Commentary on the laws of the *Mishnah*. The *Mishnah* and the *Gemara* comprise the Talmud.

Gematria: The system of numerical value assigned to each Hebrew letter, in which the sum of letters in words are said to reveal hidden connections.

Halakhah (the Way): The Jewish legal system.

Hammah: A name for the Sun meaning "heat."

Hanukkah: Feast of Lights.

Hanukkiyah: Modern Hebrew word for the *Hanukkah Menorah*.

Hasmonean: Maccabee.

Havdalah (separation): Ceremony marking the transition between the end of Sabbath and religious festivals and the beginning of the ordinary weekdays.

Heh: The fifth letter of the Hebrew alphabet; also an interrogative in Hebrew; the feminine ending with an opening that accepts light and the life-force.

Histalkut: Concentration and reintegration of Divine forces.

Hitpashtut: Spreading out, emanation.

Hodesh: The moon; Hebrew word for month and renewal.

Hokhmah (Wisdom): The second *Sefirah* at the top of the right column of the *Sefirotic* tree.

Iyyun Circle: An early group of Kabbalists who flourished in southern Europe, possibly in southern France, in the thirteenth century. Named after its most famous work, the *Sefer ha-Iyyun* (Book of Contemplation). A mysticism different from *Sefirotic Kabbalah*, it is based on thirteen Divine Attributes, not ten, and on the neo-Platonic Chariot and Palace mysteries.

Judea Resurrecta: Judea Restored.

Judenstern (Jewish Star): A special star-embellished Sabbath lamp prevalent in Germany in the late Middle Ages.

Kabbalah: A tradition, specifically the mystical tradition; receptivity.

Kaddish: Mourners' Prayer sanctifying God.

Kallah: Bride; a term for *Shekhinah* and *Shabbat*.

Kavannah: Intention (pl. *Kavannot*).

Kavod: (the Glory): God's Name or how He is known in the world, depicted by Ezekiel as a human-type figure on the Celestial Throne; sometimes synonymous with the *Shekhinah* and therefore feminine.

Kedushah: Sanctifying Prayer of God's Glory inserted in the "Standing Prayer."

Kedushat Levi: Levi Yitzhak of Berdichev, the disciple of the *Mezritcher Maggid*.

Keseh (concealment): A name for *Rosh Hashanah*, the only Jewish festival celebrated when the Moon is at her lowest ebb.

Keter (crown): Name of the Highest *Sefirah* (emanation) within the *Sefirotic* tree, usually referring to God Himself, or the first appearance of God from the *Ein-Sof*, His Unknown Essence.

Keter Elyon: The Supreme Crown, referring to God and to the Highest *Sefirah*.

Kiddush: Blessing of sanctification over wine on the Sabbath and festivals.

Kislev: Eighth month of the Hebrew year and season of *Hanukkah*.

Klippah: Membrane or shell on sparks of Divine Light, externalizing evil (pl. *Klippot*).

Knesset (The Israeli Parliament): Gathering or collectivity, as in *Knesset Yisrael,* the Collectivity of Israel; a feminine entity sometimes equated with the *Shekhinah*.

Knesset Ha-Gedolah: Parliament of the Second Temple, comprised of 120 members.

Kohanim: Jews of priestly descent through the family of Aaron.

Lekha Dodi: Sabbath-welcoming song, written by Rabbi Solomon Alkabetz (1505–1584).

Levanah: The moon in her milky white radiance.

Levites: Belonging to the priestly tribe of Levi.

Lo sivaru aish: Prohibition against kindling fire on the Sabbath; the most particularized of the Sabbath prohibitions.

Luria, Rabbi Isaac: Leading Kabbalist of Safed (1534–1572); originator of the concepts of *Tzimtzum, Breaking of the Vessels*, the exile of the *Shekhinah*, and of *Tikkun*.

Lulav: Palm branch, one of the four plants used in the festival of *Sukkot*.

The L'Vush (the Garment): Pen name and six-volume masterpiece of R. Mordecai Yaffe (1535–1612).

Malkhut (Kingdom or Queen): The tenth and lowest Kingship or emanation, typified as feminine and personified as the *Shekhinah*, Rachel, or *Knesset Yisrael*.

Ma'ariv: The Evening Prayer.

Ma'aseh: A story.

Maccabees: Hasmonean heroes at the time of *Hanukkah*.

Magen David: "Shield of David" originally shaped like a *Menorah* but associated with the hexagram in the sixth century. This "star" shape was only recently chosen as a Jewish symbol, and it is associated with the rise of the State of Israel.

Maggid of Mezeritch (Dov Baer, d. 1772): Storyteller, preacher, most prominent disciple of the Baal Shem Tov.

Ma'oz Tzur (Rock of Ages): Song sung over the kindling of the *Hanukkah* lights.

Marheshvan (Heshvan): The eighth month of the Hebrew year.

Mashpiah: The active partner, the Giver, the one who influences.

Matrona: Mother aspect of God.

Menorah: The seven-branched candelabra of Temple days and the eight-branched candelabra of *Hanukkah*.

Merkavah (chariot): A concept of the Talmudic mystics, based on the visions of Ezekiel, who envisioned the Divine realm as a series of chambers of palaces and chariots.

Mesuhsah (transparent light): One of the three additional Higher lights of pseudo-Hai HaGaon concealed in the "Root of Roots," either in *Keter* or in the *Ein-Sof*.

Metatron: A transfiguration of Enoch whose body metamorphosed into pure fire and whose spirit transformed into an angel who mediates between God and man. His name is derived from *mater* or *matrona*, the mother aspect of God.

Mezuzah: Cylindrical box on right door post containing special verses that affirm faith in God and protect against evil influences.

Midrash: Rabbinic compilation of biblical interpretations that elucidate legal points and teach moral lessons.

Mikabel: The Receiver, usually feminine.

Mikveh: Body of fresh water used for purification by ritual immersion.

Minhah: The Afternoon Prayer.

Mishkan: Sanctuary, dwelling place of the *Shekhinah* in the desert.

Mishnah (repetition or learning): Earliest code of Jewish law, ca. 200 C.E., codified by Judah the Prince.

Mitzvah (commandment): Divine mandates in Jewish law; also, benevolent acts (pl. *Mitzvot*).

Mizrach: East; a wallmarker pointing in the direction of the Temple site.

Mudra (muzra): Sanskrit seal of imprinted code of hand positions reenacting episodes in the life of Buddha; in Tantra *Sakti*, the feminine counterpart of the god.

Muktzah: Category of objects forbidden to be used or even touched on *Shabbat*.

Musaf: The Additional Prayer said on the Sabbath and Festivals and on *Rosh Hodesh*.

Nachmanides: Moses ben Nachman; also known as Nachmani and the Ramban (1194–1270); Sephardic philosopher, Kabbalist, and commentator.

Nefesh (life): The lowest (animal) grade of soul, said to be centered in the blood and the belly.

Ne'ilah: Closing service of *Yom Kippur* that seals the judgment; a name for the *Shekhinah*.

Ner: Lamp or candles (pl. *Nerot*).

Ner Tamid: The Eternal Light introduced in the sixteenth century as a special feature of the interior of the synagogue. It arose from the idea that the lights of the *Menorah* were kindled continuously.

Ner Huppah: Bridal tapers used in the procession circling the Bride to light up her face and make certain she is the right woman.

Neshamah: Higher soul.

Neshamah Yeterah: Additional soul of *Shabbat*.

Neshamah-Ruah: Marriage of male and female components of the soul, which creates a *nur*, a lamp.

Nisan: the first month of Spring and time of Passover.

Or: Light (pl. *orot*).

Oral Torah: The Oral Law developed by the Rabbis out of the Written Law, the Five Books of Moses, consisting of the Talmud, *Mishnah, Gemara*, and the responsa on points of *halakhah*; also includes *Midrash*, the more experiential part of the Jewish heritage.

Partzuf (face or facet of God): Representation of a stage in the reintegration of the Divine Image that constitutes *Tikkun* (pl. *Partzufin*).

Pesah (Passover): Spring festival beginning on the fifteenth of Nisan and commemorating the Exodus of Israelites from Egypt; the biblical recounting of the avenging angel who kills the Egyptian first-born but "passes over" the homes of Israelites, whose children and animals were spared.

Penimi Kadmon (inner primordial light): According to Pseudo-Hai HaGaon, the highest of the three hidden roots or lights concealed in the *Ein-Sof*.

Pharisees: Rabbis in conflict with the Sadducees; Second Temple antihierarchical rabbinic movement, which championed the pursuit of holiness for ordinary people through observance of the Torah.

Piyyut: Religious poem, usually from the Middle Ages.

Rambam: Acronym for Rabbi Moses ben Maimon (Maimonides) (1135–1204); rabbinic authority, philosopher, royal physician, and codifier.

Rashi: Rabbi Solomon ben Isaac, foremost Bible commentator who lived in Troyes, France, in the twelfth century.

Returning Light: Reversal of the light of the emanations to its source in the *Ein-Sof*.

River Nehar Denur: River of Flame.

Rosh Hodesh: New Month Festival.

Rosh Hashanah: New Year.

Rotsen: (God's) Will.

Ruach: Breath; middle grade of the soul.

Sadducees: Priestly hierarchy; sect of the latter half of the second Temple, ca. 200 B.C.E.; wealthy elite of priests and aristocrats who dominated Temple worship and the rule of the *Sanhedrin.*

Sandalphon: One of the most exalted angels (Ezekiel 1:15), mediating between earth and heaven; a transfiguration of Elijah.

Sanhedrin: Assembly of scholars that served as the supreme political, religious, and judicial body in Palestine during the Roman period.

Sefirot: The ten emanations or Divine Powers that constitute the revealed aspects of God; term first found in the *Sefer Yetzirah,* which refers to *Sefirot Belimah,* closed *Sefirot.*

Sifat Emet: R. Yehudah Aryeh Leib (1847–1905), first Rabbi of Ger, an important Hasidic thinker.

Idra Zutta (the Lesser Assembly): Conclusion of the *Zohar* (III: 287b–296b) that describes the death scene of R. Shimon bar Yohai and his last words to his followers. As a companion discourse to the death of Moshe, the early Kabbalists called it *Idra de-Ha'azinu.*

Sephardim: Jews from Spain and Portugal and their descendants, including Jews from the Middle East, North Africa, Italy, and Greece.

Serugin: Micrography, miniature Hebrew script.

Shaar Hashamayyim: Heaven's Gate, Jerusalem.

Shaharit: The Morning Prayer.

Shaddai: The Almighty; the God who sets limits to the proliferation of nature.

Shaken: Neighbor or dwelling; root of the word *Shekhinah.*

Shalom Bayyit: Domestic harmony.

Shaked (almond): The *Menorah*'s resemblance to an almond tree; also, God's watchfulness.

Shammas: Beadle in a synagogue; ninth servitor-light on the *Hanukkah Menorah*, used to kindle the other eight, which are holy and not to be touched.

Shammash: A name for the Sun in His capacity as God's Great Servant.

Sheheheyanu: Blessing thanking God for keeping us in life and enabling us to make the blessing; also recited while savoring a new experience.

Shekhinah: The Divine Presence in the natural world, typified as feminine.

Shema: The most familiar of all prayers recited by Jews, declaring the unity of God.

Shemoi: God's name.

Shiviti: A decorative plaque placed on the eastern wall to indicate the orientation of prayer toward Jerusalem.

Siddur: Prayer book of Ashkenazic Jews.

Shofar: Ram's horn stirring Jews to repentance during *Elul*, the month preceding *Rosh Hashanah* and the period of *Yomim Noraim*; also sounded on the New Moon and other religious occasions.

Shulkhan Arukh: The "Prepared Table"; Code of Jewish law by Joseph Karo, a 16th-century Kabbalist.

Sifre: A rabbinic commentary on Numbers and Deuteronomy.

Simhat Torah (rejoicing with the Torah): The holiday marking the annual completion of reading the Torah in the synagogue.

Soheret: The Precious Stone bartered in the market place; also, the *Shekhinah*.

Soferim: Scribes; also, name of minor talmudic tractate.

Sukkah: Open-air booth covered with branches commemorating the Israelites' faith during their wanderings in the desert.

Sukkot: Feast of Tabernacles celebrated after the "Days of Awe" in *Tishri*, the seventh month of the Hebrew year.

Talmud: Code of Jewish law, lore, philosophy, and ethics compiled between 200 and 500 C.E. in Palestine and Babylonia. The two centers, Babylon and Jerusalem, each produced a codex.

Tallit: Prayer shawl with *Tzitzit* (fringes) attached to the four corners and worn during the morning prayers.

Tallit Katan: A small, four-cornered undergarment with fringes.

Tanna: Mishnaic teacher, 400 B.C.E.–200 C.E.

Tanya: The "Bible" of the Lubavitch *Hasidim* (*Likkutei Amarim*) by the First Lubavitcher Rebbe, Rabbi Shneor Zalman of Liadi.

Tashlikh: Ceremony casting sins into fresh water on *Rosh Hashanah*.

Tefillah: Prayer.

Tefillin: Phylacteries worn by male Jews on the head and the arm during weekday morning prayers. In them is handwritten parchment with verses from Exodus 13:1–10, Exodus 13:11–16, Deuteronomy 6:4–9, and Deuteronomy 11:13–21.

Tetragrammaton: The 42-letter name of God.

Tevet: The tenth month of the Hebrew year.

Tiferet (Splendor): The *Sefirah* of Beauty and physical attraction, typified as masculine, which emits light and life-force into the physical realm of *Malkhut*. The sixth *Sefirah*, linked to Jacob, is in the middle of the central column of the *Sefirot*.

Tihelet: The blue of the *tzitzit* (fringes).

Tikkun: Redemption and "fixing" of the world; reintegration of the fragments of the *Shekhinah* Light, according to Lurianic *Kabbalah*.

Torah: Divine Wisdom, the Sophia; also, Revelation of the Divine Law, the Written Torah, and the Oral Torah.

Tzaddik: Saint; man in his perfect state who maintains the harmony of Creation and of God within Creation.

Tzayyar: Artist, painter.

Tzel: Shadow or astral body.

Tzimtzum: Self-contraction of God's light, creating a void to allow Creation to appear.

Tzinor: Vessel.

Tzitzit: Ritual fringes on the four corners of the *Tallit*.

Urim and Tummim: The *ephod* or apronlike garment of the High Priest set with twelve precious stones and engraved with the names of the twelve tribes.

Vav: Sixth letter of the Hebrew alphabet; phallic third letter of the Divine Name leading into the feminine opening of the physical world.

Yahrzeit: Annual commemoration of death.

Yedidyah: Beloved of God, a name of King Solomon.

Yehidah: The highest root of the five scales of the soul, buried alone within the Divine.

Yerah: Wanderer, a name for the Moon.

Yesod: The ninth *Sefirah*, the phallic *Vav* of the Divine Name, leading into the female opening of *Malkhut*.

Yod: The tenth number of the Hebrew alphabet; also the Ten *Sefirot* within God Himself and within man.

Yom Kippur: Day of Atonement.

Yomim Noraim: The Days of Awe; the season that includes *Rosh Hashanah*, the Ten Days of Penitence, and *Yom Kippur*.

Zah: A quality of crystal clear light, one of the three additional Upper Lights of Pseudo-Hai HaGaon rooted in either *Keter* or the *Ein-Sof*.

Ze'ir Anpin (the "Short Face"): The "Impatient One," God in immanence descending to *Malkhut*.

Zohar: The Book of Splendor; the Bible of *Kabbalah*, purportedly written by R. Shimon bar Yohai during the second century C.E. but pinpointed by scholars as having been written down, possibly by Moses de Leon, in the thirteenth century.

BIBLIOGRAPHY

Abrahams, I. (1896). *Jewish Life in the Middle Ages.* London: E. Goldston.
_____ (1934). *Festival Studies: Being Thoughts on the Jewish Year.* London: E. Goldston.
Akiva ben Joseph (1970). *Sefer Yetzirah (Book of Formation).* Trans. K. Stenring. New York: Ktav.
Albeck, H., and Yalon, H., eds. (1952–1956). *Shishah Sidrei Mishnah.* 6 vols. Jerusalem: Bialik Institute.
Alnaqua, I. ben Joseph (1929). *Menorat Ha-Maor.* Parts 1–4. Ed. H. G. Enelow. New York: Bloch.
Alstat, P. (1972). Lights are kindled in Bergen-Belsen. *American Examiner/ The Jewish Week.* 30 Nov.–6 Dec.
Altmann, A. (1943). Gnostic themes in rabbinic cosmology. In *Essays in Honor of J. H. Hertz,* ed. I. Epstein, p. 121. London: E. Goldston.
Arendt, H. (1958). *The Human Condition.* New York: Doubleday.
Ashlag, Y. L. (1943). *Talmud Eser Sefirot.* New York: The Kabbalah Foundation.
_____ (1945–1953). *HaZohar im Sulam.* 18 vols. Jerusalem.
_____ (1969). *The Kabbalah: A Study of the Ten Luminous Emanations of Rabbi Isaac Luria.* Trans. L. I. Krakovsky. Jerusalem: Research Center of Kabbalah.

—— (1970). *Introduction to the Zohar.* Vol. 1. Jerusalem: Research Center of Kabbalah.

Baal Shem Tov (Besht) (1791). Letter to Rabbi Gershon of Kutov, Koretz (Trans. and ed. Norman Lamm). *Tradition* 14:110–125.

Babylonian Talmud (1886). Vilna: Romm.

Bahya ben Asher (1964). *Kitvei HaRamban.* 2 vols. Ed. C. D. Chavel. Jerusalem: Mossad Harav Kook.

Barash, A. (1943). *Menorat Ha-Zahav (The Golden Candelabrum).* Tel Aviv: Masadah Press.

Bension, A. (1932). *The Zohar in Moslem and Christian Spain.* New York: Hermon Press, 1974.

Ben Adret, S. Anonymous commentary on the ten *sefirot.* MS. British Library 755, fol. 93b. MS. Berlin 122, fol. 96a.

Berditchevsky, M. J. ben Gorion (1966). *Mimekor Yisrael.* Tel Aviv: Dvir.

Bialik, C. N., and Ravnitzky, J. C. (1907). *Sefer Aggadah.* 2 vols. Tel Aviv: Dvir, 1960.

Blatter, J., and Milton, S. (1981). *Art of the Holocaust.* New York: Routledge and Kegan Paul.

Braude, W. G., trans. (1959). *Midrash on Psalms.* 2 vols. New Haven: Yale University Press.

—— (1968). *Pesikta Rabbati.* 2 vols. New Haven: Yale University Press.

—— (1975). *Pesikta de Rav Kahana.* Philadelphia: Jewish Publication Society.

—— (1981). *Tanna de Vei Eliyahu.* Philadelphia: Jewish Publication Society.

Buber, S., ed. (1885). *Midrash Tanhuma.* Vilna.

—— (1891). *Midrash Tehillim (Schocher Tov).* Vilna.

—— (1893). *Midrash Mishle (Shocher Tov).* Lemberg.

Budge, E., and Wallis, A. (1978). *Amulets and Superstitions.* New York: Dover Books.

Campbell, J. (1956). *The Hero with a Thousand Faces.* Bollingen Series, no. 17. Princeton: Princeton University Press.

—— (1975). *The Masks of God: Creative Mythology.* New York: Penguin-Viking, 1978.

Cassirer, E. (1953). *Language and Myth.* Trans. S. K. Langer. New York: Dover Books.

Charles, R. H., ed. (1913). *The Apocrypha and Pseudepigrapha of the Old*

Testament. Oxford, England: Clarendon Press. (The Book of Adam and Eve, vol. 1, pp. 123–154; The Book of Wisdom of Ben Sira, vol. 1, pp. 268–517. Greek Apocalypse of Baruch, vol. 2, pp. 527–541. Wisdom of Solomon, vol. 1, pp. 518–568.)

Cohen, A., trans. (1965). *Talmud: Minor Tractates, Massektoth Ketannoth, Derekh Eretz Zuta.* London: Soncino Press.

Corbin, H. (1978). *The Men of Light in Iranian Sufism.* Boulder, CO: Shambhala.

Cordovero, M. (The *Ramak*) (1591). *Pardes Rimmonim.*

_____ (1976). *The Palm Tree of Deborah.* Trans. L. Jacobs. New York: Sepher-Hermon Press.

Dan, J. (1980). *Kabbalat R. Asher Ben David: Interpretation of the Tetragrammaton. (Shem Hamiforash).* A seminar pamphlet. Jerusalem: Hebrew University.

Dan, J., and Kiener, R. C. (1986). *The Early Kabbalah.* Ramsey, NJ: Paulist Press.

David ben Yehuda he-Hasid (1982). *The Book of Mirrors (Sefer Mar'ot ha-Zove'ot).* Ed. D. C. Matt, Brown Judaic Studies. Chico, CA: Scholars Press.

Dawood, N. J., trans. (1974). *Koran.* Edinburgh, Scotland: Harmondsworth.

Dubos, R. (1968). *So Human an Animal.* New York: Scribner's.

_____ (1981). *Celebrations of Life.* New York: McGraw-Hill.

Eban, A. (1968). *My People: The Story of the Jews.* New York: Random House, 1984.

Eisenstein, J. D., ed. (1915). *Otzar Midrashim.* 2 vols. New York: Eisenstein.

Elimelekh, R. of Lizhensk (1867). *Noam Elimelekh.* Lemberg.

Enelow, H. G. (1927). *Midrash Hashem* quotations in Alnaqua's *Menorat Ha-Maor. Hebrew Union College Annual* 4:311–343.

Epstein, I., ed. (1948). *Talmud.* London: Soncino Press.

Freedman, H., and Simon, M., trans. and ed. (1959). *Midrash Rabbah.* 10 vols. London: Soncino Press.

Friedlander, G., trans. (1852). Pirke de Rabbi Eliezer. New York: Sepher Hermon, 1965.

Friedmann, M., ed. (1902). *Tanna de Vei Eliyahu.* Vienna:

Ganzfried, S. (1961). *Code of Jewish Law (Kitzur Shulkan Arukh).* Vol. 2. Trans. H. E. Goldin. New York: Hebrew Publishing Company.

Gikatilla, J. (1976). *Sha'are Orah*. Ed. J. Ben-Shlomo. Jerusalem: Mossad Harav Kuk.

Ginzberg, L. (1909). *The Legends of the Jews*. 7 vols. Trans. H. Szold. Philadelphia: Jewish Publication Society.

Goldshmidt, L., ed. (1894). *Baraita de-Ma'aseh Bereishit*. Trans. from the Ethiopian into Aramaico Argentorati.

Gollancz, H. (1912). *The Book of Protection*. London: Oxford University Press.

Goodenough, E. R. (1954). *Jewish Symbols in the Greco-Roman Period*. Vol. 4. New York: Pantheon.

Goodman, P. (1976). *Hanukkah Anthology*. Philadelphia: Jewish Publication Society.

Gottlieb, W. (1948). *From Days of Old (Mi'Mei Kedem): Stories and Sayings from Talmud and Midrash*. London: Central Council of Jewish Religious Education in the United Kingdom.

Green, A. (1987). The Song of Songs in early Jewish mysticism. *Orim* 2: 49–62.

Green, A., and Holtz, B. (1977). *Your Word Is Fire*. Leiden: E. J. Brill.

Gruenwald, I. (1980). *Apocalyptic and Merkavah Mysticism*. Leiden: E. J. Brill.

Grunwald, M. (1904). Magen David. In *The Jewish Encyclopaedia*, vol. 3. ed. I. Singer, p. 202. New York: Funk & Wagnalls.

Hacohen, S., and Shragai, E. (1950). *Perakim le-Hanukkah*. Israel: Israel Military Rabbinate, Israel Defense Forces.

Halevi, Y. (1924). *Selected Poems*. Trans. N. Salaman. Philadelphia: Jewish Publication Society.

Handelman, S. A. (1982). *The Slayers of Moses: The Emergence of Rabbinic Interpretation in Modern Literary Theory*. Albany, NY: State University of New York Press.

Hanukkah. In *Encyclopaedia Judaica*, vol. 7, pp. 1280–1286. New York: Macmillan, 1971.

Hartmann, G. H., and Budick, S. (1986). *Midrash and Literature*. New Haven: Yale University Press.

Hasmonean. In *Encyclopaedia Judaica*, vol. 7, pp. 1455–1459. New York: Macmillan, 1971.

Heinemann, J. (1970). *Drashot B'Tzibbur B'Tkufat Ha-Talmud*. Jerusalem: Mossad Bialik.

Herzl, T. (1925). *The Menorah* (trans. B. L. Pouzzner). *The Menorah Journal* 1:264–267.

Heschel, R. Abraham Joshua of Apt (1863). *Ohebh Yisra'el.* Zitomir.

Heschel, A. J. (1951). *The Sabbath: Its Meaning for Modern Man.* New York: Farrar, Straus and Giroux.

Hirsch, S. R. (1964). *The Pentateuch with Commentary.* 5 vols. Trans. I. Levy. London: Soncino Press.

Hoffman, E. (1981). *The Way of Splendor.* Boulder, CO: Shambhala.

Horodetsky, S. A., ed. (1920). *Shivhei Ha-Besht.* Tel-Aviv.

Horowitz, I. (1860). *Shne Luhot Ha-Brit (SHELAH).* 3 vols. Lemberg.

Ibn Gabbai, Meir (1560). *Tola'at Ya'akov.* Cracow: 1932.

_____ (1562:Padua). *Avodat Hakodesh.* Jerusalem: 1954.

_____ (1890). *Sefer Derekh Emunah.* Cracow: 1932.

Ibn Gabirol, S., (1972). *Keter Malkhut.* Ed. M. J. Bernardette. New York: Foundation for the Advancement of Sephardic Studies and Culture.

Idel, M. (1988). *Kabbalah: New Perspectives.* New Haven: Yale University Press.

_____ (1988). *The Mystical Experience in Abraham Abulafia.* Trans. J. Chipman. Albany, NY: State University of New York Press.

_____ (1988). *Studies in Ecstatic Kabbalah.* Albany, NY: State University of New York Press.

Israel ben Benjamin of Belzyce (1657). *Yalkut Hadash.* Prague: Jacob Bak's sons.

Jacobs, L. (1976). *Hasidic Thought.* New York: Schocken.

_____ (1978). *Hasidic Prayer.* New York: Schocken.

Jaffe, A. (1977). The lighted tree. In *A Well of Living Waters: Festschrift for Hilde Kirsch,* ed. R. Head et al., pp. 129–130. Los Angeles: C. J. Jung Institute.

Jellinek, A., ed. (1877). *Bet ha-Midrash.* 6 vols. Reprinted. Jerusalem: 1938.

Jerusalem Talmud (1948). New York: Shulsinger.

Josephus, Flavius (1937–1953). *The Life; Against Apion; The Jewish War; Antiquities.* 9 vols. Trans. H. St. J. Thackeray, R. Marcus, and H. Feldman. London: W. Heinemann.

Jove, ed. (1977). *New Testament.* In *The Holy Bible,* King James version. New York: Delair Publishing.

Jung, C. (1960). *The Structure and Dynamics of the Psyche.* Vol. 12 of *Collected Works.* New York: Pantheon.

Kadushin, M. (1969). *A Conceptual Approach to the Mekhilta.* Philadelphia: Jewish Publication Society.

Kaplan, A. (1982). *Meditation and Kabbalah.* New York: Weiser.

Keneally, T. (1982). *Schindler's List.* New York: Simon & Schuster.

Klapholz, J. S., ed. (1968). *Sippurei Eliyahu ha-Navi.* 2 vols. Tel Aviv: Dvir.

Klingender, F. (1971). Animals in art and thought to the end of the Middle Ages. *American Journal of Archaeology* 77:115.

Kuk, A. I. (1938). *Lights of Holiness.* Jerusalem: Mossad Harav Kuk.

———— (1950). *Orot Ha-Kodesh.* 3 vols. Ed. R. D. Kahan. Jerusalem: Mossad Harav Kuk.

———— (1964). *Orot Ha-Torah.* Jerusalem: Mossad Harav Kuk.

———— (1978). *The Lights of Penitence: The Moral Principles; Essays, Letters, and Poems.* Trans. and ed. B. Z. Bokser. New York: Paulist Press.

———— (1986). Selected letters. In *Igrot Ha-Re'iyah,* trans. T. Feldman. Ma'alot Adumim, Israel: Ma'alot Publications of Yeshivat Birkhat Moshe.

Langer, J. (1961). *Nine Grates.* London: James Clarke & Co.

Lefébure, E. (1907). *La main de Fathma. Bulletin de la Société de Géographic d'Alger* 12:411–417.

Leftwich, J. (1976). *Israel Anthology.* Philadelphia: Jewish Publication Society.

Levi Isaac of Berditchev (1986). *Kedushat Levi.* Tel Aviv: Morshah Publishers.

Levy, H. (1945). A note on the fate of the sacred vessels of the second temple. *Kedem* 11:123.

Luria, S. (1807). *Amude Shlomo.* Kopys.

Luzzato, M. H. (1806). *Mesilat Yesharim.* Luneville, France: Abraham Prizek and his son Yekl.

L'vush Ha-Tichelet of Mordecai, Yaffe (1965). 6 vols. New York: Grosz Brothers.

Maccabees I-IV. In *Encyclopaedia Judaica,* vol. 11, pp. 656–662. New York: Macmillan, 1971.

Maggid of Mezeritch (Dov Baer). *Imrei Tzaddikim.*

———— (1792). *Likkutei Yekarim.* Lemberg.

———— (1901). *Or HaEmet.* Written down by his disciple, Levi Yitzhak of Berdichev. Zhitomir, Poland.

Maharal, Judah Loew ben Bezalel. (1958). *Ner Mitzvah Al Hanukkah.* Part 2 of *Or Hadash.* Bnai Brak, Israel. Reprint from the Prague original.

Maimonides (1958). *Hilkhot Hanukkah and Beth Habehirah.* In *Mishneh Torah,* 14 vols. Jerusalem: Mossad Harav Kuk.

———— (1961). *The Code of Maimonides.* Vol. 3 of *The Book of Seasons.* Trans. S. Ganzfried and H. Klein. New Haven: Yale University Press.

———— (1963). *Guide for the Perplexed.* Trans. S. Pines. Chicago: University of Chicago Press.

Mandelbaum, B., ed. (1962). *Pesikta de Rav Kahana.* 2 vols. New York.

Margoliot, R., trans. (1951). *The Bahir.* Jerusalem: Mossad Harav Kuk.

Margulies, E., ed. (1913). *Pesikta Rabbati.* Warsaw: Eisenstadt.

Margulies, M., ed. (1947). *Midrash Ha-Gadol* on the Pentateuch. Jerusalem: Mossad Harav Kuk.

Matt, D. C. (1983). *The Zohar: The Book of Enlightenment.* Ramsey, NJ: Paulist Press.

Mayer, L. A. (1967). *Bibliography of Jewish Art.* Ed. Otto Kurz. Jerusalem: Magnes Press, Hebrew University.

Menahem Nachum of Tchernobyl (1960). *Sefer Meor Enayim* and *Yismach Lev.* Jerusalem: Magnes Press.

Meshullam of Zhabaraz (1863). *Likkutim Yekarim.* Lemberg.

Metzger, T., and Metzger, M. (1982). *Jewish Life in the Middle Ages.* New York: Alpine Fine Arts.

Mordecai of Tchernobyl (1971). *Likkutei Torah.* Jerusalem.

Myers, C. (1974). *The Tabernacle Menorah.* Master's Thesis. Brandeis University.

Midrash Sifra (1545). Venice: Daniel Bomberg.

Mikraot Gedolot: Torah (1958–1959). 2 vols. Jerusalem: Schocken.

Nachman of Bratzlav (1850). *Likkutei Etzot.* Zolkiew: Saul Meyerhoffer.

———— (1874). *Likkutei Moharan.*

———— (1922). *Sippurei Ma'asiyot.* Ed. S. A. Horodetzky.

Nachmanides (1963–1964). *Kitvei Ramban.* Ed. C. D. Chavel. Jerusalem: Mossad Harav Kuk.

———— (1959). *Perush al Ha-Torah.* 2 vols. Ed. C. D. Chavel. Jerusalem: Mossad Harav Kuk.

Narbonne, M. (1852). *Commentary on Moreh Nevuchim* 1:46. Vienna.

Narkiss, B. (1959). The history of the *Hanukkah* lamp. *Youth Aliyah Review* (Winter):279–320.

Narkiss, M. (1939). Introduction in English. In *Menorat Ha-Hanukkah*

(The *Hanukkah* Lamp). Jerusalem: Bezalel Museum.

Namenyi, E. (1960). *The Essence of Jewish Art (Esprit de l'Art Juif)*. Trans. E. Rodit. New York: T. Yoseloff.

Neumann, E. (1956). *Amor and Psyche: The Psychic Development of the Feminine—A Commentary on the Tale by Apuleius*. Trans. R. Manheim. London: Routledge and Kegan Paul.

—— (1969). *Depth Psychology and a New Ethic*. Trans. E. Rolfe. New York: Putnam Sons.

Newman, L. (1938). *Hasidic Anthology*. New York: Scribner's.

Patai, R. (1978). *The Hebrew Goddess*. New York: Behrman House.

Philo (1937). *The Decalogue*. Trans. F. H. Colson and G. H. Whitaker. Cambridge, MA: Harvard University Press.

Plato (1937). Symposium. In *The Dialogues of Plato,* vol. 2, trans. B. Jowett, pp. 315–318. New York: Random House.

—— (1969). *The Republic*. Trans. P. Shorey. London: Heinemann.

Previous Lubavitcher Rebbe (1980). *Bosi I'Gani*. New York: Empire Press.

Rosary. In *Abingdon Dictionary of Living Religions,* ed. K. Crim, p. 630. Nashville: Abingdon, 1981.

Rosary. In *The New Westminster Dictionary of Liturgy and Worship,* ed. J. G. Davies, pp. 471–472. Philadelphia: Westminster Press, 1986.

Rosary. In *Westminster Dictionary of Christian Spirituality,* ed. G. S. Wakefield, p. 339. Philadelphia: Westminster Press, 1983.

Rosen, M. (1973). *The Paper Bridge*. Rev. Ed. Wolf Gottlieb. Trans. C. Kormos. Bucharest.

Roth, C. (1959). *History of Italian Renaissance Jewry*. Philadelphia: Jewish Publication Society.

Rothenberg, J., ed. (1978). *A Big Jewish Book*. New York: Doubleday.

Russell, E. H. (1975). Parapsychic luminosities. *Quadrant* 8:49–71. (Reprinted by C. G. Jung Foundation for Analytical Psychology, New York, 1975.)

Saunders, E. D. (1960). *Mudra: A Study of Symbolic Gestures in Japanese Buddhist Sculpture*. Bollingen Series, no. 43. Princeton: Princeton University Press.

Schaya, L. (1977). *L'Homme et l'Absolu selon la Kabbale*. Paris: Dervy-Livres.

Schechter, S., ed. (1886). *Aggadot Shir HaShirim*. Cambridge, England: Cambridge University Press.

—— (1887). *Aboth de Rabbi Natan*. Vienna.

_____ (1902). *Midrash Ha-Gadol.* Cambridge, England: Cambridge University Press.

Shneur Zalman of Liadi (1884). *Likkutei Torah.* Vilna: L. L. Matz.

_____ (1973). *Sefer Tanya (Likkutei Amarim).* Trans. N. Mindel. New York: Kehot Publication Society.

Scholem, G. (1941). *Major Trends in Jewish Mysticism.* Jerusalem: Schocken.

_____ (1971). *The Messianic Idea in Judaism.* New York: Schocken.

_____ (1974). *Kabbalah.* New York: Quadrangle.

_____ (1987). *Origins of Kabbalah.* Ed. R. J. Zwi Werblowsky. Trans. A. Arkush. Philadelphia: Jewish Publication Society.

Septuagint Version of the Old Testament (1879). Trans. and ed. L. C. L. Brenton. London: Zondervan.

Smith, Margaret (1928). *Rabi'ah the Mystic and Her Fellow Saints in Islam.* Cambridge, England: Cambridge University Press.

Smith, Morton (1953). Review of *Jewish Symbols in the Greco-Roman Period* by E. R. Goodenough. *Anglican Theological Review* 36:1–11, 218–220.

_____ (1957–1958). The image of God: notes on the Hellenization of Judaism. *Bulletin of the John Rylands Library* 40:473–512.

Slucki, H. J., ed. (1836). *Midrash Konen.* Vilna: Avraham Yitzhak ben Harav Shalom.

Sperber, D. (1967). The history of the *Menorah. Journal of Jewish Studies* 16:135.

Sperling, H., Simon, M., and Levertoff, P. P., trans. (1931–1934). *The Zohar.* London: Soncino Press.

Steinsaltz, A. (1979). *Beggars and Prayers: Adin Steinsaltz Retells the Tales of R. Nachum of Bratzlav.* Trans. Y. Hanegbi, F. Gottlieb, et. al. Ed. J. Omer-Man. New York: Basic Books.

_____ (1980). *The Thirteen-Petalled Rose.* New York: Basic Books.

Tanakh: A New Translation of the Holy Scriptures According to the Traditional Hebrew Text (1985). Philadelphia: Jewish Publication Society.

Taub, Menachem Mendel (Kalever Rebbe) (1987). In *Sefer Kol Menachem,* part 4. Bnai Brak: Kalever Yeshiva.

Tikkunei Zohar (1867). Vilna: S. Zuckerman.

Tishby, I. (1957–1961). *Mishnat ha-Zohar.* 2 vols. Jerusalem: Bialik Institute.

Trachtenberg, J. (1939). *Jewish Magic and Superstition.* New York: Behrman House.

Treves, N. H. (1560). *Siddur* (Commentary on *Ha-Aderet veha-Emunah*), fol. BH. Thiengen.

Unsdorfer, S. B. (1961). *The Yellow Star*. New York: Thomas Yoseloff.

Urbah, E. E. (1975). *The Sages*. 2 vols. Jerusalem: Magnes Press.

Vishniac, R. (1983). *A Vanished World*. New York: Farrar, Straus and Giroux.

Vital, C. (1910). *Sefer Etz Hayyim*. Reprint. Jerusalem: *Ahavat Shalom*, 1982.

_____ (1979). *Sefer ha-Gilgulim*. Zolkiew.

_____ (1982). *Etz ha-Dat'at Tov*. Part II, fol. 5b. *Sefer HaCheshek and VeZot LeYehudah*. Jerusalem.

Weiss, J. (1960). The great *Maggid's* theory of contemplative magic. *Hebrew Union College Annual* 31.

Wertheimer, S. A., ed. (1914). *Otiyyot de-Rabbi Akiva*. Jerusalem: Frumkin.

Westermarck, E. (1904). The magic origin of Morrish designs. *Journal of the Anthropological Institute* 34:213.

_____ (1926). *Ritual and Belief in Morocco*. 2 vols. London: Macmillan.

Wigoder, G. (1972). *Jewish Art and Civilization*. New York: Walker.

Wischnitzer, M. (1965). *History of the Jewish Crafts and Guilds*. New York: Jonathan David.

Wischnitzer, R. B. (1930). *Origine de la lampe de Hanouka*. Revue des Études Juives 89:135–146.

Wolfson, H. A. (1948). *Philo: Foundation of Religious Philosophy*. 2 vols. Cambridge, MA: Harvard University Press.

Yaakov Yosef of Polnoye (1841). *Toledot Yaakov Yosef*. Warsaw.

_____ (1875). *Ben Porat Yosef*. Lemberg.

_____ (1950). *Ketonent Passim*. New York.

_____ (1957). *Zofnat Paneah*. New York.

Yalkut Shimoni (1973). Oxford MS. Jerusalem: Mossad Harav Kuk.

Yarden, L. (1971). *Tree of Light: A Study of the Menorah*. Ithaca, NY: Cornell University Press.

Yadin, Y. (1962). *The Scroll of the Sons of Light versus the Sons of Darkness*. London: Oxford University Press.

Yehudah Aryeh Leib of Ger (1952). *Sifat Emet: Hiddushei Torah al Kol Shabbatot Ha-Shanah ve-Ha-Moadim*. New York.

Yishmael (Rabbi) (1931). *Mekhilta de Rabbi Yishmael*. Ed. C. S. Horovitz. Frankfurt: Kaufmann.

Zimmels, H. J. (1952). *Magicians, Theologians, and Doctors.* London: E. Goldston.

Zohar Hadash (1658). Venice.

Zwartz, J. (1935). *Die Zevenarmige Kundelaar in de Romeinse Diaspora.* Amsterdam.

INDEX

489